ASSER International Sports Law Series

For further volumes:
http://www.springer.com/series/8858

Katrien Lefever

New Media and Sport

International Legal Aspects

T·M·C·Asser press

Springer

Katrien Lefever
Faculty of Law
Interdisciplinary Centre for Law and ICT
KU Leuven
Leuven
Belgium

ISSN 1874-6926
ISBN 978-90-6704-872-9 ISBN 978-90-6704-873-6 (eBook)
DOI 10.1007/978-90-6704-873-6

Library of Congress Control Number: 2012940957

Published by T.M.C. ASSER PRESS, The Hague, The Netherlands www.asserpress.nl
Produced and distributed for T.M.C. ASSER PRESS by Springer-Verlag Berlin Heidelberg

Printed on acid-free paper

Springer is part of Springer Science+Business Media (www.springer.com)

Series Information

Books in the *ASSER International Sports Law Series* chart and comment upon the legal and policy developments in European and international sports law. The books contain materials on interstate organisations and the international sports governing bodies, and will serve as comprehensive and relevant reference tools for all those involved in the area on a professional basis.

The Series is developed, edited and published by the ASSER International Sports Law Centre in The Hague. The Centre's mission is to provide a centre of excellence in particular by providing high-quality research, services and products to the sporting world at large (sports ministries, international—intergovernmental—organisations, sports associations and federations, the professional sports industry, etc.) on both a national and an international basis. The Centre is the co-founder and coordinator of the Hague International Sports Law Academy (HISLA), the purpose of which is the organisation of academic conferences and workshops of international excellence which are held in various parts of the world. Apart from the Series, the Centre edits and publishes *The International Sports Law Journal.*

Series Editors
Dr. Robert C. R. Siekmann, Director Asser International Sports Centre
e-mail: r.siekmann@asser.nl

Dr. Janwillem Soek
e-mail: J.soek@asser.nl

M. A. van der Harst LL.M.
e-mail: m.van.der.harst@asser.nl

Editorial Office
ASSER International Sports Law Centre
T.M.C. Asser Institute
P.O. Box 30461
2500 GL, The Hague
The Netherlands
www.sportslaw.nl

Foreword

The summer of 2012 is often referred to in the popular media as the Summer of Sports. High-profile sporting events followed each other in quick succession. In early June, the Spanish tennis superstar Rafael Nadal was crowned for an unprecedented seventh time as the 'king of clay' at Roland Garros in Paris. Some weeks later, his compatriots in the Spanish national football team continued their unparalleled winning streak at international tournaments during the European Championships in Poland and Ukraine. One week later, on the holy grass of Wimbledon, Roger Federer proved once again why he is the Swiss Maestro. In the Tour de France, two British riders from Team Sky mainly decided amongst themselves which one of them would ultimately take the yellow jersey home to Great Britain. Bradley Wiggins' historic victory was the ideal appetizer for the *pièce de résistance* that was about to come thereafter, the 2012 Olympic Games. During the next sixteen days, the performances of the likes of Usain Bolt, Michael Phelps or Epke Zonderland in London dominated the headlines in the media worldwide. Only when the IOC Chairman Rogge drew the curtain over the 'happy and glorious games' did the 2012 Summer of Sports come to an end.

A great deal of sports history was written in a time span of merely three months. Hundreds of millions of people all over the globe were able to follow all these sporting highlights in one way or another. Nowadays, we live in an information society. This book even speaks of an 'information rollercoaster'. The times when the only means to be directly informed about a sporting event were to actually go to the venue, to watch television or to listen to the radio belong to the past. During the last decade, the number of providers of sports content in the media has substantially increased. Moreover, new platforms such as the internet or mobile phones enable them to provide more sports. Almost inevitably, these developments in the media landscape influence the relationship between the media and the sporting world. As the public's access to sports content is valuable—which is the working hypothesis of this book—these developments also entail legal repercussions. The overall objective of this book is precisely to examine the impact of our rapidly evolving information society on the existing legal framework relating to the public's access to sports content, especially media law and competition law.

Adopting both an interdisciplinary and intra-disciplinary approach, it specifically purports to assess how competition and media law guarantee access to live and full sports coverage for the audience in the new media landscape.

The subject of this book by Ms. Lefever is important and topical. Sport and the law have long been uneasy bedfellows. Sporting federations traditionally operated under the assumption that they enjoyed complete autonomy in organizing and regulating sports and thus that they were immune to legal intervention from the 'outside world'. This general attitude may have been contested or even (successfully) challenged in court on a given concrete occasion, but ultimately it was only in a judgment of December 15, 1995 by the Court of Justice of the European Union that sporting federations would definitely lose their self-proclaimed aura of being legally 'untouchable'. In the already legendary *Bosman* case, the Court of Justice first dispelled every doubt about its previous statement that sport is part of EU law insofar as it constitutes an economic activity, before subsequently outlawing certain aspects of the traditional transfer system and also the so-called '3+2' nationality clauses in professional football in Europe for infringing the free movement rules laid down in the European Treaties. Since that day, the Court of Justice has been laden with all the sins of Israel in sporting circles. Bosman is widely regarded as the main culprit for everything that has gone wrong in professional football and beyond the last fifteen years: in particular, that the sporting and financial equilibrium between clubs is disturbed and the gap between rich and poor clubs has widened, or that many clubs no longer invest time and money in the development and training of young players. The sporting establishment has often been so occupied with criticising the *Bosman* decision and looking for ways to circumvent or overturn it, that other plausible explanations were simply overlooked or did not receive appropriate attention. More or less contemporaneously with the *Bosman* judgment, professional sports became increasingly commercialised. Revenues from the sale of the broadcasting rights of sporting events reached unprecedented heights. It is submitted that this – and the unequal distribution of this wealth—is the principal reason for the financial and sporting imbalances that have occurred over the last few years. One of the intrinsic strengths of this book is therefore its overall topic: the regulation of the laws concerning the broadcasting of sports events.

Besides this, the book also tackles several of the important concrete sub-issues in this regard. To mention but a few; firstly, it addresses the specificity of the sports sector, emphasizing the social and economic function of sport. This so-called specificity of sport is also important in legal terms. For instance, sports associations often refer—with varying degrees of success—to the argument of the specific nature of sport to justify a *prima facie* infringement of EU law or even to call for an exemption from the scope of EU law. Secondly, the book also inquires whether the freedom of expression and the right to information, enshrined in article 10 of the European Convention on Human Rights, can play a role in protecting the public's access to sports content, as consumers and as citizens. Thirdly, concerning media law, the focus is on the analysis of the 'list of major events' mechanism. Sport is an important weapon in the 'battle for the audience' between broadcasters. In an attempt to attract more viewers and more advertisement revenue, media operators often try to acquire exclusive broadcasting rights to sports events. This has led to the situation that some of these events are no longer available to all on free-to–air television. Therefore, a list of major sporting events has been drawn up that must be accessible to all viewers. The book examines the suitability and the necessity of this list. Fourthly, the book addresses a number of competition law concerns triggered by the fierce competition for these sports broadcasting rights. Through regulation and case law, the national and European competition authorities have created the conditions of open and fair competition for the sale, acquisition and exploitation of sporting broadcasting rights. The book studies whether, and if so, how, the rise of new media operators has influenced these competitive conditions. In this respect, attention is primarily paid to issues such as joint selling, sublicensing obligations and 'must-offer' obligations.

All in all, this book by Ms. Lefever deals with the right topic in the area of sports and the law, it asks many of the right questions and provides various useful insights, analysis and answers. I warmly recommend this book to broadcasters, sports governors, lawyers and all those with a general interest in the issue.

Stefaan Van den Bogaert
Professor of European Law & Director of the Europa Institute,
Leiden University, The Netherlands
Visiting Professor of European Sports Law, Vrije Universiteit
Brussel, Belgium

Contents

Chapter 1
Introduction

When do new media become old media?
Boyle and Haynes 2004, p. 3

During the past decade, the media landscape and the coverage of sports events have changed fundamentally. The emergence of new communication technologies, such as Internet and digital television, the convergence of these technologies, the multiplication of the number of devices through which content can be accessed and the rise of the active 'prosumer' have put their stamp on the way fans can consume sports content. Watching television is no longer a 'sit back and relax'-experience. Due to technological changes, everybody can now consume the sports content of his choice, on the platform he prefers and at the time he wants. To be connected with the public, sports organisations and media operators exploit all opportunities provided by the different platforms. Early in the morning, when a sports fan wakes up and switches on his mobile phone, he will receive SMS alerts or pictures about the latest sports news. On his way to work, he can listen to the radio in the car or get more information on his mobile phone in the train. At work and during lunch break, he can consult highlights on different sports websites. On his way home, he can listen to the downloaded podcast with the most recent news. And finally, in the evening, he can watch the live matches on his television set at home. Especially the year 2008 was the dawn of this 360° sports multi-platform coverage approach[1]: it was the year of a 24/7 experience of the Beijing Olympics, Wimbledon, Tour de France and EURO 2008. Although this evolution sounds very exciting, it is necessary for all actors involved, such as the public, the audiovisual media service providers, organisers of sports events, sports organisations, policy makers, etc., to be aware of the legal challenges this new media landscape is presenting.

Without a doubt, digitalisation has changed the media sector. Analogue broadcasting was characterised by scarcity. Due to spectrum scarcity and the pervasive influence of broadcasters, the perception reigned that regulatory control over television content was needed to ensure that normative goals, such as quality

---

[1] This 360° sports multi-platform coverage approach was presented by Gallop in Gallop 2008 at the Westminster eForum—The role of new media in sports and special events coverage.

K. Lefever, *New Media and Sport*, ASSER International Sports Law Series,
DOI: 10.1007/978-90-6704-873-6_1,

of content, protection of minors, were met. As a result, legislators have adopted detailed rules for broadcasters on the protection of minors, advertising, etc., while media regulators monitor whether these content requirements are respected in practice. However, the rise of digital technology has increased the information flow and the amount of channels available, using only a fraction of the valuable capacity resources that were employed in the analogue past.[2] As a result, the validity of traditional media regulation in the digital environment is questioned. Moreover, it was sometimes proposed to leave the regulation of the broadcasting market solely to competition law. According to Ungerer, for example, "*[w]e will move [...] to an environment that will be less subject to the sector specific rules built for the traditional broadcasting sector, and more to the general market regulation under competition rules*".[3] Ariño referred to this way of thinking as a trend "*to progressively abandon regulation and move towards a competition-law based model that will ultimately prevail*".[4] Furthermore, in the past, the dissemination of information was the exclusive domain of the professional media, such as television, radio and written press. Thanks to electronic devices and the Internet, audiovisual content can now be created and distributed by every citizen. Additionally, digitalisation has brought about a shift from a 'lean back'-experience of watching television and consulting information to a 'lean forward'-experience. In the past, professional media decided which information would reach the public and when it would reach the public. Currently, the public itself decides where, when and on which device it will watch television or consult information. Once again, due to the increased participation of the public in creating and distributing content, the question needs to be asked whether government intervention in the broadcasting sector is still justified. As a result, the question rises whether the premise on which media regulation was based will still serve as the basic assumption for the regulation of the media sector in the future. Or in other words, would the shift from scarcity to abundance and from mass media and passive consumers to media for mass self-communication and active 'prosumers' undermine the premises from which current media regulation starts, i.e. scarcity and one-way selection of information at the central level of the broadcaster. In this book, it will be examined whether media regulation has still a role to play in guaranteeing access to live and full sports coverage in the new media landscape.

Considering the importance of digital content regulation and the current concerns regarding access to sports content in the new digital media environment, the need for legal research is pressing. It is clear that new technologies and new media models pose challenges for industry, academics and policy makers. There exists no doubt that legal uncertainties will increase in the coming years. Hence, it is important to build a solid basis of legal expertise around this issue, so that appropriate input can be presented in sight of regulatory initiatives in a setting of

---

[2] Cowie and Marsden 1999, 54–55; Tambini and Verhulst 2001, 5–6.

[3] Ungerer 2005, 3.

[4] Arino Arino 2004, 101.

new media. Despite the omnipresence of sport in the media, the level of research focussing on the relationship between media and sports was only recently established as a significant academic field. One should realise that in the Treaty of Rome sport was not even included in the competences of the European Economic Community. Only when the Lisbon Treaty entered into force, for the first time in European history, sport has been integrated in the primary law of the EU. Unfortunately, the White Paper on Sport, the cornerstone of the European Commission's actions regarding its new power, only briefly touches upon the public's access to sports coverage. Given that the latter plays an important role when dealing with the societal function of sport, this book aims at contributing to a more in-depth analysis of the public's right to access to live and full coverage of sports events. The objective of this book is to study the impact of the rapidly changing information society on the existing legal framework guaranteeing the public's access to sports content, especially media and competition law.

Access to sports content covers a broad area of topics, going from access at downstream level to access at upstream level or access to live and full coverage of sports events to access to short news reports. However, it is not the objective of this book to examine all these issues. As already indicated above, the aim of this book is to examine how competition and media law guarantee access to live and full sports coverage for the public in the new media landscape. This implies that the following issues will not be dealt with in detail, but only be highlighted when necessary: right to short news reporting, copyright, image rights, ownership of sports broadcasting rights, etc.

This book is composed of three main parts and is followed by a conclusion. Part I gives a detailed overview of the synergies between actors of the sports/media complex and explains how the changing media landscape has driven this sports/media complex into a new dimension. Second, the specificity of the sports sector will be described. In doing so, both the economic and societal function of sport will be highlighted. This includes a description of the new Article 165 of the Treaty on the Functioning of the European Union, which is officially recognising the specificity of sport. Third, it will be examined whether sports coverage, particularly live and full coverage of sports events, could be protected under Article 10 of the European Convention on Human Rights. Fourth, the distinction between a viewer as a citizen and a viewer as a consumer will be described. In particular, it will be examined whether Article 10 of the European Convention on Human Rights protects the public's access to sports content, both in its role as consumer and citizen. Finally, the question whether the changing media landscape and the changing sports/media complex would have an impact on the regulatory process of the broadcasting sector will be touched upon. Once the concepts and the building blocks of the book are clearly demarcated in Part I, Part II will focus on the question whether the technological changes in the media landscape have influenced the way competition authorities are dealing with the public's access to sports coverage. The European Commission and national competition authorities have made use of competition rules in order to ensure that access to exclusive broadcasting rights of sports events is not unduly restricted by anti-competitive practices. In order to ensure access to those rights, competition authorities have shaped the conditions for selling, acquiring and exploiting sports broadcasting rights to establish open and effective competition. In this Part, the *UEFA Champions League* case, *German Bundesliga* case, *FA Premier League* case, *EBU/Eurovision system* case, *German public broadcaster state aid* case, *Newscorp/Telepiù* case, *Audiovisual Sport* case, *BSkyB* case and the *Telenet/Canal+* case will be discussed in detail. The *Flemish public broadcaster state aid* will be briefly highlighted. In Part III, the sector-specific measure that is in place in EU Member States to safeguard the public's right to information, namely the 'list of major events' mechanism, will be critically analysed and discussed. The aim of Part III is to evaluate in detail the 'list of major events' mechanism and to examine whether this mechanism is still adapted to guarantee the public's right to information in the digital media landscape. As a way of conclusion, Part III proposes the introduction of a 'must-broadcast' obligation in order to render the 'list of major events' mechanism more effective. In the conclusion, the findings from the previous Parts will be integrated.

References

Doctrine

Arino M (2004) Competition law and pluralism in European digital broadcasting: addressing the gaps. Commun Strateg 54:97–128

Boyle R, Haynes R (2004) Football in the new media age. Routledge, London

Gallop B (2008) The role of new media in sports and special events coverage, Westminster eForum—Beyond Beijing—Media technology at the olympic & paralympic Games, London, 23 Oct 2008

Cowie C, Marsden C (1999) Convergence navigating bottlenecks in digital pay-TV. J policy Regul Strateg Telecommun inform Media 1(1):53–67

Tambini D, Verhulst S (2001) The transition to digital and content regulation: the paradigm shift. In: Tambini D (ed) Communications: revolution and reform. IPPR, London, pp 5–20

Ungerer H (2005) Competition in the media sector: how long can the future be delayed? http://ec.europa.eu/competition/speeches/text/sp2005_015_en.pdf. Accessed 23 Aug 2010

Part I
Setting: Notions, Issues and Legal Background

This marriage between sport and television is one made in heaven

(Goldlust 1987).

In Part I, the underlying context, on which the research is built, will be delineated. The basic assumption of this book is that the public's access to live sports coverage is valuable and that it still should be guaranteed in the digital media landscape. In Part I of this book, the theoretical grounds for the study of the research assumption will be provided. This Part I is intended to serve as a background against which the following Parts should be read. It should be seen as a framework for reflexion rather than a formal legal analysis. First, synergies between the stakeholders of the sports/media complex in the analogue media market will be examined, including the background and characteristics of the digital and converging media environment and their impact on the sports/media complex. Second, the dual nature of the sports sector will be described. The economic dimension of sport will be highlighted, while the societal dimension of sport will be analysed in detail. The new Article 165 of the Treaty on the Functioning of the European Union, officially recognising the specificity of sport, will also be discussed. In other words, this chapter will emphasise the important role of sport and access thereto for our society. Third, Article 10 of the European Convention on Human Rights will be examined. In the light of the research question, it is important to analyse whether sports coverage could fall under the scope of Article 10 of the European Convention on Human Rights, whether only highlights or also live and full coverage of sports events could get protection under this Article 10 and whether States could intervene in order to protect access to live and full sports coverage. In this regard, analysis of the societal role of sport will play an important role. Fourth, when focussing on the public's access to sports content, and particularly the public's right to information, it is important to touch upon the distinction between a viewer as a citizen and a viewer as a consumer. It should be examined whether Article 10 of the European Convention on Human Rights protects the public's access to sports content, both in its role as consumer and citizen. Finally, the question will be answered whether the changing media landscape and the changing sports/media complex would have an impact on the regulatory process of the broadcasting sector.

Reference

Goldlust J (1987) Playing for keeps: sport, the media and society. Longman Cheshire, Melbourne, p 78

Chapter 2
Sports/Media Complex in the New Media Landscape

2.1 Introduction

Over the years, the sports sector and the media sector have developed a self-interest relationship. Both industries gain benefits from the complementary nature of their interests: while sport provides valuable content and audiences for media operators, the media is a revenue source and promotional tool for sport.[1] The sale of exclusive live sports broadcasting rights is an important, if not the principal, source of revenue for sports organisations and clubs (besides ticketing, marketing, etc.), whereas live sports content is decisive for media operators to create an attractive programming for their audience. Wide coverage through television, for instance, can result in significant exposure for sports leagues. Such exposure can deliver private benefits to the league and the clubs in the form of increased revenue from sponsorship and attraction of new supporters.[2] This implies that, without cameras, major sports events would have virtually no meaning at all. This interdependence among sports organisations, media conglomerates and sponsors is often referred to as the "*sports/media complex*",[3] "*media-sport-cultural-complex*"[4] or "*media-sport-production complex*".[5] In the next sections, the different roles and interests of those three key players in this sports/media complex will be described. Additionally, the public/fans will also be considered as an important actor in this complex.

---

1 Bolotny and Bourg 2006, 112.
2 Grant and Graeme 2008, 593.
3 Jhally 1989, 77.
4 Rowe 1999, 4.
5 Maguire 1991, 316.

K. Lefever, *New Media and Sport*, ASSER International Sports Law Series,
DOI: 10.1007/978-90-6704-873-6_2,

2.2 Sports/Media Complex in the Analogue Media Landscape

Over the years, a symbiotic relationship between sport and media has been developed which can be seen as a fusion among media, sport and advertising.[6] In the analogue past, the stakeholders of the sports/media complex had clearly defined roles and the win–win situation for all the actors was apparent.

2.2.1 Sports Clubs and Sports Organisations

The sports sector benefits from this sports/media complex, because it receives a well needed infusion of money from sponsors as well as media organisations.[7] As ticket sales represented the major revenue source for sports organisations in the past, the introduction of televised sports was originally feared to cause depletion in stadium attendance, because people could attend the events directly from their own living rooms. Live coverage of sports events, however, soon demonstrated not to be detrimental to attendance, but on the contrary, to have the possibility to become a fan builder.[8] As a result, Buraimo referred to televised sports as "*being a complement to stadium attendance*".[9] Sponsorship deals have also become important revenue streams for sports teams and organisations, causing sports teams and organisations themselves to now heavily rely on the support of sponsors.[10]

The sponsors' and media's increasing involvement in, and control over, sport has put the sponsors and media companies in a powerful position to dictate the characteristics of events or indeed, even to change fundamental aspects of the sport.[11] Rules have been changed or abandoned and playing conditions revised so as to enhance media coverage and attract sponsors fees. A white ball, instead of the traditional brown ball, and distinct coloured shirts were introduced to increase the watching experience of football viewers. To get the chance to broadcast as many football matches as possible, matches played at the European level were split into different shifts. The UEFA Champions League matches are played on Tuesday and Wednesday evenings and the UEFA Europa League on Thursday evenings, while in the past, they were all played on Wednesday.[12] Similar changes were made in volleyball. To make volleyball games more appealing, the International Volleyball Federation modified the scoring system. Before 1999, points could be scored only when a team had the serve and the sets went up to 15 points. To make the length of

6 Silk 2004, 233.

7 Slack and Amis 2004, 270.

8 Forrest et al. 2010, 112–135.

9 Buraimo 2006, 108.

10 PriceWaterHouseCoopers 2008, 168.

11 European Commission 1998, 12; Stead 1986, 189; Hargreaves 1986, 120.

12 Kestens 2005, 21.

the match more predictable and sensational, and thus more television friendly, the game now continues until the first team scores 25 points. Additionally, events are sometimes held at a time of the day that would not appear to be in the best interests of the athletes involved, but which fit viewer habits and thus the broadcasters' preferences.[13] During the 1994 FIFA World Cup in the United States, for example, football matches were played at the hottest time of the day so that they could be broadcast in Europe at prime time.[14] The same goes for the swimming contests during the Beijing Olympics in 2008. At the American broadcasters' request, the swimming finals were held in the morning, i.e. prime time in the United States.[15]

2.2.2 Media Companies

While sports organisations could benefit from media publicity, for broadcasters, live coverage of sports events is important, because it gives them a credibility and profile in the marketplace as well as lucrative audiences to advertisers.[16] Because the economics of broadcasting require sufficient audience size to produce adequate financial resources, audience share is the buzz word in the media sector. Viewing figures are a key indicator for the popularity of a channel. Where these figures are low it is impossible to attract advertisers or investors. To boost the viewing figures, it is crucial to put together a very attractive and appealing set of programmes, preferably not available on other channels. It is known that some content, more than others, can trigger consumers' and advertisers' attention. Sport unmistakably has this ability.[17]

Sports programming is particularly desirable for broadcasters, because of its ability to attract viewers with significant buying power that would, otherwise, be hard to reach in large numbers, i.e. young men with an above-average spending power. The problem with this group is that they watch less television than others and, thus, are much harder to reach by advertisers through television advertising. Nevertheless, given that football (in most European countries) seems to have the ability to attract this particular group of the population, broadcasters can sell advertising slots during sports programmes for a higher rate than during other programmes.[18] The advertising spots during the Super Bowl, for example, are the most expensive ones. Super Bowl broadcaster CBS Corp has sold all its television

---

[13] Stead 1986, 190.

[14] The New York Times 1990.

[15] BBC Sport 2006.

[16] Boyle and Haynes Boyle and Haynes 2000, 70.

[17] Vanderkelen 1997, 82.

[18] Commission decision, 23 July 2003, para 74; Rosner and Shropshire 2004, 139; Hoehn and Lancefield 2003, 554.

advertising around the season-finale match in February 2010, with the top spots going for more than $3 million.[19]

Additionally, the European Commission often recognised that exclusive and live sport constitutes a "*stand-alone driver content*" for new media operators to enter (and stay) in the broadcasting market.[20] In fact, most of the pay-television packages include live football as part of its content when launched.[21] Murdoch even described sport as the "*battering ram*" of his pay-television service.[22] The CEO of Premiere, further, specified this by saying that "*exclusive programming rights are the foundation for successful pay-TV—why else should viewers pay extra for television*".[23] Evidence from different countries illustrates the importance of live sport in this respect. In December 2005, for example, the German pay-television operator Premiere lost 42 % of its market value and a part of its subscriber base after having failed to buy the rights for the Bundesliga, while the new Bundesliga rights owner Unity Media's Arena attracted over 900,000 subscribers in only a few months.[24] The same goes for TPS in France, when it lost the rights to Ligue 1 matches.[25]

This intensified struggle for market share, viewers and subscribers has caused a substantial increase in demand for exclusive live sports broadcasting rights, ultimately leading to highly valued rights contracts for popular sports events. The broadcasting rights for the first English Premier League, for instance, were acquired by BSkyB for around €280 million for five seasons in 1992, or €56 million per season. In 2006, BSkyB and Setanta paid around €2.5 billion for the live broadcasting rights in the UK for three seasons, i.e. more than €830 million per season.[26] The total revenues generated by the Premier League for the 2010–2013 rights further increased by 4.5 %.[27] Likewise, the value of the European broadcasting rights to the UEFA Champions League rose from €71 million for the 1992–1994 seasons, i.e. more than €35 million per season, to €638 million for the 2006–2009 seasons, i.e. more than €212 million per season.[28]

[19] Sportbusiness International 2010a.

[20] Commission decision, 2 April 2003, para 61; Commission decision 23 July 2003, para 20.

[21] Boyle and Haynes 2004, 54–55.

[22] The Independent 1996.

[23] Premiere 2006.

[24] Hatton et al. 2007, 346.

[25] Ofcom 2008, para 3.66–3.72; Ofcom 2009, para 3.31.

[26] Ofcom 2007, 19 and 28.

[27] Financial Times 2009.

[28] Lefever and Van Rompuy 2009, 247.

2.2.3 Sponsors

Sponsors play an important role in this triangle. The concept of sports marketing is defined by Skinner as "*the process in which companies make use of popular and alternative sports, and the athletes prominent within those sports, to connect with consumers*". Skinner further indicated that a sponsorship agreement is a reciprocal arrangement, where those being sponsored (a sports organisation, an individual athlete, etc.) may receive funding and the sponsoring corporation receives the benefits of the marketing advantages of being associated with sports teams, sports events or athletes.[29] Sponsors hope that, by investing in sport, they will increase the public's awareness of their brand and consequently build their brand equity.[30]

It should be said that it is important for sponsors to be linked with clubs, events or athletes that are positively evaluated by the public. In 2009, for example, AT&T, Accenture and Gillette communicated they would no longer sponsor top golfer Tiger Woods, who announced that he would take an indefinite break from the sport after the storm over his private life. According to the different sponsors, Tiger Woods was no longer the right representative for their companies. Even though a recent University of California study suggested the total economic damage of the Tiger Woods affair to all involved parties could amount to as much as $12 billion, Nike, Wood's main sponsor, announced that it would continue to sponsor him. Phil Knight, the chairman and co-founder of the sportswear company, brushed off the scandal engulfing Woods as 'part of the game' of sponsorship deals.[31]

The most efficient way to reach as many people as possible is via media exposure. Given that one image says more than a thousand words; television coverage is for sponsors virtually obligatory nowadays. It puts them in contact with a potentially massive group of customers.[32] For example, 8 billion viewers followed EURO 2004 in Portugal[33] and worldwide television audience of more than 700 million people was expected to have watched Spain's 1-0 extra-time victory over the Netherlands during the 2010 FIFA World Cup final.[34] It is obvious that the more media coverage an event will get, the better it is for the sponsors.[35] Therefore, events such as the FIFA World Cup, the European Championship or the Olympic Games offer multiple opportunities for lucrative sponsorship deals to market brands and develop business.[36] Due to wide media exposure of these events, sponsorship fees for these events have escalated. For example, the official

29 Skinner 2010, 104–106.

30 Smith 2008, 173 and 192; X 2009, 15.

31 See e.g.: BBC News 2009a; BBC News 2009b; Guardian 2009; Telegraph 2009.

32 Hargreaves 1986, 118.

33 UEFA 2008.

34 Sportbusiness International 2010b.

35 Slack and Amis 2004, 270.

36 Commission of the European Communities 2007, SEC(2007) 935, 31

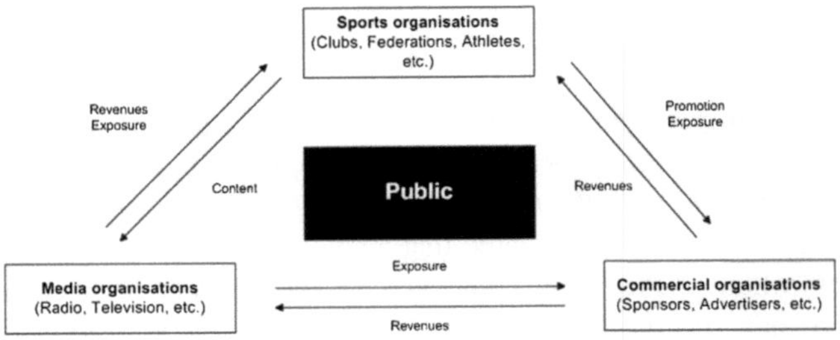

Fig. 2.1 Sports/media complex in the analogue media market (based on de Moragas et al. 2003)

partners of FIFA World Cup 2006 have spent €700 million on the tournament.[37] Coca Cola alone spent more than $70 million to be one of the top Olympic sponsors for the 2008 Beijing Games and 2006 Turin Games.[38] PriceWater-HouseCoopers determined that sponsorship revenues in sports will increase from €260 million in 2007 to €400 million in 2012.[39]

2.2.4 Public: Fans

Without question, sport is an area of human activity that greatly interests citizens, with a majority of people passionate about sport and taking part in sports activities on a regular basis.[40] Sports minded people do not only enjoy sport actively, but also passively. As a result, going to the stadium to see their favourite team play is often seen as the perfect pastime. Thanks to the media, the exploits of the athletes and the emotional experience from being in the stadium are also brought to the public at home, who is given the impression that they are live spectators in the stadium. Moreover, additional features, such as replays, different camera positions, close-ups, etc., make viewers feel part of the event, because it helps them to see things that stadium audiences often missed.[41]

2.2.5 Sports/Media Complex in the Analogue Media Landscape: Summary

Figure 2.1 reflects the intertwined relationship of the different stakeholders of the sports/media complex in the analogue media market.

[37] Guardian 2006.

[38] Businessweek 2008.

[39] PriceWaterHouseCoopers 2008, 168.

[40] Commission of the European Communities 2007b, COM (2007) 391 final, 2–3.

[41] Whitson 1998, 63; Maguire 1993, 39.

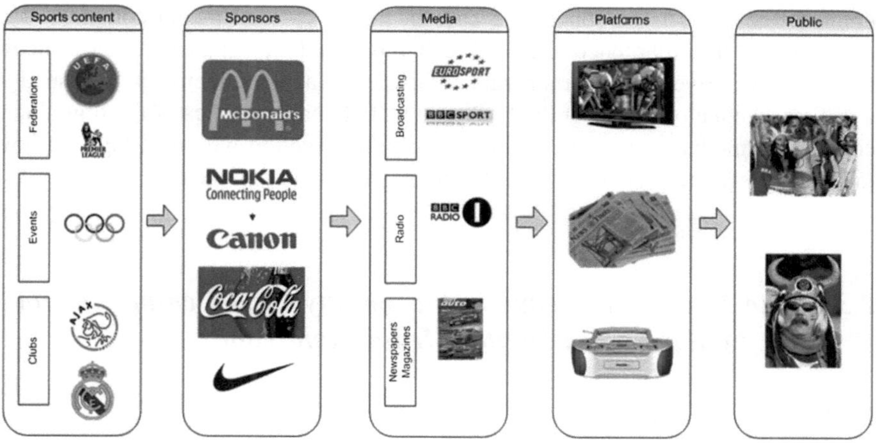

Fig. 2.2 Sports/media complex and the value chain of the analogue media sector

Stakeholders' interests of the sports/media complex could go along, but could also be opposed to each other. Given that sports organisations need revenue from both media organisations and commercial organisations, they try to sell their broadcasting rights for a very high price to media companies and try to close lucrative sponsorship deals with commercial organisations. If a pay-television operator is willing to pay a huge amount of money for exclusive sports broadcasting rights, sports organisations will probably accept that offer. However, this will not be in the interest of the commercial organisations or the public/fans. In fact, commercial organisations want to reach as many people as possible via media exposure in order to increase consumers' awareness of their products, services and brands. And the public's main interest is to have access to sports coverage on television, preferably for free or for a very low price. Given that a part of the public is not keen on or not able to pay extra for a subscription to a pay-television channel, these channels can only attract a smaller audience. For commercial organisations, this means less exposure and a possible shortfall in revenues. Nevertheless, it is possible that sports organisations will accept a lower offer from free-to-air broadcasters in order to increase stadium attendance or interest in the sport via extra media publicity. The latter is most likely in the interest of both the fans and sponsors.

Figure 2.2 reflects how the sports/media complex can be integrated in the value chain of the analogue media sector.

2.3 Sports/Media Complex in the Digital Media Landscape

Due to the evolution of media technology in the twentieth century, the sports/media complex has somehow changed, allowing the different stakeholders to take up new roles. While, in the past, the actors in the sports/media complex had clearly defined roles, this is no longer the case in the new sports/media complex. It is apparent that the emergence of digital technology and the expansion of new media markets have driven this sports/media complex into a new dimension. This section will first take a closer look at the background and characteristics of the digital and converging media environment and secondly, this section will shed light on how these new technologies have changed the sports/media complex.

2.3.1 The Media Landscape in the Twenty-First Century: From an Analogue to a Digital Media Landscape

2.3.1.1 Introduction

Until the early 1990s, watching television was a passive, sit-back-and-relax experience. People came home from work, switched on the television and watched the programmes offered by broadcasters, in a fixed order. During the last decade, the media environment and the way the public consumes information have been altered. The public today requests, besides the traditional reporting, camera shots from different angles, additional information on previous events, comments by others on a separate forum and so on. In other words, viewers no longer passively submit themselves to linear audiovisual broadcasts or fixed texts, but desire on-demand services enabling them to decide where, when and on which device they experience the event.[42] Under the impulse of technological and economic developments, this evolution will continue. This section will outline in short the impact of the main economic and technical trends in the media sector on how the public watches television.

2.3.1.2 Digitalisation

A. From Waves to Bits

In the past, television signals were exclusively broadcast as an electrical signal continuously varying in amplitude and frequency. This system, called analogue television, is currently being replaced by digital broadcasting. Digital television uses informational codes of 1s and 0s.[43] Hence, where traditional media are manufactured and shipped in a physical form or via analogue waves, digital media are broken down into intangible bits of information that are easier to manipulate, distribute and reproduce via computer-mediated communication.[44]

---

[42] Werkers et al. 2008, 43.

[43] EICTA 2008.

[44] Boyle and Haynes 2003, 96.

In case of analogue television, each individual frame of film or video is transmitted, meaning that in order to broadcast the image each complete frame must be redrawn on the screen. Whereas with digital technology only the changes from frame to frame, are transmitted, allowing more information to be sent using the same bandwidth.[45]

Hence, the most significant impact of digitalisation is the immediate expansion of capacity, effectively removing a limitation that existed in the analogue period.[46] A channel that used to carry a single analogue service can now carry up to seven higher quality digital services by satellite, cable or four terrestrially broadcast programmes.[47] Thus, replacing analogue broadcasting with a system based on digital techniques presents huge advantages in terms of efficient spectrum (or other infrastructure) usage.[48] Digital technology also offers new services, such as pay-per-view, near-video-on-demand, electronic programme guides, interactive features, etc. and improves picture and sound quality. Thanks to all these benefits, the European Commission stressed, in its i2010 action plan,[49] the crucial role of digital services in the further development of the information society.[50] Given that new Information and Communication Technologies (ICT) might be a strong driver for "*reinforcing Europe's cultural diversity by making our heritage and our cultural creations available to a wider number of citizens*",[51] the European Commission is pushing citizens to go digital as soon as possible.

B. Convergence

In the past, there were clear boundaries between different services, each being linked to their own specific infrastructure. On the one hand, broadcasting programmes were distributed via the air (terrestrial television), cable (cable television) or satellite (satellite television) to the viewers. On the other hand, the telecommunication network was used for private communication (telephony).[52] Due to the digital evolution, these clear boundaries became increasingly blurred and the telecommunications and broadcasting sectors are increasingly using the same infrastructure technologies. In practice, all different services, whether voice, data, sound or pictures, are no longer stuck to their "specialised" infrastructure, but can now be transmitted over every network.[53] The phenomenon of all networks

45 Harrison and Woods 2007, 52.
46 Commission of the European Communities 1997, COM(97) 623, 3.
47 See e.g.: European Audiovisual Observatory 1999, 6–7.
48 Commission of the European Communities 2003, COM(2003) 541 final, 5.
49 Commission of the European Communities 2005, COM(2005) 229 final.
50 Evens et al. 2010.
51 Commission of the European Communities (2005). COM(2005) 229 final, 9.
52 Valcke 2004, 20.
53 See e.g.: *Ibid.* 75; Commission of the European Communities 1997, ii.

being able to deliver any kind of service to any kind of platform is better known as "convergence".[54]

Commissioner Reding stated that "*mobile television is a key example of the digital convergence between networks, devices and content*".[55] As mobile operators are facing decreasing average revenue per user, due to intensified competition and regulatory interventions such as restricted termination tariffs and roaming fees, mobile television acts as the latest cash cow opportunity to generate new revenues. In doing so, mobile television challenges established business models by providing an innovative distribution mechanism for content delivery in order to reach new audiences or to target the traditional prime time audience at other times of the day.[56] Another example of convergence is the Internet, being able to transport text, image, video and sound.[57]

C. Interactivity

The next aspect of digitalisation is interactivity. Where traditional mass media were about the one-way flow of information, new media incorporate the ability to interact with the medium in a two-way or multilateral communication. Interactive television blurs some of the boundaries between the so-called "lean back"-experience of watching television and the "lean forward"-experience of personal computing.[58] Through interactivity, passive experiences will be transformed into something infinitely richer and more compelling giving the user some influence on the content. In practice, this usually means that, in one way or another, the system presents the user with choices.[59] In fact, Reding referred to this evolution as the transition from "*a passive "couch potato" attitude towards media, such as traditional TV or Cinema, towards an interactive consumer attitude similarly to blogging or chatting*".[60]

D. User-Generated Content

In the past, only newspapers, radio operators and television operators were able to communicate to the masses. However, the combination of cheap electronic devices

---

[54] For more information on convergence, see: Commission of the European Communities 1997, COM(97) 623.

[55] Reding 2006b, SPEECH/06/157, 2.

[56] IBM 2006, 1; Södergard 2003; Urban 2007, 48.

[57] Commission of the European Communities 1997, 3; Reding 2006a, b SPEECH, 2; Iosifidis 2002, 30.

[58] Boyle and Haynes 2003, 148.

[59] Feldman 1997, 13.

[60] Reding 2006a, SPEECH, 3.

linked to digital communication networks has resulted in the unprecedented lowering of the threshold to media content production and consequently, the blurring of the traditional allocation of tasks between producer and consumer. Whereas, in the past, audiovisual content production was a privilege largely attributed to a limited number of (professional) broadcasters (the production of content was very expensive), at the moment, audiovisual content can be created and distributed by anyone who has access to a camera (today even available in mobile phones) and a connection to the Internet. This means that broadcasters have lost their broadcasting monopoly and they are facing competition of viewers themselves putting video extracts on the web.[61] Time Magazine recognised this power shift in the media by naming 'you" as the Person of the Year in 2006.[62]

New communication technologies have clearly improved the abilities of individuals and groups to distribute the content they create and to redistribute content produced by others.[63] The content that is created in this way is referred to as "user-generated-content". As indicated by Valcke and Lenaerts, defining user-generated-content is very difficult, because there is no officially accepted definition. According to them, "*user-generated-content is understood very broadly to include all content put online by users, whether it was created by them or not*". It is, however, worthwhile to note the difference between "user-generated-content" and "user-created-content'. The latter is limited to content that was actually created by users.[64] The OECD, for example, defines user-created content as "*a) content made publicly available on the Internet; b) which reflects a certain amount of creative effort; c) which is created outside of professional routines and practices*".[65]

The OECD argued that the rise of user-generated content could lead to "*[...] increased participation and increased diversity*"[66] and that it should be seen as "*an open platform enriching political and societal debates, diversity of opinion, free flow of information and freedom of expression*".[67] Although user-generated content can be very valuable, it also has its drawbacks. The Independent Study on Indicators for Media Pluralism in the Member States, for example, emphasised that user-generated content could produce benefits, but that it could also create potential harm to pluralism (*infra*).[68]

---

[61] Werkers et al. 2008, 44.

[62] Time 2006.

[63] ICRI et al. 2009a, 12.

[64] Valcke and Lenaerts 2010, 129.

[65] OECD 2007, 4.

[66] Ibid. 5 and 35.

[67] Ibid. 6.

[68] ICRI et. al. 2009b, 9.

2.3.1.3 Liberalisation

In the past, broadcasting services as well as telecommunication services were characterised by monopolies. The standard structural form of broadcasting services in Europe was traditionally that of a monopoly, granted under the argument that some essential social, cultural and political interests would not be served by a market based, competitive broadcast system. The results of these policies and a limitation of the available spectrum resulted in a limited choice for viewers. The emergence of new infrastructure means, such as cable and satellite, allowed new players, other than the traditional public broadcasters, to enter the broadcasting market. As a result of this evolution, Member States began authorising commercially funded broadcasters to supplement public service broadcasters.[69] In addition, telecommunications were seen as natural monopoly.[70] One of the reasons exclusive rights were granted was that telecommunications systems, and in particular telephony, were seen as a public service, fulfilling the important social function of enabling people to communicate.[71] However, as indicated by Nikolinakos, this situation changed due to digitalisation, convergence and the growing international and competitive character of the telecommunications sector.[72] In order to increase the competitiveness of the European telecommunications industry, the European Commission proposed opening the internal telecommunications market to competition by means of liberalisation and harmonisation measures.

Hence, these recent policy developments towards liberalisation within the telecommunications sector and breaking up the broadcasting monopolies have fundamentally reshaped the media landscape. Previously, distinct players entered each other's territories: telecom companies started to offer digital television services; cable television operators started to offer voice and Internet services. Previously, distinct markets have merged into a broad communications industry.

2.3.2 Sports/Media Complex in the Digital Media Landscape

2.3.2.1 Sports Clubs and Sports Organisations

Sports clubs and sports organisations themselves have discovered the opportunities of new media to get in touch with their fans as well as to extract commercial values from those new services. The clubs realised that, to keep up with all the new trends and to intensify the relationship with the fans, they had to become a

---

69 ICRI et al. 2009a, 14.

70 Larouche 2000, 29.

71 Nikolinakos 2006, 21.

72 *Ibid.*

multimedia company themselves. Jakubowicz defined this trend as "disintermediation". This means that intermediaries, such as media organisations, are eliminated. Anyone can offer information and other content to be directly accessed by users and receivers. Hence, disintermediation allows sports (and other) entities to become content providers and disseminators themselves, bypassing traditional media and reaching out directly to the general public.[73]

The first step in bringing sports events, sports clubs and athletes closer to the public is the creation of a club website containing news about the club, results, team line-ups and so on. Additionally, the aim of these websites is to become a meeting point for the fans offering them opportunities to communicate on a forum with each other about issues such as the merits of different teams and players.[74] Given that the Internet is a visual platform, websites do not only offer text, but also a variety of images. With the aid of improved bandwidth, the volume of photos and video footage available on those websites has been increasing a lot.[75] This audiovisual material provides also another opportunity for clubs to attract advertisers and make profit.[76]

In order to connect with the public, clubs launched their own television or online channels offering highlights of the matches, daily news, exclusive interviews with players and coaches, live coverage of reserve games and so on. An early experiment was the launch of "MUTV" by Manchester United in 1998. MUTV was the first football television station to broadcast on a daily basis in order to promote the identity and the image of the club. This example was followed by other big clubs such as Barcelona with "Barça TV" and Real Madrid with "Real Madrid TV", as well as smaller clubs such as the Belgian team RSC Anderlecht with "RSCA TV".

Furthermore, it should be noted that a range of sports organisations are already offering video footage of their sports free of charge via YouTube. YouTube has a deal with different European football clubs such as AC Milan, Chelsea, Barcelona and Real Madrid to offer content on their platform.[77]

Finally, sports clubs and sports associations are not only active on traditional television and Internet, but they have also discovered the opportunities of mobile services. Mobile technologies represent an effective way to reach new consumers and provide value-added components to dedicated consumers. Due to the almost universal availability of mobile phones and the significant market penetration worldwide, sports organisations can reach a large and often specifically targeted audience.[78] In addition to SMS, sports clubs are able to offer sports branded ring tones, wallpapers, interactive games, match highlights, score updates, game

73 Jakubowicz 2009, 12 and 19.

74 Rowe 2004, 206.

75 Standing Committee on Environment, Communications and the Arts 2009, 12.

76 ENPA 2005, 2.

77 BBC News 2007a.

78 Santomier and Costabiei 2010, 41.

schedules, news flashes and breaking news via text messaging.[79] With "MyMadrid", Real Madrid even goes a step further. This mobile community provides to all Real Madrid fans the possibility to buy tickets, to get all the information about matches, the club as well as the players. The members of MyMadrid community will also be able to chat with each other, to give their opinion about the matches and take part in different sport events and contests.[80]

2.3.2.2 Media Companies

Not only sports clubs have become media entities. Media companies, being producers of sports programmes, have in turn acquired controlling stakes in sports organisations, being the providers of content.[81] For example, Real Madrid is part-owned by the Spanish telecommunications giant Telefonica and Paris St Germain by Canal Plus.[82] This trend is often referred to as the "vertical integration strategy in sport" or "Murdochisation". "Murdochisation" can be defined as "*a process by which corporations primarily involved in mass media or communications appropriate and integrate into their own organizations sport clubs. In doing so, the media groups gain access to and control of the competitive activities of the clubs, which they can distribute through their network*".[83] The key driver of this vertical integration trend is to secure access to sports broadcasting rights.[84] Therefore, the increasing convergence between sports organisations and media conglomerates is driving the sports/media complex to a new dimension, allowing media companies to have exclusive access and closer control of broadcasting and merchandising rights.[85]

Still, it is argued that this vertical integration process is likely to decrease broadcasting competitiveness, eliminate third parties and depress the fees for broadcasting rights. This is the reason why the Monopolies and Mergers Commission denied the takeover of Manchester United by BSkyB in 1999.[86] According to this Commission, the merger would damage competition among broadcasters and would be detrimental to the wider interests of British football, because BSkyB would have a natural advantage over competitors in the bidding contest, since a proportion of its bid would return automatically to the company through the

---

79 *Ibid.*; Boyle 2004, 73–82.

80 Eufootball.biz, 2009.

81 Gratton and Solberg 2007, 95 and 97.

82 Silk 2004, 236.

83 Horne 2006, 49–50.

84 Gerrard 2004, 258.

85 Evens and Lefever 2011, 38.

86 For more information about this decision, see: Monopolies and Mergers Commission 1999; Binmore and Harbord (2000). 142–144; Crowther 2000, 30–35; Cave and Crandall 2001, Hoehn and Lancefield 2003, 564–565.

football club.[87] This is called a "toehold effect". In practice, a toehold effect exists when a bidder in an auction has an ownership stake in the property being sold and that stake increases the bidders' chances to win the auction, even when the ownership stake is relatively small. Bidders with a toehold ownership stake have an incentive to bid above the property value since part of the bid price would be automatically reimbursed to the bidder through his ownership stake.[88] As a result, the England and Wales Premier League, for example, ruled that no media company should be allowed to own a stake over 10 % in a football club.[89] In order to protect the integrity of the sport, the UEFA furthermore stipulated a multi-ownership rule. This rule entails that a company or individual cannot directly or indirectly control more than one of the clubs participating in a UEFA club competition (*infra*).[90] National football associations too have rules preventing one company or individual from having a controlling stake in two or more clubs playing in the same competition.[91]

2.3.2.3 Sponsors

New media have come to refer a different style of marketing where sport marketers can communicate in novel ways with sports consumers (such as websites and mobile phones). However, new media marketing means more than just using up-to-date technology within a traditional marketing programme. It also refers to a novel marketing approach that recognises the complex social and technological world that sports consumers occupy. As indicated by Smith, new media marketing must do more than just use new technology to be effective. The strategy also needs to respond to the changing lifestyle and expectations of sports consumers.[92] A good example of this new way of marketing is the video featuring tennis star Roger Federer who knocks off a can of a crew member's head in true William Tell style, while shooting an ad for Gillette. This video had the Internet buzzing about the question whether his exploits were real or fake. The video has already been viewed over a million times, and we are still waiting for the Gillette commercial they were actually shooting…[93]

---

87 Dobson and Goddard 2001, 84–85.

88 Gerrard 2004, 262–263.

89 Ofcom 2007, 24.

90 Rapid Press Releases 2002, IP/02/942.

91 Cave and Crandall 2001, 22.

92 Smith 2008, 259–261.

93 See e.g.: The Daily Telegraph 2010; YouTube 2010.

2.3.2.4 Public: Fans

The sports/media complex has been altered forever by new digital media, but so has the role of the sports audience. Currently, the public is afforded the opportunity to produce their own sports content and distribute it on the World Wide Web (*supra*). The new media technologies have offered the public (including the athletes themselves) the opportunity to run their personal blogs to report and express their personal opinion on sports events. They sometimes illustrate their texts with pictures or videos, images of the game or images of the atmosphere, for example, taken at the scene.[94] Individuals now have a place next to traditional producers of sports content in the digital sports landscape.[95]

However, as the saying goes, "all that glisters is not gold". In fact, the Internet not only provides interesting original online creative content generated by new actors, it is also swarming with illegal and harmful content that infringes the rights of others. One of the problems that has been given much media attention is the fact that sports events (in all formats: text, audiovisual, radio, webcast, etc.), being covered by exclusive media licensing agreements, are now on a large scale copied by fans without the authorisation of the rights holders involved.[96] Therefore, the Premier League decided to sue YouTube, for posting user-generated videos that infringe exclusive deals with other media operators.[97] Both Viacom and the Premier League lost the case in first instance. According to the US Court, YouTube is not infringing copyright when the public is posting unauthorised videos to the site. YouTube only becomes liable for infringement when it does not immediately remove videos from its website once it has been told that these videos infringe specific copyrights.[98] During the Beijing Games in 2008, the International Olympic Committee (IOC) requested the Swedish authorities for the removal of copyrighted Olympics content illegally stored on the peer-to-peer network Pirate Bay.[99] In June 2011, The Times obtained information that Apple wants to stop iPhone users from filming live events, such as sports events or concerts, with their smartphone. According to The Times, Apple is developing software that will sense when a smartphone user is trying to record a live event. Sensors would automatically instruct the iPhone to shut down its camera function. Other features, such as texting and making calls, would still work.[100] According to The Times, the development of this software is seen as an attempt to protect the exclusive rights holders.[101]

[94] Werkers et al. 2008, 43.

[95] Mahan and McDaniel 2006, 429; Rowe 1999, 168.

[96] Werkers et al. 2008, 45.

[97] See e.g.: BBC News 2007b.

[98] United States District Court 2010.

[99] Newton 2008.

[100] Daily Mail 2011.

[101] News.com.au 2011.

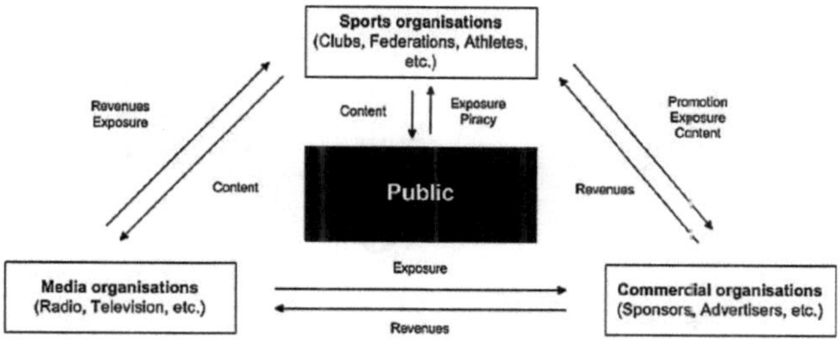

Fig. 2.3 Sports/media complex in the digital media market

However, during the 2006 FIFA World Cup, one of the new media innovations was the involvement of the public in user-generated content, which included participation and involvement through self-production of videos and pictures.[102] Furthermore, Santomier and Costabiei argued that, from a content distribution perspective, sports organisations should develop a strategy for integrating appropriately selected user-generated content with traditional sports content. In particular, sports organisations will determine which content will be made available via digital feeds to the public offering the latter the possibility to create their own services, such as a video or a blog.[103]

The evolution that users have taken up the role of creator and distributor of content created new opportunities for citizens to exercise their right to freedom of expression and information by recording and distributing information and video fragments of important events on the one hand, but, on the other hand, the opportunity for citizens to violate the exclusive rights of broadcasters who offer the events.[104]

2.3.3 Sports/Media Complex in the Digital Media Landscape: Summary

Figure 2.3 shows the intertwined relationship of the different stakeholders of the sports/media complex in the digital media market:

This figure reflects the new reality that everybody can or has become content producer. Not only media organisations are interested in broadcasting sports events, commercial organisations, the public and the sports organisations too are offered the possibility to produce their own sports content. As a result, new conflicting interests have emerged in this changed media landscape. Sports content is now wanted more than ever. For example, supporters who use digital cameras or

[102] Santomier and Costabiei 2010, 43.

[103] Ibid. 47.

[104] Werkers et al. 2008, 44.

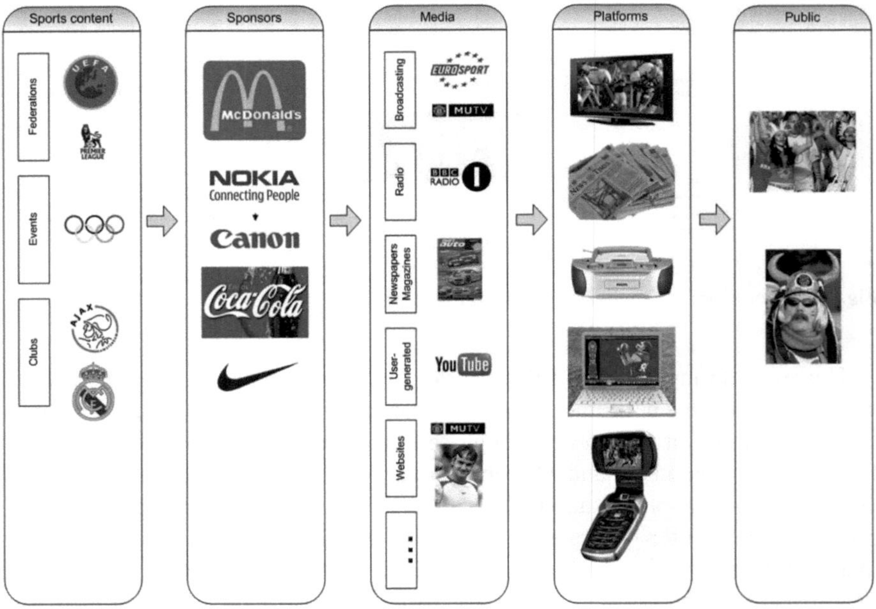

Fig. 2.4 Sports/media complex and the value chain of the digital media sector

smartphones during games and upload content may violate exclusive contracts which sports organisations have agreed upon.[105] In fact, this is actually the main fear of the sports organisations wanting to guarantee that only the rights holding broadcasters could cover the sports event. Naturally, the sports content would be devaluated without this exclusivity and this would of course result in lower prices for the broadcasting rights. However, as indicated above, some sports organisations have embraced the opportunities created by user-generated content. They realised that user-generated content could create opportunities apart from threats. In fact, user-generated content could reach new fans leading to an increased interest in their sport. Furthermore, given that sports organisations can take over the role of multimedia companies themselves, they can eliminate media organisations as the main and only source of sports coverage and can directly reach out to the public. It is, however, important that these new content providers recognise that broadcasting, editing and generating sports content does have legal consequences which need to be taken into account. Depending on the role they will fulfil (audiovisual media service provider, e-publisher or platform provider), media obligations and risk of liability will be different.[106] Given that the old and traditional balance between the public, media organisations, commercial organisations

[105] Lefever and Werkers 2010, 217.

[106] For more information about the new media players and their new obligations, see: Lefever and Werkers 2010, 214–219.

and sports organisations is under pressure, the question rises how the legislator should deal with these new evolutions in order to enhance new media operators' access and the public's access to live sports content. This will be discussed in the following Parts.

Figure 2.4 reflects how the sports/media complex can be integrated in the value chain of the digital media sector. The main difference with the analogue value chain is that the public is included as a media provider and thus, that user-generated content is put on the same level as professional media.

References

Legislation and Policy Documents

European Union

Commission Staff Working Papers

Commission of the European Communities (2007) Commission staff working document—The EU and sport: background and context—Accompanying document to the white paper on sport. SEC(2007) 935, 11 July 2007

European Commission (1998) Commission staff working paper—The development and prospects for community action in the field of sport. http://ec.europa.eu/sport/library/doc/a/doc252_en.pdf. Accessed 19 Aug 2010

Communications

Commission of the European Communities (2003) Communication from the Commission to the European Parliament, the Council, the Economic and Social Committee and the Committee of the Regions on the transition from analogue to digital broadcasting (from digital 'switchover' to analogue 'switch-off'). COM(2003) 541 final, 17 Sept 2003

Commission of the European Communities (2005) Communication from the Commission to the European Parliament, the Council, the Economic and Social Committee and the Committee of the Regions—"i2010—A European Information Society for growth and employment". COM(2005) 229 final, 1 June 2005

Decisions

Commission decision of 2 April 2003 declaring a concentration to be compatible with the common market and the EEA Agreement (Case No COMP/M. 2876—Newscorp/Telepiù) *OJ* (2004) L 110/73

Commission decision of 23 July 2003 relating to a proceeding pursuant to Article 81 of the EC Treaty and Article 53 of the EEA Agreement (2003) COMP/C.2-37.398—Joint selling of the commercial rights of the UEFA Champions League. *OJ*, L 291/25

Green Papers

Commission of the European Communities (1997) Green paper on the convergence of the telecommunications, media and information technology sectors, and the implications for regulation. COM(97)623, 3 Dec 1997

White Papers

Commission of the European Communities (2007) White paper on sport. COM (2007)391 final, 11 July 2007

Press Releases

Rapid Press Releases (2002) Commission closes investigation into UEFA rule on multiple ownership of football clubs. IP/02/942

Speeches

Reding V (2006a) Television is going mobile—and needs a pan European policy approach, SPEECH/06/157

Reding V (2006b) Digital convergence: a whole new way of life, SPEECH

UK

Consultations

Ofcom (2007) Summary of UK sports rights - Annex 10 to pay TV market investigation consultation. http://stakeholders.ofcom.org.uk/binaries/consultations/market_invest_paytv/annexes/annex_10.pdf. Accessed 18 Aug 2010

Ofcom (2008) Pay TV second consultation—Access to premium content. http://stakeholders.ofcom.org.uk/binaries/consultations/second_paytv/summary/condoc.pdf. Accessed 18 Aug 2010

Ofcom (2009) Pay TV phase three document: proposed remedies. http://stakeholders.ofcom.org.uk/binaries/consultations/third_paytv/summary/paytv_condoc.pdf. Accessed 18 Aug 2010

Reports

Standing Committee on Environment, Communications and the Arts (2009) The reporting of sports news and the emergence of digital media. http://www.aph.gov.au/Senate/committee/eca_ctte/sports_news/report/report.pdf. Accessed 18 Aug 2010

Case Law

UK

Monopolies and Mergers Commission (1999) British Sky Broadcasting Group plc and Manchester United plc. A report on the proposed merger. http://www.competition-commission.org.uk. Accessed 18 Aug 2010

US

United States District Court—Southern District of New York, Viacom vs. YouTube and Premier League vs. YouTube. (2010) http://static.googleusercontent.com/external_content/untrusted_dlcp/www.google.com/en/us/press/pdf/msj_decision.pdf. Accessed 18 Aug 2010

Doctrine

BBC News (2007a) YouTube makes international move, 19 June 2007. http://news.bbc.co.uk/2/hi/technology/6757525.stm. Accessed on 18 Aug 2010
BBC News (2007b) Sport puts up fight to protect rights, 11 July 2007. http://news.bbc.co.uk/2/hi/business/6268854.stm. Accessed 18 Aug 2010
BBC News (2009a) Major sponsor Gillette to 'limit' Tiger Woods's role, 12 Dec 2009. http://news.bbc.co.uk/2/hi/americas/8409841.stm. Accessed 18 Aug 2010
BBC News (2009b) Accenture ends Tiger Woods sponsorship deal, 14 Dec 2009. http://news.bbc.co.uk/2/hi/8411091.stm. Accessed 18 Aug 2010
BBC Sport (2006) IOC debates 2008 pool finals move, 22 June 2006, http://news.bbc.co.uk/sport2/low/other_sports/swimming/5104686.stm. Accessed 18 Aug 2010
Binmore K, Harbord D (2000) Toeholds, takeovers and football. Eur Compet Law Rev 21(2):142–144
Bolotny F, Bourg JF (2006) The demand for media coverage. In: Wladimir A, Szymanski S (eds) Handbook of the economics of sport. Edward Elgar, Cheltenham, pp 112–133
Boyle R (2004) Mobile communications and the sports industry: the case of 3G. Trends Commun 12(2):73–82
Boyle R, Haynes R (2000) Power play: sport, the media and popular culture. Longman, Harlow
Boyle R, Haynes R (2003) New media sport. In: Bernstein A, Blain N (eds) Sport, media, culture: global and local dimensions. Cass, London, pp 95–114
Boyle R, Haynes R (2004) Football in the new media age. Routledge, London
Buraimo B (2006) The demand for sports broadcasting. In: Wladimir A, Szymanski S (eds) Handbook of the economics of sport. Edward Elgar, Cheltenham, pp 100–111
Businessweek (2008) Coke's Going for the gold, 3 Sept 2008. http://www.businessweek.com/careers/managementiq/archives/2008/09/cokes_going_for.html. Accessed 18 Aug 2010
Cave M, Crandall R (2001) Sports rights and the broadcast industry. Econ J 111:4–26
Crowther P (2000) Broadcasters v. regulators: the threat to football from media company ownership of football clubs. Soccer Soc 1(3):30–35
Daily Mail (2011) Now Apple wants to block iPhone users from filming live events with their smartphone. 16 June 2011. http://www.dailymail.co.uk/sciencetech/article-2004233/Apple-files-patent-block-iPhone-users-filming-live-events-smartphone.html. Accessed 16 June 2011

De Moragas M et al (2003) The impact of the Internet on the sports industry. SportCongress, Barcelona, pp 15–16
Dobson S, Goddard J (2001) The economics of football. Cambridge University press, New York
ENPA (2005) ENPA response to the issue paper for audiovisual conference in Liverpool: Right to information and right to short reporting. http://ec.europa.eu/avpolicy/docs/reg/modernisation/issue_papers/contributions/ip2-enpa.pdf. Accessed 18 Aug 2010
Eufootball.biz (2009) Real Madrid launch mobile community, 24 Sept 2009. http://www.eufootball.biz/Technology/7567-real_madrid_launch_mobile_community.html. Accessed 23 Aug 2010
European Audiovisual Observatory (1999) Developments in digital television in the European Union. http://www.obs.coe.int/online_publication/expert/00002497.pdf.fr. Accessed 18 Aug 2010
Evens T et al (2010) Attracting the un-served audience: the sustainability of long tail-based. business models for cultural television content. New Media Soc 12:1005–1023
Evens T, Lefever K (2011) Watching the soccer game: broadcasting rights for the European digital television market. J Sport Soc Issues 35(1):33–49
Feldman T (1997) An introduction to digital. Routledge, London
Financial Times (2009) Sky wins extra package of live TV football, 7 Feb 2009. http://www.ft.com/cms/s/0/15a1f2fa-f4b9-11dd-8e76-0000779fd2ac.html?ftcamp=rss&nclick_check=1. Accessed 18 Aug 2010
Forrest D, Simmons R, Szymanski S (2010) Broadcasting, attendance and the inefficiency of cartels. In: Szymanski S (ed) Football economics and policy. Palgrave Macmillan, London, pp 112–135
Gerrard B (2004) Media ownership of teams: the latest stage in the commercialization of team sports. In: Slack T (ed) The commercialisation of sport. Routledge, London, pp 247–266
Ginesta Portret X, Sopena Palomar J (2008) The global media sports complex and its resistances: the case of the Spanish media clubs. IAMCR World Congres, Stockholm, 20–25 July 2008
Grant A, Graeme R (2008) Does television crowd out spectators?: new evidence from the Scottish Premier League. J Sports Econ 9:592–605
Gratton C, Solberg HA (2007) The economics of sports broadcasting. Routledge, London
Guardian (2006) The new World Cup rule: take off your trousers, they're offending our sponsor, 19 June 2006. http://www.guardian.co.uk/media/2006/jun/19/marketingandpr.worldcup2006. Accessed 18 Aug 2010
Guardian (2009) Nike stands by sponsorship of Tiger Woods despite 'indiscretions', 14 Dec 2009. http://www.guardian.co.uk/sport/2009/dec/14/nike-sponsorship-tiger-woods. Accessed 18 Aug 2010
Hargreaves J (1986) Sport, power and culture: a social and historical analysis of popular sports in Britain. Polity press, Cambridge
Harrison J, Woods L (2007) European broadcasting law and policy. Cambridge University Press, Cambridge
Hatton C, Wagner C, Armengod H (2007) Fair play: how competition authorities have regulated the sale of football media rights in Europe. ECLR 28(6):346–354
Hoehn T, Lancefield D (2003) Broadcasting and sport. Oxf Rev Econ Policy 19(4):552–568
Horne J (2006) Sport in consumer culture. Palgrave Macmillan, New York
IBM (2006) Primetime for mobile television: extending the entertainment concept by bringing together the best of both worlds. IBM Institute for Business Value, New York. http://www-935.ibm.com/services/us/gbs/bus/pdf/ibv-ge510-6275-02.pdf. Accessed 18 Aug 2010
ICRI et. al. (2009a) Independent study on indicators for media pluralism in the member states—towards a risk-based approach. Final report—annex I: user guide. http://ec.europa.eu/information_society/media_taskforce/doc/pluralism/study/user_guide_09.pdf. Accessed 18 Aug 2010
ICRI et. al. (2009b) Independent study on indicators for media pluralism in the member states—towards a risk-based approach. Final report. http://ec.europa.eu/information_society/media_taskforce/doc/pluralism/study/final_report_09.pdf. Accessed 19 Aug 2010

Iosifidis P (2002) Digital convergence: challenges for European regulation. Public 9(3):27–48
Jhally S (1989) Cultural studies and the sports/media complex. In: Wenner L (ed) Media, sports and society. Sage, London, pp 70–97
Jakubowicz K (2009) A new notion of media?—background text, 1st Council of Europe Conference of Ministers Responsible for Media and New Communication Services, Reykjavik, 28–29 May 2009. http://www.ministerialconference.is/media/images/a_new_notion_of_media_web_version.pdf. Accessed 18 Aug 2010
Kestens S (2005) De mediatisering van de voetbalsport: de websites en televisiezenders van de grote Europese voetbalploegen. Master thesis social science, Promotor: Prof. Dr. Guy De Meyer, Leuven
Larouche P (2000) Competition law and regulation in European telecommunications. Hart, Oxford
Lefever K, Van Rompuy B (2009) Ensuring access to sports content: 10 years of EU intervention. time to celebrate? J Media Law 2:243–268
Lefever K, Werkers E (2010) Digital sports content: the rise of new media players and the legal consequences in terms of obligations and liability risks. Entertain Law Rev 6:214–219
Maguire J (1991) The media-sport production complex: the case of American football in Western European Societies. European Journal of Communication 6:315–335
Maguire J (1993) Globalization, sport development, and the media/sport production complex. Sport Sci Rev 2:29–47
Mahan J, McDaniel S (2006) The new online arena: sport, marketing, and media converge in cyberspace. In: Raney A, Bryant J (eds) Handbook of sports and media. Erlbaum, Mahwah (N.J.), pp 409–431
News.com.au (2011) Apple patent will stop you filming concerts, sports events on iPhone (2011) http://www.news.com.au/technology/apple-patent-will-stop-you-filming-concerts-sports-events-on-iphone/story-e6frfro0-1226076805416. Accessed 17 June 2011
Nikolinakos N (2006) EU competition law and regulation in the converging telecommunications, media and IT sectors. Kluwer Law International, Alphen a/d Rijn
OECD (2007) Participative web: user-generated content. http://www.oecd.org/dataoecd/57/14/38393115.pdf. Accessed 18 Aug 2010
Premiere (2006) Annual report 2005. http://info.sky.de/inhalt/static/download/aktie/gj2005/premiere_ag_annual_report_2005.pdf. Accessed 18 Aug 2010
PriceWaterHouseCoopers (2008) At the dawn of new traditions. Entertainment & Media Outlook towards 2012. Trends in the Netherlands 2008–2012. http://submit.pwc.com/Extweb/onlineforms.nsf/docid/0C1E3760C0ED03EF802574CC0046B6E1/$file/PwC_EMOutlook08.pdf. Accessed 18 Aug 2010
Rosner S, Shropshire K (2004) The business of sports. Jones and Bartlett Publishers, Sudbury
Rowe D (1999) Sport, culture and the media: the unruly trinity. Open University Press, Buckingham
Rowe D (2004) Sport, culture and the media: the unruly trinity, 2nd edn. Open University Press, Maidenhead
Santomier J, Costabiei A (2010) New media challenges in the twenty-first century. In: Hamil S, Chadwick S (eds) Managing football: an international perspective. Elsevier, Amsterdam, pp 37–54
Silk M (2004) Televised sport in a global consumer age. In: Slack T (ed) The commercialisation of sport. Routledge, London, pp 226–246
Skinner J (2010) Sports marketing and Sponsorship. In: Hamil S, Chadwick S (eds) Managing football: an international perspective. Elsevier, Amsterdam, pp 103–117
Slack T, Amis J (2004) 'Money for nothing and your cheques for free?' A critical perspective on sport sponsorship. In: Slack T (ed) The commercialisation of sport. Routledge, London, pp 269–286
Smith A (2008) Introduction to sport marketing. Elsevier, Amsterdam
Smart B (2008) Not playing around: global capitalism, modern sport and consumer culture. In: Giulianotti R, Robertson R (eds) Globalization and sport. Blackwell, Malden, pp 113–134

Södergard C (2003) Mobile television—technology and user experience.VTT Publications: Finland

Sportbusiness International (2010a) Super Bowl ads exceed 2009 prices, 2 February 2010. http://www.sportbusiness.com/news/171730/super-bowl-ads-exceed-2009-prices?utm_source=sbinsl&utm_medium=email&utm_campaign=feb2. Accessed 18 Aug 2010

Sportbusiness International (2010b) FIFA: Over 700m viewers for World Cup final, 12 July 2010. http://www.sportbusiness.com/news/178947/fifa-over-700m-viewers-for-world-cup-final?utm_source=sbinsl&utm_medium=email&utm_campaign=july12. Accessed 18 Aug 2010

Stead D (1986) Sport and the media. In: Houlihan B (ed) Sport and society: a student introduction. Sage, London, pp 184–200

Telegraph (2009) Tiger Woods: affairs may have cost sponsors' shareholders $12bn, 29 Dec 2009. http://www.telegraph.co.uk/sport/golf/tigerwoods/6907788/Tiger-Woods-affairs-may-have-cost-sponsors-shareholders-12bn.html. Accessed 18 Aug 2010

The Daily Telegraph (2010) Federer trick shot - real or fake, 19 Aug 2010. http://www.dailytelegraph.com.au/sport/federer-trick-shot-real-or-fake/story-e6frexni-1225907302001. Accessed 27 Oct 2010

The Independent (1996) Sport is Murdoch's 'battering ram' for pay TV, 16 October 1996. http://www.independent.co.uk/sport/sport-is-murdochs-battering-ram-for-pay-tv-1358686.html. Accessed 18 Aug 2010

The New York Times (1990) Networks Wary on '94 World Cup Rights, 5 July 1990. http://www.nytimes.com/1990/07/05/business/networks-wary-on-94-world-cup-rights.html. Accessed 18 Aug 2010

Time (2006) Time's person of the year: you, 13 Dec 2006. http://www.time.com/time/magazine/article/0,9171,1569514,00.html. Accessed 18 Aug 2010

UEFA (2008) UEFA EURO 2008 in figures, 24 May 2008. http://www1.uefa.com/MultimediaFiles/Download/MediaRelease/Competitions/MediaServices/70/28/54/702854_DOWNLOAD.pdf. Accessed 18 Aug 2010

Urban A (2007) Mobile television: is it just a hype or a real consumer need? Obs J 1(3):45–58

Valcke P (2004) Digitale Diversiteit. Convergentie van Media-, Telecommunicatie- en Mededingingsrecht. Larcier, Brussels

Valcke P, Lenaerts M (2010) Looking for the author, the editor and the publisher in UGC: new models for legal liability of UGC intermediaries. Int Rev Law Comput Technol 24(1): 119–131

Vanderkelen P (1997) Supersport—Structurele en programmatorische doorlichting van een betaalsportzender in Vlaanderen. Master thesis social science, Promotor: Prof. Dr. D. Biltereyst, Leuven

Werkers E, Lefever K, Valcke P (2008) One world one dream? Sports blogging at the Beijing Olympic Games. ISLJ 3–4:42–51

Whitson Dd (1998) Circuits of promotion: media, marketing and the globalization of sport. In: Wenner L (ed) Mediasport. Routledge, Londen, pp 57–72

Newton J (2008) Take Pirate Bay Olympics posts down!, IOC. http://www.p2pnet.net/story/16769. Accessed 18 August 2010

X (2009) Sports broadcasting in the digital era. Commun Law Bull 27(4):15–20

YouTube (2010) Amazing Roger Federer trickshot on Gillette ad shoot. http://www.youtube.com/results?search_query=federer+trick+shot+gillette&aq=4. Accessed 27 Oct 2010

Chapter 3
Specificity of Sport: The Important Role of Sport in Society

3.1 Introduction

As indicated by, for example, Reding, sport is characterised by a dual nature: sport embraces both an economic and a societal dimension or function.[1] In this chapter, we will take a closer look at both dimensions of sport. In doing so, the importance of sport in our society will be discussed in-depth. The latter is needed, because this analysis will play an important role in this chapter when dealing with the question of whether States should guarantee access to sports coverage under Article 10 of the European Convention on Human Rights.

3.2 Economic Dimension of Sport

Over the years, sport has become much more than just a game or winning medals. The sports sector has transformed into an important economic activity and became big business. The cost of becoming an official sponsor of a team or major sports events is higher than ever before (*supra*), the value of sports broadcasting rights has increased sharply (*supra*) and the same goes for the transfer fees and salaries of professional athletes. The vast amount of money flowing into sports due to professionalisation and commercialisation demonstrates that sport has, transformed into an important economic sphere. In 2011, the global sports market was valued at $118.7 billion.[2]

Although sports government bodies often have argued that, due to its legal autonomy, law and sport are two different worlds,[3] the European Court of Justice

[1] Reding 2002, SPEECH/02/440.
[2] PricewaterhouseCoopers 2011, 4.
[3] See e.g., Chappelet 2010.

K. Lefever, *New Media and Sport*, ASSER International Sports Law Series,
DOI: 10.1007/978-90-6704-873-6_3,

has already established in the 1970s that sport is subject to Community law, insofar as it constitutes an economic activity within the meaning of Article 2 of the EC Treaty. Article 2 of the EC Treaty stated the following: "*the Union shall set itself the following objectives: to promote economic and social progress and a high level of employment and to achieve balanced and sustainable development, in particular through the creation of an area without internal frontiers, through the strengthening of economic and social cohesion and through the establishment of economic and monetary union, ultimately including a single currency in accordance with the provisions of this Treaty*". This Article is repealed by the Lisbon Treaty and is replaced, in substance, by Article 3 of the Treaty on European Union.[4]

The principle that sport is subject to Community law, insofar as it constitutes an economic activity was enunciated for the first time in the *Walrave* case.[5] In para 8 of the *Walrave* case, the European Court of Justice stated that "*Community law does not apply to rules of 'purely sporting interest' which as such has nothing to do with an economic activity*". Over the years, this principle is affirmed and reiterated in different cases such as *Dona* case,[6] *Bosman* case,[7] *Deliege* case[8] and *Lehtonen* case.[9] According to Blanpain, it is self-evident that the law is applicable to sport, like any other activity, and that sports organisers, like everyone else, have to follow the law.[10]

Although those first cases stating that sport could be subject to Community law were decided on the basis of the freedom of movement of persons, services and capital, it has also long been established by the European Commission and the Community Courts that economic activities in the context of sport do fall within the scope of EU competition law, notably Articles 101 (restrictive agreements between undertakings) and 102 (abuse of a dominant position) of the Treaty on the Functioning of the European Union (hereafter: TFEU).[11,12] The latter has been explicitly confirmed by the European Court of Justice in the *Meca Medina* case in 2006.[13,14]

---

4 Consolidated version of the Treaty on European Union. *OJ* (2008). C 115/13.

5 CJ, Walrave and Koch v. Union Cycliste Internationale, para 4.

6 CJ, Donà v Mantero, para 12.

7 CJ, Union Royale Belge des Sociétés de Football Association ASLB v. Jean Marc Bosman, para 73 (1995) (hereafter *Bosman* case).

8 CJ, Christelle Deliège v Ligue Francophone de Judo et Disciplines ASBL and others, para 41.

9 CJ, Jyri Lehtonen and Castors Canada Dry Namur-Braine ASBL v Fédération royale belge des sociétés de basketball ASBL (FRBSB), para 32.

10 Blanpain 2008, 2.

11 Consolidated version of the Treaty on the Functioning of the European Union. *OJ* (2008) C 115/47.

12 Commission of the European Communities 2007, SEC(2007) 935, 63.

13 GC, David Meca-Medina and Igor Majcen v. Commission of the European Communities (2004) (hereafter: GC, *Meca Medina* case); CJ, David Meca-Medina and Igor Majcen v. Commission of the European Communities (2006) (hereafter: CJ, *Meca Medina* case).

14 Commission of the European Communities 2007, SEC(2007) 935, 35.

Before the *Meca Medina* landmark decision, the European Commission, when applying competition rules in the sports sector, drew a dividing line between, on the one hand, 'purely sporting' rules, i.e. sporting rules that are necessary for its organisation or for the organisation of competitions, such as the length of a match, the size of a ball, etc., and, on the other hand, economic activities generated by sports, such as the sale and acquisition of sports broadcasting rights. The European Commission specified those two levels of activity as follows: "*the sporting activity strictly speaking, which fulfils a social, integrating and cultural role that must be preserved and to which in theory the competition rules of the EC Treaty do not apply*", and "*a series of economic activities generated by the sporting activity to which the competition rules of the EC Treaty apply*".[15] In 2006, in its first ever ruling on the application of European competition law to sport, the European Court of Justice rejected this long accepted dichotomy. The European Court of Justice stated that "*it is apparent that the mere fact that a rule is purely sporting in nature does not have the effect of removing from the scope of the Treaty the person engaging in the activity governed by that rule or the body which has laid it down*".[16] The European Court of Justice further clarified that "*even if those rules do not constitute restrictions on freedom of movement because they concern questions of purely sporting interest and, as such, have nothing to do with economic activity, that fact means neither that the sporting activity in question necessarily falls outside the scope of Articles 81 EC and 82 EC nor that the rules do not satisfy the specific requirements of those articles*".[17] This implies that no categories of sporting activities are a priori excluded from the application of Articles 101 and 102 of the TFEU. Instead, it must be determined on a case-by-case basis whether the specific requirements of Articles 101 and 102 of the TFEU are met, irrespective of the alleged "*purely sporting*" nature of the rule (*infra*).[18] Moreover, the European Court of Justice ruled that "*in holding that rules could thus be excluded straightaway from the scope of those Articles solely on the ground that they were regarded as purely sporting with regard to the application of Articles 39 EC and 49 EC, without any need to determine first whether the rules fulfilled the specific requirements of Articles 81 EC and 82 EC, [...] the Court of First Instance made an error of law*".[19]

This ruling also contains a methodology of applying competition law to organisational sporting rules. The European Court of Justice spelled out that competition rules cannot be assessed in abstract.[20] In assessing the compatibility of a specific rule with competition law account should be taken of "*the overall context in which the decision of the association of undertakings was taken or*

---

15 Rapid Press Releases 1999, 2.

16 CJ, *Meca Medina* case, para 27.

17 *Ibid.*, para 31.

18 Kienappel and Stein, 7.

19 CJ, *Meca Medina* case, para 33.

20 *Ibid.*, para 42.

produces its effects and, more specifically, of its objectives. It has then to be considered whether the consequential effects restrictive of competition are inherent in the pursuit of those objectives [...] and are proportionate to them".[21] When the European Court of Justice applied these principles in the *Meca Medina* case, it indicated that "*anti-doping rules at issue and the magnitude of the penalties applicable if they are breached are capable of producing adverse effects on competition because they could [...] result in an athlete's unwarranted exclusion from sporting events*".[22] However, the general objective of anti-doping rules is to combat doping in order for competitive sport to be conducted fairly with equal chances for athletes, to protect athletes' health, the integrity and objectivity of competitive sport and ethical values in sport.[23] Furthermore, the restrictions caused by the anti-doping rules, in particular as a result of penalties, were considered to be inherent in the organisation and proper conduct of competitive sport.[24] Finally, the European Court of Justice carried out a proportionality test examining whether the rules went beyond what is necessary to achieve those objectives as regards (i) the threshold for the banned substance in question and (ii) the severity of the penalties. It failed to identify such disproportionate effects.[25]

This decision has provoked a lot of (negative) reactions from the sports sector. Gianni Infantino, the Director Legal Affairs of UEFA, for example, has qualified this decision as a 'Pandora box'. According to him "*it seems that in most cases 'sporting activity' will be deemed to fall under the Treaty. On the other hand, many sports rules can be described as representing conditions for 'engaging in' sport. Probably, only the rules concerning the size of the ball or the kind of advertisement allowed on the kit will outside the scope*".[26] However, the European Commission stressed that this decision is of paramount importance for the application of competition law to the sports sector. This judgment, containing an authoritative interpretation of the anti-trust provisions in the context of organisational sporting rules by the European Court of Justice, represents a significant contribution to legal certainty in this area.[27]

3.3 Societal Dimension of Sport

Sport is more than an economic business. Sport is also characterised by a societal dimension fulfilling an important and vital role in our society. The European Court of Justice emphasised that sporting activities, and in particular football, are of

---

21 *Ibid.*

22 *Ibid.*, para 47.

23 *Ibid.*, para 43; Commission of the European Communities 2007, SEC(2007) 935, 37.

24 CJ, *Meca Medina* case, paras 44–45; Commission of the European Communities 2007, SEC(2007) 935, 37.

25 CJ, *Meca Medina* case, paras 47–55.

26 Infantino 2006, 5–6.

27 Commission of the European Communities 2007, SEC(2007) 935, 35.

"*considerable social importance*".[28] These societal sports features and qualities are often referred to as the 'specificity of sport'.

3.3.1 Specificity of Sport: Introduction

It is often recognised that sport brings people together, regardless of their age or social origin. Due to its capacity to reach out to everybody, the European institutions have attributed different functions that sport has in our society: a health-promotion role, an educational role, a social role, a recreational role and a cultural role.[29] First, sport can perform an educational function giving a view of values in life, such as competitiveness and fair play. Second, sport offers an opportunity to improve people's health and it is an effective means of combating certain illnesses. Third, sport is a tool to combat racism, discrimination, violence and to promote a more open and tolerant society. In other words, sport provides a ground for social inclusion. Fourth, sport gives people an additional opportunity to put down roots, to integrate better and to create a sense of belonging. And finally, sporting activities are important leisure occupations and provide personal and collective entertainment.[30] In the Opinion of the Committee of the Regions on 'Equal opportunities and sport',[31] Tarschys, a former Secretary-General Council of Europe, was quoted saying that "*the hidden face of sport is the thousands of enthusiasts who find in their football, rowing, athletics and rock-climbing clubs, a place for meeting and exchange, but above all the training ground for community life. In this microcosm, people learn to take responsibility, to follow rules, to accept one another, to look for consensus, to take on democracy. Seen from this angle, sport is par excellence the ideal school for democracy*". Hence, in other words, as indicated by the European Commission, "*sport is a suitable tool for promoting a more inclusive society and for combating intolerance, racism, violence, alcohol and drug abuse; sport can also assist in the integration of people excluded from the labour market*".[32]

As indicated in the White Paper on Sport, active citizenship, for example, could be promoted through sport and its values. According to the European Commission, participation in a team, principles such as fair-play, compliance with the rules of the game, respect for others, solidarity and discipline could reinforce active citizenship.[33] In the 2004 Eurobarometer, the European Union citizens indicated that team spirit is a value that is promoted the most by sport. Team spirit is followed by

---

[28] *Bosman* case, para 106.

[29] European Commission 1998, 5–6; Commission of the European Communities 2007, SEC(2007) 935, 7–8.

[30] European Commission 1998, 5–6.

[31] Committee of the Regions 2007.

[32] European Commission 1998, 6.

[33] Commission of the European Communities 2007, SEC(2007) 935, 16; Commission of the European Communities 2007, COM (2007) 391 final, 7.

discipline, friendship, effort, self-control, fair play.[34] According to Blatter, for example, "*FIFA's Fair Play campaign involves much more than simply promoting fair play on the pitch during a competition. FIFA is committed to encouraging fair play in society too, beginning with our future—with children*".[35]

Furthermore, sport could create social cohesion. As indicated above, the European institutions have recognised that sport plays an important role in bringing people together (*supra*). In the literature, many authors have also indicated that sport has the ability to promote a shared sense of belonging. Bodin, Robène & Héas, for example, pointed out that "*sport [...] brings people together and allows them to relate to one another*".[36] Parrish noted that sport often could be seen as a tool for social inclusion.[37] According to Goldlust, the social significance of sports events lies in their capability of creating a sense of communality.[38] In other words, some sports events have the ability to appeal both to the committed sports fan and the viewer who becomes interested for reasons of an ideological nature, connected with national pride and identification with a wider collective experience.[39] Sports events can bring people together in different ways. They create the possibility for people to share their experience with other people. Instead of watching a major sports event alone, everybody is gathered around the television set at home or in the pub. Hence, such an event brings people together and stimulates conversations for days after the event with friends, at the office and even with strangers.[40] Furthermore, after winning an important game, people come out into the streets and celebrate the victory together creating a feeling of togetherness and solidarity. Moreover, journalists address their audience in terms of national belongingness, referring to "*our*" chances, "*we*" won and celebrating "*a great day for our country*".[41]

Additionally, according to Rowe and Bernstein, in countries divided by class, gender, ethnic, religious, regional and other means of identification, there are few opportunities for the citizens of a nation to develop a strong sense of collective consciousness of being one. However, international sporting events provide an opportunity for people to experience that exclusive sense of belonging to their "*imagined community*".[42] For example, in 1998, France won the FIFA World Cup with half the team composed of African born players. This multi-ethnic team was said to symbolise a new, more inclusive definition of "*Frenchness*".[43] The same

---

34 European Commission 2004, 7.

35 FIFA 2010.

36 Bodin et al. 2005, 17.

37 Parrish et al. 2010, 46.

38 Goldlust 1987, 129.

39 Boyle and Haynes 2000, 68.

40 Gratton and Solberg 2007, 173.

41 Whannel 1992, 136.

42 Rowe 2004, Bernstein 2007, 653.

43 Boyle and Haynes 2000, 159.

goes for the Belgian citizens. The year 2008 was characterised by a governmental crisis in Belgium due to the dissensions between the northern and the southern part of Belgium. However, during the Beijing Olympics, the citizens felt a sense of belonging when the Belgian women took the Women's 4 × 100 m silver medal. Journalists considered this victory and medal as a proof of a united Belgium: "*Four girls: north, south, black, white, Flemish, French, laughing, crying, and friendship. A mix of Belgium 2008*".[44] Boardman and Hargreaves-Heap referred to this as the "*positive social network externalities*" of the broadcasting of sports events.[45] Given that sport could create a feeling of togetherness and participation, it could also contribute to more integrated societies.[46] In the 2004 Eurobarometer, 73 % of the European Union citizens view sport as a means of promoting the integration of immigrant populations.[47] Based on this observation, it can be argued that guaranteeing the public's access to live and full sports content is important for the development of our democratic society and the individual citizens (*supra*).

Furthermore, the European institutions and literature have granted sport an important role in fostering a national identity.[48] However, the link between sport and national identity is questioned by some authors. The question that is often raised is whether sport can still create a national identity when local competitions are populated by foreign players and international teams by diasporas that return home for a few matches a year.[49] The same question is also raised by Bairner: "*to what extent is the linkage between sport and national identity likely to be weakened as a result of major transformations in global society?*".[50] In other words, in the past, the clubs in the leading national leagues were traditionally composed of fellow nationals and locally developed players. Hence, they were connected with the communities in which their fans lived. Now, players move from one club to another creating a difficulty for fans to feel identified with their club and players. According to Roche, however, the symbolic identifications of local fans with these "*new*" clubs seem to have often, ironically, intensified in spite of this. This is partly because the characters of the leagues that clubs are competing in are changing. In the past, clubs were competing in national leagues, and, thus, representing the locality to the nation, while the leading clubs are now also competing in competitions such as UEFA's Champions League. In such a European-level super-league, clubs represent both their locality and also their nation, on the European stage.[51] Furthermore, Mandelzis and Bernstein doubted whether this feeling of being one would last forever. For example, when Hapoel Bnei Sakhnin,

[44] Sporza 2008; Le Soir 2008.

[45] Boardman and Hargreaves-Heap 1999, 168.

[46] Commission of the European Communities 2007, COM (2007) 391 final, 7.

[47] European Commission 2004, 8.

[48] See e.g. Harrison and Woods 2007, 9; EU Sport Forum 2010, 3; Parrish et al. 2010, 46.

[49] Miller et al. 2001, 43.

[50] Bairner 2001, 1.

[51] For more information, see: Roche 2001, 89–90; Hundley and Billings 2010.

a football club representing an Arab town, won the Israeli State Cup in 2004, this success was seen as a symbol for a new Israel. Although this victory provided a "*ray of light*" and a "*sign*" of hope in the Israeli political conflict, in the end, it did not change anything for the Arab minority in Israel.[52]

In the workshop report about the social function of sport, it was indicated that both active and passive sport participation can contribute to the social function of sport.[53] Active sports participation refers to physical participation in sport. It is mostly seen as a source of fun and entertainment, but it can also contribute to personal growth and (inter)personal skills, encourage team building, etc. (*supra*). In other words, active sports participation plays an important role in the creation of social cohesion. Passive sports participation includes watching sports events on television and talking about the events and it can also contribute to bring people together and to create social inclusion. As indicated by different authors, a necessary precondition for the achievement of these social goals is that sport would be available and affordable to all citizens.[54] In other words, the importance of live and full sports coverage on free-to-air television (*infra*) may not be underestimated when dealing with the social function of sport. According to Iosifidis and Smith, unlike pay-television, free-to-air broadcasters are uniquely placed to maximise the social and cultural value attached to sport.[55] Furthermore, one should realise that sports on television could also have a positive effect on the active participation of the youth. Especially youth participation in sport is driven by watching professionals during the World Cup, Tour de France or the Olympic Games. In Belgium, for example, Kim Clijsters and Tom Boonen were an inspiration for children to engage in playing sport, because they want to become the new Kim Clijsters or Tom Boonen. As a result, thanks to the success of Boonen and Clijsters, both cycling and tennis organisations attracted more members.

However, sports organisations do not always support the idea that their sport should be broadcast on free-to-air television (*infra*). Nevertheless, they should understand that when they refer to the societal role of sport in order to get reduced VAT rates or public funding (*infra*), this argument cuts at both sides and, thus, that it also should be taken into account when dealing with live sports coverage on free-to-air television. Given that sport plays an important societal role in our society and is crucial to the well-being of our society, financial support of governments is accepted. As indicated by the European Commission, "*[t]he vast majority of sporting activities takes place in non-profit-making structures, many of which depend on public support to provide access to sporting activities to all citizens in a discrimination-free environment*".[56] In the accompanying document to the White Paper on Sport, the European Commission accepts public financial

---

52 Mandelzis and Bernstein 2010.

53 Van Bottenburg and Van Sterkenburg 2005, 3.

54 See e.g., Iosifidis and Smith 2011; Harrison and Woods 2007, 9.

55 Iosifidis and Smith 2011.

56 Commission of the European Communities 2007, SEC(2007) 935, 27.

support for sport as long as it is provided within the limits imposed by Community law. This accompanying document includes an overview of the different forms public support for sport can take: direct subsidies from public budgets, subsidies from fully or partly state-owned gambling operators, or direct revenues resulting from a licence to provide gambling services, special tax rates, loans with lower interest rates, public financing of sport facilities, payment for the construction or renovation of sport facilities by the local council, etc.[57] In the field of indirect taxation, the EU's VAT Directive[58] provides the possibility for Member States to exempt certain sport-related services and, where exemption does not apply, the possibility to apply reduced rates in some cases.[59] In this regard, the European Commission has indicated that the question of allowing a Member State to avoid a VAT bill for a given sports event, such as the World Cup and Olympic Games, is a recurrent issue.[60] To host the FIFA World Cup, the governments are contractually obliged, as part of the host country agreement, to pass laws which exempted FIFA from VAT and corporation tax. In other words, the host countries should guarantee that the entire World Cup event should be free of tax for FIFA.[61] In order to host the 2018 FIFA World Cup in Holland and Belgium, the Dutch Government accepted that FIFA and FIFA Subsidiaries could benefit from a full tax exemption. The Government Guarantee No. 3 Document explicitly states that "*the exemption [...] shall encompass all revenues, profits, income, expenses, costs, investments and any and all kind of payments, in cash or otherwise [...]*".[62] However, some Belgian political parties objected to the strict conditions imposed by FIFA for organising the 2018 World Cup. The spokesman of the Holland Belgium Bid replied that no laws or rules should be amended and that international tax law should be respected.[63] Because sport is characterised by an important societal function, in Belgium, sports clubs can recover 80% of the advance tax payment.[64] However, in April 2011, five football clubs of the Belgian Pro League announced that they would sell their broadcasting rights separately from the other 11 clubs of the Pro League. The Belgian member of the European Parliament Belet, advocating the collective selling of sports broadcasting rights in the Report on the future of professional football in Europe,[65] threatened that these five football clubs

---

[57] *Ibid.*, 26–27.

[58] Council Directive of 28 November 2006 on the Common System of Value Added Tax, 2006/112/EC. *OJ* (2006) L 347/1.

[59] Commission of the European Communities 2007, COM (2007) 391 final, 12.

[60] Commission of the European Communities 2007, SEC(2007) 935, 30.

[61] See e.g., BBC News Business 2010; Guardian 2010.

[62] Rijksoverheid 2010.

[63] See e.g., Het Nieuwsblad 2010.

[64] Tax regime for paid athletes Act of 4 May 2007; Royal Decree of 20 December 2007.

[65] European parliament 2007, A6-0036/2007.

would lose this tax advantage when they sold their broadcasting rights individually.[66]

Admittedly, there can also be a dark side to sports and, thus, the foregoing should be read with some caution. For example, sport is often associated with hooliganism.[67] Following the exit from the competition of their team, hooligans damage property and infrastructure or stone buses transporting rival fans. Or even worse, they start fighting with the police force or rival fans or become aggressive against passers-by who have no connection with the match.[68] Furthermore, the sports sector is often being criticised over doping. Due to the increasing pressure for athletes to improve their performances, they start taking prohibited substances.[69] Furthermore, as indicated by Chalip, sport does not only unite people but it can also have negative consequences exacerbating ethnic or cross-national tensions.[70] In this regard, different studies have analysed the English media coverage of the EURO 1996 and, in particular, the match of the English national team against the German national team. They came to the same conclusion: aggressive and anti-Germany xenophobia language was used by the English press.[71] Or during important sports events, attempts are sometimes made to use these events to express sub-nationalist identities. For example, the 1976 Olympic Games in Montreal and the 1992 Olympic Games in Barcelona, respectively for Quebec and Catalan nationalists, were an opportunity to cohere around sport against their host states.[72] Or during the FIFA World Cup, Catalan football fans wear the jersey of the national selection but they attach their regional flag to the Spanish flag or English football fans try to symbolise the non-existent English nation by the flag of St. George.[73] Finally, in sport and football in particular, homophobia is still a widespread phenomenon.[74] As indicated by Anderson, sport remains so homophobic that many athletes are convinced that the hyper masculinity exhibited in sports nullifies the possibility of gays even existing in their sport.[75] However, a recent study of Anderson indicated a decline of homophobia in sport.[76] A 2009 survey, issued by Sport/Voetbalmagazine and sent out to all Belgian professional football players, revealed that 67.8% of these players even believes that there is no place for gay men in football.[77] In the sports world, racism, in terms of limited

---

66 STVV 2011.

67 Bodin et al. 2005, 19.

68 Garland and Rowe 1999, 80; Bodin et al. 2005, 20.

69 See e.g., Burns 2006 (ed); Thieme and Hemmersbach 2010 (eds).

70 Chalip 2006, 9.

71 Garland and Rowe 1999, 80–95; Maguire et al. 1999, 439–454.

72 Hargreaves 2000, 8; Rowe 2003, 287; Delanty and Kumar 2006, 264.

73 Rowe 2003, 287; Castro-Ramos 2008, 707.

74 Paul 2011, 125.

75 Anderson 2005, 13.

76 Anderson 2011, 250–268.

77 Sport/Voetbalmagazine 2009.

work opportunities, verbal abuse and harassment, is a reality too.[78] As indicated by Gardiner, "*[r]acism has been a part of sport as long as sport has been played*".[79]

Nevertheless, these arguments can again be put into perspective. In 1999, the first European anti-racist football network, "*Football Against Racism in Europe—FARE*", was founded. As indicated by the European Commission, more than 40 different organisations including anti-racist sport projects, fan clubs, players' unions, football associations and ethnic minority groups from different European countries affirmed their commitment to fight all forms of discrimination in football.[80] Pillay, United Nations High Commissioner for Human Rights, stated that "*fear, intolerance and xenophobia can all be combated with diametrically opposed values of fair play and cooperation that are so central to team sports such as football*". According to her, the clear message of the football World Cup in South Africa should be that there is no place for racism and intolerance in sport.[81] In fact, FIFA used the quarter final matches of the World Cup in South Africa to make an unequivocal statement against racism to millions of people around the world. Each team captain read a declaration encouraging players, officials and fans around the world to say "*no*" to any and all forms of racism. Additionally, teams and match officials were standing behind a banner displaying the unequivocal message "*Say no to racism*". According to Blatter, it is part of the social responsibility of FIFA to use the World Cup competition to raise awareness of the pressing social issues, such as racism.[82] Previous World Cups were also characterised by FIFA's fight against racism.[83]

3.3.2 Specificity of Sport Before the Lisbon Treaty

In the Treaty of Rome ("*EC Treaty*"), which formed the basis for the establishment of the European Economic Community, sport was not included within its competence. Back then, sport was no high priority on the European political agenda, because it was seen as an activity mainly practiced by amateurs, being a leisure-time activity.[84] As a result, the EC Treaty did not contain any reference to the specificity of sport. Despite the absence of a designated competence with regard to sport in the EC Treaty and although the European institutions may act only within the limits of the competences conferred upon it by the Treaties, the Community institutions have taken several actions in the field of sport in the past.

---

[78] Gardiner and Welsh 2009, 134.

[79] Gardiner et al. 2006, 130.

[80] Commission of the European Communities 2007, SEC(2007) 935, 20.

[81] Pillay 2010.

[82] Africa Business.com 2010.

[83] FIFA 2007.

[84] Szyszczak 2007, 10.

This book, however, will only focus on those actions taken by the institutions dealing with access to sports coverage.

However, in other documents, the specificity of sport has been recognised. During the 1980s–1990s, the cultural and social function of sport came to the foreground. In 1985, the importance of sport to contribute to the development of a European identity and a sense of belonging was acknowledged in Adonnino's Report "*A People's Europe*".[85] In September 1998, the European Commission issued a working paper in which it explicitly identified the five functions of sport (*supra*).[86] In 1997, the Declaration on Sport,[87] accompanying the Amsterdam Treaty pointed out the following: "*The Conference emphasises the social significance of sport, in particular its role in forging identity and bringing people together. The Conference therefore calls on the bodies of the European Union to listen to sports associations when important questions affecting sport are at issue. In this connection, special consideration should be given to the particular characteristics of amateur sport*". The declaration on the specific characteristics of sport and its social function in Europe of which account should be taken in implementing common policies, better known as the Nice Declaration on Sport, stressed that "*[e]ven though not having any direct powers in this area, the Community must, in its action under the various Treaty provisions, take account of the social, educational and cultural functions inherent in sport and making it special, in order that the code of ethics and the solidarity essential to the preservation of its social role may be respected and nurtured*".[88] The specificity of sport has also been recognised in the 2007 White Paper on Sport: "*the case law of the European courts and decisions of the European Commission show that the specificity of sport has been recognised and taken into account*".[89] In its accompanying document to the White Paper on Sport, the European Commission stressed that "*Community Courts and the Commission have consistently taken into consideration the particular characteristics of sport setting it apart from other economic activities that are frequently referred to as the 'specificity of sport'*".[90] Although the European Commission affirmed that "*in line with established case law, the specificity of sport will continue to be recognised*", it underlined that "*[the specificity of sport] cannot be construed so as to justify a general exemption from the application of EU law*".[91]

---

[85] European Parliament 1985, S7/85.

[86] European Commission 1998, 5–6.

[87] Treaty of Amsterdam amending the Treaty on European Union, the Treaties establishing the European Communities and certain related acts—Declarations adopted by the Conference—Declaration on sport. *OJ* (1997) C 340/136.

[88] Council of the European Union 2000.

[89] Commission of the European Communities 2007, COM (2007) 391 final, 221.

[90] Commission of the European Communities 2007, SEC(2007) 935, 35.

[91] Commission of the European Communities 2007, COM (2007) 391 final, 13.

3.3.3 *Specificity of Sport After the Lisbon Treaty*

3.3.3.1 Article 165 of the TFEU

The Treaty establishing a Constitution for Europe[92] of 2004 contained the first legal basis for actions in the sports field: Article I-17 and III-282. During the process of ratification of this Treaty by the Member States, however, French and Dutch voters rejected this Treaty in different referenda, hindering the adoption of this Treaty. The sports competence was nevertheless retained in the 2007 (Reform) Treaty of Lisbon.[93] With the entry into force of the Lisbon Treaty on 1 December 2009, for the first time in European history, sport was integrated in the primary law of the EU and the specificity of sport was officially recognised in the Treaty.

Article 165 of the TFEU states:

> [...] the Union shall contribute to the promotion of European sporting issues, while taking account of the specific nature of sport, its structures based on voluntary activity and its social and educational function. Union action shall be aimed at: developing the European dimension in sport, by promoting fairness and openness in sporting competitions and cooperation between bodies responsible for sports, and by protecting the physical and moral integrity of sportsmen and sportswomen, especially the youngest sportsmen and sportswomen. The Union and the Member States shall foster cooperation with third countries and the competent international organisations in the field of education and sport, in particular the Council of Europe. In order to contribute to the achievement of the objectives referred to in this Article: the European Parliament and the Council, acting in accordance with the ordinary legislative procedure, after consulting the Economic and Social Committee and the Committee of the Regions, shall adopt incentive measures, excluding any harmonisation of the laws and regulations of the Member States—the Council, on a proposal from the Commission, shall adopt recommendations.

Article 6 of the TFEU states that the "*Union shall have competence to carry out actions to support, coordinate or supplement the actions of the Member States. The areas of such action shall, at European level, be: [...] sport*". In other words, Article 165 of the TFEU makes sport part of the coordinating, complementary and supporting action competences of the EU giving the EU the power to adopt soft law in the field of sport.[94] Although Blatter has welcomed the recognition of the specificity of sport in this Article,[95] others argue that, since the European Union will not have a power to harmonise, the importance of the introduction of this Article in the Treaty should not be overestimated.[96] Given that any harmonisation of the Member States' laws and regulations is explicitly prohibited, Van den Bogaert and Vermeersch, for example, argued that the role of the Union in the field

---

[92] Treaty establishing a Constitution for Europe. *OJ* (2004) C 310/01.

[93] Article 149 of Treaty of Lisbon amending the Treaty on European Union and the Treaty establishing the European Community. *OJ* (2007) C 306/01.

[94] Mestre 2005, 83; Siekmann 2008, 48.

[95] See e.g., FIFA 2009.

[96] See e.g., Van den Bogaert and Vermeersch 2006, 821–840; Parrish et al. 2010, 12.

of sport will remain limited and that competence in this context would rest primarily with the Member States and the sporting federations.[97] They also stated that, given that the introduction of this sports provision would not bring about major changes in the EU approach to sport in the near future, i.e. the application of the competition law rules and the free movement provisions would proceed, the importance of such an Article would be partially symbolical, legitimising Community action already taken in the field of sport.[98] Nevertheless, those two authors regretted the total exclusion of harmonising measures. According to Van den Bogaert and Vermeersch, it could be possible that harmonisation at supranational level might actually be the solution to a particular problem without those actions automatically being in contradiction with the EU limited competence in sporting affairs. In the fight against doping, for example, the Union could arguably fulfil a useful complementary role by providing a legal framework for the uniform implementation in all Member States of arrangements agreed upon at international level (e.g. within the World Anti-Doping Agency).[99]

Hendrickx added that, in principle, the incentive measures that could be taken do not exclude certain forms of regulation and could, therefore, be confined with legally binding acts.[100] Likewise, the Study on the Lisbon Treaty and EU Sports Policy stated that "*measures to harmonise such areas can be taken despite this type of prohibition so long as the harmonising measures are nominally based on another Treaty competence*".[101] Despite a similarly worded prohibition of harmonisation in the field of, for example, public health, the EU has in practice achieved convergence in legislation through other legal bases. The European Court of Justice, in the *Tobacco Advertising II* judgment, stated that when the recourse to Article 114 of the TFEU [ex 95 EC] as a legal basis is fulfilled, "*the Community legislature cannot be prevented from relying on that legal basis on the ground that public health protection is a decisive factor in the choices to be made*".[102] In other words, as indicated in the Study on the Lisbon Treaty and EU Sports Policy, "*even though the public health competence could not be relied upon to prohibit tobacco advertising, since it expressly excluded harmonising measures, the limit applied only to the public health competence and thus did not preclude other competences that potentially allowed such measures to be adopted*".[103] Hence, according to the authors of the study, "*it seems unlikely that Article 165(4) TFEU will prevent*

97 Van den Bogaert and Vermeersch 2006, 838; Vermeersch 2009, 79.

98 Van den Bogaert and Vermeersch 2006, 839; Van den Bogaert 2010, 271.

99 Van den Bogaert and Vermeersch 2006, 838; Vermeersch 2009, 79–80.

100 Hendrickx 2008, 15.

101 Parrish et al. 2010, 26.

102 CJ, Federal Republic of Germany v European Parliament and Council of the European Union, para 92 (2006).

103 Parrish et al. 2010, 26.

harmonising legislation with impacts on sport so long as that legislation is formally based on a Treaty article other than Article 165 TFEU".[104]

In the past, as indicated by Hendrickx, the specificity of sport was often used as "*an argument for exceptions or exemptions with regard to sporting issues under European Union law*".[105] In the first decisions dealing with sports-related issues, the European Court of Justice stated that sport was subject to Community law insofar as it constitutes an economic activity. Or in other words, sport does not fall under Community law, unless it concerns an economic activity (*supra*). As a result, the Courts were able to exclude certain matters from the scope of the Treaty. In other words, the specificity of sport was mainly used as a defence mechanism. Given that the specificity of sport is officially recognised in Article 165 of the TFEU, Hendrickx suggested that the concept could be turned into a more positive notion changing the way the Courts would deal with sports-related matters.[106]

According to Hendrickx, "*the notion of specificity of sport cannot be used as a sort «standard clause» or «style formula» to exclude sport from any further requirement of justifying limitations on the free movement of workers*". As a result, a mere reference to the specificity of sport by the European Courts and European institutions in their decisions would not be sufficient. Hence, they should put forward the specific reasons justifying an exemption.[107] Advocate General Sharpston formulated it as follows: "*[t]he specific characteristics of sport in general, and football in particular, do not seem to me to be of paramount importance when considering whether there is a prohibited restriction on freedom of movement. They must, however, be considered carefully when examining possible justifications for any such restriction—just as the specific characteristics of any other sector would need to be borne in mind when examining the justification of restrictions applicable in that sector*".[108] In other words, a simple reference to Article 165 of the TFEU is not sufficient. Whether the specificity of sport could play a role in a decision should be analysed in *concreto*.

In the course of 2010, the European Commission planned to present its ideas and to make proposals for the implementation of the new provisions.[109] In the framework of this process, the European Commission launched a public consultation on the EU's strategic choices for the implementation of the new EU competence in the field of sport in April 2010 in order to obtain input for the European Commission's future proposals.[110] In January 2011, this consultation was followed

---

[104] *Ibid.*, 27.

[105] Hendrickx 2010, 26.

[106] *Ibid.*, 26; Hendrickx 2008, 16.

[107] Hendrickx 2010, 26.

[108] CJ, Olympique Lyonnais SASP v Olivier Bernard & Newcastle United FC, Opinion of Advocate General Sharpston (2009).

[109] European Commission 2010a.

[110] European Commission 2010b, c.

by the adoption of the European Commission's first communication on sport entitled "*Developing the European Dimension in Sport*".[111] This communication contains proposals aiming at strengthening the societal, economic and organisational dimensions of sport[112] The European Commission explicitly stressed that it will respect the autonomy of the sports organisations and the competences of the Member States in this area. Nevertheless, it is also accepted that action at EU level can provide added value.[113] It is important to indicate that this communication pays little attention to the public's access to sports content and the sale, acquisition and exploitation of broadcasting rights and the fact that these rights should be licensed respecting the Internal Market and competition law.[114]

3.3.3.2 Article 165 of the TFEU and the European Court of Justice: The Bernard Case

In the *Bernard* case,[115] the European Court of Justice referred for the first time to Article 165 of the TFEU. The question that rises is whether the European Court of Justice, relying on this new Article, did change its way of decision making.

In this case, the European Court of Justice had to examine whether the rules according to which a "*joueur espoir*" may be ordered to pay damages if, at the end of his training period, he would sign a professional contract, not with the club which provided his training, but with a club in another Member State, constitute a restriction within the meaning of Article 45 of the TFEU [ex Article 39 TEC] and, if so, whether that restriction is justified by the need to encourage the recruitment and training of young players.[116] According to the European Court of Justice, "*those rules are a restriction on freedom of movement for workers guaranteed within the European Union by Article 45 TFEU*".[117] However, the European Court of Justice added that "*a measure which constitutes an obstacle to freedom of movement for workers can be accepted only if it pursues a legitimate aim compatible with the Treaty and is justified by overriding reasons in the public interest. Even if that were so, application of that measure would still have to be such as to ensure achievement of the objective in question and not go beyond what is necessary for that purpose*".[118] The European Court of Justice stressed that "*the*

---

[111] Commission of the European Communities 2011, COM(2011) 12 final. This communication is accompanied by the following Staff Working Document: Commission of the European Communities 2011, SEC(2011) 66/2.

[112] Rapid Press Releases 2011, IP/11/43.

[113] Commission of the European Communities 2011, COM(2011) 12 final, 3.

[114] *Ibid.*, 8–9.

[115] CJ, Olympique Lyonnais SASP v Olivier Bernard & Newcastle United FC 2009 (hereafter: *Bernard* case).

[116] *Bernard* case, para 17.

[117] *Ibid.*, para 37.

[118] *Ibid.*, para 38.

considerable social importance of sporting activities and in particular football in the European Union, the objective of encouraging the recruitment and training of young players must be accepted as legitimate".[119] In paragraph 40 of the judgement, the European Court of Justice made its first reference to the new "*sports Article*": "*[i]n considering whether a system which restricts the freedom of movement of such players is suitable to ensure that the said objective is attained and does not go beyond what is necessary to attain it, account must be taken [...] of the specific characteristics of sport in general, and football in particular, and of their social and educational function. The relevance of those factors is also corroborated by their being mentioned in the second subparagraph of Article 165(1) TFEU*". The European Court of Justice recognised that "*the prospect of receiving training fees is likely to encourage football clubs to [...] train young players*"[120] and that "*the clubs which provided the training could be discouraged from investing in the training of young players if they could not obtain reimbursement of the amounts spent for that purpose where, at the end of his training, a player enters into a professional contract with another club*".[121]

According to Colucci, although the European Court of Justice took into account the new Article 165 of the TFEU in its decision-making process, the outcome of the judgment is not different from that in the past. In its previous decisions, the European Court of Justice already referred to the specificity of sport.[122] In this regard, it is important to note that the application of Article 165 of the TFEU has not resulted in a general exemption. Although the European Court of Justice decided that "*a scheme providing for the payment of compensation for training where a young player, at the end of his training, signs a professional contract with a club other than the one which trained him can, in principle, be justified*",[123] the French rule providing a scheme for the payment, not of compensation for training, but of damages[124] "*went beyond what was necessary to encourage recruitment and training of young players and to fund those activities*".[125] The authors of the Study on the Lisbon Treaty and EU Sports Policy formulated it as follows: "*[ECJ's] reference [to Article 165 of the TFEU] was not an attempt to justify treating sport in a particular, different way, but merely provided further support for justifications already accepted prior to the Treaty reforms*" and that "*whilst the Bernard case did not explore the constitutional boundaries of the EU's new sporting competence, [...] the Court provided few reasons to believe that the new*

119 *Ibid.*, para 39.
120 *Ibid.*, para 40.
121 *Ibid.*, para 44.
122 Colucci 2010.
123 *Bernard* case, para 45.
124 *Ibid.*, para 46.
125 *Ibid.*, para 48.

sporting competence has any substantial impact on the pre-existing acquis which applies to sport".[126]

Although it seems correct that the outcome of the judgment is not different from that in the past, the importance of Article 165 of the TFEU may not be underestimated. Since the entry into force of the Lisbon Treaty, the specificity of the sport became officially recognised and could not be questioned anymore. As a result, when taking decisions, the European institutions have to take into account that the sports sector is not only an economic business, but that it is also characterised by a societal dimension (*supra*).

References

Legislation and Policy Documents

European Union

Treaties

Consolidated version of the Treaty on European Union. *OJ* (2008) C 115/13

Consolidated version of the Treaty on the functioning of the European Union. *OJ* (2008) C 115/47

Treaty establishing a constitution for Europe. *OJ* (2004) C 310/01

Treaty of Amsterdam amending the Treaty on European Union, the Treaties establishing the European Communities and certain related acts—declarations adopted by the conference—declaration on sport. *OJ* (1997) C 340/136

Treaty of Lisbon amending the Treaty on European Union and the Treaty establishing the European Community. *OJ* (2007) C 306/01

Commission Staff Working Papers

Commission of the European Communities (2007) Commission staff working document—the EU and sport: background and context—accompanying document to the white paper on sport. 11 July 2007, SEC(2007) 935

Commission of the European Communities (2011) Commission staff working document—sport and free movement—accompanying document to the communication from the commission to the European Parliament, the council, the Economic and Social Committee and the Committee of the Regions, developing the European dimension in sport. SEC(2011) 66/2

European Commission (1998) Commission staff working paper—the development and prospects for community action in the field of sport. http://ec.europa.eu/sport/library/doc/a/doc252_en.pdf. Accessed 19 Aug 2010

[126] Parrish et al. 2010, 28.

Communications

Commission of the European Communities (2011) Communication from the commission to the European Parliament, the council, the Economic and Social Committee and the Committee of the Regions, developing the European dimension in sport. 18 January 2011, COM(2011) 12 final

Declarations

Council of the European Union (2000) Declaration on the specific characteristics of sport and its social function in Europe, of which account should be taken in implementing common policies, presidency conclusions, Nice European Council Meeting, 7–9 Dec 2000

Directives

Council Directive of 28 November 2006 on the common system of value added tax, 2006/112/EC. *OJ* (2006) L 347/1

Opinions

Committee of the Regions 2007. Opinion of the committee of the regions on 'Equal opportunities and sport'. *OJ* (2007) C305/53

Reports

European Parliament (1985). Report from the ad hoc committee on a People's Europe. *OJ* (1985) C 175/273, S7/85

European Parliament (2007) Report on the future of professional football in Europe. 13 December 2007, A6-0036/2007

White Papers

Commission of the European Communities (2007) White paper on sport. 11 July 2007, COM (2007) 391 final

Press Releases

Rapid Press Releases (1999) Commission debates application of its competition rules to sports. IP/99/133

Rapid Press Releases (2011) Commission strengthens the European dimension of sport, 18 January 2011, IP/11/43

Speeches

Reding V (2002) Sport and television: moving towards more balanced relations. SPEECH/02/440

Miscallanious

European Commission (2004) Special eurobarometer—the citizens of the European Union and sport. http://ec.europa.eu/public_opinion/archives/ebs/ebs_213_summ_en.pdf. Accessed 22 Apr 2011

European Commission (2010a) Sport—Lisbon Treaty provisions on sport enter into force. http://ec.europa.eu/sport/news/news873_en.htm. Accessed 18 Aug 2010

European Commission (2010b) Sport—Commission's public consultation on sport. http://ec.europa.eu/sport/news/news945_en.htm. Accessed 18 Aug 2010

European Commission (2010c) Strategic choices for the implementation of the new EU competence in the field of sport—EU-wide public consultation—report. http://ec.europa.eu/sport/library/doc/a/100726_online_consultation_report.pdf. Accessed 18 Aug 2010

Belgium

Legislation

Royal Decree of 20 December 2007 amending KB/WIB 92 [Koninklijk besluit tot wijziging van het KB/WIB 92 in uitvoering van artikel 2756, laatste lid, van het Wetboek van de inkomstenbelastingen 1992], Belgian State Gazette 31 Dec 2007

Tax regime for paid athletes act of 4 May 2007 [Wet betreffende het fiscaal statuut van de bezoldigde sportbeoefenaars], Belgian State Gazette, 15 May 2007

Case Law

Court of Justice

CJ, Christelle Deliège v Ligue Francophone de Judo et Disciplines ASBL and others, 11 April 2000, joined cases C-51/96 and C-191/97, *ECR* (2000) I-02549

CJ, David Meca-Medina and Igor Majcen v. Commission of the European Communities, 18 July 2006, Case C-519/04, *ECR* (2006), I-06991

CJ, Donà v Mantero, 14 July 1976, Case 13/76, *ECR* (1976) 1333

CJ, Federal Republic of Germany v European Parliament and Council of the European Union, 12 Dec 2006, Case C-380/03, *ECR* (2006) I-11573

CJ, Jyri Lehtonen and Castors Canada Dry Namur-Braine ASBL v Fédération royale belge des sociétés de basketball ASBL (FRBSB), Case C-176/96, *ECR* (2000) I-02681

CJ, Olympique Lyonnais SASP v Olivier Bernard & Newcastle United FC, Case C 325/08, opinion of advocate General Sharpston, 16 July 2009

CJ, Olympique Lyonnais SASP v Olivier Bernard & Newcastle United FC, 16 March 2010, Case C 325/08, not yet published in the ECR

CJ, Union Royale Belge des Sociétés de Football Association ASLB v. Jean Marc Bosman, 15 Dec 1995, Case C 415/93, *ECR* (1995) I-04921

CJ, Walrave and Koch v. Union Cycliste Internationale, 12 Dec 1974, Case 36/47, *ECR* (1974) 1405

General Court

GC, David Meca-Medina and Igor Majcen v. Commission of the European Communities, 30 Sept 2004, Case T-313/02, *ECR* (2004) II-3291

Doctrine

Africa Business.com (2010) World Cup quarter finalists "say no to racism". http://africabusiness.com/2010/07/01/world-cup/. Accessed 22 Apr 2011

Anderson E (2005) In the game: gay athletes and the cult of masculinity. State University of New York Press, Albany

Anderson E (2011) Updating the outcome: Gay athletes, straight teams, and coming out in educationally based sport teams. Gender Soc 25:250–268

Bairner A (2001) Sport, nationalism, and globalization: European and North American perspectives. State university of New York Press, Albany

BBC News Business (2010) World Cup: to tax or not to tax?, 11 May 2010. http://www.bbc.co.uk/news/10091277. Accessed 24 Apr 2011

Bernstein A (2007) 'Running nowhere': national identity and media coverage of the Israeli football team's attempt to qualify for EURO 2000. Israel Aff 13(3):653–664

Blanpain R (2008) The future of sports in Europe—specificity of sport: a legal perspective. In: Blanpain R et al (eds) The future of sports law in the European Union: beyond the EU reform treaty and the white paper. Kluwer, Deventer, pp 1–8

Boardman A, Hargreaves-Heap S (1999) Network externalities and government restrictions on satellite broadcasting of key sporting events. J Cult Econ 23:167–181

Bodin D et al (2005) Sport and violence in Europe. Council of Europe, Strasbourg

Boyle R, Haynes R (2000) Power play: sport, the media and popular culture. Longman, Harlow

Burns C (ed) (2006) Doping in sports. Nova Science, New York

Castro-Ramos E (2008) Loyalties, commodity and fandom: Real Madrid, Barça and Athletic fans versus 'La Furia Roja' during the World Cup. Sport Soc 11(6):696–710

Chalip L (2006) Towards a distinctive sport management discipline. J Sport Manag 20:1–21

Chappelet JL (2010) Autonomy of sport in Europe. Council of Europe Publishing, Strasbourg

Colucci M (2010) The Bernard case: a brief overview, conference on the Bernard case (ECJ, C-325/08): judgment and impact on the sports world, Brussels, 29 Apr 2010

Delanty G, Kumar K (2006) The Sage handbook of nations and nationalism. Sage, London

EU Sport Forum 2010 (2010) Report EU sport forum 2010. http://ec.europa.eu/sport/library/doc/b1/sport_forum_madrid_report_11_05_10.pdf. Accessed 21 Oct 2010

FIFA (2007) Anti-Racism at the 2006 FIFA World Cup, 11 May 2007. http://www.fifa.com/aboutfifa/worldwideprograms/footballforhope/news/newsid=518222.html. Accessed 22 Apr 2011

FIFA (2009). Lisbon Treaty gives a boost to sport, 30 Nov 2009. http://www.fifa.com/aboutfifa/federation/releases/newsid=1141618.html. Accessed 18 Aug 2010

FIFA (2010) The world unites in fair play and respect, 2 Sept 2010. http://www.fifa.com/aboutfifa/worldwideprograms/releases/newsid=1293362.html. Accessed 22 Apr 2011
Gardiner S, Welsh R (2009) Sport, racism and the limits of 'colour blind' law. In: Carrington B, McDonald I (eds) 'Race', sport, and British society. Routledge, New York, pp 133–152
Gardiner S, O'Leary J, Welch R (2006) Sports law. Cavendish, London
Garland J, Rowe M (1999) War minus the shooting?: Jingoism, the English Press, and Euro 96. J Sport Soc Iss 23:80–95
Goldlust J (1987) Playing for keeps: sport, the media and society. Longman Cheshire, Melbourne
Gratton C, Solberg HA (2007) The economics of sports broadcasting. Routledge, London
Hargreaves J (2000) Freedom for Catalonia?: Catalan nationalism Spanish identity and the Barcelona Olympic Games. Cambridge University Press, Cambridge
Harrison J, Woods L (2007) European broadcasting law and policy. Cambridge University Press, Cambridge
Hendrickx F (2008) Future directions of EU sports law. In: Blanpain R et al (eds) The future of sports law in the European Union: beyond the EU reform treaty and the white paper. Kluwer, Deventer, pp 9–20
Hendrickx F (2010) Justification of training compensation in European football: Bosman and Bernard compared. Eur Sports Law Policy Bull 1:19–33
Het Nieuwsblad (2010) François Colin weerlegt kritiek op WK 2018, 4 Aug 2010. http://www.nieuwsblad.be/article/detail.aspx?articleid=DMF20100804_103. Accessed 24 Apr 2011
Hundley H, Billings A (eds) (2010) Examining identity in sports media. Sage, Los Angeles
Infantino G (2006) Meca-Medina: a step backwards for the European sports model and the specificity of sport? http://www.uefa.com/multimediafiles/download/uefa/keytopics/480391_download.pdf. Accessed 18 Aug 2010
Iosifidis P, Smith P (2011) The European television rights market: balancing culture and commerce, private television conference, Brussels, 28 Apr 2011
Kienappel P, Stein A (2007) The application of Articles 81 and 82 EC in the sport sector. Competition Policy Newsl 3:6–14
Le Soir (2008) Le 4 × 100 m, un relais qui vaut de l'or, 22 Aug 2008. http://www.lesoir.be/dossiers/pekin_2008/article_630634.shtml. Accessed 22 Aug 2008, no longer available
Maguire J et al (1999) Weltkrieg III?: Media coverage of England versus Germany in Euro 96. J Sport Soc Iss 23:439–454
Mandelzis L, Bernstein A (2010) Cup of hope: narrating the identity of the Arab minority in a Jewish state through football, IAMCR conference, Braga, 19 July 2010
Mestre A (2005) Sport in the European constitution. Int Sports Law J 1–2:83–84
Miller T, Lawrence G, McKay J (2001) Globalization and sport: playing the world. Sage, London
Parrish R et al (2010) The Lisbon Treaty and EU Sports Policy—study. http://www.europarl.europa.eu/activities/committees/studies/download.do?language=en&file=32471. Accessed 14 Oct 2010
Paul J (2011) Can gays kick a ball? On homophobia in soccer. In: Groneberg M, Funke C (eds) Combatting homophobia: experiences and analyses pertinent to education. Lit Verlag, Berlin, pp 125–135
Pillay N (2010) Opinion piece—racism and the football world cup. http://www.un.org/wcm/webdav/site/sport/shared/sport/pdfs/Press%20Interviews%20%26%20Articles/Racism%20and%20the%20Football%20World%20Cup_Pillay_4_June_2010.pdf. Accessed 22 Apr 2011
PricewaterhouseCoopers (2011) Back on track? The outlook for the global sports market to 2013. http://www.pwc.com/gx/en/entertainment-media/pdf/Global-Sports-Outlook.pdf. Accessed 16 Jan 2012
Rijksoverheid (2010) Government guarantee no. 3. http://www.rijksoverheid.nl/documenten-en-publicaties/brieven/2010/04/20/government-guarantee-no-3-tax-exemption.html. Accessed 24 Apr 2011
Roche M (2001) Citizenship, popular culture, and Europe. In: Stevenson N (ed) Culture and citizenship. Sage, London, pp 74–98

Rowe D (2003) Sport and the repudiation of the global. Int Rev Sociol Sport 38:281–294

Rowe D (2004) Sport, culture and the media: the unruly trinity, 2nd edn. Open University Press, Maidenhead

Siekmann R (2008) Is sport 'special' in EU law and policy? In: Blanpain R et al (eds) The future of sports law in the European Union: beyond the EU reform treaty and the white paper. Kluwer, Deventer, pp 37–49

Sport/Voetbalmagazine (2009) Homo's niet welkom in het voetbal, 9 June 2009. http://sportmagazine.rnews.be/nl/sport/nieuws/homo-s-niet-welkom-in-het-voetbal/article-1194699092519.htm. Accessed 18 July 2011

Sporza (2008) Kranten bedanken de estafettemeisjes, 23 Aug 2008. http://www.sporza.be/cm/sporza.be/Olympia/atletiek/080823_4x100_krantenoverzicht. Accessed 23 Aug 2008, no longer available

STVV (2011) Selectieve verontwaardiging bij Europarlementslid Ivo Belet over de tv-rechten, 17 Apr 2011. http://www.stvv.com/nl/nieuws/hotnews/d/detail/persbericht-selectieve-verontwaardiging-bij-europarlementslid-ivo-belet-over-de-tv-rechten. Accessed 17 Apr 2011

Szyszczak E (2007) Is sport special? In: Bogusz B, Cygan A, Szyszczak E (eds) The regulation of sport in the European Union. Elgar, Cheltenham, pp 3–32

The Guardian (2010) World Cup 2018: England's five lucky escapes, 3 Dec 2010. http://www.guardian.co.uk/football/2010/dec/03/world-cup-2018-england-lucky-escapes. Accessed 24 Apr 2011

Thieme D, Hemmersbach P (eds) (2010) Doping in sports. Springer, Heidelberg

Van Bottenburg M, Van Sterkenburg J (2005) The social function of sport, the EU & Sport—matching expectations, Brussels, 14–15 June 2005. http://ec.europa.eu/sport/library/doc/c5/doc322_en.pdf. Accessed 20 Aug 2010

Van den Bogaert S (2010) De zaak Bernard: het Hof van Justitie laat opleidingsvergoedingen toe in het voetbal. NtEr 8:265–272

Van den Bogaert S, Vermeersch A (2006) Sport and the EC Treaty: a tale of uneasy bedfellows. Eur Law Rev 31(6):821–840

Vermeersch A (2009) Europese spelregels voor sport Overzicht van het Europees sportbeleid in wording en de toepassing van het Europees recht op sport. Maklu, Antwerpen

Whannel G (1992) Fields in vision: television sport and cultural transformation. Routledge, London

Chapter 4
Article 10 of the European Convention on Human Rights and the Public's Right to Information Regarding Sports Events

4.1 Introduction

The European Court of Human Rights has always reiterated that "*the freedom of expression constitutes one of the essential foundations of a democratic society and one of the basic conditions for its progress and for each individual's self-fulfilment*".[1] Moreover, journalists are often referred to as the "watchdogs of our society".[2] This implies that the press, because they have a major influence on what citizens know, believe and feel, play a central role in the functioning of modern democratic societies and in the development and transmission of social values, which means it is its right and duty to inform the public on matters of public interest. Hence, it is apparent that the freedom of expression and the right to information are two preconditions for a well-functioning democracy.

The principle of freedom of expression and the public's right to information has been enshrined in different documents at the European level as well as at the international level. Article 10 of the European Convention on Human Rights (ECHR)[3] constitutes the very cornerstone for the protection of freedom of expression for the European Union:

> *1. Everyone has the right to freedom of expression. This right shall include freedom to hold opinions and to receive and impart information and ideas without interference by public authority and regardless of frontiers. This article shall not prevent States from requiring the licensing of broadcasting, television or cinema enterprises.*
> *2. The exercise of these freedoms, since it carries with it duties and responsibilities, may be subject to such formalities, conditions, restrictions or penalties as are prescribed by law and are necessary in a democratic society, in the interests of national security, territorial integrity or public safety, for the prevention of disorder or crime, for the*

---

[1] See e.g. ECHR, Handyside v. the United Kingdom, para 49 (hereafter *Handyside* case); ECHR, Perna v. Italy, 6 May 200, para 39 (hereafter: *Perna* case).
[2] See e.g. ECHR, Goodwin v. the United Kingdom, para 39.
[3] Council of Europe 1950.

K. Lefever, *New Media and Sport*, ASSER International Sports Law Series,
DOI: 10.1007/978-90-6704-873-6_4,

protection of health or morals, for the protection of the reputation or the rights of others, for preventing the disclosure of information received in confidence, or for maintaining the authority and impartiality of the judiciary.

This fundamental right is also explicitly included in Article 11 of the Charter of Fundamental Rights of the European Union.[4] At international level, it is expressed in Article 19 of the Universal Declaration of Human Rights (UDHR)[5] as well as in Article 19 of the International Covenant on Civil and Political Rights (ICCPR).[6] In the next paragraphs, Article 10 of the ECHR will be analysed.

4.2 Article 10, § 1 of the ECHR: Freedom of Expression and the Right to Information Without Interference by Public Authority

4.2.1 What is Protected Under Article 10, § 1 of the ECHR

4.2.1.1 Protection Regardless of the Content, the Form or the Type of Medium Used[7]

A. Introduction

Article 10 of the ECHR is characterised by its broad scope of application. Although the European Court of Human Rights has always underlined the importance of the freedom of expression and the right to information for the individual self-fulfilment, it has never given a clear, qualitative definition of what could (not) be classified as information from an Article 10 perspective. In fact, in the *Groppera* case, the European Court of Human Rights did not consider it "*necessary to give [...] a precise definition of what is meant by 'information' and 'ideas'*".[8] However, the European Court of Human Rights has indicated that the freedom of expression and the right to information does not only protect information or ideas that are favourably or inoffensive, but also those that offend, shock or disturb.[9] While the European Court of Human Rights has recognised that nearly anything counting as 'expression' could fall within the scope of Article 10 of the ECHR (with the exception of those expressions which attack the basics of

---

4 European Union 2000, Charter of Fundamental Rights of the European Union. *OJ* (2000) C 364/1.

5 United Nations 1948, Universal Declaration of Human Rights.

6 United Nations 1966, International Covenant on Civil and Political Rights.

7 This subsection is a revised and updated version of a part of the following article: Lefever et al. 2010, 396–407.

8 ECHR, Groppera Radio AG and others v. Switzerland, para 55 (hereafter: *Groppera* case).

9 See e.g.: *Perna* case, para 39; *Handyside* case, para 49.

democracy, such as Nazi speech[10]), it has also recognised that various types of expression may have varying degree of importance in a democratic society.[11] Therefore, the European Court of Human Rights has traditionally attached different levels of legal protection to different categories of expression, with primacy for expression that is predominantly political in character and considerably less protection for expression that is mainly commercial (*infra*).[12] The fact that political expression is given priority can be explained by its fundamental role in a democratic society.[13]

Furthermore, Article 10 of the ECHR protects not only the substance of the ideas and information expressed, but also the form in which they are conveyed.[14] The European Court of Human Rights formulated it as follows: "*Article 10 [...] applies not only to the content of information but also to the means of transmission or reception since any restriction imposed on the means necessarily interferes with the right to receive and impart information*".[15] Given that this provision is formulated in a technologically neutral way, this implies that all means of dissemination (print, television, radio, Internet, etc.) are covered.[16]

To summarise, in principle, any expression of opinion regardless of its content (artistic expressions,[17] expressions of commercial nature,[18] light music,[19] etc.), its form (written text, picture, image or action to express an idea, etc.) or the type of media used (print, television, radio, Internet, etc.) is protected under Article 10 of the ECHR.[20]

B. Access to Coverage of Sports Events Protected under Article 10 of the ECHR

With regard to the broadcasting sector, the European Court of Human Rights stated in the *Groppera* case that "*broadcasting of programmes over the air and cable retransmission of such programmes are covered by the right enshrined in Article 10 of the ECHR, without there being any need to make distinctions according to the content of the programmes*".[21] In the same sense, in Autronic v. Switzerland, the European Court of Human Rights made clear that the right to information under Article 10 of the ECHR also encompasses the freedom to receive uncoded

---

10 See e.g.: ECHR, Garaudy v. France.

11 Fenwick and Phillipson 2006, 44; Cucereanu 2008, 19.

12 Closs and Nikoltchev 2005, 2.

13 Cucereanu 2008, 19.

14 See e.g. ECHR, Jresild v. Denmark, para 31 (hereafter *Jresild* case); *Perna* case, para 39.

15 ECHR, Autronic AG v. Switzerland, para 47 (hereafter: *Autronic AG v. Switzerland* case).

16 *Ibid.*, para 47.

17 ECHR, Müller and Others v. Switzerland, para 27 (hereafter *Müller* case).

18 ECHR, Verlag GmbH and Klaus Beermann v. Germany, para 26 (hereafter: *Verlag GmbH* case).

19 *Groppera* case, para 54.

20 See e.g.: Voorhoof 1995, 45–54.

21 *Groppera* case, para 55.

television programmes.[22] Furthermore, in the *Verlag GmbH* case, the European Court of Human Rights stated that "information of a commercial nature cannot be excluded from the scope of Article 10 of the ECHR" and that "Article 10 of the ECHR does not apply solely to certain types of information".[23] Recently, in the 2008 *Khurshid Mustafa and Tarzibach v. Sweden* case, the European Court of Human Rights stressed that "*the freedom to receive information does not extend only to reports of events of public concern, but covers in principle also cultural expressions as well as pure entertainment. The importance of the latter types of information should not be underestimated, especially for an immigrant family [...] who may wish to maintain in contact with the culture and language of their country of origin*".[24] In other words, the right to receive information also contains the right to receive entertainment television programmes. According to Herr, the European Court of Human Rights gives a message that the right of the public to have access to any type of information for private purposes is a Convention priority.[25]

Hence, given that the European Court of Human Rights does not give a qualitative interpretation of the notion 'information', and given that *inter alia* light music, artistic expression, entertainment and commercials is covered by Article 10 of the ECHR, the European Court of Human Rights applies a very broad interpretation of information. However, it is not difficult to see that sport belongs to a 'lower' category of information than political speech[26] or state-held official documents (*infra*), which are needed for public debate in a pluralistic, democratic society. Nevertheless, there is no reason whatsoever to assume that the coverage of sports events would not be grasped by this notion. This finding is even strengthened by the formulation of Article 19 ICCPR, which speaks of "*information and ideas of all kinds*". The United Nations Human Rights Committee (UNHRC), in its recent general comment No. 34 on Article 19 ICCPR, also stresses that the right to information includes the right of the general public to receive mass media output, without making a distinction as to the type of that output.[27]

C. Live and Full Coverage of Sports Events Protected under Article 10 of the ECHR

In 1996, Luciana Castellina[28] said that "*watching a football match on television is a human right*".[29] Although sports fans would heavily support this vision, others

[22] *Autronic AG v. Switzerland* case, para 47.

[23] *Verlag GmbH* case, para 26.

[24] ECHR, Khurshid Mustafa and Tarzibach v. Sweden, para 44 (hereafter: *Khurshid Mustafa* case).

[25] Herr 2011.

[26] Harris et.al. 2009, 455–457.

[27] Human Rights Committee 2011, para 18.

[28] Luciana Castellina was the President of the Parliament's Committee on Culture, Youth, Education and the Media during the period 22.07.1994–15.01.1997.

[29] Lewis and Taylor 2003, 325.

argue that the right to information included in Article 10 of the ECHR is not a legal basis to justify a claim to watch sports events live and full, but only justify the right to watch short news reports of sports events.[30] Hence, the question rises whether live and full access to sports events is 'valuable' enough to support a serious claim for protection under Article 10 of the ECHR, when access to these events is made difficult or even impossible.

There is no doubt that the broadcast of highlights of sports events will be protected under Article 10 of the ECHR (*infra*). The aim of such short reports is providing information on specific events for the people unable to watch the live coverage (*infra*). Given that live and full coverage exceeds a purely informative objective, in this view, Article 10 of the ECHR seems only to provide a legal basis to the right to watch highlights of sports events. However, the concept 'information' does not only refer to knowledge communicated or received concerning a particular fact or circumstance or to the mere transfer of data. When we take a look at the European Court for Human Rights' decisions, the European Court of Human Rights uses a broader definition with regard to the information and the right to information. According to the European Court of Human Rights, the right to information embraces everything that can play an important role in the development of a democratic society and the development of the citizens (*supra*). As indicated in Chap. 2, sport can fulfil this role. Sport has the ability of representing and strengthening national or regional identity by giving people a sense of belonging to a group. It unites players and spectators giving the latter the possibility of identifying with their nation. In other words, as indicated by the European Commission, sport contributes to social stability and is an emblem for culture and identity (*supra*).

However, to create a sense of belonging and a collective experience shared among all viewers, sports should be experienced by a large number of people simultaneously and live and in communal social spaces at home or pubs or at 'live sites' located in public squares and parks.[31] In other words, full and direct access to sports events can be approached as a means of promoting civil participation in our democratic society, by enabling citizens to participate fully in public discourse about these events. Admittedly, the type of debate in pursuance of major sports events is not as important for procedural democracy (i.e. democratic procedure, structure and organisation) as political discourse (the type of 'key' public discourse that receives a very high level of protection, the reason also why access to state-held public documents is highly protected (*supra*)).[32] Yet, as Weinstein holds, public discourse (in the sense of discourse in the public interest) is not only speech concerning the organisation, but also concerning the culture of society.[33] It has been made plausible that the live experience of important sports events can contribute significantly to the latter type of public discourse. However, attempting

---

[30] Scheuer and Strothmann 2004, 5.

[31] See e.g.: Saltzman 2000, 2; Gratton and Solberg 2007, 208; Hutchins and Rowe 2009.

[32] Barendt 2005, 25–26.

[33] Weinstein 2009, 23–62.

to make plausible that, therefore, the public would have a right of access to full and live coverage on free-to-air television of any sports event that is transmitted, would maybe too challenging (*infra*).

4.2.1.2 Protection of all Phases in the Communications Chain

As mentioned before, the media play an essential role in a democratic society imparting information and ideas on all matters of public interest. Not only do the media have the task of imparting such information and ideas, the public has a corresponding right to receive this information.[34] The European Court of Human Rights has recognised this right as being a fundamental part of Article 10 of the ECHR. In the *Sunday Times* case, the European Court of Human Rights explicitly referred for the first time to "*the right of the public to be properly informed*" as being a fundamental part of Article 10 of the ECHR.[35] In later cases, the European Court of Human Rights has repeatedly reiterated "*the right to receive information*",[36] "*public had a legitimate interest in being informed*"[37] and "*the public's right to be informed of a different perspective*".[38] Moreover, the European Court of Human Rights pointed out that "*the freedom to receive information [...] basically prohibits a government from restricting a person from receiving information that others wish or may be willing to impart to him*".[39] Hence, Article 10 of the ECHR protects all the phases in the communications chain, starting from the holding of opinions, the imparting of information and ideas to others, the reception of such information and ideas, to even the negative freedom not to receive any information at all.[40]

Article 19 of the ICCPR even seems to go further by explicitly protecting the active right of 'seeking' information. In its recent draft of general comment No. 34 on Article 19 ICCPR, the United Nations Human Rights Committee (UNHRC) has also reinforced a firm right to information.[41] Unlike Article 19 of the UDHR, Article 10 of the ECHR does not explicitly provide for the right to 'seek information'.[42] As a result, in the *Leander* case, the European Court of Human Rights has stated that Article 10 of the ECHR does not confer on the individual a right of access to a register containing information on his or her personal position, nor does it embody an obligation for the government to impart information or

---

[34] See e.g.: *Jresild* case, para 31.

[35] ECHR, Sunday Times v. the United Kingdom, para 66 (hereafter: *Sunday Times* case).

[36] See e.g. ECHR, Timpul Info-Magazine and Anghel v. Moldova, para 31 (hereafter: *Timpul Info-Magazine* case).

[37] ECHR, Colombia and others v. Turkey, 25 June 2002, Application no. 51279/99, para 64.

[38] ECHR, Sener v. Turkey, para 46.

[39] *Guerra* case, para 53.

[40] Helberger 2005, 68; Voorhoof 1996, Voorhoof 2004, 912–918.

[41] Human Rights Committee 2010, 4.

[42] Dommering 2008, 48.

administrative documents to the individual.[43] The same goes for the *Guerra* case where the European Court of Human Rights has reiterated that "*freedom to receive information cannot be construed as imposing on a State [...] positive obligations to collect and disseminate information of its own motion*".[44] However, Hins and Voorhoof have always argued that "*a positive obligation for the State to supply relevant information and to give access to official documents regarding matters of public interest is inherent in that article*".[45] A very recent trend in Europe is the explicit recognition of a firm general right of access to public documents.[46] As Hins and Voorhoof hold, "*access to information on issues of general interest allows the public to have an adequate view of, and to form a critical opinion on, the state of the society in which they live*".[47] The new Convention on Access to Official Documents,[48] likewise considering "*the importance in a pluralistic, democratic society of transparency of public authorities*",[49] obliges all subscribing parties to guarantee the right of everyone to have access to "*all information recorded in any form, drawn up or received and held by public authorities*", and to take the necessary measures thereto.[50] In addition, the Human Rights Committee has recently emphasised that Article 19 of the ICCPR embraces a general right of access to information held by public bodies. This Committee adds that State parties should enact the necessary procedures to give effect to the right of access to information.[51] The European Court of Human Rights too has recently given a strong Article 10 protection to access to public documents. In a judgement of 2007, the European Court of Human rights stated that "*[p]articularly strong reasons must be provided for any measure affecting this role of the press and limiting access to information which the public has the right to receive*".[52] According to Voorhoof and Cannie, with this statement, the European Court of Human Rights recognised at least implicitly a right of access to information, and thus seems to be willing to reconsider its previous approach.[53] In the spring of 2009, the European Court of Human Rights, in two judgements, explicitly recognised the right of access to official documents. In those judgements, the European Court of Human Rights considered that when public bodies hold information that is needed for public debate, the refusal to open access to documents in this matter is to be regarded as a violation of the right to freedom of expression and information.

43 ECHR, Leander v. Sweden, para 74.; Voorhoof and Cannie 2010, 416.

44 *Guerra* case, para 53.

45 Hins and Voorhoof 2007, 114.

46 Voorhoof and Cannie 2010, 416.

47 Hins and Voorhoof 2007, 114.

48 Council of Europe 2008, Convention on Access to Official Documents.

49 Preamble of the Council of Europe Convention on Access to Official Documents.

50 Article 2 of the Council of Europe Convention on Access to Official Documents.

51 Human Rights Committee 2010, 6.

52 *Timpul Info-Magazine* case, para 31.

53 Voorhoof and Cannie 2010, 416.

The European Court of Human Rights had made clear that the state has an obligation not to impede the flow of information sought by a journalist or an interested citizen and that access to original documentary sources for legitimate historical research is an essential element of the exercise of the right to freedom of expression.[54] More specifically, the European Court of Human Rights considers that "*obstacles created in order to hinder access to information of public interest may discourage those working in the media or related fields from pursuing such matters. As a result, they may no longer be able to play their vital role as "public watchdogs"*".[55] Hence, the existence of a positive obligation for the State to actively supply relevant information and to give access to official documents regarding matters of public interest is today no longer questioned.[56]

4.2.2 No Interference by Public Authority Allowed

4.2.2.1 Negative Obligation

The freedom of expression and right to information has the character of an abstention right. In other words, Article 10 of the ECHR includes a prohibition for States to intervene.[57] The notion 'intervention' covers any form of interference coming from any authority exercising public power and duties or being in the public service, such as courts, prosecutors' offices, police, any law enforcing body, intelligence services, central or local councils, Governmental departments, army's decision-making bodies, public professional structures and so on.[58] The European Court of Human Rights formulated it as follows: "*the responsibility of a State under the Convention may arise for acts of all its organs, agents and servants. [...] In particular, the obligations of a Contracting Party under the Convention can be violated by any person exercising an official function vested in him*".[59] Nicol, Millar and Sharland have indicated that interference by a public authority also includes restrictions which are imposed by a private body which is exercising public law functions.[60] A wide range of restrictions or sanctions has been considered as interferences with the individual's or the media's exercise of freedom of expression or right to information: the prohibition, refusal or withdrawal of a licence to broadcast, a penal sanction for the publication of specific information, withdrawal of circulation or destruction of copies of a publication, a

54 See e.g.: ECHR, Kenedi v. Hungary, 26 May 2009; Voorhoof and Cannie 2010, 416.

55 ECHR, Társaság a Szabadságjogokért v. Hungary, para 38.

56 Lefever et al. 2010, 403.

57 See e.g.: Voorhoof 1995, 51.

58 Macovei 2004, 24; Voorhoof 2004, 922.

59 ECHR, Wille v. Liechtenstein, para 46.

60 Nicol et al. 2009, 20.

prohibition to participate in a radio or television programme, criminal sanctions and so on.[61]

Although Article 10, § 1 of the ECHR obliges States to refrain from intervening, this Article also states that it "*shall not prevent States from requiring the licensing of broadcasting, television or cinema enterprises*". In other words, States are permitted to control by a licencing system the way in which broadcasting is organised in their territories. However, the European Court of Human Rights added that "*[i]t does not provide that licensing measures shall not otherwise be subject to the requirements of paragraph 2 (article 10–2), for that would lead to a result contrary to the object and purpose of Article 10 (article 10) taken as a whole*".[62] In paragraph 60 of the *Groppera* case, the European Court of Human Rights indicated why this sentence was included in Article 10: "*The insertion of the sentence in issue [...] was clearly due to technical or practical considerations such as the limited number of available frequencies and the major capital investment required for building transmitters. It also reflected a political concern on the part of several States, namely that broadcasting should be the preserve of the State*". Due to technical developments, public broadcasting monopolies could be classified as contrary to Article 10 of the ECHR.[63] In 1993, the European Court of Human Rights stated that "*a public monopoly [...] imposes the greatest restrictions on the freedom of expression, namely the total impossibility of broadcasting otherwise than through a national station*".[64]

As indicated in Article 34 of the ECHR, any person, non-governmental organisation or group of individuals claiming to be the victim of a violation of its fundamental rights can go to Court.

4.2.2.2 Positive Obligations and Horizontal Effect

A. General Introduction

As indicated by Voorhoof, the European Court of Human Rights has extended the scope of Article 10 of the ECHR by attributing a horizontal effect to Article 10 and by recognising positive obligations for Member States to protect these fundamental rights.[65] In other words, the State and public authorities can also have a positive obligation under Article 10 of the ECHR to actively protect the realisation of the freedom of expression and the right to information.[66] One should realise that negative obligations (*supra*) have always been regarded as inherent in

---

[61] See e.g.: Voorhoof 1995, 52; Macovei 2004, 20.

[62] *Groppera* case, para 61.

[63] Macovei 2004, 16.

[64] ECHR, Informationsverein Lentia and others v. Austria, para 39 (hereafter: *Lentia* case).

[65] Voorhoof 2009, 7.

[66] See e.g.: Mowbray 2004; Akandji-Kombe 2007.

the European Convention, which is not true for the positive obligations. However, over the years, the European Court of Human Rights has attributed a dual character, a negative and a positive, to the provisions of the ECHR.[67] In the *Özgür Gündem* case, the European Court of Human Rights formulated it as follows: "*[g]enuine, effective exercise of this freedom [of expression] does not depend merely on the State's duty not to interfere, but may require positive measures of protection, [...]*".[68] The same reasoning could be found in the *VGT Verein gegen Tierfabriken* case: "*in addition to the primarily negative undertaking of a State to abstain from interference in Convention guarantees, "there may be positive obligations inherent" in such guarantees. The responsibility of a State may then be engaged as a result of not observing its obligation to enact domestic legislation*".[69] Recently, in the 2008 *Khurshid Mustafa and Tarzibach v. Sweden* case, the European Court of Human Rights gives new evidence that a State's positive obligation to guarantee access to information is not restricted to public (state-held) documents. In this case, the applicants had been forced by their landlord, with support of the Swedish judiciary, to move from their rented flat because they refused to remove a satellite antenna, in breach of the tenancy agreement. The European Court of Human Rights observed that the satellite dish enabled them to receive television programmes, not only including political but also social news, from their country of origin (Iraq). According to the European Court of Human Rights, "*the freedom to receive information does not extend only to reports of events of public concern, but covers in principle also cultural expressions as well as pure entertainment. The importance of the latter types of information should not be underestimated, especially for an immigrant family [...] who may wish to maintain in contact with the culture and language of their country of origin*".[70] After having considered all relevant elements, it judged that the interference with the applicants' right to freedom of information was not necessary in a democratic society (in the sense of Article 10, § 2 of the ECHR). Thus, Sweden had failed to fulfil its positive obligation to protect the right of the applicants to receive information.[71] In determining whether a positive obligation exists, the European Court of Human Rights has emphasised that "*regard must be had to the fair balance that has to be struck between the general interest of the community and the interests of the individual, the search for which is inherent throughout the Convention*".[72] As indicated by Harris, O'Boyle and Warwick, the relevant factors that could be considered are the following: the kind of expression rights at stake, their public interest nature, their capacity to

---

[67] Akandji-Kombe 2007, 5–6.

[68] ECHR, Özgür Gündem v. Turkey, para 43 (hereafter:. *Ozgyr Gundem* case).

[69] ECHR, VGT Verein gegen Tierfabriken v. Switzerland, para 45 (hereafter: *VGT Verein gegen Tierfabriken* case).

[70] *Khurshid Mustafa* case, para 44.

[71] *Ibid.*, para 50.

[72] *Ozgyr Gundem* case, para 43.

contribute to public debates, the availability of alternative venues for expression, the weight of countervailing rights of others or the public.[73]

As stated by Voorhoof, another aspect of the State's positive obligation to protect and promote the freedom of expression and right to information could be found in the indirect horizontal effect of Article 10 of the ECHR.[74] At first sight, interference in the individual's right by another private person or by a non-governmental organisation could not to be considered as interference by public authorities. As a result, in principle, such a complaint is not admissible under the scope of this Article. However, the European Court of Human Rights has indicated that positive obligations exist for States to protect person's rights from the acts of other private parties.[75] In the *Ozgyr Gundem* case, the European Court of Human Rights formulated it as follows: "*effective exercise of this freedom does not depend merely on the State's duty not to interfere, but may require positive measures of protection, even in the sphere of relations between individuals*".[76] More recently, the European Court of Human Rights stated that "*the Court is not in theory required to settle disputes of a purely private nature. [However,] it cannot remain passive where a national court's interpretation of a legal act, be it a testamentary disposition, a private contract, a public document, a statutory provision or an administrative practice appears unreasonable, arbitrary, discriminatory or, more broadly, inconsistent with the principles underlying the Convention*".[77] However, in the *VGT Verein gegen Tierfabriken* case, the European Court of Human Rights has explicitly stated that it "*does not consider it desirable, let alone necessary, to elaborate a general theory concerning the extent to which the Convention guarantees should be extended to relations between private individuals inter se*".[78] According to the European Court of Human Rights, under Article 1 of the ECHR, each Contracting State of the ECHR "*shall secure to everyone within [its] jurisdiction the rights and freedoms defined in [...] [the] Convention*".[79] Hence, as indicated by Harris and others, although the European Court of Human Rights refrained from formulating a general theory on positive obligations, the European Court of Human Rights has consistently recognised that individuals can effectively exercise their rights among themselves.[80] As a result, this implies that complaints from the public, if exclusive contracts closed between sports organisations and broadcasters would interfere with their right to information, could be admissible under Article 10 of the ECHR.

---

73 Harris et al. 2009, 446.

74 Voorhoof 1995, 59.

75 See e.g.: Voorhoof 1995, 51; Akandji-Kombe 2007, 14.

76 *Ozgyr Gundem* case, para 43.

77 *Khurshid Mustafa* case, para 33.

78 *VGT Verein gegen Tierfabriken* case, para 46.

79 *Ibid.*, para 45.

80 Harris et al. 2009, 446.

B. Obligation to Guarantee Access to Live and Full Sports Coverage

Given that States have the positive obligation to actively protect the public's right to information, the question that needs to be answered is whether an obligation for the state or public authority to intervene could exist in order to ensure the public's access to live and full coverage of sports events. In determining whether a positive obligation exists, the state should examine whether a fair balance could be achieved between the different interests at stake (*supra*). Regarding access to sports content, the interests of the public should be weighted against the freedom of programming of the broadcasters and the right to property of the rights holding sports federations or sports clubs. In doing so, different relevant factors could be considered. Although it is not the aim to do this exercise in detail, some relevant elements of this discussion will be highlighted in the following section (*infra*). As indicated by Helberger, when States would decide that such protection is needed, Article 10, § 2 of the ECHR should be respected (*infra*).[81]

4.3 Article 10, § 2 of the ECHR: Restrictions Regarding the Freedom of Expression and the Right to Information

As other fundamental freedoms, freedom of expression is not an absolute right either and can, therefore, be subject to restrictions imposed by the Member State.[82] The unrestricted exercise of a freedom could, otherwise, cause unacceptable abuses and harm of other people that cannot be tolerated in a democratic society.[83] In other words, public authorities are allowed to intervene with the freedom of expression and the right to information by imposing restrictions, conditions or sanctions when they cumulatively fulfil the following conditions: 1) the restriction has to be 'prescribed by law'; 2) the restriction has to be 'necessary in a democratic society' and 3) the restriction has to be in pursuance of one or more of the :legitimate aims' listed in Article 10, § 2 of the ECHR.

4.3.1 Prescribed by Law

First, the European Court of Human Rights should determine whether the restriction is 'prescribed by law'. According to the European Court of Human Rights, the word "law" in the expression 'prescribed by law' covers not only formal law, directly

[81] Helberger 2005, 69.

[82] *Thorgeir* case, para 63.

[83] Rozakis 2008, 2.

emanating from Parliament, but also unwritten law, deontological code and so on.[84] This condition implies that the regulation must be adequately accessible and adequately foreseeable, *i.e.* it must be formulated with sufficient precision to reasonably foresee the consequences that a given action may entail.[85] An unpublished provision cannot satisfy the first condition; an unclear and contradictory rule cannot satisfy the second.[86] In the European Court of Human Rights' view, "*the scope of the concepts of foreseeability and accessibility depends to a considerable degree on the content of the instrument in issue, the field it is designed to cover and the number and status of those to whom it is addressed*".[87] Hence, if States decide to intervene in order to guarantee the public's access to live and full broadcasts of sports events, the rule should be adequately accessible and adequately foreseeable.

4.3.2 Legitimate Aim

Second, the legitimate grounds upon which restrictions can be allowed are enumerated by § 2 of this Article in a limitative list: "*national security, territorial integrity or public safety, for the prevention of disorder or crime, for the protection of health or morals, for the protection of the reputation or rights of others, for preventing the disclosure of information received in confidence, or for maintaining the authority and impartiality of the judiciary*".

Voorhoof argued that the extensiveness of this list indicates a justification of all kinds of interferences by public authorities to the freedom of expression and information. According to him, the jurisprudence of the European Court of Human Rights makes clear that in all cases concerning the freedom of expression and information, the restrictions imposed were estimated as falling under one or the other of the legitimate aims or values as enumerated in § 2.[88]

In the *Groppera* case, for example, the European Court of Human Rights has incorporated the principle of media pluralism into the protection of the rights of others within article 10, § 2 of the ECHR. In this case, the governments submitted that the interference with the freedom of expression could be allowed under 'the protection of the rights of others', because the interference's objective was to ensure pluralism, in particular of information. According to the European Court of Human Rights, this objective could, indeed, be grasped by the protection of the rights of others.[89]

---

84 *Sunday Times* case, para 47; Voorhoof 1995, 57.
85 *Sunday Times* case, para 49.
86 Dommering 2008, 43.
87 *Groppera* case, para 68.
88 See e.g.: Voorhoof 1995, 58.
89 *Groppera* case, para 69–70; Marauhn 2007, 117.

Furthermore, the European Court of Human Rights has indicated different times that the broadcasters' freedom of programming could be legitimately limited by rules included in the broadcasting regulation. Recital 5 of the Audiovisual Media Services Directive[90] specifies that the growing importance of audiovisual media services for societies and democracy, in particular by ensuring freedom of information, diversity of opinion and media pluralism, justifies the application of specific rules to these services. Advertising rules, for example, were labelled by the European Court of Human Rights as pursuing a legitimate aim included in Article 10, § 2 of the ECHR. In the *VgT Verein Gegen Tierfabriken* case, the European Court of Human Rights stated that advertising rules aim at "*the "protection of the... rights of others" within the meaning of Article 10 § 2 of the Convention*".[91] In the *TV Vest* case too, the European Court of Human Rights held that advertising rules could be justified in order to protect the rights of others.[92] In the recent *Sigma Radio Television* case, the Cyprus Government argued that the interference with the broadcaster's freedom of expression pursued the protection of rights of others. In particular, viewers, including children, should be protected from abusive practises.[93] The European Court of Human Rights agreed with the government that "*the interference pursued at least one of the legitimate aims set out in paragraph 2 of Article 10, namely, the protection of the rights of others*".[94] The European Court of Justice followed the same reasoning. In the *RTL Television* case,[95] for example, the European Court of Justice stated that advertisement rules "*may amount to a restriction on the freedom of expression*".[96] However, "*[s]uch a restriction appears [...] to be justified under Article 10(2) of the ECHR*".[97]

As indicated by Barendt, this broad interpretation of the notion "the protection of the rights of others" would enable States to justify positive programme requirements.[98] Based on these observations, rules guaranteeing the public's access to live and full coverage of (certain) sports events could probably also fall under this legitimate aim.

---

[90] European Parliament and Council Directive of 10 March 2010 on the coordination of certain provisions laid down by law, regulation or administrative action in Member States concerning the provision of audiovisual media services (Audiovisual Media Services Directive). *OJ* (2010) L 95/1.

[91] *VgT Verein Gegen Tierfabriken* case, para 61–62.

[92] ECHR, TV Vest AS & Rogaland Pensjonistparti v. Normay, para 29 (hereafter: *TV Vest* case).

[93] ECHR, Sigma Radio Television Ltd. V. Cyprus, para 183 (hereafter: *Sigma Radio Television* case).

[94] *Sigma Radio Television* case, para 196.

[95] CJ, RTL Television GmbH v Niedersächsische Landesmedienanstalt für privaten Rundfunk Judgment (hereafter: *RTL Television* case).

[96] *RTL Television* case, para 68.

[97] *Ibid.*, para 69.

[98] Barendt 1992, 19.

4.3.3 Necessary in a Democratic Society

Third, the restriction has to be 'necessary in a democratic society'. The adjective 'necessary' is not synonymous with 'indispensable', neither has it the flexibility of such expressions as 'admissible', 'ordinary', 'useful', 'reasonable' or 'desirable', but it requires a 'pressing social need'.[99] Hence, the test of 'necessity in a democratic society' requires the European Court of Human Rights to determine whether the 'interference' corresponds to a 'pressing social need' whether it was proportionate to the legitimate aim pursued and whether the reasons given by the national authorities to justify it are relevant and sufficient.[100] In assessing whether such a 'need' exists and what measures should be adopted to deal with it, the national authorities are left a certain margin of appreciation. This power of appreciation is not, however, unlimited but goes hand in hand with supervision by the European Court of Human Rights, whose task it is to give a final ruling on whether a restriction is reconcilable with freedom of expression as protected by Article 10.[101] The scope of this margin of appreciation is not identical in each case, but will vary according to the context. Relevant factors include the nature of the Convention right in issue, its importance for the individual, the nature of the activities concerned, etc.[102] The European Court of Human Rights could also take into consideration a comparative element: if the relevant legislation or litigious interference is in conformity with the situation in different Contracting Parties of the Council of Europe, this can weight heavily in determining its democratic necessity, as the main purpose of the Convention is to lay down certain international standards in their relations with persons under their jurisdiction.[103] In the light of this study, the question should be raised whether interference by a State or by a public authority to guarantee access to coverage of (certain) sports events could be classified as necessary in a democratic society.

First, the public interest nature of the information and its capacity to contribute to the public debate should be analysed. As already indicated different times, access to live and full coverage of sports events can play an important role in our society. Sports events can bring people together, create a sense of belonging and stimulate conversations (*supra*). However, a necessary precondition for these achievements is that sport is simultaneously and live accessible to all citizens. In other words, to give the public the chance to feel "one" and to discuss certain events of public interest, access to the broadcasting of these events should not be restricted to a limited number of people (*supra*). Although the type of debate in

---

[99] See e.g.: *Sunday Times* case, para 59.

[100] ECHR, Bladet Tromsø and Stensaas v. Norway, para 58 (hereafter: *Bladet* case); *Sunday Times* case, para 62.

[101] See e.g.: *Groppera* case, para 72; *Bladet* case, para 58; para 39; *Lentia* case, para 35.

[102] See e.g. ECHR, Buckley v. the United Kingdom, para 74; ECHR, Laskey, Jaggard and Brown v. the United Kingdom, para 42.

[103] Voorhoof 1995, 62.

pursuance of sports events is not as important for procedural democracy as political discourse, public interest discourse concerning the culture of society is also important for the development of a democratic society (*supra*). As a result, access to live and full sports coverage could be protected under Article 10 of the ECHR.

Second, the countervailing rights should be weighted. Rights holders could argue that their property rights are affected by such interference (*infra*).[104] However, we can observe that restrictions to private properties in order to realise specific social benefits are a current and accepted practise. In this regard, an intervention to guarantee access to the broadcasting of sports events could also be defended on the grounds that sport performs an important social function.[105] Broadcasters could argue that broadcasting regulation contains different rules 'infringing' their freedom of programming. However, these infringements were often considered justified under Article 10, § 2 of the ECHR. The different quota regulations of the Audiovisual Media Services Directive,[106] for example, encroach the broadcasters' freedom of programming, since the duty to broadcast European works has an influence on the content of the programme and the programme schedule. However, as indicated by Castendyk, this restriction is considered to be justified under Article 10, § 2 of the ECHR.[107] Furthermore, in the *Sigma Radio Television* case, the European Court of Human Rights needed to deal with an annulment request of 25 decisions of the Cyprus Radio and Television Authority in which fines were imposed on Sigma Radio Television. Sigma Radio Television was convicted for the following breaches of the advertising rules: advertisements for children's toys, the duration of advertising breaks, the placement of sponsors' names during news programmes and product placement in a comedy series.[108] The European Court of Human Rights considered that the impugned interference was proportionate to the aim pursued, being the protection of consumers and children from unethical advertising practises, including surreptitious advertising and the importance of ensuring that viewers were informed on the true content of the broadcasts by the use of appropriate acoustic and visual warnings, and that the reasons given to justify it were relevant and sufficient. As a result, the European Court of Human Rights stressed that the interference with the broadcaster's freedom of expression can reasonably be regarded as having been necessary in a democratic society for the protection of the rights of others.[109]

In addition, the European Court of Human Rights should evaluate the proportionality of the interference or restriction. In doing so, the European Court

---

[104] GC, FIFA v European Commission, para 135–136; GC, FIFA v European Commission, para 132–133; GC, UEFA v European Commission, para 173–174.

[105] Craufurd Smith and Bottcher 2002, 113; Parrish and Miettinen 2009, 26.

[106] Article 16 & 17 of the AVMS Directive.

[107] Castendyk 2008, 443.

[108] *Sigma Radio Television* case, para 14–19.

[109] *Ibid.*, para 200–201.

of Human Rights will examine whether a restriction is "*proportionate to the legitimate aim pursued*".[110] As a result, any interference disproportionate to the legitimate aim pursued will not be deemed necessary in a democratic society.[111] As indicated by Voorhoof, in evaluating the proportionality, the European Court of Human Rights takes into consideration the degree of interference in the applicant's right with regard to the effect, a restriction has on the exercise of his freedom of expression or right to information. To decide whether interference is proportionate to the legitimate aim pursued, the European Court of Human Rights will take into account the case as a whole.[112] Furthermore, when dealing with the proportionality question, it should be repeated that attempting to make plausible that the public would have a right of access to full and live coverage on free-to-air television of every sports event would probably not be proportionate and, thus, too challenging. However, it might not be unthinkable that in certain circumstances such right could be defended for specific sports events. For example, for events of major importance for society or when the broadcasting rights are concentrated in the hands of one powerful player (*infra*). Additionally, it could be suggested that the broadcasting of short news reports about or highlights of the sports events could be labelled as alternative sources available to access the content, and thus be the only proportionate interference. The latter vision is supported by Craufurd Smith and Bottcher. According to these authors, full coverage of sports events exceeds the scope of Article 10 of the ECHR. According to them "*the extent that the public has a genuine need for information about sporting events this may be met by brief news reports or at most, highlights*".[113] However, as indicated above, the aim of such short broadcasts is purely to provide information on events for people unable to watch the live coverage, while the full and live broadcasts of sports events can contribute to a certain type of public discourse which is important for the development of the society. From that perspective, it can be argued that short news reports cannot be labelled as an alternative source.

Based on the foregoing, my conclusion is that States can intervene in order to protect the public's access to live and full sports coverage. States can provide adequate sector specific regulation, in particular broadcasting regulation (*infra*) or competition authorities, being a public authority or an authority exercising public power can intervene (*infra*).

---

[110] See e.g. *Handyside* case, para 49.; *Jersild* case, para 31; *Perna* case, para 39.

[111] Council of Europe 2007, 9.

[112] Voorhoof 1995, 60–61; Voorhoof 2009, 1–2, 43.

[113] Craufurd Smith and Bottcher 2002, 112–114.

References

Legislation and Policy Documents,

International

United Nations

United Nations (1948) Universal declaration of human rights, 10 December 1948. http://www.un.org/en/documents/udhr/. Accessed 18 Aug 2010

United Nations (1966) International covenant on civil and political rights, 16 December 1966. http://www2.ohchr.org/english/law/ccpr.htm. Accessed 18 Aug 2010

Human rights committee (2010) Draft general comment No. 34, CCPR/C/GC/34/CRP.2

Human rights committee (2011) General comment No. 34, CCPR/C/GC/34. http://www.psw.ugent.be/cms_global/uploads/publicaties/dv/UNHRCgeneral-comment34-20110725DVf.pdf. Accessed 17 Aug 2011

European Union

Charters

European Union (2000). Charter of fundamental rights of the European Union. *OJ* (2000) C 364/1

Directives

European Parliament and Council Directive of 10 March 2010 on the coordination of certain provisions laid down by law, regulation or administrative action in Member States concerning the provision of audiovisual media services (Audiovisual Media Services Directive). *OJ* (2010) L 95/1

Council of Europe

Conventions

Council of Europe (1950). Convention for the protection of human rights and fundamental freedoms, CETS No. 005, 04 November 1950. http://conventions.coe.int/Treaty/en/Treaties/Html/005.htm. Accessed 18 Aug 2010

Council of Europe (2008) Convention on access to official documents, 27 November 2008. https://wcd.coe.int/ViewDoc.jsp?id=1377737&Site=CM. Accessed 21 Aug 2010

Case Law

Court of Justice

CJ, RTL Television GmbH v Niedersächsische Landesmedienanstalt für privaten Rundfunk Judgment, Case C-245/01, 23 October 2003, *ECR* I-12489

European Court of Human Rights

ECHR, Handyside v. the United Kingdom, 7 December 1976, Application no. 5493/72
ECHR, Sunday Times v. the United Kingdom, 26 April 1979, Application no. 6538/74
ECHR, Leander v. Sweden, 26 March 1987, Application no. 9248/81
ECHR, Müller and Others v. Switzerland, 24 May 1988, Application no. 10737/84
ECHR, Verlag GmbH and Klaus Beermann v. Germany, 20 November 1989, Application no. 10572/83
ECHR, Groppera Radio AG and others v. Switzerland, 28 March 1990, Application no. 10890/84
ECHR, Autronic AG v. Switzerland, 22 May 1990, Application no. 12726/87
ECHR, Informationsverein Lentia and others v. Austria, 24 November 1993, Application no. 13914/88; 15041/89; 15717/89; 15779/89; 17207/90
ECHR, Jresild v. Denmark, 23 September 1994, Application no. 15890/89
ECHR, Goodwin v. the United Kingdom, 27 March 1996, Application no. 17488/90
ECHR, Buckley v. the United Kingdom, 25 September 1996, Application no. 20348/92
ECHR, Laskey, Jaggard and Brown v. the United Kingdom, 19 February 1997, Application nos. 21627/93, 21826/93, 21974/93
ECHR, Bladet Tromsø and Stensaas v. Norway, 20 May 1999, Application no. 21980/93
ECHR, Wille v. Liechtenstein, 28 October 1999, Application no. 28396/95
ECHR, Özgür Gündem v. Turkey, 16 March 2000, Application no. 23144/93
ECHR, Sener v. Turkey, 18 July 2000, Application no. 26680/95
ECHR, VGT Verein gegen Tierfabriken v. Switzerland, 28 June 2001, Application no. 24699/94
ECHR, Sigma Radio Television Ltd. V. Cyprus, 21 July 2011, Applications nos. 32181/04 and 35122/05
ECHR, Colombia and others v. Turkey, 25 June 2002, Application no. 51279/99
ECHR, Perna v. Italy, 6 May 2003, Application no. 48898/99
ECHR, Garaudy v. France, 24 June 2003. Application no. 65831/01
ECHR, Timpul Info-Magazine and Anghel v. Moldova, 27 November 2007, Application no. 42864/05
ECHR, TV Vest AS & Rogaland Pensjonistparti v. Normay, 11 December 2008, Application no. 21132/05
ECHR, Khurshid Mustafa and Tarzibach v. Sweden, 16 December 2008, Application no. 23883/06
ECHR, Társaság a Szabadságjogokért v. Hungary, 14 April 2009
ECHR, Kenedi v. Hungary, 26 May 2009

General Court

GC, FIFA v European Commission, 17 February 2011, Case T-68/08 (not yet published in ECR)
GC, FIFA v European Commission, 17 February 2011, Case T-385/07 (not yet published in ECR)
GC, UEFA v European Commission, 17 February 2011, Case T-55/08 (not yet published in ECR)

Doctrine

Akandji-Kombe JF (2007) Positive obligations under the European Convention on Human Rights. A guide to the implementation of the European Convention on Human Rights—Human rights handbooks, No. 7. Strasbourg: Council of Europe. http://www.echr.coe.int/NR/rdonlyres/1B521F61-A636-43F5-AD56-5F26D46A4F55/0/DG2ENHRHAND072007.pdf. Accessed 15 July 2011

Barendt E (1995) Broadcasting law: a comparative study. Clarendon, Oxford

Barendt E (1992) Fundamental freedoms. In: Dommering E et al (eds) Information law towards the 21st century. Kluwer, Deventer, pp 13–25

Castendyk O (2008) Article 4 TWFD. In: Castendyk O et al (eds) European media law. Kluwer Law International, Alphen a/d Rijn, pp 429–455

Closs W, Nikoltchev S (2005) Political debate and the role of the media. European Audiovisual Observatory, Strasbourg

Council of Europe (2007) Freedom of expression in Europe: case law concerning article 10 of the European convention on human rights. Council of Europe, Strasbourg

Craufurd Smith R, Bottcher B (2002) Football and fundamental rights: regulating access to major sporting events on television. European Public Law 8(1):107–133

Cucereanu D (2008) Aspects of regulating freedom of expression on the internet. Intersentia, Antwerpen

Dommering E (2008) Article 10 ECHR. In: Castendyk O et al (eds) European media law. Kluwer Law International, Alphen a/d Rijn, pp 35–81

Harris D et al (2009) Law of the European convention on human rights. Oxford University Press, Oxford

Herr R (2011) Can human rights law support access to communication technology? a case study under article 10 of the right to receive information. http://papers.ssrn.com/sol3/papers.cfm?abstract_id=1860824&. Accessed 18 Aug 2011

Fenwick H, Gavin P (2006) Media freedom under the human rights act. Oxford University Press, Oxford

Gratton C, Solberg HA (2007) The economics of sports broadcasting. Routledge, London

Helberger N (2005) Controlling access to content—Regulating Conditional Access in Digital Broadcasting. Kluwer Law International, The Hague

Hins W, Voorhoof D (2007) Access to state-held information as a fundamental right under the European Convention on Human Rights. European Constitutional Law Review 3:114–126

Hutchins B, Rowe D (2009) From broadcast scarcity to digital plenitude: The changing dynamics of the media sport content economy. Television New Media 10:354–370

Lefever K et al. (2010) Watching live sport on television: a human right? The right to information and the list of major events regime. E.H.R.L.R. 4:396-407

Lewis A, Taylor J (2003) Sport: law and practice. Butterworths, London

Macovei M (2004) A guide to the implementation of Article 10 of the European Convention on Human Rights—human rights handbooks No. 2. Strasbourg: Council of Europe. http://www.humanrights.coe.int/aware/GB/publi/materials/947.pdf. Accessed 14 July 2011

Marauhn T (2007) Freedom of expression, freedom of assembly and association. In: Ehlers D (ed) European fundamental rights and freedoms. De Gruyter Recht, Berlin, pp 97–129

Mowbray A (2004) The development of positive obligations under the European Convention on Human Rights by the European Court of Human Rights. Hart, Oxford

Nicol A et al (2009) Media Law & Human Rights. Oxford University Press Sharland, Oxford

Parrish R, Miettinen S (2009) Sports broadcasting in community law. In: Blackshaw I et al (eds) TV Rights and Sport. Legal Aspects. T.M.C. ASSER press, The Hague, pp 9–33

Rozakis C (2008) The European protection of freedom of expression: some recent restrictive trends, seminar on the European Protection of freedom of expression, Strasbourg, 10 October 2008. http://www-ircm.u-strasbg.fr/seminaire_oct2008/docs/Introduction_Christos_Rozakis.pdf. Accessed 18 Aug 2010

Saltzman R (2000) Television news access to exclusively owned sporting events: a comparative study. Sports Lawyers Journal 7:1–28

Scheuer A, Strothmann P (2004) Sports as reflected in European media law Part I. Iris Plus. http://www.obs.coe.int/oea_publ/iris/iris_plus/iplus4_2004.pdf.en. Accessed 19 August 2010

Voorhoof D (1995) The media in a democratic society. Article 10 of the European convention on human rights. In: Council of Europe (European Media Law Forum) (ed), Legal problems of the functioning of media in a democratic society. Llubljana, pp 39–74

Voorhoof D (1996) Art.10 EVRM en de vrijheid van de media. Jaarboek Mensenrechten 1995–1996. Maklu Uitgevers, Antwerpen/Apeldoorn

Voorhoof D (2004) Artikel 10—Vrijheid van meningsuiting. In: Vande Lanotte J, Haeck Y (eds), Handboek EVRM—Deel 2 Artikelsgewijze commentaar Volume I. Intersentia, Antwerpen, pp 837–1050

Voorhoof D (2009) Freedom of expression under the European Human Rights System. Inter-Am Eur Hum Rights J 2(1–2):3–48

Voorhoof D, Cannie H (2010) Freedom of expression and information in a democratic society: The added but fragile value of the European convention on human rights. Int Comm Gazette 72:407–423

Weinstein J (2009) Extreme speech, public order, and democracy: lessons from the masses. In: Hare I, Weinstein J (eds) Extreme speech and democracy. Oxford University Press, Oxford, pp 23–62

Chapter 5
The Public in Its Role as Citizen and Consumer

5.1 Introduction

With regard to broadcasting, when referring to the public or the viewers, a distinction is often made between citizens versus consumers,[1] civic culture versus consumer culture,[2] or more generally, constitutional citizenship versus consumer citizenship.[3] Harrison and Woods, for example, stated that "*the viewer can be regarded as either a market-based consumer or as a citizen with rights of access to certain content*".[4] In other words, as formulated by Cooper, "*the needs of citizens cannot be reduced to the needs of consumers*".[5] Given that, as indicated by Harrison and Woods, "*[m]any of us are both consumer and citizen*"[6] and, as indicated by Sunstein, "*[c]onsumers are not citizens and it is a large error to conflate the two*",[7] these two notions should be analysed in detail. It is important to examine whether access to sport for the public, both in its role as citizen and consumer, could be protected under Article 10 of the ECHR.

5.2 The Viewer as Consumer

First of all, a viewer is a consumer. According to different authors, consumers reside in the commercial, market-based domain.[8] As indicated by Harrison and Woods, in this commercial domain, "*[i]nformation is not necessarily a public*

[1] See e.g.: Born and Prosser 2001, 657–687; Harrison and Woods 2007, 7–10.
[2] Keum et al. 2004, 369.
[3] Freedland and Sciarra 1998, 10–11.
[4] Harrison and Woods 2007, 7–10.
[5] Cooper 2003, 13.
[6] Harrison and Woods 2007, 8.
[7] Sunstein 2001, 122.
[8] Harrison and Woods 2007, 7–10; Helberger 2008, 5.

K. Lefever, *New Media and Sport*, ASSER International Sports Law Series,
DOI: 10.1007/978-90-6704-873-6_5,

resource to be disseminated on behalf of the public good, but is private property to be exploited for financial gain".[9] In other words, when talking about protecting the consumers' interest, consumers will be referred to in terms of economic goals, such as choice, price, quality of service and value for money, in particular through promoting open and competitive markets.[10] Helberger described a consumer as "*someone who measures quality in terms of quantity, maximum pleasure and price*".[11]

In this economic-driven domain, viewers are seen as individuals with only their own interest in mind.[12] As a result, Richards emphasised that the consumer's concern is that "*[they] are supplied with what [they] as individuals [...] want to watch or what [they] want to have an option to watch*".[13] As a result, consumers are prepared to pay an extra subscription fee in order to have access to their preferred content.[14] A study conducted by Accenture, for example, found that the proportion of viewers/consumers willing to pay for some content is continuing to grow.[15] In other words, as formulated by Born and Posser, the objective of broadcasters in a market-based domain is to respond to pre-existing and individual audience tastes by offering specialised and niche content. Hence, when taking into account consumers' interest, broadcasting becomes an essentially commercial activity.[16] As indicated by Harrison and Woods, the content diet of consumers is quite different from that of the citizens: "*[n]o content type is excluded from their diets, although particular groups of consumers tend to focus on a narrower range of programmes, reflecting pre-existing interests and consumption patterns*".[17] Hence, sport could be part of the consumer's diet. The fact that the public wants to pay for sports coverage can be illustrated by the success of sports channels only available on a pay-television basis.[18]

5.3 The Viewer as Citizen

While the consumer resides in the commercial domain, the viewer, as a citizen, resides in the public domain.[19] A strong and robust public domain is often described as a necessary precondition for the development of a democratic society

[9] Harrison and Woods 2007, 7.

[10] Dawes 2007, 8; Livingstone and Lunt 2007, 5 and 7.

[11] Helberger 2008, 5.

[12] See e.g.: Richards 2004; Helberger 2008, 5.

[13] Richards 2004.

[14] Harrison and Woods 2007, 9.

[15] Accenture 2009, 6.

[16] Born and Prosser 2001, 659 and 7679.

[17] Harrison and Woods 2007, 7 and 9.

[18] Ofcom 2007, 31, 2008, Section 5.

[19] See e.g.: Born 2001, 657–687; Harrison and Woods 2007, 7.

where free communication and discussion of ideas is guaranteed.[20] Given that a constant interaction of information on different topics has to take place in the public domain, the citizen, as indicated by Harrison and Woods, "*requires that certain civic functions are fulfilled by broadcasters*".[21] Therefore, the audiovisual sector needs to offer access to information on issues of general interest allowing the citizens/public to have an adequate view of, and to form a critical opinion on, the state of the society in which they live and, thus, fulfil its democratic responsibilities.[22] However, as stated by Born and Prosser, the media should not only be seen as having an informative role, but also as having a cultural role by constructing a shared identity. In this case, it is the broadcaster's task to create a sense of belonging between people of different backgrounds, with different tastes and interests.[23] In order to inform the citizens and to create an identity, citizens should have access to programmes having social, political and civic assets and values, such as news, current affairs, documentaries and sport (*supra*).[24] Different studies have shown that news is an effective tool to inform viewers about public interest affairs and that news programmes have the ability of activating citizens and creating a social consciousness.[25] Additionally, the European institutions and literature have granted sport an important role in creating a national identity, bringing people together and uniting the nation. Hence, the broadcasting of sport events is an important mechanism through which an involved citizenry can be developed, and through which a sense of national identity may be fostered (*supra*).

Moreover, it is often argued that this valuable content should be available to all citizens. Born and Posser, for example, stressed that "*the citizenship perspective requires a focus equally on commonality*".[26] Likewise, Harrison and Woods emphasised that "*[s]uch content should be available to all and enjoyed communally*".[27] Sports, for example, will only have the ability of creating a shared experience when a large number of people will have access to the coverage of the sports events on television (*supra*). Harrison and Woods even added that this content should be freely accessible (*infra*).[28] In other words, when talking about protecting the citizens' interest, such as access to content and sports coverage, citizens will be referred to in terms of Article 10 of the ECHR (*supra*). In order to guarantee the citizen's access to sports content, media law contains specific

[20] Rheingold 1998; Hugenholtz and Guibault 2006, 2.

[21] Harrison and Woods 2007, 7–8.

[22] Born and Prosser 2001, 674; Hins and Voorhoof 2007, 114.

[23] Born and Prosser 2001, 672 and 674.

[24] Harrison and Woods 2007, 7–10.

[25] For an overview of such studies, see: Keum et al. 2004, 369–391.

[26] Born and Prosser 2001, 671.

[27] Harrison and Woods 2007, 7.

[28] Ibid. 7.

Table 5.1 Broadcasting sector: consumer versus citizen

Consumer's interest	Citizen's interest
Economic focus	Cultural/political focus
Individual	Community
Private interests	Public interests
Wants	Needs
Short-term focus	Long-term focus
Niche content, such as sport, movies, etc.	News, current affairs, sport, etc.
Price	Freedom of speech/right to information (Article 10 of the ECHR)
Quality of service	Content standards
Competition law	Media law

provisions dealing with this issue. In this regard, Part III of this book will take a closer look at the 'list of major events' mechanism (*infra*).

In order to clarify the difference between those two concepts in another way, Cooper gave the following example: "*[t]he distinction between the commercial marketplace and the forum for democratic discourse becomes readily apparent when we respond to the advice frequently given by the most ardent advocates of pure economics to the complaint of mediocrity in the media. When the poor quality of the media product is brought up, they give a good free market response — "If you do not like what is on the tube, turn it off." An okay answer for consumers is very bad for citizens. It may be perfectly acceptable for consumers to be forced to vote with their dollars and turn off commercial entertainment, but it is not acceptable for citizens to be turned off by the poor quality of civic discourse, and then have no comparable alternative to which they can turn*".[29]

5.4 The Viewer: Summary

As can be concluded from the previous sections and as indicated by Born and Posser, "*the two conceptions [consumer and citizen] imply radically different visions of the nature of the television viewer*".[30] Table 5.1 indicates how the consumer and the citizen could be contrasted in the broadcasting sector.[31]

As can be concluded from this section, the public's access to sports coverage covers both the viewer's interests as a consumer (choice, price) and as a citizen (free access to live and full sports coverage). In the following Parts, it will be examined how the regulatory framework of the broadcasting sector, in particular

[29] Cooper 2003, 14.

[30] Born and Prosser 2001, 658.

[31] See e.g.: Richards 2004; Livingstone and Lunt 2007, 6; Dawes 2007, 9.

media and competition law, deal with public's access to sports content, in their role as citizen and/or consumer, in the changed media landscape.

References

Legislation and Policy Documents

UK

Consultations

Ofcom (2007) Pay TV market overview—Annex 8 to pay TV market investigation consultation. http://stakeholders.ofcom.org.uk/binaries/consultations/market_invest_paytv/annexes/a8.pdf. Accessed 25 Aug 2011

Ofcom (2008) Consumer research on pay TV—Annex 10 to second pay TV market investigation consultation. http://stakeholders.ofcom.org.uk/binaries/consultations/second_paytv/annexes/annex10.pdf. Accessed 25 Aug 2011

Doctrine

Accenture (2009) Television: entering the era of mass-fragmentation. http://www.accenture.com/NR/rdonlyres/277C838F-2ED7-4173-9E1D-17AE90B04300/0/Accenture_2009_Consumer_Broadcast_Survey.pdf%20. Accessed 2 Dec 2010

Born G, Prosser T (2001) Culture and consumerism: citizenship, public service broadcasting and the BBC's fair trading obligations. Mod L Rev 64(5):657–687

Cooper M (2003) Media ownership and democracy in the digital information age. http://cyberlaw.stanford.edu/attachments/mediabooke.pdf. Accessed 26 Nov 2010

Dawes S (2007) Reducing the difference between citizens and consumers: a critical discourse analysis of the communications white paper 2000. networking knowledge. J MeCCSA Postgrad Netw 1(2). http://journalhosting.org/meccsa-pgn/index.php/netknow/article/viewFile/30/68. Accessed 26 Nov 2010

Freedland M, Sciarra S (eds) (1998) Public services and citizenship in European law: public and labour law perspectives. Clarendon, Oxford

Harrison J, Woods L (2007) European broadcasting law and policy. Cambridge University Press, Cambridge

Helberger N (2008) From eyeball to creator—toying with audience empowerment in the Audiovisual Media Service Directive. http://www.ivir.nl/publications/helberger/From%20eyeball%20to%20media%20literate%20viewer.pdf. Accessed 20 May 2011

Hins W, Voorhoof D (2007) Access to State-held information as a fundamental right under the European Convention on Human Rights. Eur Const L Rev 3:114–126

Hugenholtz B, Guibault L (2006) The future of the public domain: an introduction. In: Guibault L, Hugenholtz B (eds) The future of the public domain: identifying the commons in information law. Kluwer Law International, Alphen aan den Rijn

Keum H et al (2004) The citizen-consumer: media effects at the intersection of consumer and civic culture. Political Commun 21:369–391

Livingstone S, Lunt P (2007) Representing citizens and consumers in media and communications regulation. The ANNALS of the American Academy of Political and Social Science. http://eprints.lse.ac.uk/996/1/Representing_citizens_and_consumers_in_media_and_communications_regulation_(LSERO).pdf. Accessed 26 Nov 2010

Rheingold H (1998) The virtual commmuninity. www.rheingold.com/vc/book. Accessed 30 Nov 2010

Richards E (2004) Speech to Westminster Media Forum on the ofcom review of public service broadcasting, 24 April 2005. http://media.ofcom.org.uk/2004/05/25/speech-to-westminster-media-forum-ofcom-review-of-public-service-broadcasting/. Accessed 26 Nov 2010

Sunstein C (2001) Republic.com. Princeton University Press, Princeton

Chapter 6
Changing Sports/Media Complex and Its Impact on the Regulatory Process of the Broadcasting Sector

6.1 Introduction

The broadcasting sector in Europe is mainly regulated at national level. However, some measures have been adopted at the EU level to create a single market in broadcasting (*infra*). The following legal instruments are applicable to broadcasting at EU level: Audiovisual Media Services Directive (*infra*), Charter of Fundamental Rights, Electronic Communications Framework and various specific instruments, such as the Copyright Directives.[1] Additionally, competition law will also be applied to the media sector. Competition law can play an important role in the broadcasting sector in order to keep the media market competitive resulting in increased consumer choice, better quality and lower prices to the sector (*infra*). According to the European Commission, access to (premium) content, for example, is crucial to enable competition in media markets.

As indicated in Chap. 3, Article 10 of the ECHR could cover a positive obligation for States to actively protect the public's right to live and full sports coverage. When dealing with the public's access to sports coverage, the European institutions have combined both media law, particularly the Audiovisual Media Services Directive, and competition law. In Part II and Part III, it will be examined how competition and media law deal with the public's access to sports content in the changing media landscape.

However, before we start this analysis it is important to take a look at the ongoing debate about the relevance of media law in a digital media environment. To some observers, media law is no longer needed in the digital media landscape to guarantee public interest objectives, such as the public's right to information or pluralism. They even argue that media regulation is no longer justified and propose to leave the regulation of the broadcasting market to competition law. To other observers, however, policy objectives behind existing media regulation remain

[1] For a detailed overview, see e.g. Castendyk et al. 2008, Valcke et al. 2010.

K. Lefever, *New Media and Sport*, ASSER International Sports Law Series,
DOI: 10.1007/978-90-6704-873-6_6,

valid in a changed media environment. Or in other words, is competition law able to protect both the consumer's and citizen's interests in the changed media landscape? In this section, this debate will be described in more detail.

6.2 From Scarcity to Abundance

Due to technological changes of the past two decades, the media sector has been characterised by a shift from scarcity to abundance. This evolution is often referred to as 'digital plenitude',[2] i.e. an increasing number of platforms, of content providers and an increasing amount of information available, giving the audience a wider choice over which content is consumed and where and when it is consumed. As stated by Szymanski, "*[w]ith an almost unlimited channel capacity, a given consumer can simultaneously be offered the content they are interested in without depriving other consumers the opportunity to watch their preferred content*".[3] With regard to the Olympic Games, for example, due to the opportunities provided by the Internet and digital television, the BBC has been able to increase its Olympic output from 250 h of the Sydney Games in 2000 to 1.350 h for the 2004 Games in Athens to 2.750 h for Beijing. Moreover, for the 2012 London Olympics, BBC is pursuing a multi-platform strategy, utilising video-on-demand, embedded video and mobile phones to enhance its round-the-clock television coverage.[4]

Additionally, this changed media landscape also offers other opportunities. Electronic versions of print media and individual news websites can be updated throughout the whole day. Whereas a daily newspaper may at best bring out one or more 'extras' a day, news items on the Internet can be revised countless times a day, as new information comes in.[5] For example, the score of a match or other major sports events would traditionally be disseminated to the public at scheduled television news bulletins which may be available three times a day. In the current media environment, however, the public may want and can get a news update on the score every minute and so, in response to that demand, news media organisations are providing news updates as the event happens.[6] Moreover, additional information can be added, such as old articles, archived webpages, fora, etc.

Furthermore, given that the new emerging technologies create opportunities for anyone to put any information on the World Wide Web, niche demands can be addressed.[7] For example, new media could act as alternative gateways to deliver

---

[2] Hutchins and Rowe 2009, 356.

[3] Szymanski 2006, 430.

[4] Sportcal.com 2008.

[5] Jakubowicz 2009, 17.

[6] Standing Committee on Environment, Communications and the Arts 2009, 11.

[7] Reding 2006.

culture and less known sports to a wider audience and to stimulate participation among people.[8] In other words, digital television, mobile television or the Internet could prove themselves as platforms targeting niche sports markets.

The media landscape of the twenty first century seems to be the 'manna of information'. Since the array of material available in the digital era continues to grow every day, the public can now be informed about major (sports) events '24/7' on the device they prefer, about the topic they prefer. In other words, a plenitude of information and news has become available and accessible at any place and time that suits the viewer. Hence, it is often argued that any existing constraints on access to information will disappear.[9] As a result, due to the fact that media regulation traditionally contains rules safeguarding access to information, pluralism and diversity, the validity of these rules in the digital environment is sometimes questioned. Levy, for example, formulated it as follows: "*[t]he end of spectrum scarcity, the proliferation of channels, and changes in the way in which broadcasting is consumed, are all cited in support of the case that digitalisation will render broadcasting regulation superfluous*".[10] Moreover, the 'digitopia' even proposed to leave the regulation of the broadcasting market to competition law. According to Ungerer, for example, the development of open competitive market structures is vital to guarantee pluralism in the media sector. Therefore, he emphasised that this makes "*competition law application a vital component of [...] policies in the media sector*".[11] Furthermore, Ungerer added that "*[w]e will move [...] to an environment that will be less subject to the sector specific rules built for the traditional broadcasting sector, and more to the general market regulation under competition rules*".[12] As a result, Donders said that "*there is an increasing belief in competition-related solutions for possible market failure or other problems in the media sector*" and that "*[t]he application of strict competition rules is the best option to achieve choice and thus (seemingly automatically) pluralism in the market*".[13] In other words, Ariño qualified this as a trend "*to progressively abandon regulation and move towards a competition-law based model that will ultimately prevail*".[14] Hence, according to them, the role of media law was entering a rapid decline and the best thing it could do so is stand aside.[15]

While access to information seems endless in the digital era, reality shows a different practice... Although digitalisation makes it possible to put an end to spectrum scarcity, literature warned for the increasing control of access to information in the digital era. The Committee of Ministers, for example, noted that new

---

[8] Evens et al. 2010.

[9] Mansell 1999, 156.

[10] Levy 2001, 138.

[11] Ungerer 2005a, 4.

[12] Ungerer 2005b, 3.

[13] Donders 2010.

[14] Ariño2004a, 101.

[15] Cowie and Marsden 1999, 56; Tambini 2001, 3.

bottlenecks will emerge in the area of the new communication technologies and services, such as control over conditional access systems (CAS) for digital television services.[16] A conditional access system, or a set-top box, is a technical solution for controlling access to electronic content. The operator of a conditional access system can determine who has access to which content under which conditions and terms. Access to information can be closed off for the public or made dependent of payment of an additional subscription fee. Pay-television operators, for example, use these conditional access systems to prevent unauthorised access to their content for those without a specific subscription. Additionally, the introduction of electronic programme guides (EPGs) could also create new bottlenecks. EPGs are video navigation services designed to assist the viewer in tuning, finding, selecting and recording digital television services.[17] Hence, the position of a channel in an EPG is of strategic importance for broadcasters as it could influence audience share and advertising revenues.[18] Some scholars feared that the EPG would be designed in such a way to manipulate the public's choice of programmes or channels by making it easy to find their own programmes or services while making it almost impossible to find or access a rival's service.[19] Digital sepsis argued that the providers of these new technical bottlenecks aim at controlling access to networks or content creating a new form of scarcity. They refer to the development of 'gatekeepers of access' or 'gateway monopolies'.[20] As a result, they stressed that competition law alone will not be sufficient to protect social values, such as pluralism and access to information in a digital media landscape. In other words, concerns related to the broadcasting sector could be better addressed through media regulation.[21]

6.3 From One-to-Many to Many-to-Many Communication

In the past, the dissemination of information was the exclusive domain of the professional media, such as television, radio and press. Thanks to electronic devices and access to Internet, audiovisual content can now be created and distributed by every citizen. With regard to sports events, fans can use their digital camera or smartphone to film during a game and can upload this content on their own websites or user-generated content sites. This evolution has been often

---

16 Council of Europe 1999, Recommendation No. R (99) 1 on measures to promote media pluralism.

17 Dermot 1997, 603.

18 Donders and Evens 2010..

19 Cowie and Marsden 1999, 61; Helberger 2005, 45.

20 Mansell 1999, 63; Van Loon 2000, 298; Mansell 2004, 97.

21 See e.g.: Council of Europe 1999, Recommendation No. R (99) 1 on measures to promote media pluralism; Ariño 2004b, 157; Valcke 2004, 764.

referred to as "*the democratisation of access to media*".[22] In other words, digitalisation has encouraged and contributed to, as stated by Ariño, "*greater participation in democratic processes, and [...] a new and different public sphere*".[23] The OECD stressed that the rise of user-generated content could lead to "*[...] increased participation and increased diversity*" and that it should be seen as "*an open platform enriching political and societal debates, diversity of opinion, free flow of information and freedom of expression*".[24] Additionally, digitalisation has brought about a shift from a 'lean back'-experience of watching television and consulting information, where professional media decides which information reaches the public and when it reaches the public, to the 'lean forward'-experience, where the public itself decides where, when and through which means it will watch television or consult information. This trend is often referred to as a shift from one-to-many communication to many-to-many communication[25] or from a supply-driven market to a demand-driven market.[26] This shift from mass media and passive consumers to media for mass self-communication[27] and active 'prosumers' could lead to the conclusion that one of the basic principles on which the current media regulation is based, i.e. one-way selection of information at the central level of the sender, could no longer be upheld in the future as the premise for the regulation of the media sector. Because pluralism results from access to different media, content, and opinions, it has long been said that new technology may increase the ability of individuals to distribute their opinions and to access and select content and, thus, that it would automatically lead to greater pluralism. In other words, due to these changes, the existence of media law is no longer justified, because issues such as pluralism or public's right to information have become irrelevant.[28] Unfortunately, this myth should also be refuted.

First, as indicated in the Independent Study on Indicators for Media Pluralism in the Member States, the shift from a supply-driven market to a demand-driven market "*produce[s] benefits but also create new types of potential harm to pluralism*".[29] In fact, this shift could lead to new forms of scarcity. As indicated by Verhulst, due to the fact that the public is overloaded with information, a need for new intermediaries has emerged. In the past, broadcasters filtered the information and shaped the perception by the public of the world they live in. Today, information is filtered by, for example, search engines.[30] The problem with search engines is that the results are often manipulated. Van Eijk clarified this by stating

---

22 ICRI et al. 2009a, 8.

23 Ariño 2007, 116.

24 OECD 2007, 5–6 & 35.

25 Verhulst 2006, 333; Jakubowicz 2009, 13.

26 See e.g.: ICRI et al. 2009bb, 17.

27 Castells Castells 2009, 55 & 58.

28 ICRI et al. 2009a, 9; ICRI et al. 2009b, 11 & 14.

29 ICRI et al. 2009a, 9.

30 Verhulst 2007, 115 &121–122.

that "*[t]he highest position on the list of search results is for sale and information providers use advanced methods to mislead search engines*".[31] Although search engines have a growing influence over the diversity of the media offer, the problem is that obligations about the quality, objectivity and diversity of the content do not extend to these new intermediate actors.[32] To summarise, although we have access to more information than in the past, we should realise that, currently, access to information could be manipulated and that information provided by search engines are not always objective search results.

Second, mass media were characterised by the ability of fostering a common identity and bringing people together, because the programmes and information reached the public simultaneously. As a result, it constituted a forum for public thinking and confrontation with common values.[33] However, after the multiplication of channels and increase of content offered by prosumers, audiences become more fragmented.[34] In Keen's words: "*[t]oday's media is shattering the world into a billion personalized truths each seemingly equally valid and worthwile*".[35] As a result, according to some authors, as referred to in the Independent Study on Indicators for Media Pluralism in the Member States, "*new media break down social cohesiveness, result in reduced diversity and plurality as users congregate around content and views with that reinforce their own beliefs, produce Babel, create many speakers with few listeners, [...]*".[36] Furthermore, the anonymity offered by the World Wide Web could also question the reliability of the information, because anyone, even ill-informed, can publish and share information. Given that each truth can become as true as any other, Keen stressed that this could result in a situation where the real truth will be threatened and where the civic discourse will be soured.[37] Hence, it shows that traditional broadcasters need to keep playing a key role in the digital world in offering professional content of high quality.

Third, in the past, it has often been argued that Internet would kill traditional television and, thus, that old media would be replaced by new media.[38] In December 2007, for example, a survey by Nokia predicted that up to a quarter of entertainment consumed by people in 2012 would have been created, edited and shared within their peer circle rather than coming out of traditional media groups.[39] However, de Dorlodot, general counsel of RTL Group, refuted the idea that Internet is taking over traditional television. According to him, traditional

---

31 van Eijk 2006, 2.

32 Recital 22 of the AVMS Directive.

33 Lievens 2010, 78.

34 van Dijk 2006, 171–173; IDATE et al. 2008, 173.

35 Keen 2007, 15.

36 ICRI et al. 2009b, 10.

37 Keen 2007, 15 & 17.

38 See e.g.: Chaffee and Metzger Chaffee and Metzger 2001, 365–379; Butler 2007, 4.

39 Visiongain 2008, 44.

television is not dead yet. Moreover, he believes that television will continue to be the centrepiece for audiovisual content.[40] Different studies have indeed indicated that traditional television consumption has even increased over the years and, thus, still remains the most important source of information.[41] In its recent News Corp-BSkyB report, Ofcom identified "*the television as the most popular 'main' source of U.K. news for a large proportion of the UK adult population aged 15+*".[42] A study on the future of television formulated it as follows: "*[d]espite the Internet's growing popularity, television remains the number one medium in terms of hours spent*".[43] Or in the words of Woolard: "*[t]raditional broadcasting remains a hugely sticky consumer habit*".[44] This should be clarified by the differences between television and Internet. Different studies have indicated that Internet and traditional television have—at least for the time being–different service quality. The signals of 'television' via Internet are transmitted via broadband, usually without a particular priority, reducing the quality of transmission and increasing the possibility of being subject to interferences. Traditional television signals are transmitted via an infrastructure that is reserved for the transmission of television signals. Furthermore, according to Dejonghe, although Internet content can be displayed on the television screen and television content on the laptop screen, Internet and television are two different media. Television aggregates content into shows and channels, while Internet disaggregates media products into clips. Furthermore, television is about shared emotions in familiar surroundings, whereas Internet is about individual media browsing in private or semi-public surroundings.[45] Already in 1998, Laven stated that traditional television is viewed passively, whereas Internet is a heavily interactive activity. As a result, he concluded that "*[t]he reality is that interactivity and communal viewing do not mix—except if you are the one with the remote control!*".[46]

Fourth, it is often stressed that the public prefers to watch programmes on their own schedules rather than the 'appointment' viewing that broadcasters offer.[47] Although the end of 'scheduled viewing' was often predicted, studies indicate that on-demand viewing does not cannibalise traditional, linear viewing. Moreover, it is likely that it will even not do so in the near future. Whereas the introduction of on-demand services has given the viewers more opportunities with regard to choice and control, because they are not limited to the pre-scheduled programming of broadcasters, practice shows that people prefer to see programmes when the

---

[40] de Dorlodot 2010.

[41] See e.g.: ACT 2010, 4 & 14; Deloitte 2011.

[42] Ofcom 2010a, para 4.9.

[43] Gluck and Sales 2008, 46.

[44] Woolard 2010.

[45] Dejonghe 2010.

[46] Laven 1998, 7.

[47] Gluck and Sales 2008, 8; Deloitte 2011.

others are also watching them. In a special report on television in the Economist, it was emphasised that if people do not have the possibility to watch a specific programme, they will watch it as soon as they can afterwards. Figures show that more than 50 % of recorded programmes are viewed within a day.[48] Or as stated by Dejonghe: "*we stick to traditional media rituals even when the environment is changing*".[49] According to Gripsrud, the reason lies in the primary functions of traditional television: simultaneity and liveness.[50] Likewise, Tay and Turner argued that the social role of traditional television is far from over.[51] Foster, in his Report on Future Broadcasting Regulation, stressed that conventional scheduled coverage of, in particular, sports events is still necessary, because the public "*will still value regular shared experiences with other viewers and listeners—and some types of programming will be at their most relevant and enjoyable when consumed live in real time—from news, to sport, to reality shows, [...]*".[52] Gluck and Roca Sales too affirmed that people prefer to watch sports events live and in group.[53] In its Communication Market Report, Ofcom emphasised that sports channels experience the lowest proportion of time shifted viewing.[54] Due to the fact that live sports coverage is the most appealing, it is unlikely that the coverage of sports events will be recorded in order to watch it later.[55] Hence, we can conclude that traditional linear television has still an important role to play to cover certain types of content.

Fifth, the Internet has offered the public and the fans the opportunity to become both producer and receiver of information and content. This implies that sports fans could film during sports events and upload this content on their own website or user-generated content websites. At first sight, it seems that the evolution from one-to-many to many-to-many communication has offered the fans access to a plenitude of sports coverage and sports information. However, terms and conditions of different football teams and sports organisations contain the prohibition for ticket holders to bring any equipment which is capable of recording or transmitting (by digital or other means) any audio, visual or audio-visual material or any information or data in relation to a Match.[56] Hence, these prohibitions limit the fans' and sports clubs' possibilities to upload audiovisual material of matches on the Internet. Or in other words, it limits their ability to become legitimate providers of online sports content.

---

48 The Economist 2010; IP Network 2010.

49 Dejonghe 2010.

50 Gripsrud 2004, 216.

51 Tay and Turner 2010, 31.

52 Foster 2007, para 7.3.20.

53 Gluck and Sales 2008, 48, 112 & 115; Chunovic 2008, 2–3.

54 Ofcom 2010b, 102–103.

55 X 2004, 667; Boyle 2009, 5; Ofcom 2010b, 102–103.

56 Chelsea 2012.

Hence, it is often forgotten that a substitution of old media by new media, as stated by Schuurman and De Marez, takes place at two levels: "*first, a replacement of old media technologies by new media innovations, and second, the substitution of old media practices by new media habits*".[57] As indicated above, the latter seems problematic. The report on television in the Economist formulated it as follows: "*a change in expectations is not quite the same as a change in behaviour*".[58] Or, in other words: "*[t]he saying 'old habits die hard', can clearly be applied to watching television*".[59] Zeiler, CEO of RTL Group, stated that "*[t]he basic human need to lean back, relax and be entertained remains unchanged*".[60] Given that traditional broadcasters remain important for the public, it could be dangerous, as indicated by Helberger, that regulatory policy will jump from one extreme to the other and, thus, to conclude that media regulation would no longer be needed.[61] Furthermore, although it is impossible to guarantee that the public will choose to acquire and consume pluralistic content, it is important to realise, as indicated in the Independent Study on Indicators for Media Pluralism in the Member States, that policy can "*create the preconditions for pluralistic consumption and 'encourage' citizens to consume diverse content, but never 'force' citizens to do so without infringing their freedom of choice and expression in an unjustified and disproportionate manner*".[62] Hence, as stressed by Helberger, it is still not up to the viewer to determine what kind of programmes are needed to serve public interests goals, but this is still a task of the governments.[63] As a result, regulation should still help viewers having access to important and diverse content and, thus, media law is still needed to ensure that public policy goals such as quality and diversity are met, even in a world where the information flow seems endless. Or in Iosifidis' words: "*technology might change the media environment, but that does not imply that concerns about pluralism, diversity, free speech, [...] are less valid*". It seems correct when he stressed that, with regard to the broadcasting sector, "*[a] dual model in which competition law could apply, supplemented by flexible sector-specific regulation*".[64] In other words, it could be argued that media law is still needed to guarantee the citizen's interests in the changing media landscape. Nevertheless, policy makers need to be aware that it is necessary to keep the media regulation up-to-date in order to create more legal certainty in the digital media landscape.

---

57 Schuurman and De Marez 2010.

58 The Economist 2010.

59 Berte et al. 2010.

60 ACT 2009, 10.

61 Helberger 2008, 13.

62 ICRI et al. 2009b, 17.

63 Helberger 2008, 3.

64 Iosifidis 2002, 39.

References

Legislation and Policy Documents

International

OECD

OECD (2007) Participative Web: User-Generated Content, DSTI/ICCP/IE(2006)7/FINAL. http://www.oecd.org/dataoecd/57/14/38393115.pdf. Accessed 18 August 2010

Council of Europe

Recommendations

Council of Europe (1999) Recommendation No. R (99) 1 on measures to promote media pluralism

UK

Reports

Ofcom (2010a) Report on public interest test on the proposed acquisition of British Sky Broadcasting Group plc by News Corporation. http://www.ofcomwatch.co.uk/wp-content/uploads/2011/01/Ofcom-report-News-Corp-BSkyB-merger.pdf. Accessed 15 Mar 2011

Ofcom (2010b) Communications Market Report. http://stakeholders.ofcom.org.uk/binaries/research/cmr/753567/CMR_2010_FINAL.pdf. Accessed 29 Nov 2010

Standing Committee on Environment, Communications and the Arts (2009) The reporting of sports news and the emergence of digital media. http://www.aph.gov.au/Senate/committee/eca_ctte/sports_news/report/report.pdf. Accessed 18 Aug 2010

Doctrine

ACT (2009) Annual report 2009. http://www.acte.be/EPUB/easnet.dll/GetDoc?APPL=1&DAT_IM=029395. Accessed 5 Jan 2011

ACT (2010) Annual report 2010. http://www.acte.be/EPUB/easnet.dll/GetDoc?APPL=1&DAT_IM=029395. Accessed 5 Jan 2011

Arino M (2004) Competition law and pluralism in European digital broadcasting: addressing the gaps. Commun Strateg 54:97–128

Ariño M (2004) Digital war and peace: regulation and competition in European digital broadcasting. Eur Public Law 10(1):135–160

Ariño M (2007) Content regulation and new media: a case study of online video portals. Commun Strateg 66:115–135

Berte K et al. (2010) Adoption versus use diffusion of iDTV in Flanders - Personalized television content as a tool to cross the chasm?, euroITV, Tampere, 9–11 June

Boyle R (2009) Why Sport matters: new challenges in the digital age. http://olympicstudies.uab.es/lec/pdf/boyle.pdf. Accessed 6 Dec 2010

Butler J (2007) Television: critical methods and applications, 3rd edn. Erlbaum, Mahwah

Castells M (2009) Communication power. Oxford University Press, Oxford

Castendyk O et al (eds) (2008) European media law. Kluwer Law International, Alphen a/d Rijn

Chaffee S, Metzger M (2001) The end of mass communication? Mass Commun Soc 4(4):365–379

Chelsea (2012) Terms and conditions. http://www.chelseafc com/page/ToutInfoDetails/0,,10268 ~ 1945402,00.html. Accessed 16 Jan 2012

Chunovic L (2008) The future of televised sports in the digital age. http://www.transmedia institute.com/reports/TheFutureOfTelevisedSports.pdf. Accessed 6 Dec 2010

Cowie C, Marsden C (1999) Convergence navigating bottlenecks in digital pay-TV. J Policy, Regul Strateg Telecommun Inf Media 1(1):53–67

de Dorlodot V (2010) Our strategy in the digital age, digital broadcasting markets and contents regulation conference, florence, 19 Nov 2010. http://www.florence-school.eu/portal/page/portal/FSR_HOME/COMMUNICATIONS_MEDIA/Policy_events/Workshops/2010_Archive/Broadcasting/DE%20DORLODOT%20Digital%20Broadcasting%20Markets.pdf. Accessed 30 Nov 2010

Dejonghe E (2010) New media: social rituals, technological innovations, disruptive business models, Postgraduate Studies in ICT and Media Law, Leuven, 8 Dec 2010

Deloitte (2011) Deloitte defines the main trends for 2011 in the telecommunications, media and technology sector, http://www.deloitte.com/assets/Dcom-Belgium/Local%20Assets/Documents/EN/be_press_tmt-predictions-2011.pdf. Accessed 16 Feb 2011

Dermot N (1997) Bottlenecks in pay television. Impact on Europe market development in Europe. Telecommun Policy 21(7):597–610

Donders K (2010) Under pressure? An analysis of the impact of European State aid policy on public service broadcasting. Marginalisation or revival as public service media?. PhD Thesis, Promotor: Prof. Dr. Pauwels Caroline, Brussel, (in press)

Donders K and Evens T (2010) Broadcasting and its distribution in Flanders, Denmark and the United States: an explorative and future-oriented analysis–A research report for SBS Belgium (not published)

Evens T (2010) Attracting the un-served audience: the sustainability of long tail-based business models for cultural television content. New Media Soc 12(6):1005–1023

Gluck M, Sales R (2008) The Future of Television? Advertising, technology and the pursuit of audiences. http://www.learcenter.org/pdf/FutureofTV.pdf. Accessed 6 Dec 2010

Gripsrud J (2004) Broadcast television: the chances of its survival in a digital age. In: Spigel L, Olsson J (eds) Television after TV: essays on a medium in transition. Duke University Press, Durham, pp 210–223

Helberger N (2005) Controlling access to content—regulating conditional access in digital broadcasting. Kluwer Law International, The Hague

Helberger N (2008) From eyeball to creator–toying with audience empowerment in the audiovisual media service directive. http://www.ivir.nl/publications/helberger/From%20eyeball%20to%20media%20literate%20viewer.pdf. Accessed 20 May 2011

Hutchins B, Rowe D (2009) From broadcast scarcity to digital plenitude: the changing dynamics of the media sport content economy. Telev New Media 10:354–370

ICRI et al. (2009a) Independent study on indicators for media pluralism in the member states—towards a risk-based approach. final report. http://ec.europa.eu/information_society/media_taskforce/doc/pluralism/study/final_report_09.pdf. Accessed 19 Aug 2010

ICRI et al. (2009b) Independent Study on Indicators for Media Pluralism in the Member States—Towards a Risk-Based Approach. Final Report—Annex I: User Guide. http://ec.europa.eu/

information_society/media_taskforce/doc/pluralism/study/user_guide_09.pdf. Accessed 18 Aug 2010

IDATE et al. (2008) User-created-content: supporting a participative information society. http://ec.europa.eu/information_society/eeurope/i2010/docs/studies/ucc-final_report.pdf. Accessed 18 Aug 2010

Iosifidis P (2002) Digital convergence: challenges for European regulation. Public 9(3):27–48

IP Network (2010) Television 2010. International key facts. http://www.ipb.be/index.php?option=com_content&task=showarticle&id=14182&Itemid=404&lang=nl. Accessed 10 Dec 2010

Jakubowicz K (2009) A new notion of media?—Background text, 1st Council of Europe Conference of Ministers Responsible for Media and New Communication Services, Reykjavik, 28–29 May 2009. http://www.ministerialconference.is/media/images/a_new_notion_of_media_web_version.pdf. Accessed 18 Aug 2010

Laven P (1998) Predicting the future of broadcasting. EBU technical review. http://tech.ebu.ch/docs/techreview/trev_276-laven.pdf. Accessed 10 Dec 2010

Keen A (2007) The cult of the amateur: how today's internet is killing our culture and assaulting our economy. Doubleday/Currency, New York and London

Levy D (2001) Europe's digital revolution: broadcasting regulation, the EU and the nation. Routledge, London

Lievens E (2010) Protecting children in the digital era—The use of alternative regulatory instruments. Martinus Nijhoff Publishers, Leiden/Boston

Mansell R (1999) New media competition and access. The scarcity-abundance dialectic. New Media & Soc 1(2):155–182

Mansell R (2004) Political economy, power and new media. New Media Soc 6(1):96–105

Reding V (2006) Foreword. In Richards E et al. (eds), Communications the next decade—A collection of essays prepared for the UK office of communications. http://stakeholders.ofcom.org.uk/market-data-research/research-publications/comms-next-decade/foreword/. Accessed 18 Aug 2010

Foster R (2007) Future broadcasting regulation. http://webarchive.nationalarchives.gov.uk/+/http://www.culture.gov.uk/NR/rdonlyres/A86E7A41-52F2-452B-B9BF-EB08B5E0EFFF/0/FutureBroadcastingRegulation.pdf. Accessed 28 Nov 2010

Schuurman D, De Marez L (2010) The chasm between having and using—Adoption versus use diffusion of iDTV in Flanders [not published]

Sportcal.com (2008) BBC in Multi-platform mode to ensure full coverage of 2012 games, 27 Oct 2008. www.sportcal.com. Accessed 20 Jan 2010

Szymanski S (2006) The economic evolution of sport and broadcasting. Aus Econ Rev 39(4):428–434

Tambini D (2001) Introduction. In: Damian Tambini (ed) Communications: revolution and reform. IPPR, London

Tay J, Turner G (2010) Not the apocalypse: television futures in the digital age. Int J Digit Telev 1(1):31–50

The Economist (2010). The lazy medium—how people really watch television, 29 Apr 2010. http://www.economist.com/node/15980817. Accessed 1 Dec 2010

Ungerer H (2005a) Competition rules and the media: are they determinant or complementary?, 1 Apr 2005. http://ec.europa.eu/competition/speeches/text/sp2005_004_en.pdf. Accessed 23 Aug 2010

Ungerer H (2005b) Competition in the media sector: how long can the future be delayed?, 19 Jan 2005. http://ec.europa.eu/competition/speeches/text/sp2005_015_en.pdf. 3 Accessed 23 Aug 2010

Valcke P (2004) Digitale Diversiteit. Convergentie van Media-, Telecommunicatie- en Mededingingsrecht. Larcier, Brussels

Valcke P et al. (2010) The EU regulatory framework applicable to broadcasting. In: Garzaniti L, O'Regan M (eds), Telecommunications, broadcasting and the internet. EU competition law & regulation-3rd edn. Thomson Sweet & Maxwell, London, pp. 263–330

van Dijk J (2006) The network society: social aspects of new media, 2nd. Sage, London

van Eijk N (2006) Search engines: seek and ye shall find? The position of search engines in law. Iris Plus. http://www.obs.coe.int/oea_publ/iris/iris_plus/iplus2_2006.pdf. Accessed 30 Nov 2010

Van Loon A (2000) Freedom versus access rights in a European context. In: Marsden C (ed) Regulating the global information society. Routledge, London, pp 285–303

Verhulst S (2006) The regulation of digital content. In: Lievrouw L, Livingstone S (eds) Handbook of new media—social shaping and social consequences of ICTs. Sage Publications, London, pp 330–349

Verhulst S (2007) Mediation, mediators, and new intermediaries. In: Napoli P (ed) Media diversity and localism: meaning and metrics. LEA Publishers, Mawhaw, pp 113–137

Visiongain (2008) Mobile social networking & user generated content- market insight 2008

Woolard C (2010) Key regulatory challenges: the content economy, MeCCSA Annual Conference 2010, 6 Jan 2010. http://media.ofcom.org.uk/2010/01/15/speech-outline-lse-meccsa-plenarykey-regulatory-challenges-the-content-economy/. Accessed 10 Dec 2010

X (2004) The Future of Sports Television. Fordham Intell. Prop. Media & Ent. L.J., vol. 14, 667. http://iplj.net/blog/wp-content/uploads/2009/09/Symposium-PANEL-I-THE-FUTURE-OF-SPORTS-TELEVISION.pdf. Accessed 6 Dec 2010

Chapter 7
Conclusion Part I

Without any question, we stand in the middle of a new era. Due to the digitalisation process, the media sector has entered a new era. Given that the cost of content production has been lowered drastically, everybody could become content producer. Moreover, new media platforms, such as Internet and smartphones, have provided content providers new means to distribute their content. Hence, the ability for professional and non-professional content creators to communicate and distribute materials via websites, blogs, virtual communities, etc., has increased. For decades, the sports and media sector have been building solid synergies aimed at developing an entwined relationship offering a win–win situation for all parties involved: sport will offer broadcasters the possibility to attract viewers and advertisers, while broadcasters offer sports organisations exposure and revenue. In the past, the roles of the different stakeholders of the sports/media complex were clearly defined. However, it comes as no surprise that, due to the development and spread of new media and communication technologies, the old and traditional balance between the actors of the sports/media complex came under pressure. As Rowe once described: "*the mutual relationship between sports and broadcasting has been described as 'the happiest of marriages', but as this happens in all long-lasting relationships, there appear some points of tension, compromise and disagreement*".[1] Sports clubs tried to become media companies themselves by offering club channels, mobile content and websites to their fans. When discovering the opportunities of new media, sports clubs bypassed traditional media and reached out directly to their fans. Furthermore, the role of the fans/public in the sports/media complex has also been altered. In the past, they passively submitted themselves to linear broadcasts of sports events. Currently, the public, when having access to the Internet and digital cameras, become potential producers of sports content. The main question that rises is whether and how this changing media landscape, characterised by an abundance of information, would have an

---

[1] Rowe 1999, 32.

K. Lefever, *New Media and Sport*, ASSER International Sports Law Series,
DOI: 10.1007/978-90-6704-873-6_7,

impact on the legal frameworks guaranteeing the public's access to sports content, in particular the public's right to information with regard to sports events

When dealing with sports issues, lawyers and policy makers should take due account of the two dimensions of sport. Over the years, the sports sector has become a fast-growing economic sector. The vast amount of money flowing into sports, due to professionalisation and commercialisation, has increased. An important part of the economic value of sports is linked with the sale of broadcasting rights. However, sport is much more than big business. It has been recognised that sport has a significant societal role to play in our society. In particular, sport has been attributed five functions: an educational, a public health, a social, a cultural and a recreational function. This societal dimension of sport is referred to as the 'specificity of sport'. With the entry into force of the Lisbon Treaty, the European Union has acquired a competence regarding sport. Furthermore, Article 165 of the TFEU has officially recognised the specificity of sport. The fact that other sectors can display a similar dual nature is without prejudice to our conclusion that the European institutions, when dealing with the public's access to sports content, and in particular the public's right to information with regard to sports events, the societal role of sport can, since the inclusion of Article 165 in the Treaty, no longer be denied. As a result, access to sports content should be promoted. Without a doubt, the freedom of expression and the right to information, included in Article 10 of the ECHR, play an essential role in order to achieve this. The European Court of Human Rights has considered the freedom of expression and the right to information an important foundation for the development of a democratic society and each individual. The European Court for Human Rights applies a broad definition of the notion 'information', particularly everything that can play an important role in the development of a democratic society and the development of the citizens. Although the European Court of Human Rights has never given a definition of the notion 'information', sports coverage, being characterised by a social dimension, could be grasped by this notion. Reding, for example, stated that regarding sport, the audiovisual sector has an important influence on our system of values and social cohesion.[2] Furthermore, both highlights as well as live and full coverage of sports events could be protected under Article 10 of the ECHR. Given that it is difficult to create a collective experience via the broadcast of highlights, live and full access to the coverage of sports events should be available to the public. In other words, full and direct access to sports events can be approached as a means of promoting civil participation in our democratic society. Article 10 of the ECHR contains both a negative as a positive obligation for States. The latter obligation obliges Member States to actively protect fundamental rights of the citizens, while the former obligation prohibits States to intervene. When States would decide to actively protect the public's right to live and full sports coverage, the criteria of Article 10, § 2 of the ECHR should be respected. In this regard, it should be taken into account that in

[2] Reding 2002, SPEECH/02/440.

order for the intervention to be proportionate, only live and full access to certain events should be ensured. In the following Parts, it will be examined how competition and media law are dealing with the public's right to information regarding sports content in the new media landscape.

With regard to broadcasting, a distinction is often made between the viewer as a citizen and the viewer as a consumer. The viewer as a consumer resides in the market-based domain. When talking about protecting the consumers' interest, viewers will be referred to in terms of economic goals, such as choice, price, quality of service and value for money. The viewer as a citizen resides in the public domain where free communication and discussion of ideas take place. In order to take part in these discussions, access to specific content and information, such as news, current affairs, documentaries and sport, should be guaranteed. When dealing with the research question of this book, it is important to emphasise that the public's access to sports coverage covers both the viewer's interests as a consumer and as a citizen. As a consumer, access to sports coverage will be referred to in terms of economic goals, such as choice, price, quality of service, while as a citizen, access to sports coverage will be referred to in terms of Article 10 of the ECHR, in particular their right to information.

In the last two decades, due to technological evolutions, the characteristics of the media sector have been altered from scarcity to abundance. As a result, the changed media landscape seems to be the 'manna of information' for the viewer, both in its role as citizen and consumer. Given that any constraints on access to information will disappear, the validity of traditional media regulation, containing rules safeguarding access to information, pluralism and diversity, has been questioned. Moreover, there was even an increasing belief to leave the regulation of the broadcasting market to competition law. Although it is sometimes suggested that these new evolutions in the media landscape (from scarcity to abundance and from one-to-many communication to many-to-many communication) put media regulation under pressure, it has been indicated that traditional public interest goals in the media sector, such as the public's right to information, remain valid in a changed media environment and are not called into question by technological developments. Moreover, the empowerment of the viewer and the change in behaviour is often overestimated. Given that the replacement of old media by new media is not always followed immediately by the substitution of old media practices by new media habits, it would be too dangerous to conclude that the raison d'être of media regulation has disappeared. Or in other words, it could be argued that media law is still needed to guarantee the citizen's interests in the changing media landscape. Given that both competition and media law are still needed to protect the viewers' interests in the broadcasting sector, the following Parts will examine in detail the impact of new media on competition and media law which are both guaranteeing the public's access to sports content.

References

Legislation and Policy Documents

European Union

Speeches

Reding V (2002) Sport and television: moving towards more balanced relations. 1 Oct 2002, SPEECH/02/440

Doctrine

Rowe D (1999) Sport, culture and the media: the unruly trinity. Open University press, Buckingham

Part II
Competition Law

In my time, it was the army generals running Brazil who tried to pick the team. Today, it's the sponsors, the businessmen, the media moguls. The World Cup final is the world's biggest tv show.

In the last two decades, exclusive broadcasting rights prices for live coverage of sports events have been drastically inflated as a result of revolutionary technological and policy developments within the broadcasting field (*supra*). In Europe, this heavy competition for live sports broadcasting rights has raised several policy questions concerning both competition and content (*infra*) issues. Long-term exclusive contracts of sports broadcasting rights, for example, may foreclose new media markets and, thus, impede competition. Limiting competition in the broadcasting market could also have a negative impact on the public: limited choice, lower quality and higher prices. Regarding sports broadcasting rights, the European Commission and national competition authorities have shaped the conditions for selling, acquiring and exploiting these exclusive rights in order to establish open and effective competition. In this Part, it will be analysed how competition authorities, when shaping these conditions, have dealt with the development of new media and whether the development of new media have had an impact on the way competition authorities dealt with the public's access to sports content, and in particular the public's right to information.

The first chapter of Part II will give a short and general overview of the application of competition law to the audiovisual media sector: antitrust rules, State aid rules and merger regulation. Furthermore, this chapter will examine how the specificity of the sports sector and the broadcasting sector could or should (not) be taken into account in competition decisions and whether the public's right to information/citizen's interest (*supra*) can be considered in the context of competition law. The more general question whether non-efficiency considerations can play a role in the application of Article 101 of the TFEU will not be dealt with. This question is already the subject of ongoing PhD research by Van Rompuy at VUB (Van Rompuy 2011).

Carlos Alberto Perreira, Brazil's 1994 World Cup winning coach quoted in The Independent 1998.

The second chapter of Part II will focus on a remedies package imposed on joint selling bodies under the EU antitrust rules prohibiting anti-competitive agreements and practices (Article 101 of the TFEU). Over the last few years, the European Commission has adopted several important antitrust decisions to ensure that access to sports broadcasting rights is not unduly restricted by agreements concerning joint selling of exclusive broadcasting rights. Primarily, the European Commission's major decisions with regard to joint selling agreements, i.e. the *UEFA Champions League* case, the *German Bundesliga* case and *the FA Premier League* case, will be discussed. In addition, two national competition decisions, one from the Belgian Competition Council and one from the German Competition Council, will be touched upon when relevant.

The third chapter of Part II will focus on the sublicensing remedy, which is being used to deal with the issue of unused broadcasting rights. The first section of this chapter will examine the EBU/Eurovision system case with regard to joint buying agreements. In this case, the European Commission made use of a sublicensing obligation in order to grant a joint buying organisation, an exemption under Article 101 (3) of the TFEU. Next, this chapter will take a look at the sublicensing obligation imposed in the *German public broadcaster* case, being a state aid case. The *Flemish public broadcaster state* aid case will also be highlighted.

The fourth chapter of Part II will take a look at the practice of imposing must-offer obligations on vertically integrated companies, active as a pay-television operator as well as a distributor, in order to foster competition in the pay-television market. The different types of must-offer obligations and their implications will be demonstrated by the *Newscorp/Telepiù* case, *Audiovisual Sport* case, *BSkyB* case and the *Telenet/Canal+* case.

Through chapters two until four, the following question will be answered: did the development of new media have an impact on the way competition law/ competition authorities are dealing with the public's access to sports events, in particular their right to information with regard to sports content? When answering this question, it will be examined whether those authorities make a distinction between, on the one hand, the consumers' interests and, on the other hand, the citizens' interests (*supra*). In doing so, various remedies, as mentioned above, will be looked at in more detail and will be dealt with in separate chapters in order to highlight the specific nature of each remedy. The 'joint selling remedies' package has an influence on the way the exclusive sports broadcasting rights are auctioned/ sold, while the sublicensing obligation and the must-offer obligation have an influence on the way broadcasters will exploit their acquired rights. Furthermore, the sublicensing obligation and the must-offer obligation differ, because a sublicensing obligation will be imposed when broadcasting rights would remain unused, while a must-offer obligation will be imposed even when the rights holding broadcaster is using the rights itself.

It should be noted that the cases discussed in this Part II only concern those which involve exclusive broadcasting rights of football events. The sale of exclusive broadcasting rights of other sports, such as volleyball, cycling, etc. or other sports events, such as Olympic Games, will not be dealt with, because the different 'landmark' decisions that will be analysed in this Part are football-related decisions.

Reference

Van Rompuy B (2011) Is efficiency all that counts? The role of non-efficiency considerations in the application of Article 101 TFEU. The case of the audiovisual sector. PhD thesis, Promotor: Prof. Dr. Caroline Pauwels, Brussel (forthcoming)

Chapter 8
Competition Law: General Introduction

8.1 Competition Law: Relevant Provisions

In the following chapters, competition decisions with regard to the selling, buying and exploitation of exclusive sports broadcasting rights will be described in more detail. Before analysing those decisions, it is important to give a short introduction to the most relevant provisions concerning the topic of this research: Article 101 of the TFEU, i.e. rules prohibiting distortion of competition by undertakings, Article 107 of the TFEU, i.e. rules dealing with State aid and merger regulation, i.e. rules dealing with mergers and acquisitions control. Before those provisions will be discussed, it is important to first elaborate on the relevant markets for the selling, buying and exploitation of sports broadcasting rights, because, as indicated by Wachtmeister, correct definition of the relevant market will be crucial to the assessment of competition cases.[1]

8.1.1 Relevant Markets for Selling, Buying and Exploiting Sports Broadcasting Rights

Determining the relevant markets is of key importance for the application of competition law. Whether a competition decision will be taken on the basis of antitrust rules, State aid rules or merger regulation, the decision will be founded on the definition of the relevant markets. As indicated by the European Commission, "*market definition is a tool to identify and define the boundaries of competition between firms. It serves to establish the framework within which competition policy is applied by the Commission. The main purpose of market definition is to identify in*

[1] Wachtmeister 1998, 21.

K. Lefever, *New Media and Sport*, ASSER International Sports Law Series,
DOI: 10.1007/978-90-6704-873-6_8,

a systematic way the competitive constraints that the undertakings involved face".[2] In other words, the objective of market definition is to identify the actual competitors of the undertakings concerned in order to determine the degree of market power of a firm.[3]

8.1.1.1 Product and Geographic Markets

To determine whether a restriction of competition exists, the relevant product and geographic markets need to be defined. A relevant product market comprises "*all those products and/or services which are regarded as interchangeable or substitutable by the consumer, by reason of the products' characteristics, their prices and their intended use*".[4] Those markets can be defined by using the test of substitutability of products, i.e. the extent to which consumers are able and willing to switch to a substitute product in response to a hypothetical small (in the range 5–10 %) but permanent relative price increase.[5] Additionally, the supply-side substitutability should also be taken into account when defining markets.[6] The question that needs to be answered is whether it would be economic for other suppliers to switch production in case of a small price increase. If the answer would be positive, both products may be in the same market.[7] A relevant geographic market comprises "*the area in which the undertakings concerned are involved in the supply and demand of products or services, in which the conditions of competition are sufficiently homogeneous and which can be distinguished from neighbouring areas because the conditions of competition are appreciably different in those area*".[8] Geographic markets are also defined by making use of the demand and supply substitutability test.

8.1.1.2 Product and Geographic Markets: Sale, Acquisition and Exploitation of Sports Broadcasting Rights

Over the years, the European Commission has defined different markets in the sector of the sale, acquisition and exploitation of sports broadcasting rights. It is important to realise that the market definitions were defined in the context of specific cases at a given

[2] Commission notice on the definition of relevant market for the purposes of Community competition law1997, para 2.

[3] Bavasso 2003, 103.

[4] Commission notice on the definition of relevant market for the purposes of Community competition law 1997, para 7.

[5] *Ibid.*, para 18.

[6] *Ibid.*, paras 20–23.

[7] Jones and Sufrin 2008, 79–81.

[8] Commission notice on the definition of relevant market for the purposes of Community competition law1997, para 8.

point in time. Thus, nothing would prevent the European Commission or the national competition authorities from further subdividing these markets in the future.[9]

With regard to the definition of product and geographic markets, a distinction is usually made between the upstream markets, i.e. the markets where rights owners and, increasingly, sports rights agencies sell rights to media companies and, downstream markets, i.e. the markets where media companies deliver content to the public.[10]

As regards downstream product markets, due to the different types of distinctiveness of the business model (subscription v. advertisement based), type of contents (thematic v. general channels), programme scheduling and functionalities of the new services,[11] the European Commission has always distinguished a market for pay-television (including pay-per-channel and pay-per-view[12]) versus a market for free-to-air television. As emphasised in different European Commission's decisions, in case of pay-television, which is usually financed through subscription, there is a trade relationship between the broadcaster and the viewer as subscriber; whereas in case of free-to-air television, which is financed by advertising or by State contributions, there is a trade relationship between the broadcaster and the advertiser or the State.[13] However, this distinction was subject to criticism. Some authors argued that a distinction based on the statement that pay-television operators compete for subscribers whereas free-to-air broadcasters compete for viewers seems artificial and rigid. According to them, both compete for input (programming rights), for audience and for the sale of services (including advertising). Moreover, they state that in the future pay-television could be financed from a mixture of sources, so that a distinction based on 'funding' could become blurred.[14] The European Commission tackled the idea of separate markets for analogue and digital television, given that digital television is only a further development of analogue television.[15] The European Commission has also recognised a separate market for traditional media versus a market for new media such as mobile rights and Internet rights.[16]

At the upstream level, the European Commission has traditionally segmented the purchasing activity for sports broadcasting rights into separate markets according to the nature of the content that allow broadcasters to compete against each other.[17] Therefore, the European Commission has identified three types of separate markets:

---

[9] Geradin 2005, 7.

[10] *Ibid.*, 7; Kienappel and Stein 2007, 10.

[11] Mendes Pereira 2003, 31.

[12] Commission decision, 27 May1998 (hereafter: *Bertelsmann* case), para 18.

[13] See e.g. *ibid.*, para 18; Commission decision, 3 March 1999 (hereafter: *TPS* case), para 25.

[14] Nitsche 2001, 116; Ariño 2004a, 156.

[15] See e.g.: *TPS* case, para 26; *Bertelsmann* case, para 18.

[16] Commission decision, 19 January 2005 (hereafter: *German Bundesliga* case), para 18.

[17] Geradin 2005, 7; Subiotto and Graf 2003, 593.

1) Broadcasting rights for major sports events versus broadcasting rights for other television programmes. The European Commission has justified this segmentation by referring to the specific features of sports broadcasting rights and sports events as compared with film and other programme rights. First, sports programmes covering widely popular sports or major international events are often able to achieve high audience ratings and attract advertisements. Second, the broadcasting rights for sport events must be acquired in advance of the event, but their attractiveness may change considerably depending on the actual participation and success of teams or participants appealing to national or regional audiences.[18]
2) Broadcasting rights for football games versus broadcasting rights for other sports games. The market for football broadcasting rights must be distinguished from the market for other sports broadcasting rights, due to football's preeminence as the singularly most popular sport across most Member States and beyond.[19]
3) Broadcasting rights for football events that are played regularly throughout every year (such as the domestic leagues, the Champions League, etc.) versus broadcasting rights for football events that do not take place regularly (such as the World Cup, etc.).[20]

With regard to the geographic markets, the European Commission considered that the downstream markets are of a national character or at least confined to linguistic regions.[21] The same goes for the geographical upstream markets.[22]

8.1.2 Antitrust Rules

Although European competition law is built up out of different building blocks (antitrust rules—Articles 101–102 of the TFEU, merger control–Regulation 139/2004, State aid control—Article 107 of the TFEU and liberalisation—Article 106 of the TFEU), the media and sports sector have mainly dealt with the antitrust rules, based on Articles 101 (dealing with the potential anticompetitive impact of agreements between independent market operators) and 102 (dealing with the abuse of a dominant market position) of the TFEU. In this chapter, the analysis of the antitrust rules will be limited to Article 101 of the TFEU, because this Article

---

[18] *Bertelsmann* case, para 18.

[19] Commission of the European Communities 2001, para 19.

[20] See e.g.: Commission decision, 23 July 2003 (hereafter: *UEFA Champions League* case), para 59, 62–63 Case No COMP/M. 2876–Newscorp/Telepiù). *OJ* (2004) L 110/73 (hereafter: *Newscorp/Telepiù* case), para 65.

[21] *UEFA Champions League* case, para 90; *Bertelsmann* case, para 23; *Bundesliga* case, para 19.

[22] *UEFA Champions League* case, paras 87–89; *Bundesliga* case, para 19; Commission decision, 2 April 2003 (hereafter: *Newscorp* case), paras 62 & 67.

is the basis for the most relevant decisions with regard to the selling and buying of exclusive sports broadcasting rights that will be discussed later (*infra*).

The assessment of Article 101 of the TFEU consists of two elements. First, it has to be clarified whether an agreement between undertakings, which is capable of affecting trade between Member States, has an anticompetitive object or effect (Article 101 (1) of the TFEU). Secondly, it needs to be examined if a restrictive agreement also produces procompetitive benefits that could outweigh the restricting effects (Article 101 (3) of the TFEU).[23]

8.1.2.1 Article 101 (1) of the TFEU: Scope and Basic Principles

According to Article 101 (1) of the TFEU "*the following shall be prohibited as incompatible with the common market: all agreements between undertakings, decisions by associations of undertakings and concerted practices which may affect trade between Member States and which have as their object or effect the prevention, restriction or distortion of competition within the common market, and in particular those which:*

(a) directly or indirectly fix purchase or selling prices or any other trading conditions;
(b) limit or control production, markets, technical development, or investment;
(c) share markets or sources of supply;
(d) apply dissimilar conditions to equivalent transactions with other trading parties, thereby placing them at a competitive disadvantage;
(e) make the conclusion of contracts subject to acceptance by the other parties of supplementary obligations which, by their nature or according to commercial usage, have no connection with the subject of such contracts".

To fully understand the scope of Article 101 (1) of the TFEU, a limited overview of the constituent elements of this Article will be given.[24]

A. Undertakings and associations of undertakings

Article 101 (1) of the TFEU applies to (associations of) undertakings. Although the TFEU does not contain a definition of the term 'undertaking', the European Court of Justice has defined the concept 'undertaking' as "*every entity engaged in economic activity regardless of the legal status of the entity and the way it is financed*".[25] An economic activity encompasses any activity that involves "*offering goods or services on the market*".[26] Because professional sports clubs

[23] European Commission 2004, para 11.

[24] For a more detailed analysis of Art. 101 of the TFEU, see e.g.: Jones and Sufrin 2008; Van Bael and Bellis 2010.

[25] CJ, Klaus Höfner and Fritz Elser v. Macroton GmbH

[26] CJ, Commission of the European Communities v Italian Republic, para 7.

and governing bodies engage in economic activities, the European Commission has in different decisions stated that they can be classified as undertakings within this meaning.[27] Consequently, associations of, for example, football clubs are associations of undertakings and may also be undertakings themselves so far as they engage in economic activities,[28] notwithstanding the fact that some of these entities are non-profit making bodies.[29]

B. Agreement, decision, concerted practices

As with the other terms, the TFEU does not contain a definition of the notions 'agreement', 'decisions' and 'concerted practices'. Given that Article 101 (1) of the TFEU prohibits joint and not individual conduct, the reference to 'agreement', 'decision' and 'concerted practice' requires some elements of collusion between independent undertakings.[30] The different Community Courts have defined those terms very widely. Agreements do not have to be legally enforceable agreements. Nor do they need to be in writing or even still in force if such an agreement continues to pursue its effects. The term also covers so-called 'gentlemen agreements', standard conditions of sale, trade association rules and trademark delimitation agreements. For an agreement to exist, it is sufficient if the undertakings involved "*have expressed their joint intention to conduct themselves on the market in a specific way*".[31] This implies that all kinds of practices occurring in vertical and horizontal relationships between market players active on different levels of production could be considered as 'agreement', 'decision' or 'concerted practice'.[32]

In the context of sports events, the European Commission found that regulations of UEFA, such as the joint selling agreements dealing with sports broadcasting rights (*infra*), constitute decisions taken by an association of associations of undertakings.[33]. The European Commission illustrated this as follows: "*[t]he regulations of the UEFA Champions League provide the regulatory basis for the manner in which the commercial rights of the UEFA Champions League are sold. [...] The Regulations of the UEFA Champions League are binding on the national football associations and on the football clubs*".[34]

C. Prevention, restriction or distortion of competition

As indicated by Jones and Sufrin, the question whether an agreement prevents, restricts or distorts competition is the heart of Article 101 (1) of the TFEU.[35] Article

27 See e.g.: *UEFA Champions League* case, paras 106-108; *Bundesliga* case, para 21.

28 *UEFA Champions League* case, para 109.

29 Van Rompuy and Pauwels 2009, 288.

30 Jones and Sufrin 2008, 148.

31 CJ, SA Hercules Chemicals NV v. Commission, para 256.

32 Elspass and Kettner 2008, 129.

33 *Ibid.*; *UEFA Champions League* case, para 109

34 *UEFA Champions League* case, para 110.

35 Jones and Sufrin 2008, 181.

101 (1) of the TFEU includes an indicative, non-exhaustive list of the types of agreement that will prevent, restrict or distort competition. The European Commission and the European Courts have given the terminology a wide interpretation. In general, agreements are caught by Article 101 (1) of the TFEU when they are likely to have an appreciable adverse object or impact on the parameters of competition on the market such as price, output, product quality, innovation, etc.[36]

D. Affection of trade between Member States

Article 101 (1) of the TFEU will only apply if trade between Member States is affected. This jurisdictional requirement defines the boundary between the areas respectively covered by Community and national law.[37] According to the European Court of Justice, an agreement is to be capable of affecting trade between Member States if it is foreseeable that "*the agreement in question may have an influence, a direct or indirect, actual or potential on the pattern of trade between Member States suffices*".[38]

The broad definition of this concept does not have any problems in the case of sport. Rules originating from European or international sporting federations are applicable in several countries and are likely to affect trade between Member States. Furthermore, the sole fact that the undertakings in question come from the same Member State does not automatically imply that only trade within this Member State is affected. On the contrary, the European Commission considered that if an agreement is to operate across the territory of an entire Member State this will raise a presumption of effect on interstate trade, as access to this Members State's market may be hampered by this very agreement.[39] In fact, given the international context of professional sport, rules originating from national sporting federations might also affect trade between Member States.[40] Therefore, it should be noted that even agreements relating to the sale of rights to national sport events (e.g. national football leagues) do satisfy this requirement.[41]

8.1.2.2 Article 101 (3) of the TFEU

If an agreement falls within the scope of Article 101 (1) of the TFEU, this does not imply that this agreement is automatically prohibited. Article 101 (1) of the TFEU is supplemented by Article 101 (3) of the TFEU which is giving scope for exemption. In order to secure entitlement to exemption, four criteria must be

---

[36] *Ibid.*, 182; Pace 2007, 77–78.

[37] CJ, Établissements Consten S.à.R.L. and Grundig-Verkaufs-GmbH v Commission, para 341.

[38] CJ, Franz Völk v S.P.R.L. Ets J. Vervaecke, para 5/7.

[39] See e.g.: Commission decision, 22 March 2006 (hereafter: *FA Premier League* case), para 31; Elspass and Kettner 2008, 135.

[40] Vermeersch 2007, 251.

[41] Lefever and Van Rompuy 2009, 250.

satisfied. In short, agreements, decision and concerted practices as defined in Article 101 (1) of the TFEU that comply with the objectives set out in this paragraph 3 are valid and enforceable.[42]

According to Article 101 (3) of the TFEU: "*the provisions of paragraph 1 may, however, be declared inapplicable in the case of:*

—any agreement or category of agreements between undertakings,
—any decision or category of decisions by associations of undertakings,
—any concerted practice or category of concerted practices,
which contributes to improving the production or distribution of goods or to promoting technical or economic progress, while allowing consumers a fair share of the resulting benefit, and which does not:
(a) impose on the undertakings concerned restrictions which are not indispensable to the attainment of these objectives;
(b) afford such undertakings the possibility of eliminating competition in respect of a substantial part of the products in question".

Since May 2004, the European Commission's exemption monopoly under Article 101 (3) of the TFEU and the system whereby undertakings had to notify their agreements has been abolished.[43] First, undertakings no longer have to notify agreements in order to benefit from an exemption under Article 101 (3) of the TFEU. They must now themselves assess whether their agreements and practices satisfy the four criteria ('self-assessment'). This implies that when UEFA, for example, would decide to also centralise the sale of broadcasting rights for the qualifying matches of international tournaments,[44] the sports organisation itself has to decide whether this new way of selling could be exempted. Investigations are only initiated *ex officio* or upon complaint.[45] Secondly, national competition authorities and national courts are now also empowered to fully apply Article 101 of the TFEU. Related to sports broadcasting rights, it will now be the task of the national competition authorities to, for example, oversee whether the sale, acquisition and exploitation of broadcasting rights to national sporting events complies with the exemption criteria under Article 101 (3) of the TFEU.[46]

8.1.3 Merger Regulation

Due to the recent evolution of the media sector, a tendency for companies in the media sector to join forces can be identified. Consequently, one of the main concerns is that mergers do not restrict markets and that access to key elements,

---

[42] Elspass and Kettner 2008, p. 136.

[43] Council Regulation No 1 2003.

[44] Sportbusiness International 2011. Until now, the qualifying stages are sold individually by the national leagues.

[45] Weatherill 2006, 14; Jones and Sufrin 2008, 125; Faull and Nikpay 2007, 88–89.

[46] Lefever and Van Rompuy 2009, 251.

such as sports content, is not affected. Hence, in addition to Article 101 of the TFEU, merger regulation also seems to play an important role in guaranteeing access to sports content for the public as well as for new media operators (*infra*).

8.1.3.1 Introduction

Although merging entities will often state that the main motivation for their merger is that the new entity will be more efficient (e.g. exploitation of economies of scale in production, economies of scope, marketing efficiencies), the acquisition or strengthening of a position of market power through a merger could also have negative effects resulting in a distortion of competition.[47] The latter could harm consumers through, for example, higher prices, reduced choice or less innovation.

In order to permit effective control of all concentrations in terms of their effect on the structure of competition, the European legislator realised that a specific legal instrument was necessary.[48] A general power to control mergers is not expressly contained in the TFEU.[49] Instead, the merger regulation, obliging prior notification of mergers with a Community dimension, is set out in Council Regulation 139/Council Regulation No 2004.[50] The objective of merger control is to enable competition authorities to prevent harmful effects on competition by deciding whether two or more commercial companies may merge, combine or consolidate their businesses into one. To ensure effective control, undertakings are obliged to give prior notification of the concentrations.[51] In order to fully grasp the scope of the merger regulation, a limited overview of the constituent elements of this regulation will be given.[52]

8.1.3.2 Notification

If the annual turnover of the combined businesses exceeds specified thresholds in terms of global and European sales, the proposed merger must be notified to the European Commission, which must examine it.[53] Below these thresholds, the national competition authorities in the Member States may review the merger.[54]

---

[47] Rosenthal and Francis 2009, 291–314.

[48] Recital 7 of the Council Regulation No 4064/89 ; Recital 6 of the Council Regulation No 139/2004 (hereafter: EC Merger Regulation).

[49] Lenaerts and Van Nuffel 2005, 257; Jones and Sufrin 2008, 109.

[50] EC Merger Regulation.

[51] Recital 34 of the EC Merger Regulation, Article 4 of the EC Merger Regulation.

[52] For an in-depth analysis of the EC Merger Regulation, see e.g.: Jones and Sufrin 2008; Van Bael and Bellis 2010.

[53] Article 4 & 6 (1) of the EC Merger Regulation.

[54] Recital 12 of the EC Merger Regulation.

After the notification, the European Commission or the national competition authorities will examine the proposed mergers in order to see whether the concentration would raise serious doubts about its compatibility with the common market in the European Union or in the national Member States, respectively.[55]

8.1.3.3 Commitments, Conditions and Obligations

If the concentration does not raise competition concerns, the merger will be approved unconditionally. If the concentration does raise competition concerns and no commitments aimed at removing the impediment are proposed by the merging firms, the merger will be prohibited.[56] However, as indicated by Goyder, the outcome of a merger notification is not necessarily that the transaction is either blocked or cleared in its entirety.[57] Even if the competition authorities find that competition concerns could arise, the parties involved may propose modifications to the original concentration plan and offer commitments removing those competition concerns.[58] Where the competition authorities find that, following those modifications, a notified concentration no longer raises doubts with regard to competition, they shall give conditional clearance for the merger to go ahead.[59] Afterwards, they will monitor whether the merging companies fulfil their commitments and may intervene if they do not.[60] It is important to note that parties do not have to prove that their commitments eliminate the competition concerns identified. It is up to the competition authorities, if they want to reject the commitments, to demonstrate that they do not resolve the identified competition concerns.[61]

In order to ensure that the undertakings concerned comply with the commitments they have entered into vis-à-vis the competition authorities, the latter may attach to their decisions conditions and obligations.[62] It is important to be aware of the difference between 'conditions' and 'obligations' within a remedy package. A condition is of primary importance, since it is the (or one of the) measures required to ensure the maintenance, after the merger, of effective competition. If it is breached, the original decision no longer stands and heavy fines can be imposed. An obligation, by contrast, represents the steps which the parties are obliged to take in order to implement the conditions agreed, including often the appointment of a trustee to supervise divestiture of assets. If an obligation is not complied with,

---

55 Article 6 of the EC Merger Regulation; Jones and Sufrin 2008, 956.

56 European Commission 2011a.

57 Goyder 2003, 382.

58 Rose and Roth 2008, 725; Jones and Sufrin 2008, 1077.

59 Article 6 (2) & 8 (2) of the EC Merger Regulation.

60 European Commission 2011a.

61 Jones and Sufrin 2008, 1078.

62 Recital 30, Article 6 (2) & 8 (2) of the EC Merger Regulation.

the undertaking concerned can be punished by a periodical penalty, but such a breach does not involve the revocation of the decision.[63] Those conditions and obligations are more commonly referred to as 'remedies'. In practice, remedies can be either structural, behavioural or a mixture of both. However, it should be noted that it is not always easy to characterise commitments as either structural or behavioural. It is often stated that behavioural remedies, such as the sublicensing of broadcasting rights and ensuring access to essential inputs,[64] relate to the behaviour of the parties, while structural remedies, such as the reduction in the scope and/or duration of rights of exclusive access,[65] relate to the divestiture of specific assets.[66, 67] Furthermore, a structural remedy is of immediate effect and should not be capable of being reversed in the future, whereas a behavioural remedy will normally operate only for a fixed period of time and can be varied or terminated as the result of a major change of circumstances.[68]

As indicated above, competition authorities may attach conditions to their clearing decision in order to facilitate market entry by competitors. The Notice on remedies specifies that, while being the preferred remedy, divestitures or the removal of links with competitors are not the only remedy possible to eliminate certain competition concerns.[69] This implies that also other types of commitments may be accepted. In a number of cases, for example, the European Commission and national competition authorities have accepted remedies foreseeing the granting of access to key infrastructure, networks, key technology, including patents, know how or other intellectual property rights, and essential inputs to third parties on a non-discriminatory and transparent basis.[70] It is important to note that access remedies will only be imposed if they are equivalent in their effects to divestiture. Given the limited effectiveness of some access remedies in the past, this approach has to ensure that access remedies will be designed in a way that they will be used effectively.[71] The must-offer obligation that will be analysed can be classified as a behavioural access remedy (*infra*).

---

63 Goyder 2003, 384; Commission notice on remedies 2008, para 20; Article 6 (3), Article 8 (4) (b), Article 8 (5) (b) & Article 8 (7) (a) of the EC Merger Regulation.

64 Commission notice on remedies 2008, paras 62–66.

65 *Ibid.*, paras 67–68.

66 *Ibid.*, paras 22–57.

67 Jones and Sufrin 2008, 1079; Rose and Roth 2008, 728 & 730.

68 Goyder 2003, 383.

69 Commission notice on remedies 2008, para 60.

70 *Ibid.*, para 62.

71 Rapid Press Releases 2008, IP/08/1567.

8.1.4 State Aid Rules

As indicated by Donders, "*State aid control was considered to be the weak pillar of European competition policy*". Now, however, State aid control by the European Commission is at the heart of the European integration process.[72] The objective of State aid control is to ensure that government interventions do not distort competition and trade inside the EU.[73] Braun formulated this as follows: "*[t]he aim of EC competition policy in the field of State aid is to establish a proper balance between the necessity and the admissibility of public interventions in the market on the one hand and the protection of fair competition on the other hand*".[74] To achieve this objective, Articles 107–109 of the TFEU deal with State aids that could distort competition. The following sections will elaborate very briefly on these State aid rules.[75]

8.1.4.1 General Prohibition of State Aid

As indicated by, for example, Schütte and Braun, the TFEU does not give a definition of the notion 'State aid'. Instead, Article 107 (1) of the TFEU lists the characteristics under which State aid is incompatible with the common market.[76] According to Article 107 of the TFEU, "*any aid granted by a Member State or through State resources in any form whatsoever which distorts or threatens to distort competition by favouring certain undertakings or the production of certain goods shall, in so far as it affects trade between Member States, be incompatible with the internal market*". Direct subsidies, tax shelters, ad hoc payments, loans, tax exemptions, etc. are examples that can be labelled as State aid.[77] State aid as defined in Article 107 (1) of the TFEU is prohibited, save to the extent that the aid is permitted by other TFEU provisions.[78]

8.1.4.2 Exemptions

Although the basic principle of the State aid rules is a general prohibition of State aid, there are exceptions on the general ban.[79] Following the wording of Article 107 (2) of the TFEU, some aid granted by a Member State shall be compatible

---

[72] Donders 2010.

[73] European Commission 2011b.

[74] Braun 2008, 213.

[75] For an in-depth analysis of Article 107-109 of the TFEU, see e.g.: Quigley 2009; 2009a (ed).

[76] Schütte 2006, 23; Braun 2008, 213.

[77] See e.g.: Plender 2004,3–40; Nicolaides et al. 2005; Rydelski (ed.) 2006.

[78] Bacon 2009b, 24.

[79] European Commission 2011b; Donders 2010.

with the common market. According to Article 107 (2) of the TFEU the following aid shall be compatible with the common market: "*(a) aid having a social character, granted to individual consumers, provided that such aid is granted without discrimination related to the origin of the products concerned; (b) aid to make good the damage caused by natural disasters or exceptional occurrences; (c) aid granted to the economy of certain areas of the Federal Republic of Germany affected by the division of Germany, in so far as such aid is required in order to compensate for the economic disadvantages caused by that division*". Braun emphasised that once it is established that the aid falls within one of the exceptions of Article 107 (2), "*the European Commission must not withhold its authorization and must regard it as compatible with the common market*".[80] In other words, the exemptions in Article 107 (2) of the TFEU are mandatory. If the State aid falls within one of the categories specified in this Article, the European Commission is required to approve it and has no discretion.[81] According to Oldale and Piffaut, however, the majority of cases are not assessed under Article 107 (2), but under Article 107 (3) of the TFEU.[82]

Under Article 107 (3), the European Commission has discretion to permit aid to be granted or not.[83] The European Commission has only the possibility to accept the aid proposed by the Member State if it contributes to the achievement of the Community objectives and interests set out in Article 107 (3) of the TFEU.[84] According to Article 107 (3) of the TFEU the following aid may be considered to be compatible with the internal market: "*(a) aid to promote the economic development of areas where the standard of living is abnormally low or where there is serious underemployment, and of the regions referred to in Article 349, in view of their structural, economic and social situation; (b) aid to promote the execution of an important project of common European interest or to remedy a serious disturbance in the economy of a Member State; (c) aid to facilitate the development of certain economic activities or of certain economic areas, where such aid does not adversely affect trading conditions to an extent contrary to the common interest; (d) aid to promote culture and heritage conservation where such aid does not affect trading conditions and competition in the Union to an extent that is contrary to the common interest; (e) such other categories of aid as may be specified by decision of the Council on a proposal from the Commission*".

For the media sector, Article 107 (3) (d) of the TFEU is important asserting that State aid can be compatible with the common market if it "*promote(s) culture and heritage conservation where such aid does not affect trading conditions and competition in the Union to an extent that is contrary to the common interest*". In other words, this means that the distortion of competition in and trade between

80 Braun 2008, 221.

81 Oldale and Piffaut 2009, 15.

82 *Ibid.*

83 Schütte 2006, 25.

84 Braun 2008, 221.

Member States can be accepted in so far as the aid measure scrutinised addresses cultural and heritage conservation issues.[85] With regard to the application of State aid rules to the funding of public service broadcasters, the European Commission has issued a communication emphasising that "*[s]tate aid to public service broadcasters usually does not differentiate between cultural, democratic and educational needs of society. Unless a funding measure is specifically aimed at promoting cultural objectives, Article 87(3)(d)*[86] *would generally not be relevant*".[87]

In recent years, public broadcasters' usage of public money to bid for sports broadcasting rights has been criticised by private broadcasters questioning the behaviour of public broadcasters in sports broadcasting rights markets.[88] As a result, the European Commission needed to examine many complaints about the financing system of the public broadcasters not being in line with the State aid rules and, in particular, whether public service broadcasters could use their funding to acquire sports broadcasting rights (*infra*).

8.2 Competition Law and Non-Economic Considerations

8.2.1 Introduction

Given that the media sector is about offering and transmitting content to the public, securing exclusive broadcasting rights to valuable content, such as sports events, is important to acquire market share. As a result, the demand for live sports content has increased over the years, ultimately leading to highly valued rights contracts for popular sports events (*supra*). Although these contracts are seldom profitable, broadcasters remain extremely interested in sports broadcasting rights, because of their promotional opportunities, branding power and audience building effects.[89] Moreover, as indicated by the European Commission, "*exclusive possession of a majority of such content rights gives broadcasters a market position that renders the successful emergence of new competing broadcasting services very difficult*".[90] Hence, from a competition point of view, ensuring access to broadcasting rights (upstream level) has been a central focus of attention.[91] However, access issues in the broadcasting sector are not only of an economic nature, but they are also connected with the socio-political dimensions of broadcasting (downstream

---

85 Psychiogopoulou 2006, 4; Donders 2010.

86 Now: Article 107 (3) (d) of the TFEU.

87 European Commission 2009, para 35.

88 Donders 2010.

89 Evens and Lefever 2011, 38.

90 European Commission 2003, 31–32.

91 Ariño 2004b, 21.

level).[92] The European Court of Human Rights, for example, has reiterated different times that the broadcasting sector, and the media in general, have the obligation to ensure the proper functioning of a democracy, which means it is their right and duty to inform the public on matters of public interest. Not only do the media have the task of imparting information, the public has a right to receive this information in order to have an adequate view of, and to form a critical opinion on, the state of the society in which they live (*supra*).

The question that rises is the extent to which competition authorities could and/or should take into account considerations related to these socio-political dimensions of the broadcasting sector, or in other words, the citizens' interest, when analysing access to exclusive sports broadcasting rights. Hence, can those authorities include non-economic considerations in their competition decisions? The following subsections will explore whether a media policy objective, especially the public's right to information, can be considered when applying competition law.

8.2.2 Objectives of Competition Law

Title VI of the TFEU, containing the competition rules, does not specify the specific objectives of competition law, nor does this Title contain a definition of the notion competition. In its XXIXth Report on Competition Policy, the European Commission underlined the two main objectives of European competition law. The first objective of competition policy is the maintenance of competitive markets. Hence, EU competition policy serves as an instrument to encourage industrial efficiency, the optimal allocation of resources, technical progress and the flexibility to adjust to a changing environment. The second objective of EU competition policy is the single market objective. Given that an internal market is an essential condition for the development of an efficient and competitive industry, competition law tries to prevent anticompetitive practices from undermining the single market's achievements.[93]

The European Commission has often indicated that high-competitive markets will normally deliver the best outcomes for the consumers. The European Commission has, for example, formulated that "*the aim of the Community competition rules is to protect competition on the market as a means of enhancing consumer welfare and of ensuring an efficient allocation of resources*".[94] In its XXIXth Report on Competition Policy, the European Commission has specified that "*the protection of the interests of consumers, and therefore of European citizens, is at the heart of Community competition policy*".[95] In its XXXIInd Report

---

92 *Ibid.*, 6–7.

93 European Commission 1999, paras 2–3.

94 European Commission 2004, para 33.

95 European Commission 1999, 10.

on Competition Policy, the European Commission added that "*one of the main purposes of European competition policy is to promote the interests of consumers, that is, to ensure that consumers benefit from the wealth generated by the European economy*".[96] In other words, former Competition Commissioner Kroes stressed that "*[f]ree competition" is not an end in itself—it is a means to an end*".[97]

As observed by Valcke and Ariño, a frequently heard comment about the application of competition law is that it is an instrument based only on economic criteria pursuing the above-mentioned objectives.[98] Odudu, for example, states that "*non-efficiency cannot be considered within competition law*" and that "*[t]he task of Union competition law is much more modest [...]. There are limits to what competition can hope to achieve*".[99] As a result, competition and the so-called non-economic goals are often contrasted or even considered mutually exclusive.[100] Hence, this could imply that the assessment of competition issues in certain sectors would only depend on the economic position of the companies on the relevant markets. With regard to the media sector, for example, this would imply that competition authorities are unable, in their assessments, to take into account substantive issues or cultural interests linked to the dissemination of information.[101] Although some authors argued that competition law is not an appropriate tool to handle the public interest and cultural aspects of audiovisual media, other authors stated that such an approach appears to underestimate the potential benefits of competition for different sectors, such as, for example, the media sector.

8.2.3 Competition Law and Cross-Sectional Provisions

Whilst the core objectives of competition law are primarily taken into account in competition decisions, different authors argue that competition law cannot be implemented in a vacuum.[102] Valcke, for example, pointed out that the idea that competition decisions could not consider the specific socio-political aspects of the broadcasting sector is based on an overly one-sided view to competition law.[103] Ariño even considered such an approach as "*naïve*". Moreover, she stressed that "*over-reliance on economic efficiency as the driving force behind the Commission's analysis runs the risk of ignoring other considerations that are equally*

[96] *Ibid.*, 20.

[97] Kroes 2007, 1.

[98] Valcke 2004, 767–768; Ariño 2004c, 54, 97 & 103; Ariño (2004a), 157.

[99] Odudu 2010, 11.

[100] Vedder 2009, 51.

[101] Valcke 2004, 768.

[102] See e.g.: Monti 2002, 1057; Valcke 2004, 769; Ariño 2004c, 121.

[103] Valcke 2004, 768.

important".[104] Monti too suggested that "*the consideration of non-competition factors in competition law is legitimate and significant*".[105] Steenbergen and Cseres stressed as well that competition policy should consider other objectives than the mere economic ones.[106] The European Commission even stated that "*it would [...] be wrong to look at the Community's competition policy in isolation from its other policies. Where the Commission under the competition rules has to assess agreements, practices, [...], it will take a more favourable view if they pursue an objective which is in line with the Community's policy in the relevant area*".[107] Hence, it seems that other Community policies and factors could also play an important role in competition cases and affect competition decisions. In other words, according to these authors, competition authorities should take into account objectives that are not directly related to competition. This holistic approach seems to be consolidated in Article 7 of the TFEU stating that "*the Union shall ensure consistency between its policies and activities, taking all of its objectives into account and in accordance with the principle of conferral of powers*".

Moreover, according to different authors, the inclusion of 'cross-sectional clauses' or 'policy-linking clauses' in the TFEU is designed to facilitate this process.[108] These TFEU cross-sectional clauses require that their respective objectives should be considered when implementing Community policies in other areas.[109] Article 147 of the TFEU [ex 127 TEC], for example, states that "*the objective of a high level of employment shall be taken into consideration in the formulation and implementation of Union policies and activities*". The same goes for environmental protection. Article 11 of the TFEU [ex 6 TEC] states that "*environmental protection requirements must be integrated into the definition and implementation of the Union policies and activities*". With regard to the audiovisual sector, the cross-sectional cultural Article 167 (4) of the TFEU [ex Article 151 TEC] states that "*the Union shall take cultural aspects into account in its action under other provisions of the Treaties, in particular in order to respect and to promote the diversity of its cultures*". According to Valcke, this provision is not only a political obligation, but a sound legal basis for the Community to take into account cultural considerations when creating audiovisual policy.[110] Although this provision does not require that cultural objectives would get priority over other objectives, it means that those objectives should be protected from a strict application of the Treaty provisions related to competition law and the freedom principles.[111] Steenbergen and Townley recognised that

---

[104] Ariño 2004c, 103.

[105] Monti 2002, 1095.

[106] Cseres 2005, 245; Steenbergen 2008, 136.

[107] Commission of the European Communities 1991, 39.

[108] Deckert 2000, 176; Monti 2002, 1057; Monti 2007, 91; Townley 2010, 47–51.

[109] See e.g.: Ariño 2004c, 103; Valcke 2004, 772; Monti 2007, 91.

[110] Valcke 2004, 772.

[111] *Ibid.*, 772.

competition authorities need to take into account those 'other' objectives when applying competition rules.[112]

It should be noted that, although new Article 165 (1) of the TFEU states that "*the Union shall contribute to the promotion of European sporting issues, while taking account of the specific nature of sport, its structures based on voluntary activity and its social and educational function (emphasis added)*", it is not a cross-sectional clause like the other ones. Van den Bogaert and Vermeersch clarified this by saying that "*the Union would only be obliged to take into account the specific nature of sport when it undertakes direct action in sport on the basis of Art. III-282*".[113] According to Van Rompuy and Pauwels "*this provision would have no immediate bearing to the application of the competition rules*".[114] Stewart emphasised that sport's special characteristics should not be taken into account when applying other EU policies, because this provision is not a horizontal integration clause.[115] However, the authors of the Study on the Lisbon Treaty and EU Sports Policy stated that although Article 165 of the TFEU does not require sporting issues to be taken into account when making policies in other areas, this Article does not prohibit the EU from doing so.[116]

Hence, according to different authors, as indicated above, competition authorities could and even should take into account non-economic considerations and other goals of the Community when applying competition rules. The next question that needs to be answered is how the competition authorities should balance the economic and non-economic considerations in their decisions. Or as questioned by Monti: "*what significance these [non-economic] factors should have in the decision making-process*".[117]

According to Monti, these factors should have less weight than the core considerations of competition law, but it would be unacceptable that these factors could only be taken into account when a decision has already been reached that an agreement should benefit from an exemption because it satisfies the core competition criteria. As a result, he argued that "*it would be unlawful for the Commission to exempt an agreement that fostered a particular Community policy, but failed to achieve the core aims of EC competition policy*". Additionally, he said that "*an agreement which contributes to a Community policy but is inefficient [...] should not be exempted. But an agreement which results in increased efficiency and which contributes to other community goals is exempted because the combination of these two benefits outweighs the restriction of competition*".[118] Cseres added that "*the broad and open formulation of article [101] (3) makes it possible to balance*

[112] Steenbergen 2008, 142; Townley 2010, 155–159.

[113] Van den Bogaert and Vermeersch 2006, 839.

[114] Van Rompuy and Pauwels 2009, 297.

[115] Stewart 2009, 226.

[116] Parrish et al. 2010, 10 & 61.

[117] Monti 2002.

[118] *Ibid.*, 1070–1071.

the core values of competition [...] with certain non-competition policy objectives".[119] When we take a look at the Guidelines on the application of Article 81 (3) of the Treaty (now Article 101 (3) of the TFEU),[120] paragraph 42 formulates it as follows: "*[g]oals pursued by other Treaty provisions can be taken into account to the extent that they can be subsumed under the four conditions of Article 81(3)*". In the Study on the Lisbon Treaty and EU Sports Policy, it is explicitly stated that Article 165 of the TFEU "*does not adjust the proposition that the grounds for exempting a sporting practice must be located within the exemption criteria contained in Article 101(3) TFEU. The reference to the 'specific nature of sport' contained with Article 165 cannot be cited as the reason for exempting a practice should the 101(3) exemption criteria not be satisfied*".[121]

8.2.4 Competition Law and Particularities of Sectors

Just as it is sometimes argued that competition authorities should take into account non-economic objectives, they could also consider specific non-economic features of sectors when taking their decisions. The European Court of Justice, for example, has explicitly affirmed that competition law does permit the special characteristics of certain branches of the economy to be respected.[122] The competition decisions in the following subsections are illustrations of cases where competition authorities did so and, thus, refute the claims that competition regulation can only deal with economic considerations.

8.2.4.1 Particularities of the Sports Sector

A. Introduction

It has been and it is still sports bodies' greatest concern that the 'specificity of sport' (*supra*) would insufficiently or even not be taken into account when competition law will be applied. As indicated before, in its White Paper on Sport, the European Commission has explicitly stated that "*the case law of the European courts and decisions of the European Commission show that the specificity of sport has been recognised and taken into account*".[123] In its accompanying document to the White Paper on Sport, the European Commission stressed that "*Community Courts and the Commission have consistently taken into consideration the*

119 Cseres 2005, 253.

120 European Commission 2004.

121 Parrish et al 2010, 29.

122 CJ, Verband der Sachversicherer e.V. v Commission, para 15.

123 Commission of the European Communities 2007a, COM 2007)391 final, 13.

particular characteristics of sport setting it apart from other economic activities that are frequently referred to as the "specificity of sport"".[124] Although the European Commission affirmed that "*in line with established case law, the specificity of sport will continue to be recognised*", it underlined that "*[the specificity of sport] cannot be construed so as to justify a general exemption from the application of EU law*".[125] Colucci rephrased this as follows: "*the specificity of sport is not an exception to community law*".[126] Or in Zylberstein's words: "*[w]hile Article 165 TFEU sets in the stone of EU constitutional law the need to take account of the specific characteristics of sport, this does not mean that it will legitimise sporting rules that violate the most fundamental rules of EU law. Recognition of the specificity of sport should not be confused with its exemption from the scope of the Treaty*".[127]

The accompanying document to the White Paper on Sport contains distinctive features of the sports sector that could be of relevance when, for example, assessing the compliance of organisational sporting rules with competition law: 1) interdependence between competing adversaries, 2) uncertainty as to the result, 3) pyramid structure, and 4) educational, public health, social, cultural and recreational functions of sport.[128] The following subsections will briefly indicate where these specific features of sport were taken into account in different competition decisions. The subsections will not deal with the fourth feature. The fourth feature was discussed in more detail in Part I of this book. It is important to note that the European Commission stressed that those rules pursuing legitimate objectives and being inherent and necessary for the organisation of sport will be found in violation of Articles 101 and/or 102 of the TFEU when they would go beyond what is necessary.[129]

B. Interdependence between competing adversaries-Uncertainty as to the result

Given that sport is organised on the basis of clubs, teams or at least two athletes competing, mutual interdependence between competitors is a common feature of the sports sector. As a result, it comes as no surprise that the UEFA stressed that "*football clubs are not truly independent competitors*".[130] However, it is also more generally accepted that the sports sector distinguishes itself from other industries, because the aim of the game is not to eliminate the weaker competitor.

---

124 Commission of the European Communities 2007a, SEC2007b 935, 35.

125 Commission of the European Communities 2007a, COM 2007a 391 final, 13.

126 Colucci 2008, 25.

127 Zylberstein 2010, 65.

128 Commission of the European Communities 2007a, SEC(2007) 935, 35–36.

129 *Ibid.*, 70.

130 *Uefa Champions League* case, para 125.

In other words, the objective of team A is not to take market share from team B in order to effect team B's ultimate withdrawal from the market.[131]

Hence, sports competition cannot take place unilaterally. It requires the league to co-ordinate activity over such issues as setting fixtures and establishing the rules of the games. Whilst these forms of co-ordinated activity are not commonly permitted in other industries, Parrish and Mietinnen stated that "*it is eminently reasonable to allow for limited cartelisation in sport*".[132] The European Commission recognised that 'rules of the game', such as rules fixing the length of matches or the number of players on the field, are likely not to breach the competition rules if they are inherent and proportionate to the objectives pursued.[133]

To maintain the interest of the spectators, sport requires uncertainty of result. In order to create greater outcome uncertainty, redistributive mechanisms are put in place in the sports sector. The fact that sports teams, clubs and athletes have a direct interest not only in there being other teams, clubs and athletes, but also in their economic viability as competitors sets the sports sector also apart from other industries where competition between firms serves the purpose of eliminating inefficient firms from the market. It is apparent that it is perhaps the only sector in the economy where there is need for a certain degree of solidarity between the participants.[134] Given that a team needs to compete with other teams, a championship can only be successful if there is a sufficient number of clubs competing against each other. This may justify a certain degree of redistribution of money earned, notably from richer clubs to poorer clubs as well as from professional athletes to amateur sport.[135] Toft, when he was Principal Administrator of the DG Competition, stated that "*the Commission accepts such solidarity measures as part of the special character of sport. The Commission would not as such interfere with the manner in which solidarity measures are financed*".[136] In the *UEFA Champions League* case, the European Commission stressed that "*it is desirable to maintain a certain balance among the football clubs playing in a league because it creates better and more exciting football matches [...]. The Commission recognises that a cross-subsidisation of funds from richer to poorer may help achieve this*".[137]

---

131 Commission of the European Communities 2007b, SEC(2007) 935, 36; Parrish and Miettinen 2008, 2–3.

132 Parrish and Miettinen 2008, 2.

133 Commission of the European Communities 2007a, SEC(2007) 935, 39; Commission of the European Communities 2007b, COM (2007) 391 final, 13.

134 Toft 2003, p. 4; Commission of the European Communities 2007a, SEC(2007) 935, 36; Parrish and Miettinen 2008, 3.

135 Van Bael and Bellis 2010, 1486.

136 Toft 2003, 5.

137 *Uefa Champions League* case, para 165.

C. Integrity of competition

In the *ENIC* case,[138] the European Commission has accepted the objective of protecting the integrity of the competition in the interest of the public.[139] In this case, the UEFA 'multiple ownership of sport clubs/teams' rule, i.e. a rule according to which a company or individual cannot directly or indirectly control more than one of the clubs participating in a UEFA club competition, had raised concerns under EC competition law. The European Commission decided, however, that "*the object of the contested rule is not to distort competition*". The European Commission considered that "*the main purpose of the rule is to protect the integrity of the competition and to avoid conflicts of interests that may arise from the fact that more than one club controlled by the same owner or managed by the same person play in the same competition*".[140] Monti added that "*although the rule could theoretically be caught by Article 81 of the EU Treaty, it is intended to ensure that sporting competitions are fair and honest, which is in the interest of the public and football fans in particular*".[141]

D. Pyramid structure

In the European Model of Sport, the European Commission described in detail the pyramid structure of the organisation of sport in Europe.[142] The clubs form the foundation of the pyramid allowing everybody to engage in sport. The next level of this pyramid is formed by the regional federations. Those federations are responsible for organising regional championships for their members, i.e. the clubs, or coordinating sport on a regional level. National federations, organising national championships and acting as regulatory bodies, represent the next level of the pyramid. As there is only one national federation for each discipline, they have a monopolistic position. The top of the pyramid is formed by the European Federations.

This specific organisation of the sports sector has been challenged relying on competition law. In the *Mouscron* case,[143] for example, the principle of territoriality, i.e. clubs participating in a competition must be localised in the territory of the federation organising the competition,[144] was questioned. The European Commission took the view that the 'home and away from home' rule, i.e. a rule requiring each club to play its home match at its own ground, could be qualified as a sporting rule falling outside the scope of the competition rules. The European Commission found that the organisation of football on a national territorial basis

---

138 Commission decision, 25 June 2002 (hereafter: *ENIC* case); Rapid Press Releases 2002, IP/02/942.

139 Van Bael and Bellis 2010, 1490.

140 *ENIC* case, para 28.

141 Rapid Press Releases 2002, IP/02/942..

142 European Commission 1998, 2–4.

143 Commission decision, 9 December 1999; Rapid Press Releases 1999, IP/99/965.

144 Van Bael and Bellis 2010, 1488.

was not called into question by Community law and considered the rule indispensable for the organisation of national and international competitions in view of ensuring equality of chances between clubs.[145]

8.2.4.2 Particularities of the Audiovisual Media Sector

In 2001, then Competition Commissioner Monti explicitly recognised that "*[…] competition rules […] are the same across virtually all sectors of the economy. They apply to media and telecoms, just as they apply to pharmaceuticals and perfumes. However, in the audio-visual sector we should remember that the competition rules are set in an economic context marked by a number of particular features*".[146] In its Resolution on the development of the audiovisual sector, the Council of Ministers invited the European Commission "*to continue and to make more effective its contribution to the development of the audiovisual sector based on an approach that integrates the cultural, competitive and industrial dimensions of the sector*".[147] According to Georgio Monti, this resolution suggests that the Council considers that competition enforcement by the European Commission should be sensitive to inter alia the cultural dimension of this sector.[148] The European Commission indeed acknowledged that socio-cultural objectives of the media sector, i.e. freedom of expression, public's right to information and a high quality of output and media plurality, could provide a backdrop to the application of the competition rules.[149] Ariño believed that "*in communications markets, the goal of competition law is not only to safeguard a competitive market process […], but also to ensure a democratic communications order*".[150] Hence, when intervening in the media market, competition authorities could and should consider the peculiarities of communications markets.[151]

As already indicated in Part I, freedom of expression and information, pluralist media and independent journalistic reporting can help democracy to take root and to develop in a country.[152] As a result, media pluralism is a concept that generates a broad respect for its undisputed value and importance for the democratic process as well as cultural identity formation.[153] In its Competition Policy Newsletter of 1999,

---

[145] Rapid Press Releases 1999, IP/99/965; Commission of the European Communities 2007a, SEC(2007) 935, 71.

[146] Monti 2001, SPEECH/01/578.

[147] Council 2002.

[148] Monti 2007, 105–106.

[149] Monti 2001, SPEECH/01/578.

[150] Ariño 2004c, 97.

[151] See e.g.: Nitsche 2001, 97; Ariño 2004c, 103.

[152] Voorhoof and Cannie 2010, 421.

[153] Klimkiewicz 2008, 81.

the European Commission has indicated that, in the case of television, the goal of media plurality must, therefore, always be kept in mind when applying competition rules.[154] As a result, some authors have indicated that competition decisions, even though the competition rules leave less scope for taking into account non-economic considerations, have indirectly contributed to non-economic policies, such as pluralism, by keeping markets open and competitive, by preventing undue concentration of markets, and by remedying abusive behaviour.[155]

Although competition decisions could indirectly influence pluralism, the Belgian Competition Council has taken this principle explicitly into account in one of its decisions. The president of the Belgian Competition Council found a *prima facie* abuse of dominance in the behaviour of the largest Flemish media group VMMa (owning a commercial broadcaster, radio stations, newspapers, magazines and websites) towards its competitor, the second largest newspaper group in Flanders (VUM) when trading advertising space or time ('barter agreements'). Preliminary measures were imposed to prevent VMMa from abusing its dominant position in one market, i.e. the television advertising market, in order to strengthen the position of associated companies in another market, i.e. newspapers and magazines market. According to the Belgian Competition Council, due to such practices, the pluriformity of the Dutch speaking press in Belgium could be endangered and accordingly damage the general economic interest.[156] Hence, this decision perfectly illustrates how competition authorities (can) take into account the specificities of the media sector. However, the Court of Appeal annulled this decision, because there was no proof of the *prima facie* abuse of dominance.[157]

References

Legislation and Policy Documents

European Union

Communications

European Commission (2009) Communication from the commission on the application of state aid rules to public service broadcasting. *OJ* (2009) C 257/1

---

154 Linsey Mc Callum 1999, 7.

155 Nitsche 2001, 6; Hitchens 2006, 208; ICRI et al. 2009a, 3.

156 Belgian Competition Council 2003, 100–126; ICRI et al. 2009b, 71.

157 Court of Appeal of Brussels 2004.

Commission Staff Working Documents

Commission of the European Communities (2007) Commission staff working document—The EU and Sport: background and context—Accompanying document to the White Paper on Sport. 11 July 2007, SEC(2007) 935

Decisions

Commission decision, of 27 May 1998 relating to a proceeding pursuant to Council Regulation (EEC) No 4064/89 (Case No IV/M.993—Bertelsmann/Kirch/Premiere). *OJ* 1999 L 53/1

Commission decision of 3 March 1999 relating to a proceeding pursuant to Article 85 of the EC Treaty (Case No IV/36.237-TPS). *OJ* (1999) L 90/6

Commission decision of 9 December 1999 (Case 36851–Lille/UEFA (Mouscron)) (not published)

Commission decision of 25 June 2002 (Case COMP/37806–ENIC/UEFA). http://ec.europa.eu/competition/antitrust/cases/decisions/37806/en.pdf. Accessed 19 August 2010

Commission decision of 23 July 2003 relating to a proceeding pursuant to Article 81 of the EC Treaty and Article 53 of the EEA Agreement, COMP/C.2-37.398—Joint selling of the commercial rights of the UEFA Champions League. *OJ* (2003) L 291/25

Commission decision of 2 April 2003 declaring a concentration to be compatible with the common market and the EEA Agreement (Case No COMP/M. 2876—Newscorp/Telepiù), Annex Commitments to the European Commission—Part I—Interpretations. *OJ* (2004) L 110/73

Commission decision of 19 January 2005 relating to a proceeding pursuant to Article 81 of the EC Treaty and Article 53(1) of the EEA Agreement, Case COMP/C-2/37.214—Joint selling of the media rights to the German Bundesliga. *OJ* (2005) L 134/46

Commission decision of 22 March 2006 relating to a proceeding pursuant to Article 81 of the EC Treaty (Case COMP/C-2/38.173—Joint selling of media rights to the FA Premier League)

Notices

Commission notice on the definition of relevant market for the purposes of Community competition law. *OJ* (1997) C 372/5

Commission notice on remedies acceptable under Council Regulation (EC) No 139/2004 and under Commission Regulation (EC) No 802/2004. *OJ* (2008) C 267/1

Notifications

Commission of the European Communities (2001). Notification of 26 September 2001 pursuant to Article 4 of Council Regulation No. 4064/89 Case No. (COMP/M.2483 Canal+/RTL/GJCD/JV), 13 November 2001

Regulations

Council Regulation No 4064/89 of 21 December 1989 on the control of concentrations between undertakings. *OJ* (1990) L 257/13

Council Regulation No 1/2003 of 16 December 2002 on the implementation of the rules on competition laid down in Arts 81 and 82 of the Treaty. *OJ* (2003) L1/1

Council Regulation No 139/2004 of 20 January 2004 on the control of concentrations between undertakings (the EC Merger Regulation). *OJ* (2004) L 24/1

Resolutions

Council Resolution on the development of the audiovisual sector. *OJ* (2002) C 32/4

White Papers

Commission of the European Communities (2007) White Paper on Sport. 11 July 2007, COM (2007) 391 final

Reports

Commission of the European Communities (1991) XXIst Report on Competition Policy 1991. http://bookshop.europa.eu/is-bin/INTERSHOP.enfinity/WFS/EU-Bookshop-Site/en_GB/-/EUR/ViewPublication-Start?PublicationKey=CM7392247. Accessed 18 August 2010

European Commission (1999) XXIXth Report on Competition Policy 1999. http://ec.europa.eu/competition/publications/annual_report/1999/en.pdf. Accessed 18 August 2010

European Commission (2003) XXXIIIrd Report on Competition Policy 2003., http://ec.europa.eu/competition/publications/annual_report/2003/en.pdf. Accessed 18 August 2010

Press releases

Rapid Press Releases (1999) Limits to application of treaty competition rules to sport: commission gives clear signal, 9 December 1999, IP/99/965

Rapid Press Releases (2002). Commission closes investigation into UEFA rule on multiple ownership of football clubs, 27 June 2002, IP/02/942

Rapid Press Releases (2008) Mergers: commission revises remedies notice and amends merger implementing regulation, 22 October 2008, IP/08/1567

Speeches

Monti M (2001) Does EC competition policy help or hinder the European audiovisual industry. 26 November 2001, SPEECH/01/578

Toft T (2003) TV rights of sports events. 15 Jan 2003. http://ec.europa.eu/comm/competition/speeches/text/sp2003_002_en.pdf. Accessed 19 Aug 2010

Miscallanious

European Commission (1998) The European Model of Sport. http://ec.europa.eu/sport/library/doc/a/doc248_en.pdf. Accessed 19 August 2010

European Commission (2004). Guidelines on the application of Article 81(3) of the Treaty. OJ (2004) C 101/97

European Commission (2011a). Competition—mergers. http://ec.europa.eu/competition/mergers/overview_en.html. Accessed 16 January 2012

European Commission (2011b). Competition—State Aid. http://ec.europa.eu/competition/state_aid/overview/index_en.html. Accessed 16 January 2012

Case law Court of Justice

CJ, Établissements Consten S.à.R.L. and Grundig-Verkaufs-GmbH v Commission, 13 July 1966, Joined Cases 56/64 and 58/64, *ECR* (1966) 299

CJ, Franz Völk v S.P.R.L. Ets J. Vervaecke, 9 July 1969, C 5-69; *ECR* (1969) 295

CJ, Verband der Sachversicherer e.V. v Commission, 27 January 1987, Case 45/85, *ECR* (1987) 405

CJ, Commission of the European Communities v Italian Republic, 16 June 1987, C 118-85, *ECR* (1987) 2599

CJ, Klaus Höfner and Fritz Elser v. Macroton GmbH, 23 April 1991, C-41/90, *ECR* (1991) I-01979

CJ, SA Hercules Chemicals NV v. Commission, 17 December 1991, T-7/89, *ECR* (1991) II-1711

Belgium

Belgian Competition Council (2003) Decision no. 2003-V/M-20 of 20 March 2003, Tijdschrift van Rechtspraak van de Raad voor de Mededinging, vol 1: 100–126

Court of Appeal of Brussels (2004) A.R. nr. 2003/MR/12 and 2003/MR/13, 10 March 2004 http://economie.fgov.be/fr/ binaries/2003MR12_VMMa_Persgroep_Aurex_DeMorgen_VUM_tcm326-29093.pdf. Accessed 29 March 2011

Doctrine

Ariño M (2004a) Digital war and peace: regulation and competition in european digital broadcasting. Eur Public Law 10(1):135–160

Ariño M (2004b) Pluralism in digital broadcasting: myths, realities and the boundaries of European intervention. http://userpage.fu-berlin.de/jmueller/its/conf/berlin04/Papers/Arino.pdf. Accessed 18 August 2010

Ariño M (2004c) Competition law and pluralism in European digital broadcasting: addressing the gaps. Commun Strateg 54: 97–128

Bacon K (ed) (2009a) European Community law of state aid. Oxford University Press, Oxford

Bacon K (2009b) The definition of State aid. In: Bacon K (ed) European Community law of state aid. Oxford University Press, Oxford, pp 23–102

Bavasso A (2003) Communications in EU antitrust law: market power and public interest. Kluwer Law International

Braun JD (2008) Article 87 EC. In: Castendyk O et al (eds) European media law. Kluwer Law International, Alphen a/d Rijn, pp 207–244

Colucci M (2008) Sport in the EU Treaty—In the name of specificity and autonomy. In: Blanpain R et al (eds) The future of sports law in the European Union: beyond the EU reform treaty and the White paper. Kluwer, Deventer, pp 21–36

Cseres K (2005) Competition law and consumer protection. Kluwer Law International, The Hague

Deckert M (2000) Some preliminary remarks on the limitations of European Competition Law. Eur Rev Priv Law 1: 173–185

Donders K (2010) Under pressure? An analysis of the impact of European State aid policy on public service broadcasting. Marginalisation or revival as public service media?. PhD Thesis, Promotor: Prof. Dr. Caroline Pauwels, Brussel, (in press)

Elspass M, Kettner M (2008) Article 81 EC. In: Castendyk O et al (eds) European media law. Kluwer Law International, Alphen a/d Rijn, pp 123–149

Evens T, Lefever K (2011) Watching the soccer game: broadcasting rights for the European digital television market. J Sport Soc Issues 35(1): 33–49

Faull J, Nikpay A (2007) The EC law of competition, 2nd edn. Oxford University Press, Oxford

Geradin D (2005) Access to content by new media platforms: a review of the competition law problems. http://www.coleurope.be/content/gclc/documents/GCLC%20Working%20Paper%2001-04.pdf. Accessed 18 August 2010

Goyder D (2003) EC competition law, 4th edn. Oxford University Press, Oxford

Hitchens L (2006) Broadcasting pluralism and diversity: a comparative study of policy and regulation. Hart Publishing, Oxford

ICRI et al. (2009a) Independent study on indicators for media pluralism in the member states—towards a risk-based approach. Final Report. http://ec.europa.eu/information_society/media_taskforce/doc/pluralism/study/final_report_09.pdf. Accessed 19 August 2010

ICRI et al. (2009b) Independent study on indicators for media pluralism in the member states—towards a risk-based approach. Final Report—Annex III: Country Reports—Belgium. http://ec.europa.eu/information_society/media_taskforce/doc/pluralism/study/belgium.pdf. Accessed 19 August 2010

Jones A, Sufrin B (2008) EC competition law: text, cases, and materials—3rd edn. Oxford University Press, Oxford

Kienappel P, Stein A (2007) The application of Articles 81 and 82 EC in the sport sector. Compet Policy Newsletter 3: 6–14

Klimkiewicz B (2008) Media pluralism and enlargement: the limits and potential for media policy change. In: Ward D (ed) The European Union and the Culture Industries. Ashgate, London, pp 81–104

Kroes N (2007) La libre concurrence n'est pas une fin en soi…. Concurrences, vol. 3, n°13833: 1–2

Lefever K, Van Rompuy B (2009) Ensuring access to sports content: 10 years of EU intervention. Time to celebrate? J Media Law 2:243–268

Lenaerts K, Van Nuffel P (2005) Constitutional law of the European Union, 2nd edn. Sweet & Maxwell, London

Mc Callum L (1999) EC competition and digital pay-television. Compet Policy Newsletter 1: 4–16

Mendes Pereira M (2003) Recent consolidation in the European pay-TV sector. Compet Policy Letter 2: 29–39

Monti G (2002) Article 81 EC and public policy. Common Mark Rev 39: 1057–1099

Monti G (2007) EC Competition Law. Camebridge University Press, Camebridge

Nicolaides P et al (2005) State aid policy in the European Community: a guide for practitioners. Kluwer Law International, The Hague

Nitsche I (2001) Broadcasting in the European Union: the role of public interest in competition analysis. TMC Asser instituut, 's-Gravenhage

Odudu O. (2010) The wider concerns of competition law. Oxford J Leg Stud http://ojls.oxfordjournals.org/cgi/reprint/gqq020?ijkey=n2re3VxieYucTJS&keytype=ref. Accessed 25 August 2010

Oldale A, Piffaut H (2009) Introduction to State aid law and policy. In: Bacon K (ed) European Community law of state aid. Oxford University Press, Oxford, pp 3–22

Pace L (2007) European antitrust law: prohibitions, merger control and procedures. Elgar, Cheltenham

Parrish R, Miettinen S (2008) The sporting exception in European Union law. T.M.C. ASSER institute, The Hague

Parrish R et al. (2010) The Lisbon Treaty and EU Sports Policy – Study. http://www.europarl.europa.eu/activities/committees/studies/download.do?language=en&file=32471. Accessed 14 October 2010

Plender R (2004) Definition of Aid. In: Biondi A (ed) The law of state aid in the European Union. Oxford University Press, Oxford, pp 3–40

Psychiogopoulou E (2006) EC state aid control and cultural justification. Leg Issues Econ Integ 33(1): 3–28

Quigley C (2009) European state aid law and policy. Hart, Oxford

Rose V, Roth P (2008) European community law of competition, 6th edn. Oxford University Press, Oxford

Rosenthal M, Francis D (2009) Merger control in the telecommunications sector. In: Koenig C et al (eds) EC Competition and telecommunications law, 2nd edn. Kluwer Law International, Alphen a/d Rijn, pp 227–341
Sanchez Rydelski M (ed) (2006) The EC state aid regime: distortive effects of state aid on competition and trade. Cameron May, London
Schütte M (2006) The notion of state aid. In: Sanchez Rydelski M (ed), The EC state aid regime: distortive effects of state aid on competition and trade. Cameron May, London, pp 23–54
Sportbusiness International (2011) UEFA to centralise TV rights as Platini secures second term, 23 March 2011. http://www.sportbusiness.com/news/183294/uefa-to-centralise-tv-rights-as-platini-secures-second-term. Accessed 4 May 2011
Steenbergen J (2008) Het mededingingsbeleid en het Verdrag van Lissabon. SEW 4:136–143
Stewart S (2009) The development of sports law in the European Union, Its globalisation, and the competition law aspects of European sports broadcasting rights. Sports Lawyers J 16:183–229
Subiotto R, Graf T (2003) Analysis of the principles applicable to the review of exclusive broadcasting licences under EC competition law. World Compet 26(4):589–608
The Independent (1998) Football: The mysterious shadow of the Ronaldo affair, 7 August 1998. http://www.independent.co.uk/sport/football-the-mysterious-shadow-of-the-ronaldo-affair-1170160.html. Accessed 18 August 2010
Townley C (2010) Article 81 EC and public policy. Hart Publishing, Oxford and Portland
Valcke P (2004) Digitale Diversiteit. Convergentie van Media, Telecommunicatie-en Mededingsrecht. Larcier, Brussels
Van Bael I, Bellis JF (2010) Competition law of the European Community, 5th edn. Kluwer Law International, The Hague
Van den Bogaert S, Vermeersch A (2006) Sport and the EC Treaty a tale of uneasy bedfellows. E.L. Rev. 31(6):821–840
Van Rompuy (2011) Is efficiency all that counts? The role of non-efficiency considerations in the application of Article 101 TFEU. The case of the audiovisual sector. Ph.D thesis, Promotor: Prof. Dr. Caroline Pauwels, Brussel, forthcoming
Van Rompuy B, Pauwels C (2009) The recognition of the specificity of sport in the European Commission's Article 81 EC decisional practice related to sports media rights. In: Parrish R et al (eds) EU, Sport, Law and Policy: Regulation. Re-regulation and Representation. T.M.C. Asser Press, The Hague, pp 281–298
Vedder H (2009) Of Jurisdiction and Justification. Why Competition is Good for 'Non-Economic' Goals, But May Need to be Restricted. The Competition Law. Review 6(1): 51–75
Vermeersch A (2007) All's fair in sport and competition? The application of EC competition rules to sport. J Contemp Eur Res 3(3): 238–254
Voorhoof D, Cannie H (2010) Freedom of Expression and Information in a Democratic Society: The Added but Fragile Value of the European Convention on Human Rights. Int Commun Gazette 72: 407–423
Wachtmeister AM (1998) Broadcasting of sports events and competition law. Compet Policy Newsletter 2: 18–28
Weatherill S (2006) The sale of rights to broadcast sporting events under EC law. ISLJ 3–4: 3–27
Zylberstein J (2010) The Oliver Bernard judgment: a significant step forward for the training of players. Eur Sports Law and Policy Bulletin 1: 51–66

Chapter 9
Joint Selling Remedies Package

9.1 Introduction

The practice of joint selling refers to arrangements by which sports clubs ensign the selling of their broadcasting rights to their national or international sports associations, who then sell the rights on their behalf to broadcasters limiting them to broadcast those rights in their own territory. In contrast to the joint selling practice, there are also clubs selling their rights individually. In Spain, for example, broadcasters have to negotiate the exclusive broadcasting rights with the individual football clubs. It is often argued that individual selling of broadcasting rights would favour the stronger teams in a league owning more valuable property. The discussion about the pros and contras of individual or joint selling falls outside the scope of this book.

The joint selling mechanism can be illustrated as in Fig. 9.1.

Traditionally, sports associations sold all broadcasting rights in one large exclusive contract to a single broadcaster in each territory. Hence, joint selling mechanisms could impede competition by favouring the incumbent broadcasters and allowing them to foreclose new media providers from competition. Therefore, this practice has attracted the attention of the European Commission and national competition authorities. With regard to the joint selling of exclusive broadcasting rights of sports events (in particular football games), the European Commission has taken three important decisions on the basis of Article 101 of the TFEU, namely the *UEFA Champions League* decision, the *German Bundesliga* decision and the *FA Premier League* decision. When analysing these decisions, it will be examined how the changing information society has had an impact on the way competition law is guaranteeing the public's access to sports content.

However, before the principles set out in these decisions are discussed, it is important to indicate that the principle of territorial exclusivity has been questioned. Exclusivity is often achieved by limiting the viewing of the broadcast to one specified territory. This implies that broadcasters that have acquired broadcasting rights are

K. Lefever, *New Media and Sport*, ASSER International Sports Law Series,
DOI: 10.1007/978-90-6704-873-6_9,

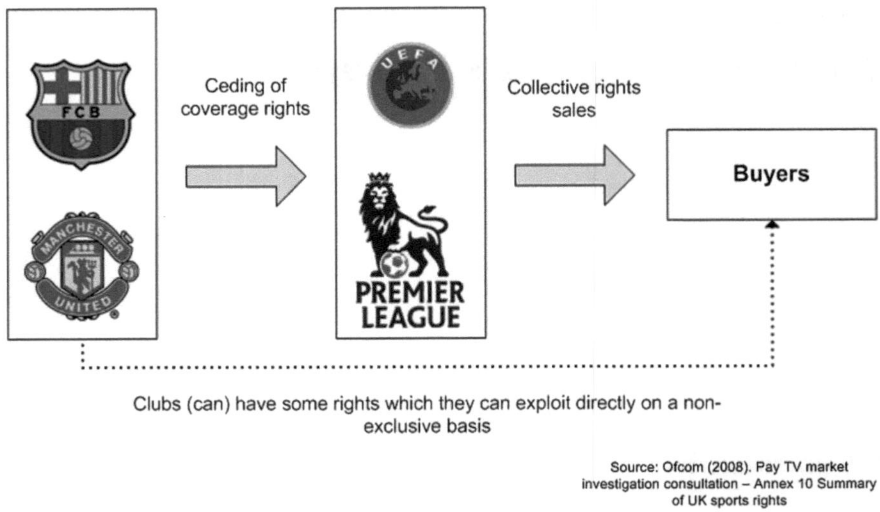

Fig. 9.1 Joint selling mechanism

limited to broadcast those matches in their respective countries. In order to guarantee this territorial exclusivity, they encrypt their broadcasting signal so it can only be received by their own customers within their assigned territory. However, a problem occurs when, for example, foreign broadcasting equipment and foreign viewing cards are imported for use, thereby by-passing the feed of the officially licensed broadcasters for a specific country. In the UK, for example, Karen Murphy, a pub owner, received the Premier League matches from a Greek broadcaster NOVA, which had a license to broadcast within Greece. She had a satellite dish, a decoder box and a NOVA viewing card that enabled her to receive and view programmes transmitted by NOVA. Publicans (or other consumers) buy these foreign decoders, because they are significantly cheaper than purchasing the equivalent official Sky or ESPN subscription. It has been argued that the Premier League's exclusive contracts infringe competition law and freedom of services by restricting the ability of a rights holding broadcaster to screen live pictures outside their own designated territory and by restricting the public to buy foreign decoders to view live Premier League matches. Conversely, the Premier League argued that such territorial restrictions are needed to protect the value of Premier League product. In the joined cases *Football Association Premier League v. QC Leisure* and *Karen Murphy v. Media Protection Services,*[1] the European Court of Justice stated that national legislation which prohibits the import, sale or use of foreign decoder cards is contrary to the freedom to provide services and cannot be justified either in light of the objective of protecting intellectual property rights or by the objective of encouraging the public to attend

[1] CJ, Football Association Premier League Ltd and Others v. QC Leisure and Others and Karen Murphy v. Media Protection Services Ltd.

football stadiums.[2] Furthermore, the Court of Justice emphasised that a system granting territorial exclusivity is also contrary to European Union competition law if the license agreements prohibit the supply of decoder cards to television viewers who wish to watch the broadcasts outside the Member State for which the license is granted.[3] A detailed analysis of this decision falls outside the scope of this book.[4]

9.2 Article 101 (1) of the TFEU and Joint Selling Agreements

9.2.1 Exclusive Contracts

In the broadcasting sector, granting exclusive broadcasting rights is an accepted and established commercial practice.[5] The only way media operators can convince viewers to tune into their audiovisual services is to offer an attractive programming not being available in the programming of other broadcasters. Hence, exclusive broadcasting rights can help broadcasters to build up audiences, to improve the image of the channel, to attract new subscribers or advertisers and to differentiate themselves from other broadcasters by broadcasting events not available on other channels. Without exclusivity, any competing channel could broadcast the same event at the same time. Accordingly, the television audience and subsequent ratings would be split between the two channels, which would devalue the product.[6] As a result, exclusivity is often seen as crucial to protect the value of existing content and to create the financial incentives necessary for the production of future content.[7] In other words, for the rights holders, exclusivity protects the value of rights, while for the purchasers, exclusivity maximises profitability and allows them to invest with greater confidence in innovative programming.[8]

Although exclusive contracts prohibit other broadcasters from showing specific content, the European Court of Justice decided that an exclusive broadcasting license does not, *in se* prevent, restrict or distort competition, because they are a legitimate way to guarantee the value of the programme.[9] This principle was affirmed by the European Commission in the European Model of Sport, saying that "*the Commission does not believe that exclusive broadcasting rights are*

[2] *Ibid.*, para 117, 124–125.

[3] *Ibid.*, para 146.

[4] For more information about this decision, see e.g.: Geey and Day 2006, 10–12; Thorntona and Takaseb 2008, 181–186; Stewart 2009, 216–217; Geey 2009a, b; Massey 2009, 38–39; Bavasso and Dominic 2010, 239–240.

[5] European Commission 1998a, b, para 4.1.1.

[6] Saltzman 2000, 2.

[7] Subiotto and Graf 2003, 590.

[8] Parrish and Miettinen 2008, 146; 2009, 12.

[9] CJ, Coditel SA and others v Ciné-Vog Films SA and others, para 16

anticompetitive per se".[10] Monti has also reiterated this principle in different speeches.[11]

9.2.2 Individual Circumstances of Exclusive Contracts

Although the exclusive exploitation of broadcasting rights in itself does not breach Article 101 of the TFEU, the individual circumstances of this practice could raise competition concerns.[12] Competition questions arise when broadcasters acquire exclusive sports broadcasting rights for an excessively long duration including a wide range of broadcasting rights (for traditional media as well as for new media services). As regards the joint selling practice in the sports sector, for example, the European Commission has argued that the sale of all broadcasting rights in one large exclusive contract to a single broadcaster constitutes a horizontal restriction of competition under Article 101 (1) of the TFEU. The reasons for this were threefold.

First, joint selling arrangements prevent the individual football clubs from individually marketing their rights, thus, preventing competition between the football clubs and also between the sports associations and the football clubs. This implies that third parties only have one single source of supply, forcing them to purchase the relevant rights under the conditions jointly determined in the context of the invitation to bid, which is issued by the joint selling body. According to the European Commission this means that "*the joint selling body restricts competition in the sense that it determines prices and all other trading conditions on behalf of all individual football clubs*". In the absence of the joint selling agreement the football clubs would set prices and conditions independently of one another and in competition with one another.[13]

Second, all rights of one sports event are bundled and sold in one huge package.[14] In the past, due to the strong asymmetry of value between traditional television rights and new media rights, this resulted in a situation where one established broadcaster was the financially stronger partner and *de facto* the only actor able to bid for this large rights package including all valuable rights to the exclusion of all other broadcasters.[15] Hence, the bundled offer of those rights across different platforms prevented new media operators from accessing the product and, thus, purchasing meaningful rights.[16] Moreover, broadcasters did not

---

[10] European Commission 1998a, b, 15.

[11] Monti 2000, SPEECH/00/152, 7; Monti 2001, SPEECH/01/84, 6.

[12] Scheuer and Strothmann 2004, p. 4.

[13] Commission decision, 23 July 2003 (hereafter: *UEFA Champions League* case), paras 1, 19, 114, 128; Commission notice 2004, para 4.

[14] *UEFA Champions League* case, para 19.

[15] See e.g.: *Ibid.*, para 20; Rapid Press Releases 2002b, IP/02/1951; Toft 2003, 11.

[16] European Commission 2005, 6; Rapid Press Releases 2002b, IP/02/1951; Toft 2006b, 6.

always exploit all the acquired rights leaving some rights unused.[17] As a consequence, the market was distorted harming other actors that were interested in buying those rights, because they could not broadcast these events.[18] This tradition of holding back rights reduced considerably the amount of rights available for new entrants, thus, hindering them from rolling out their new services. The public could also be harmed due to the limited rights that were being used.[19] Additionally, output restrictions would occur when the joint selling entity gives preferential treatment of certain media rights at the expense of other types of media rights which are withheld from the market. This method is likely to hamper the development of new media services as it may prevent players in neighbouring markets from acquiring meaningful rights.[20]

Finally, these negative effects of the joint selling agreements are even aggravated, because those rights are sold for a long period of time.[21] It is often argued that long contract duration would risk creating a situation where a successful buyer would be able to establish a dominant position on the market reducing the scope for effective *ex ante* competition in the context of future bidding rounds.[22]

9.3 Article 101 (3) of the TFEU and the Joint Selling Agreements

9.3.1 Joint Selling Agreements: Exemption Under Article 101 (3) of the TFEU

When the European Commission was, for the first time, confronted with a joint selling agreement in the *UEFA Champions League* case, the European Commission was not prepared to exempt this agreement, as it considered that the beneficial effects did not outweigh the negative impact of its inherent restrictions (*supra*).[23] As a reaction to this objection, the UEFA submitted an outline of a new joint selling arrangement.[24] At the request of the European Commission, this new arrangement was modified in a number of ways in order to benefit from an exemption under Article 101 (3) of the TFEU: unbundling of the rights, fall-back option, transparent tender procedure, limited duration of exclusive contracts

[17] *UEFA Champions League* case, para 19; Toft 2003, 11; Elspass and Kettner 2008, 144.

[18] European Commission State aid E 3/2005 (2007), para 305.

[19] Rapid Press Releases 2002b, IP/02/1951.

[20] Toft 2006b, 6.

[21] Hatton et al. 2007, 348.

[22] Toft 2006a, 6.

[23] Van den Bogaert and Vermeersch 2006, 833.

[24] *UEFA Champions League* case, para 21.

(*infra*).[25] The aforementioned list of remedies imposed on the UEFA was not an exhaustive or binding one. This implies that in future cases different or new remedies could be adopted depending on the specific circumstances of a given case.[26] In a speech, Toft explicitly stated that the remedies of the *UEFA Champions League* case would be "*insufficient to ensure that effective competition is maintained on the market*" in the *FA Premier League* case.[27] As a result, in this case, the European Commission accepted the following commitments: 'no conditional bidding' commitment, 'no single buyer' commitment and monitoring by a trustee (*infra*). In the following sections, the different amendments and their objective will be discussed in more detail.

9.3.1.1 Transparent Tender Procedure

As referred to by Subiotto and Graf, the way in which exclusive sports broadcasting rights are licensed may influence the assessment of an exclusive license.[28] Therefore, in order to reduce the risk of foreclosing the market, the European Commission has underlined, in the three different cases, that the award of the rights should follow a transparent and non-discriminatory procedure.[29]

In the *UEFA Champions League* case, for example, the UEFA has indicated that it will evaluate the bids in accordance with the following objective criteria: (a) price offered for the rights package or packages, (b) acceptance by the bidder of all relevant broadcast obligations, (c) level of audience penetration of the bidder in the contract territory, (d) proposed method of delivery or transmission, (e) proposed promotional support offered for the UEFA Champions League, (f) production capability and host broadcast expertise, (g) combination of rights packages offered in the contract territory, (h) balance between free-to-air television and pay-television.[30] In addition, this joint sales body will publish criteria on the standards which broadcasters must satisfy for broadcasting the Champions League[31] and will guarantee a reasonable time limit in which parties can submit their bids.[32]

As indicated by Toft, the obligation to organise such an open tender procedure is accepted as a good remedy "*as it gives all potential buyers an opportunity to*

---

[25] *Ibid.*, paras 23, 197.

[26] Kienappel and Stein 2007, 11.

[27] Toft 2006a, 7.

[28] Subiotto and Graf 2003, p. 600.

[29] *UEFA Champions League* case, para 27; *German Bundesliga* case, para 27; *FA Premier League* case, para 32 (f); Commission decision, 22 March 2006, Annex: Commitments of the FAPL (hereafter: *FA Premier League* case, Annex: Commitments of the FAPL), para 7.2.

[30] *UEFA Champions League* case, para 30.

[31] *Ibid.*, para 28.

[32] *Ibid.*, para 29.

compete for the rights".[33] In the *UEFA Champions League* case, it was formulated as follows: "*giving all qualified broadcasters an equal opportunity to bid for the rights in the full knowledge of the key terms and conditions*".[34] Subiotto and Graf emphasised that without this equal opportunity for all broadcasters to acquire the rights, concerns about possible foreclosure would increase.[35]

In the UK, in addition to this obligation, the FAPL proposed that the selling and awarding of the exclusive rights of the Premier League shall be overseen by a trustee that reports back to the European Commission to ensure that the tender procedure is undertaken in a fair, reasonable a non-discriminatory manner.[36]

9.3.1.2 Limited Duration of Exclusive Contracts

Although the European Commission acknowledges the need for a certain degree of exclusivity to protect the value of sports rights, long contract durations could limit competition. Exclusive contracts concluded for a long period of time could create a situation where a successful buyer would be able to establish a dominant position on the market reducing the scope for effective *ex ante* competition in the context of future bidding rounds. The risk of this long-term market foreclosure is addressed by requiring the joint selling entity to limit the duration of the exclusive rights contracts to no more than three seasons.[37]

As stressed by Toft, although three seasons were accepted in several cases, three seasons or 3 years is not an absolute period.[38] A standard duration for exclusive contracts cannot be determined, because each agreement and each market has its own characteristics. In some cases, a longer duration of exclusive arrangements can prove to be justified, particularly when an operator wishes to enter a new market with an innovative service or to introduce a new technology requiring very high risk and heavy investments. In 1993, for example, a 5-year exclusive broadcasting contract between the English Football Association, the BBC and BSkyB was found to be proportionate as BSkyB was a new entrant in the satellite broadcasting market.[39] It should also be realised that, as underlined by Subiotto and Graf, "*the absolute duration of the licence will be less of an issue than the number of events covered by the licence*". A broadcasting license for two

33 Toft 2006b, 7.

34 *UEFA Champions League* case, para 27.

35 Subiotto and Graf 2003, p. 600.

36 *FA Premier League* case, para 36 (e) 37 (a); *FA Premier League* case, Annex: Commitments of the FAPL, paras 7.8–7.14; Kienappel and Stein 2007, 13

37 See e.g.: Toft 2003, 10; *UEFA Champions League* case, para 25; *German Bundesliga* case, para 27; *FA Premier League* case, para 32 (e); *FA Premier League* case, Annex: Commitments of the FAPL, para 2.4.

38 Toft 2006a, 6.

39 See e.g.: Monti 2000, SPEECH/00/152, 7; Toft 2003, 10; Subiotto and Graf 2003, 598.

Summer Olympics, for example, would have a duration of 8 years but would only cover two events.[40]

9.3.1.3 Unbundling of Broadcasting Rights

In addition to the regulatory barriers that will be discussed in Part III, business models of incumbents could hamper the public's as well as new entrants' access to content. In the past, traditional broadcasters seemed somehow reluctant to repurpose content on mobile- and Internet-based platforms, which were viewed as a threat for their own business models. Since incumbents fear for a cannibalisation of their businesses by these platforms, they tend to protect their primary markets from new competitors by acquiring all broadcasting rights in the market, even for platforms in which they have no interest.[41]

As already mentioned before, where traditional and new media rights are bundled, the European Commission appears to be concerned that broadcasters may have little incentive to exploit new media technologies since such technologies could become competing platforms for their traditional services.[42] Because established broadcasters tend to warehouse the rights acquired, market distortions can appear harming other interested parties being unable to bid for this rights package. Geradin referred to this as the 'chicken and egg' problem. To gain market share, new media operators need premium content, but to gain access to content they need significant market share.[43] In other words, content producers, on the one hand, are reluctant to invest in often expensive new content when a substantial consumer base is not certain yet. Consumers, on the other hand, hesitate to adopt new technology owing to the uncertainty about the availability of compelling content. If these two processes co-exist, content suppliers and consumers get stuck in a vicious circle.[44] Hence, joint selling mechanisms could impede competition by favouring the incumbent broadcasters and allowing them to foreclose market access to new media providers.[45]

According to the European Commission, the offer of unbundled rights packages including different packages for new media such as Internet or mobile television was the only solution to open the sports broadcasting rights marketplace for new media operators. The fact that broadcasting rights will be no longer supplied to a single operator should enhance the possibility for more and new media companies to acquire exclusive broadcasting rights with regard to sports events. In addition, "*the sale of the UEFA Champions League media rights in separate packages [...]*

40 Subiotto and Graf 2003, 598.

41 Evens et al. 2011, 34; X 2009, 17.

42 Subiotto and Graf 2003, 605.

43 Geradin 2005, 5.

44 Evens et al. 2011, 33; Evans and Schmalensee 2009.

45 Parrish and Miettinen 2009, 17; Petit 2004, 436.

should enhance the possibility for more broadcasters, including small and medium-sized companies, to obtain UEFA Champions League content".[46]

9.3.1.4 Fall-Back Option

In the past, when the original joint selling agreements were in place, the governing bodies did not always sell all the available rights which resulted in unused/unsold rights and, thus, output restrictions. Those restrictions of output could limit the consumer's choice in sports broadcasts.[47]

This risk could only be reduced by a requirement that unsold rights should not be tolerated. Therefore, in the amended joint selling agreements, the governing bodies and the European Commission reached an agreement preventing the possibility from 'hoarding' rights. This implies that every game has to be made available for purchase in each country and that if the rights are not sold jointly; the individual clubs are granted the possibility of selling the rights individually. When the entitlement to sell the rights fall back to the individual clubs, they are then at liberty to sell the rights to any interested buyer in competition with the joint selling body.[48] In the *UEFA Champions League* case, for example, the football clubs will be allowed to sell "*on a non-exclusive basis in parallel with UEFA certain media rights relating to action in which they are participating*".[49] The same goes for the *German Bundesliga* case and the *FA Premier League* case.[50]

The philosophy behind this amendment is twofold. First, the European Commission questions the efficiencies and benefits of the joint selling procedure where the joint selling body is not able to sell the rights. Second, the European Commission emphasised that "*maintaining competition between the joint selling body and the football clubs in bringing such rights to the market helps to avoid rights to sports events remaining unused, where there is demand for them*". The fall-back option will also give the football clubs the opportunity to sell broadcasting rights to free-to-air broadcasters when pay-television operators are not interested (anymore).[51] Hence, according to the European Commission, giving the football clubs the opportunity to sell the unused rights are outweighing the negative effects arising from the joint selling arrangement by the increased amount of content made available for a wider distribution.[52]

---

46 *UEFA Champions League* case, para 171.

47 Toft 2003, 11.

48 Toft 2006b, 8; Ungerer 2003, 9.

49 *UEFA Champions League* case, paras 22, 34, 38, 158–161.

50 *German Bundesliga* case, Annex Commitments of the League Association, para 6.1; *FA Premier League* case, para 32 (g); *FA Premier League* case, Annex: Commitments of the FAPL, paras 9.1 and 9.4.

51 *UEFA Champions League* case, para 159.

52 *Ibid.*, para 161.

9.3.1.5 'No conditional bidding' Commitment

In the *FA Premier League* case, in addition to the 'standard' remedies', the European Commission received a commitment from the FAPL that bids other than simple standalone bids would be disregarded, i.e. 'no conditional bidding' commitment. In other words, this 'no conditional bidding' commitment implies that the joint selling body can only accept unconditional bids per package[53] and, thus, that the joint selling body will only sell the individual rights packages to the highest standalone bidder.[54] Such blind selling would prevent a powerful buyer wanting to acquire the most valuable package(s) from offering a bonus on condition that all the valuable rights are sold to him, thus inciting initial rights owners not to sell at least some packages to competitors in the same market or operators in neighbouring markets.[55] In Belgium, however, the Competition Council did not consider the payment of bonuses for obtaining multiple or all packages as an infringement of competition law.[56]

9.3.1.6 'No Single Buyer' Commitment

To prevent that all the exclusive live broadcasting rights would be sold to one television company, the FAPL, in the *FA Premier League* case, agreed that the tendering procedures for broadcasting rights after 2006 would ensure that there are at least two broadcasters of live Premier League matches. In order to achieve this, the live rights would be sold in six packages and one buyer would not be entitled to buy all the packages, i.e. 'no single buyer' commitment.[57] In a speech, Toft explained that this commitment will only be justified "*where at the time of the tender a serious foreclosure risk already exists ex ante due to the presence of a dominant undertaking on the downstream market or where selling the rights to a single buyer would secure the winner a dominant position extending beyond the duration of the contract in question*".[58] Hence, this would prevent incumbent pay-television operators in the UK, particularly BSkyB, from buying all the packages. In Belgium, however, the Competition Council stated that there is no objection to the selling of all packages to one actor.[59]

---

[53] *FA Premier League* case, para 36 (e); *FA Premier League* case, Annex: Commitments of the FAPL, paras 7.5–7.7; Rapid Press Releases 2005b, IP/05/1441.

[54] Kienappel and Stein 2007, 12.

[55] Toft 2006a, 6; Kienappel and Stein 2007, 12.

[56] Belgian Competition Council 2005, para 34.

[57] *FA Premier League* case, para 33, 37 (c)–(d), 41; *FA Premier League* case, Annex: Commitments of the FAPL, para 3.2.

[58] Toft 2006a, 7.

[59] Belgian Competition Council 2005, para 33.

However, it is debatable whether the inclusion of the 'no single buyer' commitment, regardless of the underlying *rationale*, has in fact substantially broadened the offer of sports on television in the UK. A recent interim report on pay-television in the UK of Ofcom demonstrates the limited practical effects of the European Commission's action on consumer's choice and pricing.[60] With the help of this remedy, in 2006, BSkyB won four of the six live packages and Setanta won the other two live packages. The outcome of the 2009 auction was that BSkyB won the rights to five of the six available packages, which is the maximum available to a single bidder.[61] Setanta was only able to secure one live package for the 2010–2013 seasons.[62] Only a few months after the auction, the FAPL announced that Setanta had been unable to meet its financial obligations, and that the existing license agreement would be terminated.[63] A couple of days later, Setanta went into administration and ceased its operations in the UK market.[64] By the end of June 2009, the FAPL announced that ESPN had won the rights previously belonging to Setanta.[65] ESPN's UK sports channel will be distributed on Sky's pay-television platform.[66] As indicated by Van Rompuy, although this remedy did facilitate the entry of a new pay-television operator, Setanta, into the market, the greater competition for the live Premier League matches could not be maintained.[67]

9.3.2 Development of New Media and the Public's Access to Sports Content

9.3.2.1 Introduction

In the different press releases that accompanied the joint selling agreement decisions, the European Commission has always stressed that the aim of the amendments was to foster competition on the markets for the acquisition of sports broadcasting rights and to increase consumers' choice. The European Commission welcomed UEFA's new policy for the joint selling of media rights to the Champions League by stating that it "*will give an impulse to the emerging new media markets such as the Internet and UMTS services*" and "*represents good news for [...] fans*".[68] In January 2005, when the commitments given by the German

---

60 Ofcom 2009, paras 2.51–2.55.

61 *Ibid.*, para 2.53.

62 *Ibid.*, para 2.53.

63 *Ibid.*, para 2.54.

64 BBC News 2009; Guardian 2009.

65 Ofcom 2009, para 2.54.

66 *Ibid.*

67 Van Rompuy 2009, 119; Lefever and Van Rompuy 2009, 258.

68 Rapid Press Releases 2002a, IP/02/806; Rapid Press Releases 2003a, IP/03/1105.

Football League were rendered legally binding by a formal European Commission's decision, the former Competition Commissioner Kroes commented that, due to this decision, fans will benefit from new products and greater choice. Furthermore, she stressed that "*[t]he commitments liberalise the central marketing arrangements and maximise the rights for television and new media (UMTS, Internet)*".[69] One year later, with regard to the *FA Premier League* case, Kroes repeated that "*[t]he commitments offered by the FA Premier League therefore provide for more rights, including television, mobile and internet rights*" and "*the solution we have reached will benefit football fans*".[70] Moreover, in 2003, then Competition Commissioner Monti stated that "*by creating opportunities for broadcasters other than BSkyB now [...], the Commission is aiming to increase consumer choice in the UK*". Moreover, he added that "*for the first time, there is a real opportunity for free to air broadcasters to provide their viewers with top flight Premier League action throughout the season*".[71]

Although these statements are very promising, the question that needs to be answered is whether the public, as a consumer or as a citizen, and the new media operators actually have been taken into account when giving an exemption under Article 101 (3) of the TFEU.

9.3.2.2 Joint Selling Agreement and Competition in the Changed Media Landscape

A. Introduction

In the *UEFA Champions League* case, the European Commission explicitly recognised and accepted that the benefits generated by the amended joint selling agreements outweigh the negative effects that it deploys and, therefore, an exemption can be granted under Article 101 (3) of the TFEU.

First, the benefits for the broadcasters are *inter alia* created by the single point of sale of the UEFA Champions League rights.[72] The advantage of a single point of sale is that this allows media operators to "*provide coverage to consumers of the league as a whole and over the course of the entire season*".[73] The European Commission has accepted that "*such aggregation seems indispensable to present a worthwhile product that interests viewers*".[74] Second, it is argued that an organisation is able to create a uniformity and consistency of its product if it is sold via joint selling. Hence, in the *UEFA Champions League* case, the European

[69] Rapid Press Releases 2005a, IP/05/62.

[70] Rapid Press Releases 2006, IP/06/356, 1.

[71] Rapid Press Releases 2003b, IP/03/1748, 2.

[72] *UEFA Champions League* case, para 169.

[73] *Ibid.*, para 145.

[74] *Ibid.*, paras 1, 145 and 175.

Commission stressed that "*the joint selling of the league media products provide benefits for broadcasters in terms of a common and consistent look to the on-screen presentation of the matches [...]. This is of benefit to viewers as they are able immediately to recognise a UEFA Champions League branded media product [...]*".[75] Finally, the joint selling arrangement "*creates efficiencies, which allow media operators to invest more in new improved production and transmission technologies, quality television coverage, quality production and presentation,* etc. *It is also likely to lead to a more intensive and innovative exploitation of the rights to the benefit of the consumer*".[76]

With regard to new media operators, the European Commission has stressed that "*the sale of the UEFA Champions League media rights in separate packages [...] should enhance the possibility for more broadcasters, including small and medium-sized companies, to obtain UEFA Champions League conten*t".[77] Furthermore, as indicated before, the European Commission has emphasised that the amended joint selling agreements will give the possibility for new media operators (such as Internet and mobile services) to buy exclusive broadcasting rights. In other words, as a result of these changes, the sports broadcasting rights market could be opened for new media operators. However, although the process of unbundling media rights seeks to stimulate the roll-out of new media and to increase consumer's choice by creating the possibility for more operators to bid for the rights, they are not always offered the same opportunities as the traditional media operators. A technical concern for a decline of quality of experience is often applied to impose an embargo on broadcasting over the Internet as well as over mobile phones. Or additionally, the tender only allows new media operators to broadcast clips of the sports events.

B. Embargo

In its 2003 decision, the European Commission specified that UEFA and the clubs could "*only provide online video content one and a half hours after the match has finished*", because live streaming on the Internet would not permit the maintenance of a satisfactorily high quality.[78] Back then, this embargo had been criticised by Internet service providers. They considered that "*the embargo is too long for deferred exploitation*" and that they "*would like to have live rights*". In addition, they regretted that Internet service providers were excluded from competing for those rights.[79] The unequal treatment of these rights makes these new media services less attractive, which may undermine market development and user take-up.[80] Especially the uniqueness of sport events makes their delayed transmission

[75] *Ibid.*, paras 154–157.
[76] *Ibid.*, para 171.
[77] *Ibid.*
[78] *Ibid.*, para 40.
[79] *Ibid.*, para 98.
[80] Evens et al. 2011, 36.

less valuable for the public as it is often argued that sports should be experienced live.[81]

However, it was stressed that this technical argument could change over time, making it necessary to revisit the embargo.[82] Over the years, it is proven that this technical argument has become highly contestable as other major sports events are streamed live without loss of quality and with a delay of no longer than a few seconds. Due to these technical evolutions, UEFA decided to create the possibility for new media operators to acquire live rights (*infra*).

C. Clip rights

In the *UEFA Champions League* decision, it was specified that UEFA and the clubs have a right to provide audio/video content via UMTS services "*available maximum 5 min after the action has taken place*" (technical transformation delay).[83] But what is actually meant by the term 'action' is not completely clear. While assuming this refers to single game extracts such as a goal or a penalty, this interpretation implies that full matches are excluded from live mobile coverage. With regard to the FA Premier League, the mobile rights are also limited to a package consisting of "*clips of all Premier League Matches*"[84] and those clips can only be delivered as soon as the 'action' has occurred during the match.[85] In this decision, clips are clearly defined as "*an excerpt which contains specific content in respect of a Premier League Match, such as a goal or key incident, and which does not comprise more than thirty (30) seconds of continuous action from the Premier League Match in question*".[86] Hence, full coverage is not allowed.

Although it is often argued that the length of mobile sports coverage is limited to highlights or single actions, because of the technical constraints faced by mobile access networks or handsets, and because of concerns about the transmission quality and viewing experience, others have stressed that these length restrictions are not related to technical concerns, but instead driven by rights holders' desire to maintain rights' value. If the latter is true, for those length restrictions to be justified, it is necessary to prove that mobile rights indeed do adversely affect the value of the traditional broadcasting rights.[87] As the European Commission's Sector Inquiry into the provision of sports content over third generation mobile networks has concluded, user experience of mobile sports content fundamentally differs from traditional television coverage due to usage costs, personalisation of the viewing experience and the length of time that consumers are willing to spend

---

81 See e.g.: Rumphorst 2001, 3; Commission of the European Communities 2007, SEC(2007) 935, 79.

82 *UEFA Champions League* case, para 40.

83 *Ibid.*, para 44.

84 *FA Premier League* case, Annex: Commitments of the FAPL, para 5.1.

85 Rapid Press Releases 2003b, IP/03/1748.

86 *FA Premier League* case, Annex: Commitments of the FAPL, para 1.

87 Evens et al. 2011, 36.

to watch the content. In addition, television and mobile services are consumed in a very different manner, for technical, as well as for social reasons.[88] Previous research has demonstrated that mobile television will be used by people having no access to fixed traditional television services while, for example, being on the move. The MADUF-project[89] has also shown that the regular television viewing peaks were extended with two mobile peaks: one in the afternoon and one in the late evening.[90] Therefore, it seems that mobile television should be considered as complementary rather than as a substitute or replacement for traditional television services. This means that mobile services are used in addition to, but not instead of the main platform of sports rights broadcasting via the traditional television set.[91] As there is (so far) little evidence of direct substitution between mobile and traditional sports content services, the licensing of mobile rights (even for the whole match) should only have a limited effect on the value of other broadcasting rights.[92] Hence, if sports fans have the time and opportunity to watch a match on their traditional television set, they are not going to be satisfied with the screen of a mobile handset.[93] The same goes for sports consumption on the Internet. Given that nobody will watch a whole match on its computer when he would have the chance to watch it on a large screen television, watching sport on Internet cannot be designated as a real substitute for watching sports on a traditional television set (*supra*). Hence, new media, such as Internet or mobile television, will not kill football on television, but will rather complement traditional broadcasting by offering additional value for the public.[94] However, it should be noted that the convergence of, on the one hand, traditional television and, on the other hand, Internet is underway.[95] Today, there is still a major separation between distribution of content to the traditional television set and the content distributed to a PC. Only a very limited number of consumers have a set-top box and a broadband link fast enough to get content on the World Wide Web in high quality down to their television. Though, this is about to change. The public is becoming increasingly aware of the possibility to enjoy Web content on their big screen. As a result, broadband delivered content could become a standard part of the living room. According to Grant, "*this development will significantly alter the balance of power within the television value chain and potentially disrupt the industry in the same*

88 See e.g.: European Commission 2005, para 14.

89 MADUF (Maximizing DVB Usage in Flanders) is an IBBT-project. The objective of the MADUF-project was to generate an optimum model for providing mobile television services in Flanders via DVB-H and develop a proof of concept. For more information about this project, see: IBBT, http://www.ibbt.be/.

90 See e.g.: Evens et al. 2008, 124–130.

91 European Commission 2005, para 14; Andriychuk 2009, 88.

92 Evens et al. 2011, 36.

93 Toft 2006a, 4.

94 Boyle and Haynes 2003, 112; Wessberg 2000.

95 Independent Advisory Panel to the Secretary of State for Culture, Media and Sport 2009, para 34.

way as the internet and viewing content on the PC has changed the music and newspaper industries".[96] Viera Cast, for example, allows the public to access Internet content via a Panasonic television set. However, it should be noted that, currently, such integrated television sets often only offer access to a limited walled garden of online content. Viera Cast only streams a limited amount of online content, such as YouTube,[97] Bloomberg News, The Weather Channel, Amazon video-on-demand service, etc. Mid-2010, the social networking site Twitter was added to the services on Viera Cast.

D. Platform-neutrality

As technological convergence is blurring the boundaries between previously distinct technologies, the way some sports organisations sell their sports broadcasting rights has also changed. Instead of carving up their rights for different platforms, the new trend is selling rights on a platform-neutral basis with packages carved out by time window: live, near-live or deferred, highlights and clip rights.[98,99] The winners of each package can then exploit these rights across various platforms.

Although the FAPL stated that it shall offer "*the Live Audio-Visual Packages and the Near-Live Audio-Visual Packages on a technologically neutral basis in respect of the delivery systems and technologies by which the Core Rights in those Packages are capable of being exploited*",[100] it is important to note that mobile rights are excluded from the definition of audio-visual rights.[101] The FAPL offers "*separate Packages of (i) Live Audio-Visual Rights, (ii) Near-Live Audio-Visual Rights, (iii) Mobile Audio-Visual Rights and (iv) National Radio Rights*".[102] Therefore, given the fact that the mobile rights are not treated as audiovisual rights, this way of selling could not be considered as being completely platform-neutral.

In contrast to the FAPL rights, the Champions League rights are now sold without any restriction with regard to the platform used for their exploitation. As already referred to above, UEFA has made major changes in the rights sales format for the 2009–2012 cycle of the Champions League. The most interesting and important change is that media content rights will be granted on a complete platform-neutral basis. Consequently, successful bidders for live match rights will benefit from exclusivity across all media platforms (*infra*), including television, Internet and mobile, throughout the entire live match.[103] As a consequence, mobile rights will now include live transmission of the Champions League matches. The

---

[96] Grant 2009.

[97] According to Panasonic, the entire catalogue of YouTube videos is available, although it may take a day or two for a new one on the site to appear on Viera Cast (CNet News 2008).

[98] *German Bundesliga* case, Annex Commitments of the League Association, para 4.

[99] Evens et al. 2011, 36.

[100] *FA Premier League* case, Annex: Commitments of the FAPL, para 2.5.

[101] *Ibid.*, para 1.

[102] *Ibid.*, para 2.1.

[103] UEFA 2008.

same goes for the 2009–2012 rights of the Europa League. Instead of limiting the distribution of Europa League's content to television, the content distributors are allowed to transmit this content over a wide range of platforms.[104] According to the UEFA, due to convergence, the traditional term 'broadcaster' is no longer accurately reflecting the reality of the methods by which content is ultimately made available to the consumer. Therefore, the UEFA uses the term 'content distributor' instead of broadcaster. A 'content distributor' is an organisation with a capacity to distribute audio-visual content via any transmission technique.[105] UEFA further specifies that the content distributor is entitled to transmit the matches on its channel, its website and via mobile wireless technology.[106]

It should be noted that a platform-neutral approach of selling rights does not rule out the possibility that one incumbent acquires all packages and dominates all sports content platforms. Although it seems that it establishes a fair, open and non-discriminatory access to sports broadcasting rights, new media operators wanting live rights have to compete again with established pay-television operators and free-to-air broadcasters.[107] Hence, platform-neutrality does not necessarily provide an adequate answer to the bundling strategies used by established market players.[108] Furthermore, the risk of keeping some of the acquired rights off the market to protect other rights is maintained. In order to alleviate this concern some governing bodies impose a use obligation on the operators who have acquired the rights. In Germany, for example, when an exploiter does not exercise its acquired broadcasting rights on more than two days in a season, those rights may then be sold on a non-exclusive basis until the end of the respective football year by the home clubs concerned.[109] In contrast to the UK, where a material or persistent failure by a purchaser of a package to comply with the obligation to exploit the right will result in the termination of the agreement,[110] not using the rights of the Bundesliga shall not prejudice the further effectiveness of the agreement.[111] With regard to the Champions League rights, when a broadcaster is not planning or is not able to use some rights, the latter fall back to the UEFA and they will exploit those rights via, for example, their website or mobile service. In addition, the same practice is applied for the Europa League rights where each content distributor has the obligation to transmit the live matches which it has acquired. This implies that the content distributor has the obligation to ensure live transmission on its channel, on the Internet as well as live transmission by mobile and/or 'near-live' video clips

---

104 UEFA 2009, 3.

105 *Ibid.*, 4.

106 *Ibid.*, para 1.2.

107 Pickles 2007, 18–19.

108 Evens et al. 2011, 38.

109 *German Bundesliga* case, Annex Commitments of the League Association, para 6.4.

110 *FA Premier League* case, Annex: Commitments of the FAPL, paras 9.2–9.4.

111 *German Bundesliga* case, Annex Commitments of the League Association, para 6.4.

via mobile platforms.[112] A content distributor may use its own website or own mobile portal to broadcast the matches. Alternatively, where a content distributor chooses not to use its own platforms or does not have the means to do so, UEFA can distribute the matches on behalf of the content distributor via an end-to-end solution incorporating a live video service and will be able to assist the content distributor with the provision of mobile services.[113]

Although a trend towards a platform-neutral approach of selling could be recognised (*supra*), the Italian football association decided not to follow this trend. It issued a right's tender, dividing rights into packages defined by their technical delivery mechanism and, thus, ignoring a recent trend for a 'platform-neutral' approach, because it believed that "*the platformed-defined solution [...] better addresses the current market needs in Italy*". The rights are being offered in six exclusive packages: satellite 'platinum live' package including live and delayed transmission of all matches involving all 20 teams, satellite highlight package, 'gold live' digital terrestrial package including live and delayed coverage of matches involving 12 teams, 'silver live' digital terrestrial package including live and delayed transmission of matches played by the remaining eight teams, highlights package for free-to-air television and live radio rights.[114] Sky Italia secured the platinum satellite package for €1.16 billion for the 2010–2011 and 2011–2012 seasons.[115] However, an Italian Court, following a complaint by television channel Conto TV, blocked the awarding of this platinum package to Sky Italia, arguing that the tender was anticompetitive.[116] Although Lega Calcio, the governing body for the top two Italian football leagues, appealed this decision,[117] as a compromise, it offered a second package of satellite rights, comprising 10 min of top-tier Serie A match highlights which can be transmitted immediately after the final whistle. However, Conto TV branded this package 'worthless' compared to the one granted to Sky Italia, which comprises live and delayed transmission of all matches involving all 20 Serie A teams.[118] Milan's Court of Appeal has revoked the interim injunction against Italy's national football league, reversing the previous ruling. The football league is now free to continue negotiating broadcast rights with pay-television providers.[119] In addition, Antitrust, the Italian competition authority, opened an inquiry into whether Lega Calcio had abused its position as the central seller of the rights, because it was suspected that the rights were packaged to benefit incumbent pay-television operators and not the viewers.[120] In January

---

[112] UEFA 2009, 8, 9 and 12.

[113] *Ibid.*, 12–13.

[114] Infront 2009; Sportcal.com 2009c.

[115] Eufootball.biz 2009.

[116] See e.g.: Reuters 2009; Sportsbusiness International 2009.

[117] Reuters 2009; Sportcal.com 2010b.

[118] Sportcal.com 2010a, b.

[119] Bull 2010.

[120] See e.g.: Poncibò 2009.

2010, Antitrust closed its probe because it was satisfied with the additional satellite highlights package offered by Lega Calcio.[121]

E. User-generated content

In the *UEFA Champions League* decision, it was indicated that only "qualified broadcasters" have the opportunity to bid for the rights.[122] A qualified broadcaster is "*a television broadcast organisation that holds a television broadcast license for the relevant territory and that has the appropriate infrastructure, resources and standing to broadcast UEFA Champions League programming*".[123] For the 2009–2012 Europa League media rights, UEFA only accepted bits from content distributors.[124] The 2009–2012 Europa League tender procedure defined a content distributor as "*an organisation with a capacity to distribute audio-visual content via any transmission technique*".[125] Such organisations may include (but shall not be limited to), television broadcasters, Internet service providers, mobile network and/or IPTV operators.[126] The commitments of the German football association state that all marketers and exploiters that meet the technical conditions and qualitative criteria determined by the association are allowed to bid for the rights packages.[127] Qualitative criteria are, for example, audience share, broadcasting schedule, the start of coverage, etc.[128] Hence, in the different tenders, no attention is paid to the (growing role of) prosumers. This means that if prosumers cover sports events on the Internet without the authorisation of the rights holders, they are infringing exclusive deals concluded with other media operators. As indicated above, some sports organisations requested the removal of sports content illegally stored on websites. In order to deal with this issue, Santomier and Costabiei proposed that sports organisations should make some sports content available for the public offering them the possibility to create their own services, such as a video or a blog (supra).[129]

9.3.2.3 Joint Selling Agreement and the Public's Access to Sports Content

A. Introduction

In 2003, then Competition Commissioner Monti stated that, due to the joint selling procedure, there was a real opportunity for free-to-air broadcasters to show

---

[121] See e.g.: Guardian 2010; Eufootball.biz 2010.

[122] *UEFA Champions League* case, para 27.

[123] *Ibid.*, para 28.

[124] UEFA 2009, 5.

[125] *Ibid.*, 4.

[126] *Ibid.*, 5.

[127] *German Bundesliga* case, Annex Commitments of the League Association, para 3.4.

[128] *Ibid.*, para 3.1.

[129] Santomier and Costabiei 2010, 47.

Premier League matches.[130] However, the *FA Premier League* decision as such did not make any reference to the advantage of sports broadcast on free-to-air television for the public's right to information. And neither did the European Commission in the *UEFA Champions League* decision and *German Bundesliga* decision. The authors of the Study on the Lisbon Treaty and EU Sports Policy state it as follows: "*the exemption decision was made out with reference to the economic exemption criteria established in 101(3) TFEU and not to wider social-cultural concerns*".[131] When we take a closer look at the Article 101 (3) exercise in the *UEFA Champions League* case, it is indicated that the viewers' interests, in their role as consumer and not in their role as citizen, have been taken into account. The European Commission considered, for example, that "*[j]oint selling of the media rights of a football tournament provides an advantage for [...] viewers*".[132] In particular, "*[v]iewers [will] benefit from offered multiple forms of coverage of the UEFA Champions League. [...] A viewer is likely to wish to have a choice of being able to watch a match live in its total length and also to be informed about several matches in brief on a delayed basis at several different times*".[133] In other words, "*viewers get access to better quality media coverage [...] allowing them to watch all premium matches of every match day over the course of the entire season which are of particular interest to them*".[134] Furthermore, according to the European Commission, the joint selling practice stimulates media operators to "*invest more in new improved production and transmission technologies, quality television coverage, quality production and presentation,* etc.". This would lead to "*a more intensive and innovative exploitation of the rights to the benefit of the consumer*".[135]

In the UK, Ofcom, when deciding not to replace the current 'no single buyer' commitment by a stricter 'no single buyer' commitment, also applied a consumers' interest approach. In 2008, Ofcom proposed in its second Pay TV Consultation document to replace the current 'no single buyer' commitment by a far more aggressive rule that would prevent the FAPL from selling more than two of its six packages of live rights to one wholesale channel provider.[136] In doing so, Ofcom wanted to secure that "*no one provider has market power*".[137] However, Ofcom abandoned this idea, because the regulator realised that this option could be in detriment to the fans.[138] Ofcom specified this by stating that "*any remedy which prevents or restricts aggregation to the extent that would be necessary to eliminate*

[130] Rapid Press Releases 2003b, 2.

[131] Parrish et al. 2010, 29.

[132] *UEFA Champions League* case, para 143.

[133] *Ibid.*, para 152.

[134] *Ibid.*, para 172.

[135] *Ibid.*, para 171.

[136] Ofcom 2008, para 8.26; Ofcom 2009, para 12.8; Van Rompuy 2009, 119–120.

[137] Ofcom 2008, para 8.25.

[138] Van Rompuy 2009, 120.

market power is also likely to risk sacrificing some of these benefits. [...] It might also result in reduced convenience for some consumers, who would potentially have to take multiple subscriptions or purchase multiple set-top boxes to get the content they want".[139] If more than one platform operator acquires the broadcasting rights of the same competition, fans should take subscriptions on the different platforms and perhaps, they have to buy additional hardware, such as an additional set-top box, to be able to watch the various packages on what will now be a divergence of channels. In practice, in the UK, the consumer benefits following from Setanta's market entry were partially offset. Existing BSkyB subscribers had to buy an additional subscription at a price of at least £9.99 per month in order to watch all the Premier League matches.[140]

However, national competition decisions can be used as an example of how the public's right to information and, in particular access to sport on free-to-air television, has played an (important) role in decisions with regard to the sale of sports broadcasting rights.

B. Access to highlights on free-to-air television

As we take a closer look at the different tender procedures of the national Premier Leagues, it is apparent that the broadcasting of highlights is always reserved for free-to-air broadcasters. In 2009, Premier League chief executive Scudamore even said that "*the free-to-air highlights are a critical part of the Premier League's broadcast presence, helping the competition and our clubs reach the maximum domestic audience possible*".[141] However, pay-television operators were faced with the practice that highlights of matches that were not yet finished or just finished, were already broadcast on free-to-air television in their sports magazines making their live coverage less valuable.

In 2008, the German DFB announced that it would replace the joint selling agreement exempted by the European Commission. The DFB had agreed to sell the broadcasting rights for the first two top divisions for the seasons 2009–2015 to the Sirius Group of Leo Kirch.[142] Under the terms of the deal, Kirch promised clubs at least an annual €500 million in return, as he intended to boost the revenues from pay-television by giving them more exclusivity.[143] However, this deal would have only been if the free-to-air highlights had been pushed back into a later Saturday night slot (not before 10 p.m.).[144] To compensate those late highlights, this plan included a significant increase in the number of live free-to-air games, i.e. 12 live free-to-air matches per season on Saturday evenings.[145] However, the

[139] Ofcom 2008, para 8.27; Ofcom 2009, para 12.8.

[140] Ofcom 2009, para 12.40.

[141] Sportcal.com 2009a.

[142] Sportbusiness International 2008a.

[143] Lefever and Van Rompuy 2009, 257.

[144] Sportbusiness International 2008b.

[145] Sportcal.com 2008a, b, 2009b.

German Competition Authority strongly objected to the agreement, because the second condition for the applicability of Article 101 (3) of the TFEU, i.e. consumers must receive a fair share of the created benefits, was not fulfilled. The latter would only be true if the public would have the opportunity to choose between combined pay-television live coverage and prompt (before 8 p.m.) free-to-air coverage of the highlights of the games.[146] Sirius did not sufficiently guarantee the free-television broadcasting of highlights early on Saturday, which implied that football fans without a pay-television subscription would be worse off in comparison to the existing situation and, thus, would deprive fans the chance to watch their team.[147] Additionally, the German Competition Authority rejected the leagues revised plans, including 30-minute highlights on unencrypted digital television at 7.30 p.m. on Saturday. The DFB had proposed the half-hour highlights at 7.30 p.m. on digital television in an attempt, on the one hand, to satisfy the German Competition Authority's demands for highlights before 8 p.m. and, on the other hand, to protect the exclusivity of pay-television and the value of the broadcasting rights. Although the German Competition Authority insisted on Saturday free-to-air highlights being broadcast 'soon after the whistle' to protect the interests of the public, it rejected the proposal on the basis that the highlights would not have an acceptable reach given that the digital penetration rate was then only limited to only 40 % of the households.[148] Following the objections of the German Competition Authority, the DFB ended the cooperation with Sirius and decided to auction the rights for the 2009–2010 seasons itself.[149] This approach is a good example of a competition authority strongly considering whether the efficiencies resulting from the agreement are passed on to the actual sports fan.[150]

It is important to note that the German Competition Authority did not formally prohibit the DFL marketing model in the end, arguing that it could not prohibit the whole scheme prospectively, but only if and once the critical scenario was really implemented.[151] Because the German Competition Authority failed to issue a formal decision about the DFB's altered plans, the latter went to court. The Higher Regional Court of Düsseldorf dismissed the DFB's complaint, but called on the Competition Authority to deliver a prompt and formal decision in the future.[152]

[146] Bundeskartellamt 2008a, b.

[147] Lefever and Van Rompuy 2009, 257.

[148] See e.g.: Sportcal.com 2008b, c.

[149] Financial Times 2008; Sportcal.com 2009d.

[150] Lefever and Van Rompuy 2009, 258.

[151] Berghen et al. 2009.

[152] See e.g.: Sportcal.com 2009d, e.

In Belgium, the same discussion was held. The programme Sportweekend, after the 7 o'clock news on Sunday, was criticised by Belgacom, the rights holding platform operator, because this programme already broadcast highlights of the matches that were still going on. The same goes for the programme Studio 1, later on Sunday evening, showing highlights of matches that were just finished. As a result, Belgacom claimed that it would only buy the exclusive broadcasting rights for the 2008–2011 seasons if free-to-air broadcasters would be prohibited to broadcast highlights before the matches were finished or too soon after the matches themselves. In order to meet Belgacom's claims, highlights can only be broadcast 60 min after the matches are finished (23 p.m.). This resulted in Studio 1 being removed from the broadcast schedule and replaced by a new show Extra Time on Monday evening. In the Belgian discussion, however, the national competition authority did not intervene.

C. Access to full coverage on free-to-air television

According to the Belgian Competition Council, the European Commission attaches in its decisional practice with regard to the joint selling of broadcasting rights of football leagues high value to the viewers' interest, especially to the principle that as many viewers as possible can see as many games as possible. As a result, from this point of view, the Competition Council considered sublicenses to free-to-air channels pro-competitive.[153] Therefore, the Belgian Competition Council and the Court of Appeal approved the joint sale of broadcasting rights of the Belgian premier League to Belgacom for the 2005–2008 seasons, because the telecom incumbent was the sole candidate who granted sublicenses to free-to-air broadcasters, i.e. VRT—Flemish public broadcaster and RTBF—French public broadcaster, for the exploitation of several packages.[154] In practice, Belgacom sublicensed the highlight rights and allowed the public broadcasters to show one live game on Sunday evening.[155] It has to be said that the deal for the broadcasting of the live games was only for 18 months and had not been extended.

---

[153] Belgian Competition Council 2005, para 31 (6).

[154] *Ibid*, para 36; Court of Appeal of Brussels 2006, para 41.

[155] Court of Appeal 2007, para 41.

References

Legislation and Policy Documents

European Union

Commission Staff Working Document

European Commission (1998a) Commission Staff working paper—the development and prospects for community action in the field of sport. 29 September 1998. http://ec.europa.eu/sport/library/doc/a/doc252_en.pdf. Accessed 19 Aug 2010

Decisions

Commission decision of 23 July 2003 relating to a proceeding pursuant to Article 81 of the EC Treaty and Article 53 of the EEA Agreement, COMP/C.2-37.398—joint selling of the commercial rights of the UEFA Champions League. *OJ* (2003) L 291/25
Commission decision of 22 March 2006 relating to a proceeding pursuant to Article 81 of the EC Treaty (Case COMP/C-2/38.173—Joint selling of media rights to the FA Premier League), Annex: Commitments of the FAPL
European Commission State aid E 3/2005 (ex- CP 2/2003, CP 232/2002, CP 43/2003, CP 243/2004 and CP 195/2004)—financing of public service broadcasters in Germany, 24 April 2007, C (2007) 1761 final

Reports

European Commission (2005) Concluding report on the sector inquiry into the provision of sports content over third generation mobile networks. http://ec.europa.eu/competition/sectors/media/inquiries/final_report.pdf. Accessed 19 Aug 2010

Notices

Commission notice published pursuant to Article 19(3) of Council Regulation No 17 concerning case COMP/C.2/38.173 and 38.453—joint selling of the media rights of the FA Premier League on an exclusive basis. *OJ* (2004) C 115

Press Releases

Rapid Press Releases (2002a) Commission welcomes UEFA's new policy for selling the media rights to the Champions League, 3 June 2002, IP/02/806
Rapid Press Releases (2002b) Commission opens proceedings into joint selling of media rights to the English Premier League, 20 December 2002, IP/02/1951

Rapid Press Releases (2003a) Commission clears UEFA's new policy regarding the sale of the media rights to the Champions League, 24 July 2003, IP/03/1105
Rapid Press Releases (2003b) Commission reaches provisional agreement with FA Premier League and BSkyB over football rights, 16 December 2003, IP/03/1748
Rapid Press Releases (2005a) German Football League commitments to liberalise joint selling of Bundesliga media rights made legally binding by Commission decision, 19 January 2005, IP/05/62
Rapid Press Releases (2005b) Competition: Commission receives improved commitments from FAPL over sale of media rights, 17 November 2005, IP/05/1441
Rapid Press Releases (2006) Commission makes commitments from FA Premier League legally binding, 22 March 2006, IP/06/356

Speeches

Monti M (2000) Sport and competition. 17 April 2000, SPEECH/00/152
Monti M (2001) Competition and sport the rules of the game. 26 February 2001, SPEECH/01/84
Toft T (2003) TV rights of sports events. 15 January 2003. http://ec.europa.eu/comm/competition/speeches/text/sp2003_002_en.pdf. Accessed 19 Aug 2010
Toft T (2006a) EC Competition Law aspects: sports rights in a converging media technology environment. 30 March 2006. http://ec.europa.eu/competition/speeches/text/sp2006_002_en.pdf. Accessed 19 Aug 2010
Torben T (2006b) Developments in European law, congress sports & law. 28 April 2006. http://ec.europa.eu/comm/competition/speeches/text/sp2006_003_en.pdf. Acessed 19 Aug 2010
Ungerer H (2003) Commercialising sport—Understanding the TV Rights debate, 2 October 2003. http://ec.europa.eu/comm/competition/speeches/text/sp2003_024_en.pdf. Accessed 19 Aug 2010

Miscallanious

European Commission (1998b) The European model of sport. http://ec.europa.eu/sport/library/doc/a/doc248_en.pdf. Accessed 19 Aug 2010

UK

Consultations

Ofcom (2007) Summary of UK sports rights—Annex 10 to pay TV market investigation consultation. http://stakeholders.ofcom.org.uk/binaries/consultations/market_invest_paytv/annexes/annex_10.pdf. Accessed 18 Aug 2010
Ofcom (2008) Pay TV second consultation—access to premium content. http://stakeholders.ofcom.org.uk/binaries/consultations/second_paytv/summary/condoc.pdf. Accessed 18 Aug 2010
Ofcom (2009) Pay TV phase three document: proposed remedies. http://stakeholders.ofcom.org.uk/binaries/consultations/third_paytv/summary/paytv_condoc.pdf. Accessed 18 Aug 2010

Reports

Independent Advisory Panel to the Secretary of State for Culture, Media and Sport (2009) Review of free-to-air listed events. http://www.culture.gov.uk/images/publications/independentpanel report-to-SoS-Free-to-air-Nov2009.pdf. Accessed 19 Nov 2009, no longer available

Case law

Court of Justice

CJ Coditel SA and others v Ciné-Vog Films SA and others, 6 October 1982, Case 262/81, ECR (1982) 3381

CJ Football Association Premier League Ltd and Others v. QC Leisure and Others and Karen Murphy v. Media Protection Services Ltd, 3 February 2011, joined Cases C 403/08 and C 429/08 (not yet published in ECR)

Belgium

Belgian Competition Council (2005). Decision no. 2005-I/O-40 of 29 July 2005, Tijdschrift van Rechtspraak van de Raad voor de Mededinging, vol 3, pp 27–47

Court of Appeal of Brussels (2006) Telenet N.V. v. Liga Beroepsvoetbal V.Z.W.—28 June 2006

Doctrine

Andriychuk O (2009) Sports broadcasting rights in the digital epoch: balancing between traditional (TV) and alternative (3G) subjects of the market from the perspective of the European competition law. In: Blackshaw I et al (eds) TV rights and sport. Legal aspects. T.M.C. Asser press, The Hague, pp 81–103

Bavasso A (2003) Communications in EU antitrust law: market power and public interest. Kluwer Law International, The Hague

BBC News (2009) Setanta goes into administration, 23 June 2009. http://news.bbc.co.uk/2/hi/8115360.stm. Accessed 19 Aug 2010

Berghen M et al (2009) Germany. In the handbook of competition economics. http://www.globalcompetitionreview.com/_files/_handbooks/_18/gcr_hce09_overview_germany.pdf. Accessed 19 Aug 2010

Boyle R, Haynes R (2003) New media sport. In: Bernstein A, Blain N (eds) Sport, media, culture: global and local dimensions. Cass, London, pp 95–114

Bull R (2010) Court repeals football league injunction. http://www.globalcompetitionreview.com/news/article/27788/. Accessed 19 Aug 2010

Bundeskartellamt (2008a) Central marketing: DFL has to improve consumer involvement, 17 July 2008. http://www.bundeskartellamt.de/wEnglisch/News/Archiv/ArchivNews2008/2008_07_17.php. Accessed 19 Aug 2010

Bundeskartellamt (2008b) DFL marketing model for TV broadcasting rights does not meet competition law requirements, 24 July 2008. http://www.bundeskartellamt.de/wEnglisch/News/Archiv/ArchivNews2008/2008_07_24.php. Accessed 19 Aug 2010

CNet News (2008) Panasonic plasma TV streams YouTube, accesses Picasa photos, 20 May 2008. http://news.cnet.com/8301-17938_105-9948400-1.html. Accessed 12 July 2011

Elspass M, Kettner M (2008) Article 81 EC. In: Castendyk O et al (eds) European media law. Kluwer Law International, Alphen a/d Rijn, pp 123–149

Eufootball.biz (2009) Lega Calcio award Italian rights, 31 July 2009. http://www.eufootball.biz/Television/7379-lega_calcio_italian_rights.html. Accessed 19 Aug 2010

Eufootball.biz (2010) TV rights sales probe in Italy completed, 22 January 2010. http://www.eufootball.biz/Television/7920-tv_rights_sales_probe_italy_completed.html. Accessed 19 Aug 2010

Evans D, Schmalensee R (2009) Failure to launch: critical mass in platform businesses. http://ssrn.com/abstract=1353502. Accessed 19 Aug 2010

Evens et al (2008) Adoption versus use diffusion. Predicting user acceptance of mobile TV in flanders. In: Proceedings of international joint conference on e-business and telecommunications, Porto, 26–29 July 2009, pp 124–130

Evens T et al (2011) Access to premium content on mobile television platforms: the case of mobile sports. Telematics Inf 28:32–39

Financial Times (2008) Kirch denied media comeback, 27 September 2008. http://www.ft.com/cms/s/0/f0febecc-8c2d-11dd-8a4c-0000779fd18c.html?nclick_check=1 Accessed 18 Sept 2009, no longer available

Geey D (2009a) Ongoing broadcasting challenges for the premier league. http://www.danielgeey.com/pdf/a-ongoing-pl-challenges-art.pdf. Accessed 23 Aug 2010

Geey D (2009b) PL rights auction: economic and regulatory challenges. World Sports L Rep 1:3–5

Geey D, Day J (2006) 'Publicasting': enforcement and competition concerns. World Sports L Rept 12:10–12

Geradin D (2005) Access to content by new media platforms: a review of the competition law problems. http://www.coleurope.be/content/gclc/documents/GCLC%20Working%20Paper%2001-04.pdf. Accessed 18 Aug 2010

Grant M (2009) Digital sports rights, Westminster media forum keynote seminar: the future for broadcast sports and free-to-air events, London, 27 October 2009

Guardian (2009) Setanta goes off air with loss of more than 200 jobs, 23 June 2009. http://www.guardian.co.uk/media/2009/jun/23/setanta-goes-into-administration. Accessed 19 Aug 2010

Guardian (2010) Italy antitrust ends TV soccer rights probe, 18 January 2010. http://www.guardian.co.uk/business/feedarticle/8904613. Accessed 18 Jan 2010, no longer available

Hatton C et al (2007) Fair play: how competition authorities have regulated the sale of football media rights in Europe. Eur Compét L Rev 28(6):346–354

Infront (2009) Lega Calcio launches tender process for Serie A assisted by infront, 10 July 2009. http://www.infrontsports.com/presscenter/newsdetail/period/01.07.2009///select/football/article/lega-calcio/114/?tx_ttnews%5Bswords%5D=Italy&tx_ttnews%5BpE%5D=01.08.2009&cHash=f8ef9f3a1f. Accessed 19 Aug 2010

Kienappel P, Stein A (2007) The application of Articles 81 and 82 EC in the sport sector. Compét Policy Newslett 3:6–14

Lefever K, Van Rompuy B (2009) Ensuring access to sports content: 10 years of EU intervention. Time to celebrate? J Media L 2:243–268

Massey R (2009) The Karen Murphy reference—copyright, euro defences and the territorial licensing of TV rights. Entertain L Rev 1:38–39

Parrish R, Miettinen S (2008) The sporting exception in European Union law. T.M.C. Asser institute, The Hague

Parrish R, Miettinen S (2009) Sports broadcasting in community law. In: Blackshaw I et al (eds) TV rights and sport. Legal aspects. T.M.C. Asser press, The Hague, pp 9–33

Parrish R et al (2010) The Lisbon Treaty and EU Sports Policy—study. http://www.europarl.europa.eu/activities/committees/studies/download.do?language=en&file=32471. Accessed 14 Oct 2010

Petit N (2004) The Commission's contribution to the emergence of 3G mobile communications: and analysis of some decisions in the field of competition law. Eur Compet L Rev 25(7):429–438

Pickles J (2007) Will sport be a 'battering ram' for mobile TV? Or will carriers be put off by the battle for (changing) sports rights? Intermedia 35(3):18–20

Poncibò C (2009) The Italian Competition Authority is investigating the sale of television rights for soccer matches ("Lega Calcio"—procedure selettive lega nazionale professionisti campionati). EU Competition Laws e-bulletin, n° 29821. www.concurrences.com. Accessed 19 Aug 2010

Reuters (2009) Milan court blocks Sky Italia soccer rights win, 4 November 2009. http://uk.reuters.com/article/idUKTRE5A351920091104. Accessed 19 Aug 2010

Rumphorst W (2001) Sports broadcasting rights and EC competition law. 25 July 2001. http://www.ebu.ch/CMSimages/en/leg_p_sports_rights_wr_tcm6-4406.pdf. Accessed 19 Aug 2010

Saltzman R (2000) Television news access to exclusively owned sporting events: a comparative study. Sports Lawyers J 7:1–28

Santomier J, Costabiei A (2010) New media challenges in the twenty-first century. In: Hamil S, Chadwick S (eds) Managing football: an international perspective. Elsevier, Amsterdam, pp 37–54

Scheuer A, Strothmann P (2004) Sports as reflected in European media law part I. Iris Plus. http://www.obs.coe.int/oea_publ/iris/iris_plus/iplus4_2004.pdf.en. Accessed 19 Aug 2010

Sportbusiness International (2008a) Bundesliga TV deal could be under threat, 11 March 2008. http://www.sportbusiness.com/news/166339/bundesliga-tv-deal-could-be-under-threat Accessed 19 Aug 2010

Sportbusiness International (2008b) Kirch contract cancelled, 26 September 2008. http://www.sportbusiness.com/news/167914/kirch-contract-cancelled. Accessed 19 Aug 2010

Sportsbusiness International (2009) Sky Italia's Serie A rights deal blocked by court, 6 November 2009. http://www.sportbusiness.com/news/170888/sky-italia-s-serie-a-rights-deal-blocked-by-court. Accessed 19 Aug 2010

Sportcal.com (2008a) One free-to-air Bundesliga match per week 'makes sense', 29 February 2008. http://sportcal.com/news/news_article.aspx?previouspage=news_list.aspx&pageno=119&articleID=48122. Accessed 20 Jan 2010

Sportcal.com (2008b) DFL's TV rights packages offer more free-to-air Bundesliga games, 21 May 2008. http://sportcal.com/news/news_article.aspx?previouspage=news_list.aspx&pageno=103&articleID=60202. Accessed 20 Jan 2010

Sportcal.com (2008c) DFL readies legal firepower after latest cartel office snub, 18 August 2008. http://sportcal.com/news/news_article.aspx?previouspage=news_list.aspx&pageno=91&articleID=61778. Accessed 20 Jan 2010

Sportcal.com (2009a) BBC secures new premier league highlights deal, 28 January 2009. http://sportcal.com/news/news_article.aspx?previouspage=news_list.aspx&pageno=49&articleID=64634. Accessed 20 Jan 2010

Sportcal.com (2009b) Cartel office: Bundesliga TV model meant higher subscription fees, 4 February 2009. http://sportcal.com/news/news_article.aspx?previouspage=news_list.aspx&pageno=48&articleID=64749. Accessed 20 Jan 2010

Sportcal.com (2009c) No platform-neutral approach for Serie A in media rights tender, 10 July 2009. http://sportcal.com/news/news_article.aspx?previouspage=news_list.aspx&pageno=25&articleID=67882. Accessed 20 Jan 2010

Sportcal.com (2009d) DFL loses TV rights court case but cartel office told to change, 16 September 2009. http://sportcal.com/news/news_article.aspx?previouspage=news_list.aspx&pageno=15&articleID=69202. Accessed 20 Jan 2010

Sportcal.com (2010a) Conto TV: Serie A compromise TV rights package is 'worthless', 15 January 2010. http://sportcal.com/news/news_article.aspx?previouspage=news_list.aspx&pageno=0&articleID=71476. Accessed 20 Jan 2010

Sportcal.com (2010b) Antitrust concludes probe into Serie A rights tender, 19 January 2010. http://sportcal.com/news/news_article.aspx?previouspage=news_list.aspx&pageno=0&articleID=71521. Accessed 20 Jan 2010

Stewart S (2009) The development of sports law in the European Union, its globalisation, and the competition law aspects of European sports broadcasting rights. Sports Lawyers J 16:183–229

Subiotto R, Graf T (2003) Analysis of the principles applicable to the review of exclusive broadcasting licences under EC competition law. World compét 26(4):589–608

Thorntona P, Takaseb K (2008) Sky and the premier league v. pub landlords. Comput L Secur Rep 24(2):181–186

UEFA (2008) Media content rights sales, 16 January 2008. http://en.uefa.com/MultimediaFiles/Download/Competitions/UEFACup_/67/58/75/675875_DOWNLOAD.pdf. Accessed 19 Aug 2010

UEFA (2009) Invitation to submit offers—UEFA Europa League 2009–2012 media rights (not published)

Van den Bogaert S, Vermeersch A (2006) Sport and the EC Treaty: a tale of uneasy bedfellows. EL Rev 31(6):821–840

Van Rompuy B (2009) Fair access to exclusive sports rights still a long shot in UK pay TV market. Commun L 14(4):118–122

Wessberg (2000) Sport, television and the Internet. http://www.ebu.ch/news/press_archive/2003_and_prev/press_news_1100a.html. Accessed on 29 Dec 2011

X (2009) Sports broadcasting in the digital era. Commun L Bull 27(4):15–20

Chapter 10
Sublicensing Obligation

10.1 Introduction

The issue of 'unused rights' is a concern that has arisen in the broadcasting sector. The coverage and scheduling of sports events is often a commercial decision, primarily driven by the potential to earn advertising revenue. As a result, broadcasters are most likely to schedule programmes or events they believe will attract the largest viewing audience and, therefore, increase the potential financial return from advertisers.[1] This could result in a situation where broadcasters, although they have bought the rights to a specific sports event, decide not to broadcast it. The warehousing of unused rights can be labelled as being detrimental to the competitors' interest as well as the public's interest. The former do not get the chance to broadcast the sports event, because they do not have the rights while the latter do not get the chance to watch the sports event.

In different speeches and decisions, the European Commission has welcomed sublicensing obligations as an effective remedy to address the risk of exclusive broadcasting rights being unused and, thus, to guarantee third parties' access to broadcasting rights.[2] Hence, when a sublicensing obligation is imposed on a media player, the latter has the obligation to share all or a part of its rights with interested third parties to ensure that these rights are effectively exploited.[3]

However, it should be noted that, as indicated by the European Commission, the mere establishment of a sublicensing system is not in itself a satisfactory solution. To be effective, the value of sublicensing will depend on the terms on which sublicenses are granted.[4] First, terms must be fair, transparent, reasonable and

[1] Department of Broadband, Communications and the Digital Economy 2009, 17; FACTS 2001, 13.

[2] See e.g.: Temple Lang 1997, 39; Schaub 2002, 8.

[3] Wachtmeister 1998, 26; Subiotto and Graf 2004, 20; Tsiotsou 2005, 79.

[4] Wachtmeister 1998, 27.

K. Lefever, *New Media and Sport*, ASSER International Sports Law Series, DOI: 10.1007/978-90-6704-873-6_10,

nondiscriminatory so that wider access to the rights to other market players will be guaranteed and, thus, that the sublicensees get a real chance to compete on the market.[5] Hence, if the terms of the sublicenses are unfair or discriminatory, this obligation will not take away the restrictive character of the underlying exclusive license.[6] Interestingly, in the Notice that the European Commission issued upon sending a statement of objections to UEFA concerning the UEFA Champions League joint selling agreement (*supra*), it criticised the rudimentary sublicensing arrangements that had been in place for allowing only one other broadcaster per Member State to broadcast Champions League matches.[7] In the European Commission's view, UEFA's sublicensing system did not provide a satisfactory mitigating effect.[8] Furthermore, the terms of the sublicensing obligation must deal with the cost of the sublicensing, access to (un)edited material, embargoes on live transmission or on transmission at popular times.[9] As indicated by Wachtmeister and van den Brink, a situation where the price of the sublicenses is unregulated is not desirable. Broadcasters obtaining exclusive broadcasting rights could then charge other broadcasters excessive, and even monopolistic, prices.[10] Finally, it is important that the terms should be known in advance.[11] If the acquirer does not know what the terms of sublicenses will be, he cannot calculate precisely how much he should offer for the right to broadcast the events in question. Lange and Wachtmeister stressed that the European Commission would be unlikely to get involved in determining those terms. If this had to be regulated, it would have to be done by a national regulator, in practice, not by the European Commission.[12]

In the following section, the impact of the changing media landscape on the way competition law is dealing with the public's access to information when imposing sublicensing obligations will be analysed. Before we go further, attention should be drawn to the distinction between unused rights when broadcasters decide not to show the events and unused rights as a result of rights holders not being able to sell their rights. In order to clarify the difference, the latter will be referred to as unsold rights while the former will be referred to as unused rights.

---

[5] See e.g.: *Ibid.*, 27; Toft 2003, 15.

[6] van den Brink 2000, 118.

[7] European Commission 1999.

[8] Toft 2003, 12.

[9] See e.g.: Wachtmeister 1998, 27; van den Brink 2000, 118.

[10] Wachtmeister 1998, 27; van den Brink 2000, 118.

[11] Temple Lang 1997, 39.

[12] *Ibid.*, 40–39; Wachtmeister 1998, 27.

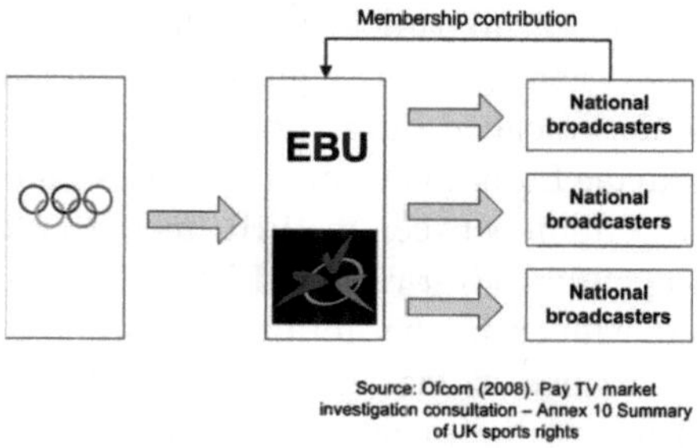

Fig. 10.1 Joint buying mechanism. *Source*: Ofcom (2008)

10.2 Sublicensing Obligation and Joint Buying Agreements

10.2.1 Introduction

Competition problems occur in situations where one entity representing several competitors is involved in the acquisition of exclusive broadcasting rights.[13] In practice, broadcasting rights for international sports events are acquired jointly by all interested members, who then share the rights and the related fee between them.[14] The joint buying mechanism can be illustrated as in Fig. 10.1.

Given that joint buying agreements could have a negative impact on competition, the European Commission decided to intervene and opened an investigation into the compatibility of this joint buying arrangement with Article 101 of the TFEU. The European Commission's approach with regard to the joint buying mechanism can be illustrated by the *EBU/Eurovision system* case. The European Broadcasting Union (EBU) is an association of national broadcasters. The EBU's purpose is to serve and support the interests of its members, to exchange content between members and to acquire a variety of sports rights on behalf of its members, i.e. better known as the joint buying mechanism.[15] Given that the European Commission's objections are similar to those expressed in the joint selling decisions, this decision will not be dealt with in detail, but only the relevant parts will be discussed.

10.2.2 Article 101 (1) of the TFEU and Joint Buying Agreement

In 1989, the EBU applied for an exemption pursuant to Article 101 (3) of the TFEU for its Eurovision system. This system is a European exchange system for television programmes, including sports programmes, in which all active members

---

[13] Elspass and Kettner 2008, 132.

[14] *EBU/Eurovision System* case, para 27.

[15] EBU 2009.

of the EBU are eligible to participate. Additionally, all the members are obliged to participate in a system of joint acquisition of broadcasting rights to international sports events, the so-called Eurovision rights.[16]

According to the European Commission, this Eurovision system restricts, on the one hand, competition between the EBU members themselves[17] and, on the other hand, the competition *vis-à-vis* non-EBU members.[18] Since the EBU members would compete with each other for the acquisition of broadcasting rights to sports events in the absence of the agreement, the European Commission found that competition between the members is "*greatly restricted if not, in many cases, eliminated*".[19] Additionally, the European Commission found that competition *vis-à-vis* non-EBU members is distorted "*as they cannot participate in the rationalisation and cost-savings achieved by the Eurovision system, which renders the broadcasting of sports events more expensive and complicated for them*".[20] Moreover, given that international sports federations often prefer to dispose of the broadcasting rights for a large area in one transaction instead of becoming involved in negotiations with numerous national broadcasters, the EBU members are given an advantage by bidding jointly.[21]

10.2.3 Article 101 (3) of the TFEU and Joint Buying Agreement

Although the joint buying agreements could restrict competition, the European Commission found the restrictions justified given the several advantages attached to the Eurovision system. First, the joint negotiation and joint acquisition of the broadcasting rights reduce the transaction costs which would be associated with a multitude of separate negotiations.[22] Second, the public was granted a fair share of the benefit, because they were able to access more high-quality sports programmes of both popular and minority sports than they would be able to do without the advantages of Eurovision (*infra*).[23] Third, the restrictions were indispensable, as the same result could not be achieved by less restrictive means.[24] Fourth, the system did not allow the participating members to eliminate competition for a substantial part of the products, because only international events (and not national

16 *EBU/Eurovision System* case, para 26.

17 *Ibid.*, para 47–49.

18 *Ibid.*, para 50–52.

19 *Ibid.*, para 48–49.

20 *Ibid.*, para 50.

21 *Ibid.*, para 51.

22 *Ibid.*, para 59.

23 *Ibid.*, para 62 & 68.

24 *Ibid.*, para 69–70.

events) were covered and there was enough competition from independent broadcasters.[25]

Due to these benefits, the European Commission adopted a decision that granted an exemption to the arrangement, albeit conditional upon the acceptance of a revised sublicensing scheme[26] enabling non-EBU members' access to the jointly acquired broadcasting rights to sports events.[27] Non-EBU members get access to the unused rights when an EBU member does not transmit any part or only a minor part of sports events.[28]

The *EBU/Eurovision System* case makes numerous references to the public mission characteristic of public service broadcasters and their specific approach to sports coverage benefiting the public.[29] Starting from the observation that increased competition from private broadcasters had moved the broadcasting rights of certain major sport events into the hands of new commercial channels,[30] the European Commission was concerned that high-quality coverage reaching the entire population was endangered.[31] In paragraph 19 of the *EBU/Eurovision System* case, the European Commission specified that "*according to whether sports programmes are more or less attractive to viewers and hence to advertisers and according to the costs and risks involved in the broadcasting of sports events, public mission-oriented broadcasters and purely commercial broadcasters often take a different approach to the broadcasting of sports events*". According to the European Commission, commercial broadcasters are more interested in mass-appeal sports events allowing them to attract advertisers and viewers, whereas public mission-oriented broadcasters also have to cover minority sports or less attractive events, as by virtue of their public mission. As a result, public mission-oriented channels normally show a broader range of sports than purely commercial channels.[32] Hence, the latter shows that media policy concerns, and thus non-economic considerations are not totally absent from the European Commission's practice.[33]

Harrison and Woods indicated that the European Commission has recognised a public interest dimension by accepting the importance of public service broadcasters' ability to provide free-to-air access to sporting events to a large public.[34]

---

25 *Ibid.*, para 77; Nitsche 2001, 94.

26 The modified access scheme for non-members can be found in: *EBU/Eurovision System* case, para 36–40.

27 *EBU/Eurovision System* case, Article 1; Lefever and Van Rompuy 2009, 254.

28 Commission decision, 10 May Commission decision of 10 May 2000 (hereafter: *Eurovision* case), Annex I EBU non-members' access to Eurovision sports programmes; Font Galarza 2000, 29.

29 *EBU/Eurovision System* case, para 5, 11, 19–20, 45, 60, 72, 74.

30 *Ibid.*, para 11.

31 Lefever and Van Rompuy 2009, 254.

32 *EBU/Eurovision System* case, para 19.

33 Ariño 2004b, 107.

34 Harrison and Woods 2007, 270–271.

Viewers who cannot afford to pay the extra subscription fees required by private commercial broadcasters would not be able to watch a given event if the event was broadcast on those commercial channels. The Eurovision system, however, enables those viewers to watch sports events by guaranteeing public broadcasters to acquire broadcasting rights and then broadcast the event on free-to-air television.[35] According to Townley, the European Commission has given a lot of weight to this non-economic consideration in this decision. Nevertheless, he regretted that the European Commission did not clarify the weight it attributed to this public policy objective in the balance.[36] Ariño argued that a greater transparency about the real objectives pursued would be desirable.[37]

Different commercial broadcasters that were unable to gain access to the Eurovision rights successfully challenged the decision before the General Court.[38] The General Court heavily criticised the European Commission for referring to the mission of providing services of general economic interest (referred to in Article 106 (2) of the TFEU [ex 86 (2) of the EC Treaty]) in order to justify the EBU being granted a special status with regard to the application of the antitrust rules.[39] As the decision in itself indicated that Article 106 (2) of the TFEU was not applicable in this case, the General Court reasoned that factors coming essentially within the ambit of this Article cannot constitute a criterion for the application of Article 101 (3) of the TFEU.[40] The General Court further annulled the decision for failing to demonstrate that the EBU membership rules were objective and sufficiently determinated so as to enable their application in a uniform and non-discriminatory manner.[41] Nevertheless, as indicated by Monti, it is important to note that the General Court has suggested in its decision a very wide scope of factors which can justify exemption under Article 101 (3) of the TFEU.[42] In paragraph 118 of this decision, the General Court explicitly admitted that "*in the context of an overall assessment, the Commission is entitled to base itself on considerations connected with the pursuit of the public interest in order to grant exemption under Article 85(3) of the Treaty*".

Consequently, in 2000, the European Commission adopted a new decision in favour of the Eurovision system.[43] This time, it carefully omitted any explicit consideration of the public mission of EBU members or the benefits of the broadcasting of sports events on public service broadcasters for sports fans.[44] As

---

[35] Mark Meltz 1999, 116–117.

[36] Townley 2010, 75.

[37] Ariño 2004a, 158.

[38] GC, Metropole télévision SA and others v. Commission (hereafter: *Metropole television* case—GC, Metropole télévision SA and others v. Commission, 11 July 1996), para 126.

[39] See e.g.: *Metropole television* case, para 117; Faull and Nikpay 2007, 1507.

[40] *Metropole television* case, para 114–124; Lefever and Van Rompuy 2009, 254.

[41] *Metropole television* case, para 102.

[42] Monti 2002, 1057.

[43] *Eurovision* case.

[44] Lefever and Van Rompuy 2009, 254–255.

an addition to the 1993 scheme, the EBU submitted a set of sublicensing rules relating to exploitation of Eurovision rights on pay-television channels in order to ensure that the joint buying agreement of the EBU would not unfairly place pay-television competitors in disadvantage. In short, a non-EBU member has the right to transmit on its pay-television channel identical or comparable competitions to those presented on the EBU member's pay-television channel.[45] As in the previous decision, the European Commission emphasised that the public was granted a fair share of the benefit because they were able to access more high-quality sports programmes of both popular and minority sports than without the advantages of the Eurovision system.[46]

Once again, the decision was annulled by the General Court.[47] The General Court disagreed with the European Commission[48] that the sublicensing scheme guaranteed competitors of EBU members sufficient access to live broadcasting rights not used by the latter.[49] According to the General Court, "*contrary to what the Commission contends, the sub-licensing scheme does not guarantee that live transmission rights which are not used by EBU members are made available to their competitors*".[50] It was shown that the provisions regarding the sublicensing of the rights for live broadcasts could only guarantee the transfer of residual rights in which the EBU members had expressed no interest.[51] The EBU nonmembers' access rules specify that "*if an event is not transmitted live by any of the members of Eurovision [...] a non-member [...] may transmit the event live*".[52] Given that an event is considered to be transmitted live "*if the majority of the principal competitions constituting it are transmitted live*",[53] this implies that an EBU member only needs to reserve the live transmission of the majority of the competitions of an event in order to refuse nonmembers competing for the same market a sublicense for live transmission of the entire event, including competitions in that event which

---

[45] Font Galarza 2000, 29; *Eurovision* case, Annex II Sublicensing rules relating to the exploitation of Eurovision rights on pay-TV channels.

[46] *Eurovision* case, para 91.

[47] GC, Metropole télévision SA and others v. Commission (hereafter: *Metropole television* case—GC, Metropole télévision SA and others v. Commission, 8 October 2002), para 86.

[48] *Eurovision* case, para 28–37, 106–110; *Eurovision* case, Annex I EBU non-members' access to Eurovision sports programmes; *Eurovision* case, Annex II Sublicensing rules relating to the exploitation of Eurovision rights on pay-TV channels.

[49] *Metropole television* case—GC, Metropole télévision SA and others v. Commission, 8 October 2002, para 79 & 83; Lefever and Van Rompuy 2009, 255.

[50] *Metropole television* case – GC, Metropole télévision SA and others v. Commission, 8 October 2002, para 79.

[51] Hatton et al. 2007, 347.

[52] *Eurovision* case, Annex I EBU non-members' access to Eurovision sports programmes, para 1.1–1.2.

[53] *Ibid.*, para 1.3.

no EBU member will transmit live.[54] Furthermore, even when an EBU member transmits less than the majority of the competitions of a sporting event on its free-to-air channel, but nevertheless broadcasts the remaining competitions of that event on its pay-television channel, the nonmember of EBU has access only to deferred transmission, unless it itself is a pay-television channel.[55] This meant that the European Commission's view that the sublicensing scheme prevented the elimination of competition in relevant market was not well founded and that, therefore, the European Commission had made a manifest error of assessment.[56] Hence, the European Commission and the EBU were forced to work on a third decision.[57]

In 2007, however, seven years after the General Court's annulment of the second exemption decision, the European Commission decided to close the case without adopting a final decision.[58] It did so by merely pointing out that, contrary to the past where EBU was the sole buyer of premium international sports rights, as a result of new entrants and the increased capacity devoted to sports broadcasts, the buying power of the EBU had recently declined. As a way of conclusion, the European Commission stressed that it "*will continue to monitor the rapidly changing media sector. Access to premium content by broadcasters and, in particular, new media operators remains a concern for the Commission*".[59] As indicated by Iosifidis and Smith, in terms of the joint buying of broadcasting rights, the biggest threat to the EBU comes from the sports organisations being keen to maximise the value of their broadcasting rights.[60] In 2009, for example, the IOC rejected EBU's bid for the exclusive broadcasting rights to the Olympic Games 2014 & 2016 and sold the rights (across all platforms) to Sportfive. Sportfive has the duty to market the broadcasting rights to individual broadcasters.[61]

10.3 Sublicensing Obligation and Public Service Broadcasters' Funding

10.3.1 Introduction

In the previous section, it is indicated how the European Commission dealt with the competition problems created by the joint buying of rights by the EBU. However, it should be noted that the market will not only be distorted when public

---

[54] *Metropole television* case—GC, Metropole télévision SA and others v. Commission, 8 October 2002, para 71.

[55] *Ibid.*, para 74.

[56] Weatherill 2007, 319.

[57] Elspass and Kettner 2008, 146.

[58] Lefever and Van Rompuy 2009, 257.

[59] European Commission 2007, 114.

[60] Iosifidis and Smith 2011.

[61] IOC 2009.

service broadcasters acquire sports broadcasting rights jointly. Indeed, the same issues can arise when public service broadcasters buy those rights individually.

As indicated by Donders, in the debate on the acquisition of sports broadcasting rights by public broadcasters, two opposite perspectives can be observed. On the one hand, private broadcasters, looking at the activities of public broadcasters from a market distortion perspective, claim that public broadcasters focus too much on popular sports events and, more importantly, increase prices on the sports broadcasting rights markets. On the other hand, public broadcasters, considering sport as a public good, maintain that covering sports events is part of their remit. They show less popular sports, they devote attention to a more extensive and in-depth coverage of sports events and they are universally available.[62]

Hence, in State aid cases, the question that often rises is whether sport falls within the remit of public broadcasters and, thus, whether public broadcasters are allowed to buy sports broadcasting rights. In an increasingly competitive market, such as the market for the acquisition of sports broadcasting rights, private broadcasters perceive the public broadcasters' presence in the sports rights markets and the public broadcasters' usage of public money to bid for sports rights as unfair competition.[63] Although an analysis of this question falls outside the scope of this book, it can be said that the European Commission has stressed that sport can be part of a broadly defined public service remit to offer a varied and balanced programme.[64]

This section will take a closer look at how the European Commission, using State aid rules, has dealt with the situation where public service broadcasters decide not to use the sports broadcasting rights in the changed media landscape. Two decisions dealing with unused sports broadcasting rights will be examined: the *Flemish public broadcaster state aid* case will be highlighted and the *German public broadcaster state aid* case will be described in more detail. Specifically, it will be analysed how competition authorities, when imposing sublicensing obligations, have dealt with the development of new media and whether this had an impact on the way competition authorities have dealt with the public's access to sports content. Although the *Flemish public broadcaster state aid* case and the *German public broadcaster state aid* also dealt with the question whether offering new media services is part of the public broadcaster's remit,[65] this question will not be touched upon in this section, because it was not linked with the exploitation of sports broadcasting rights.

---

[62] Donders 2010.

[63] *Ibid.*

[64] See e.g.: Commission decision, 22 June Commission decision of 22 June 2006, para 121;*German public broadcaster state aid* case, para 242.

[65] *German public broadcaster state aid* case, para 229–236; Commission decision, 22 February Commission decision of 22 February 2008, para 175–184.

10.3.2 *Unused Rights and The Flemish Public Service Broadcaster (VRT)*

In 2004, VRT launched Sporza, a new specialist sports channel for the 2004 sports summer. According to the Belgian government, given that sport is part of the public service broadcaster's mission, the creation of this channel was necessary to fulfil the public service broadcaster's remit. Without Sporza, too much sports events would have to be broadcast on the generalist channels of the VRT changing the regular programme schedule too drastically.[66] The VMMa, the main commercial competitor of the VRT, argued that the creation of Sporza illustrated that the VRT was overcompensated.[67] As a result, the VMMa lodged a complaint with the European Commission accusing VRT of the unlawful use of government funding.[68] Furthermore, the commercial broadcaster emphasised that this dedicated sports channel was launched in order to broadcast rights that would otherwise remain unused.[69]

Although VMMa's complaint mainly focused on the issue of sports broadcasting rights, Donders stressed that "*the European Commission's decision on the funding of Flemish public broadcaster VRT devotes considerably less attention to this issue*".[70] The European Commission indicated that with regard to the acquisition of sports broadcasting rights, the financial aid given to the VRT could have a negative effect on competition, because commercial broadcasters have to compete with public service broadcasters for exclusive broadcasting rights. Commercial broadcasters have to finance these rights based on commercial revenues only, while public broadcasters are funded by the State without having to assure the refinancing of the rights.[71] However, the fact that the Flemish government promised to ensure that the creation of additional channels is preceded by a formal entrustment of the Flemish government in the future, this, so the European Commission said, is sufficient to avoid anticompetitive practices from happening.[72] Moreover, no explicit reference is made to the problem of unused rights.

---

[66] Commission decision, 22 February Commission decision of 22 February 2008, para 60; Donders 2010.

[67] Commission decision, 22 February Commission decision of 22 February 2008, para 57.

[68] Frieda Saeys and Frédéric Antoine Saeys and Antoine 2007, 122.

[69] Donders 2010.

[70] *Ibid.*

[71] Commission decision, 22 February Commission decision of 22 February 2008, para 111.

[72] *Ibid.*, 248; Donders 2010.

10.3.3 Unused Rights and the German Public Service Broadcasters

In contrast to the previous decision, the practice of the public service broadcasters' refusal to grant sublicenses for unused rights, both for broadcasting rights of traditional media and new media, is dealt with in the *German public broadcaster state aid* case. In 2004, the European Commission received complaints from German commercial broadcasters that the German public service broadcasters acquired exclusive and extensive sports rights packages, including new media as well as pay-television rights, without fully using those rights and even refusing to grant sublicenses to third parties, which distorted competition.[73] Germany did not agree that rights remained unused. It pointed out that, as regards the Olympic Games for example, what is acquired are not broadcasted hours, but the overall events and that even if public service broadcasters had shown only a selection of all available events, the rights could not be regarded as unused.[74]

The European Commission did not consider that "*the current financing regime allows public broadcasters to structurally outbid private competitors by offering consistently and regularly prices which are significantly higher than what private operators would be able to pay and thus "empty" the market*".[75] However, with regard to possible market distortions, the fact that some sports broadcasting rights remained unused was seen as a problem. Although the European Commission recognised that "*there may be objective constraints or justifications for not using all rights potentially available*", it stressed that "*there needs to be a balance between [...] the need [of public service broadcasters] for some flexibility in the planning of events, on the one hand and market distortions that are not necessary for the fulfilment of the public service due to rights being acquired on an exclusive basis without being used and without being offered to other operators for exploitation, on the other*".[76] In its decision, the European Commission considered that the holding back of exclusive broadcasting rights could lead to market distortions not necessary for the fulfilment of the public service remit.[77] As a consequence, the European Commission clearly stated that "*state financing used for exclusive rights which the public service broadcaster cannot or does not intend to use would not, in principle, be justified [...]*".[78]

Furthermore, the European Commission considered that "*[t]here are also other situations where the question of "unused" rights require[s] further clarification such as where, due to the legal prohibition to offer pay services, public service*

[73] *German public broadcaster state aid* case, para 72 & 289.

[74] *Ibid.*, para 105 & 290.

[75] *Ibid.*, para 298.

[76] *Ibid.*, para 300.

[77] *Ibid.*, para 299 & 305.

[78] *Ibid.*, para 299.

broadcasters are not in a position to exploit payTV rights or, where due to the lack of clear entrustment as regards new media services, it is not clear whether the transmission of sports events over new platforms is covered by the public service remit".[79] According to the European Commission, pay-television has only a limited impact on free-to-air television, because of its low penetration rates.[80] As a result, the European Commission is not convinced about the argument of Germany against the sublicensing of pay-television rights, considering pay-television rights as being consumed by the exploitation of free-to-air television rights.[81] The European Commission continued by stating that when public broadcasters bought rights which they are not allowed to use, such as pay-television rights, and, thus, would risk remain unused, is in detriment to their (existing and new) competitors.[82] Hence, as described above, the main objective of this decision is to limit the adverse effects on competition by granting sublicenses to third parties when rights were not used by the public service broadcasters. Although there is no reference made to the public in this decision, indirectly the public will benefit from the sublicensing obligation, because sports events will be covered.

In addition, the European Commission observed that there is currently no system in place with clear parameters for the acquisition, use and possible sublicensing of sports rights to third parties. Moreover, there is no sufficient clarity of what is a (justified) nonuse of rights.[83] Furthermore, the European Commission stressed that, even when rights were sublicensed on several occasions to third parties, "*the current system does not ensure that such sublicenses are offered in a systematic and predictable way*".[84] Therefore, the European Commission required that the public service broadcasters' behaviour as regards the acquisition, use and possible sublicensing to third parties should be made transparent and predictable for third parties. In this respect, it is important to clarify when a right is regarded as not used as well as the circumstances and conditions under which public service broadcasters would offer such rights to other operators.[85] As regards sports broadcasting rights, Germany announced that the public service broadcasters will make their policy transparent in *inter alia* the following ways: 1) ARD and ZDF shall not leave sports rights unused, since they will either use them themselves or offer them for sublicensing to third parties. For rights acquired through the EBU, sublicenses shall be offered according to the EBU sublicensing regime under the control of a trustee, 2) unused rights shall be offered to third parties for sublicenses with public service broadcasters laying down in a transparent way the conditions under which sports rights are regarded as 'unused', 3) the transmission over the

79 *Ibid.*, para 301.

80 *Ibid.*, para 301 & footnote 120.

81 *Ibid.*, para 301.

82 *Ibid.*, para 305.

83 *Ibid.*, para 301.

84 *Ibid.*, para 302–303.

85 *Ibid.*, para 321.

digital channels of ARD and ZDF does not restrict the possibility for third parties to acquire sublicenses.[86] The European Commission welcomed these commitments and considered them to "*what is necessary for the fulfillment of the public service remit, while not leading to disproportionate effects on competition*".[87] In its press release, the European Commission summarised it as follows: "*unused sports rights which are not necessary for the fulfilment of the public service should normally be offered to third parties for sublicensing. Public service broadcasters will have to clarify which sports rights will be offered to third parties for sublicensing, and subject to which conditions*".[88]

Two years after the *German public broadcaster state aid* case, the European Commission published a communication on the application of State aid rules to public service broadcasting.[89] Paragraph 92 of this communication states that "*[...] public service broadcasters shall not engage in activities which would result in disproportionate distortions of competition that are not necessary for fulfilling the public service mission. For example, the acquisition of premium content as part of the overall public service mission of public service broadcasters is generally considered legitimate. However, disproportionate market distortions would arise if public service broadcasters were to maintain exclusive premium rights unused without offering to sublicense them in a transparent and timely manner. Therefore, the Commission invites Member States to ensure that public broadcasters respect the principle of proportionality also with regard to the acquisition of premium rights, and to provide rules for the sub-licensing of unused exclusive premium rights by public service broadcasters*".

References

Legislation and Policy Documents

European Union

Communications

European Commission 2009. Communication from the Commission on the application of State aid rules to public service broadcasting. *OJ* C 257/1.

---

[86] *Ibid.*, para 355.

[87] *Ibid.*, para 396.

[88] Rapid Press Releases 2007, MEMO/07/150.

[89] European Commission 2009.

Decisions

Commission decision of 11 June 1993 relating a proceeding pursuant to Article 85 of the EEC Treaty (IV/32.150–EBU/Eurovision System). *OJ* L 179.

Commission decision of 10 May 2000 relating to a proceeding pursuant to Article 81 EC of the Treaty (Case IV/32.150–Eurovision), L151.

Commission decision of 22 June 2006 on the ad hoc financing of Dutch public service broadcasters, C 2/2004 (EX NN 170/2003). *OJ* (2008) L 49/1.

European Commission State aid E 3/2005 (ex- CP 2/2003, CP 232/2002, CP 43/2003, CP 243/2004 and CP 195/2004) – Financing of public service broadcasters in Germany, 24 April 2007, C (2007) 1761 final.

Commission decision of 22 February 2008 on the public financing of public service broadcaster VRT, E 8/2006 (ex CP 110/2004 en CP 126/2004). http://ec.europa.eu/community_law/state_aids/comp-2006/e008-06-nl.pdf. Accessed 19 August 2010.

Reports

European Commission (2007) Report on competition policy including commission staff working document. http://ec.europa.eu/competition/publications/annual_report/2007/part2_en.pdf. Accessed 19 Aug 2010

Press releases

Rapid Press Releases (2007) State aid: Commission closes investigation regarding the financing regime for German public service broadcasters—frequently asked questions, 24 April 2007, MEMO/07/150

Speeches

Toft T (2003) TV rights of sports events. 15 January 2003. http://ec.europa.eu/comm/competition/speeches/text/sp2003_002_en.pdf. Accessed 19 Aug 2010Miscellaneous

European Commission (1999) Preliminary guidelines on the application of the competition rules to sport (not published)

Australia

Miscellaneous

Department of Broadband, Communications and the Digital Economy (2009) Sport on television: a review of the anti-siphoning scheme in the contemporary digital environment—Discussion paper. http://www.dbcde.gov.au/__data/assets/pdf_file/0010/118864/Sport_on_Television_Review_discussion_paper.pdf

Responses to discussion papers

FACTS (2001) Australian broadcasting authority's inquiry into the anti-siphoning list submission from the Federation of Australian Commercial Television Stations. http://www.freetv.com.au/

SiteMedia/w3svc087/Uploads/Documents/65db9424-80da-4a9b-b8e3-ba18b908ef12.pdf. Accessed 19 Aug 2010

UK

Consultations

Ofcom (2008) Summary of UK sports rights—Annex 10 to pay TV market investigation consultation. http://stakeholders.ofcom.org.uk/binaries/consultations/market_invest_paytv/annexes/annex_10.pdf. Accessed 18 Aug 2010

Case law

General Court

GC, Metropole télévision SA and others v. Commission, 11 July 1996, Joined Cases T-528/93, T-542/93, T-543.93 and T-546/93, *ECR* (1996) II-649

GC, Metropole télévision SA and others v. Commission, 8 October 2002, Joined Cases T-185/00, T-216/00, T-299/00 and T-300/00, *ECR* (2002) II-3805

Doctrine

Ariño M (2004a) Digital War and Peace: Regulation and Competition in European Digital Broadcasting. Eur Public Law 10(1):135–160

Ariño M (2004b) Competition Law and Pluralism in European Digital Broadcasting: Addressing the Gaps. Commun Strateg 54:97–128

Donders K (2010) Under pressure? An analysis of the impact of European State aid policy on public service broadcasting. Marginalisation or revival as public service media?. PhD Thesis, Promotor: Prof. Dr. Caroline Pauwels, Brussel (in press)

EBU (2009) European Broadcasting Union (EBU)—Who we are and what we do. http://www.ebu.ch/CMSimages/en/CorpBrochure_2009_A4_tcm6-64731.pdf. Accessed 19 August 2010

Elspass M, Kettner M (2008) Article 81 EC. In: Castendyk O et al (eds) European media law. Kluwer Law International, Alphen a/d Rijn, pp 123–149

Faull J, Nikpay A (2007) The EC law of competition, 2nd edn. Oxford university press, Oxford

Font Galarza A (2000) The Commission's assessment of the Eurovision system pursuant Article 81 EC. Compet Policy Newsletter 2:28–33

Harrison J, Woods L (2007) European broadcasting law and policy. Cambridge University Press, Cambridge

Hatton C et al (2007) Fair play: how competition authorities have regulated the sale of football media rights in Europe. ECLR 28(6):346–354

IOC (2009) IOC Agrees European Broadcast Rights Contract for 2014 and 2016 Olympic Games, 18 February 2009. http://sochi2014.com/en/sochi-live/press-center/36723/. Accessed 21 August 2010

Iosifidis P, Smith P (2011) The European Television Rights Market: Balancing Culture and Commerce, Private Television Conference, Brussels, 28 April 2011

Lefever K, Van Rompuy B (2009) Ensuring Access to Sports Content: 10 Years of EU Intervention. Time to Celebrate? J Media Law 2:243–268
Meltz M (1999) Hand it over: Eurovision, exclusive EU sports broadcasting rights, and the Article 85(3) exemption. Boston Coll Int Comp Law Rev 23(105):105–120
Monti G (2002) Article 81 EC and public policy. Common Mark Rev 39:1057–1099
Nitsche I (2001) Broadcasting in the European Union: the role of public interest in competition analysis. TMC Asser instituut, 's-Gravenhage
Saeys F, Antoine F (2007) Belgium. In: d'Haenens L, Saeys F (eds) Western broadcast models: structure, conduct, and performance. Mouton de Gruyter, Berlin, pp 105–144
Schaub A (2002) Sports and Competition: Broadcasting Rights of Sports events. 26 February 2002. http://ec.europa.eu/comm/competition/speeches/text/sp2002_008_en.pdf. Accessed 19 August 2010
Subiotto R, Graf T (2004) Licenses for new media rights under EC law on competition. Entertain Sports Lawyer 22(1):17–21
Temple Lang J (1997). Media, Multimedia and European Community Antitrust Law. http://ec.europa.eu/competition/speeches/text/sp1997_070_en.pdf. Accessed 19 August 2010
Townley C (2010) Article 81 EC and public policy. Hart Publishing, Oxford and Portland, Oregon
Tsiotsou R (2006) The Effect of European Union Regulations on Marketing Practices: The Case of European Football Broadcasting Rights. J Euromarketing 15(1):75–93
Van Den Brink J (2000) EC Competition law and the regulation of European football. Sports lawyers J 7:105–142
Wachtmeister AM (1998) Broadcasting of sports events and competition law. Compet Policy Newsletter 2:18–28
Weatherill S (2007) European Sports Law—collected papers. TMC Asser Press, The Hague

Chapter 11
Must-Offer Obligation

11.1 Introduction

As already indicated in the first chapter of this Part, over the years, European Commission and national competition authorities have dealt with an increasing number of merger cases in the media sector. Concerns have arisen that mergers could restrict access to key elements such as (sports) content. Merged entities could combine for a long period of time a portfolio of exclusive broadcasting rights related to premium content, including key sports events. Given that access to sports broadcasting rights can play an important role for new media operators to roll out their new services, this could result in a situation where an operator on one platform could foreclose third parties' access to exclusive content.[1] In order to deal with this competition issue, must-offer obligations were often imposed on the powerful merging entities. In practice, the must-offer obligation requires vertically integrated companies active as a pay-television operator as well as a distributor to offer, at wholesale or retail basis, sports broadcasting rights or specific premium content, such as Hollywood movies or sports content, to competitors. Although the must-offer obligation was traditionally imposed in the context of concentrations on the market as a result of mergers, in 2010, Ofcom (within its sectoral powers) decided to impose a must-offer obligation on BSkyB apart from merger regulation.

Although exclusive broadcasting rights have long been accepted as the only way to protect the value of those rights for the rights holders and the broadcasters' incentive to invest with greater confidence in their programmes, in recent years, as indicated by Nicita and Ramello, the European Commission and national authorities have changed the direction in their assessment of exclusivity contracts in the media sector. According to Nicita and Ramello, at the beginning of the 1990s, competition authorities seemed to share the broadcasters' view on the necessity of

[1] Commission of the European Communities 2007, SEC(2007) 935, 87; *Newscorp/Telepiù* case, para 180.

K. Lefever, *New Media and Sport*, ASSER International Sports Law Series,
DOI: 10.1007/978-90-6704-873-6_11,

exclusive rights deals; lately, their remedies are often based on the removal of exclusivity clauses and on incumbents' obligation to provide non-discriminatory access to competitors, i.e. must-offer obligation.[2]

In a 2006 speech, Toft labelled a must-offer obligation as a sublicensing obligation.[3] However, referring to a must-offer obligation as a sublicensing obligation can be very confusing. For clarity, in this book, the term 'must-offer obligation' will be used when referring to a situation where all exclusivity will be lost, while the term 'sublicensing obligation' will be used to refer to a situation where the sublicensing holder gets (in most cases) the exclusive right to broadcast the sports events.

The imposition of a must-offer obligation does not imply that the rights should be sold in a non-exclusive way. This obligation only puts a stop to the exclusive usage of broadcasting rights. In other words, the imposition of a must-offer obligation should not be confused with the shift from the sale of exclusive broadcasting rights to a single entity on one medium to the sale of those rights to multiple entities on multiple media platforms based on economic reasons.[4] The latter is described by Rowe as the replacement of the 'economics of exclusivity' by the 'economics of accessibility'. Other authors refer to this evolution as multihoming, i.e. distribution of content through several or all platforms available.[5] In the light of falling broadcasting revenues, sports organisations have been extremely wary of maintaining the current value of their products.[6] Due to the unwillingness of broadcasters to pay huge sums of fees for exclusive broadcasting rights, sports organisations questioned whether exclusive contracts would be the only affective strategy for selling their rights. As a result, as indicated by Evens, rights holders, especially in the sports business, are exploring a shared access system to premium content and provide non-exclusive content to multimedia platforms that can be accessed by means of extra payments.[7] A good example of this evolution can be found in the Netherlands. In 2008, the cable company Zesko offered approximately €45 million for highlights and live matches of the Dutch Premier League. The football clubs of the Dutch first division, better known as Eredivisie, decided, after being disappointed about the financial conditions that were offered during the bidding procedure, to exploit their broadcasting rights themselves.[8] Therefore, the Dutch Eredivisie CV, the joint company of the Premier League clubs, launched its own digital channel in cooperation with production company Endemol: Eredivisie Live. The channel shows live coverage of the matches, as well as talk shows, club reports and

[2] Nicita and Ramello 2005, 381.

[3] Toft 2006, 9

[4] Rowe 2009.

[5] Hagiu and Lee 2008, 2; Evens 2010.

[6] Geey 2004, 9.

[7] Evens 2010.

[8] Dejonghe et al. 2010, 421.

highlights of other European football leagues. For the 2010–2011 seasons, Eredivisie Live has substantially broadened its supply by acquiring the live rights of the national football cup (KNVB Beker) and the Jupiler League (second-tier division) in order to drive up subscription rate.[9] Although television providers in other countries have obtained exclusive broadcasting rights on sports events as part of their strategy to gain market share, Eredivisie Live is broadcast by all digital television operators in the Netherlands.[10] However, it should be noted that the channel's subscription price may vary among these different operators. The difference in pricing is largely down to the fact that some partners can show two games simultaneously, while others are able to show four.[11] Hence, digital viewers should not switch to another television operator to enjoy live football as all digital television operators have equal access to this channel.[12]

11.2 Development of New Media and the Public's Access to Sports Content

11.2.1 Introduction

Just as in the press releases of the joint selling decisions (*supra*), the European Commission has stressed that the aim of the must-offer remedy would be in the interest of new media operators, i.e. increasing competition, and the public, i.e. increase consumer's choice. With regard to *Newscorp/Telepiù* case, Monti stated the following: "*the Commission [...] has established the right conditions for the pay-TV market in Italy to remain open and to evolve in a competitive way on a lasting basis to the advantage of consumers*".[13] Ofcom's press release announcing the publication of the final conclusions of its investigation into the pay-television market was even titled "*delivering consumer benefits in Pay TV*". According to Ofcom, by means of this must-offer obligation, consumers' choice would increase, they would enjoy a greater range of innovative services and they would benefit from the availability of smaller, lower priced packages. Additionally, Ofcom stressed that its decision is designed to ensure fair and effective competition.[14] In the following sections, it will be analysed how competition authorities, when imposing a must-offer obligation, have dealt with the development of new media and whether the changing media landscape has had an impact on the way

[9] Eufootball.biz 2010.

[10] Sportcal.com 2008a..

[11] Sportcal.com 2008b.

[12] Lefever and Evens 2009, 31.

[13] Rapid Press Releases 2003, IP/03/478.

[14] Ofcom 2010b.

competition authorities dealt with the public's access to sports content, and particularly on the public's right to information.

11.2.2 Must-Offer Obligation and Competition in the Changed Media Landscape

The *Newscorp/Telepiù* case dealt with the merger of Italy's two satellite pay-television platforms, Telepiú and Stream, into the new entity Sky Italia. Sky Italia would be a unified satellite pay-television platform.[15] According to the European Commission, after the merger, the merged entity would have combined for a long duration an unparalleled portfolio of exclusive rights related to premium content, including key sports events, thereby foreclosing third parties from accessing premium content needed to establish competing pay-television offers.[16] According to the European Commission, this quasi-monopsonistic situation, in the absence of corrective measures, *inter alia* a must-offer obligation "*would foreclose access to content for third parties [...]*".[17] According to the European Commission, the obligation to offer content to competitors is intended to "*allow competitors of the new entity on platforms [...] to subsist or to enter in the Italian pay-TV market*".[18] Furthermore, it is stressed that "*[t]he underlying idea is that such wholesale offer will lower barriers to entry in the pay-TV market by allowing non-DTH pay-TV operators to access premium contents which would otherwise be too costly for them to purchase directly or which are locked away by means of long-duration exclusivity agreements entered into by the incumbent players with the content providers*".[19]

In the *Telenet/Canal+* case, the Belgian Competition Council had to deal with the acquisition of the Flemish pay-television activities of Canal+ by Telenet. At that time (2003), Telenet's cable infrastructure covered approximately two-third of the Dutch speaking part of Belgium[20] and Canal+ offered unique pay-television services based on the ownership of first window movie rights and the exclusive rights for live coverage of the Belgian Premier League. The Competition Council decided that this merger between a cable operator and a broadcaster of premium content in one entity could create significant difficulties for other parties to enter the broadcasting market. In order to give alternative pay-television channels and alternative infrastructures a chance to enter the Flemish broadcasting market, the Competition Council imposed three conditions upon Telenet: 1) Telenet should

---

[15] *Newscorp/Telepiù* case, para 1.

[16] Commission of the European Communities 2007, SEC(2007) 935, 87.

[17] *Newscorp/Telepiù* case, para 151.

[18] *Ibid.*, para 246.

[19] *Ibid.*, para 246.

[20] Belgian Competition Council 2003, 77.

grant new pay-television channels access to its cable networks and conditional access services on a fair, reasonable and non-discriminatory basis, 2) Telenet should offer Canal+ to alternative infrastructure operators on a fair, reasonable and non-discriminatory basis and 3) exclusive distribution agreements between Telenet and the free-to-air and pay-television channels it was distributing via its cable networks were prohibited.[21] The second condition can be referred to as a must-offer obligation. In 2007, Telenet filed a request with the Belgian Competition Council asking no longer to be obliged to offer its pay-television channel to alternative infrastructure operators. Early in 2008, the Competition Council approved the lifting of the must-offer obligation.[22] As a reaction to this decision, Belgacom lodged an appeal against this decision. In 2009, the Brussels Court of Appeal annulled this decision returning the case to the Competition Council.[23] In 2010, after a new investigation, the Competition Council decided to partly review the must-offer obligation. Telenet will still have to offer its pay-television channel to alternative platform operators, but only if Telenet would acquire all live broadcasting rights for the Belgian Jupiler Pro League matches.[24] The Court of Appeal confirmed this decision.[25]

In the UK, Ofcom was of the opinion that Sky had gained a position of market power in the wholesale markets for premium sports content and believed that it is likely to hold that position in the future, because entry barriers were such that market power was likely to persist.[26] Prior to the European Commission's intervention in 2006 (*supra*), Sky has always won all of the live Premier League rights. While the 'no single buyer' commitment prohibits the FAPL from awarding all the live Premier League rights to Sky (*supra*), Sky nonetheless won the majority of those rights in both 2006 and 2009 tender procedures.[27] Ofcom regards this as clear evidence that "*in practice, there are significant barriers to other parties winning sufficient rights away from Sky*".[28] Sky's strong bidding position, explained by the fact that Sky's established subscriber base, coupled with other factors such as its vertical integration and brand strength, creates the possibility to bid a larger amount than any other bidder.[29] As a result, Ofcom argued that Sky is likely to win the majority of those rights again during future auctions.[30] This market power gives rise to the following concern: Sky, as a vertically integrated firm, distributes its premium content in a manner that favours its own platform and its

[21] *Ibid.* 81–82.

[22] Belgian Competition Council 2008.

[23] Court of Appeal 2008.

[24] Belgian Competition Council 2010, para 116, 120 and 122.

[25] Court of Appeal 2011.

[26] Ofcom 2008, para 1.2; Ofcom 2009a, paras 1.20 and 5.19.

[27] See e.g.: Ofcom 2007, 22

[28] Ofcom 2009a, para 5.56.

[29] *Ibid.*, para 5.19 and 5.59.

[30] Ofcom 2009a, para 5.55.

own business. It does so either by denying these channels to other actors in the media sector or by making that content available on unfavourable terms.[31] In order to alleviate the concentration problems in this case, Ofcom decided that the best way to "*remove Sky's ability to act on its incentives*", was to impose a must-offer obligation implying that BSkyB needs to make its premium channels, including BSkyB's core premium sports, more widely available and at prices set by Ofcom.[32]

Hence, as can be concluded from the previous examples, limiting entry barriers and giving new media operators the chance to enter the audiovisual market is an important objective of the must-offer obligation.

11.2.3 Must-Offer Obligation and the Public's Access to Sports Content

Consumer's choice increases as the amount and variety of premium content available for consumption increase and as their price decreases.[33] However, exclusive contracts create a situation where the public is unable to exercise a real choice between different platform operators. In practice, as indicated by Ofcom, many viewers have strong preferences for particular television channels or content and they are likely to have preferences for a particular delivery platform due to their different characteristics.[34] Nevertheless, the implication of exclusive broadcasting rights is that "*consumers will have to choose between either doing without Core Premium channels, or accessing pay TV* via *a platform that would not otherwise be their preferred choice*".[35] Furthermore, Ofcom, in its pay-television consultation, determined that viewers who most value specific content are more likely to choose for the platform offering this content. This means that "*some consumers are likely to be on a platform which would not have been their first choice had premium content been equally available on another or all platforms*".[36] Consequently, with the help of the must-offer obligation, the public does not have to choose between their favourite content and a specific platform.

Although Weeds emphasised that the public would be better off under exclusivity,[37] others argued that this would not be the case at all. According to the latter, without exclusive broadcasting rights deals, competition among operators from the upstream level of premium contents acquisition will be moved to the downstream level of the quality of delivery services benefiting viewers. This non-exclusive evolution is welcomed by those authors, because operators' competitive

---

31 *Ibid.*, para 6.2–6.3; Ofcom 2008, para 1.3.

32 Ofcom 2008, par. 8.35; Ofcom 2009a, paras 8.1, 8.31–8.32.

33 Nicita and Rossi 2008, 97–98.

34 Ofcom 2009a, para 7.51.

35 *Ibid.*, para 7.52.

36 *Ibid.*, para 1.43.

37 Weeds 2009, 28–29.

advantage will not necessarily rely only on having exclusive access to valuable content, rather it could be based on the quality of services, on technological innovations, on pricing and packaging strategies, etc.[38] Nicita and Ramello further argued that a model based on shared access to premium contents "*would allow rights holder's revenues to grow with the multi-platform diffusion of information*". Hence, "*in such a world, the profitability of the incumbent operators will not depend on artificial barriers to entry, rather on the competitive capacity they will be able to exercise with respect to the technology implemented and the quality of services distributed to customers*".[39] Hagiu added that exclusive arrangements may harm viewers at the expense of industry profits. Not only are certain subscribers to the excluded platform foreclosed from accessing the content, but platforms broadcasting exclusive content can also sustain higher prices to their subscribers.[40] Hence to summarise, as Harbord and Ottaviani formulated: "*[a] ban on exclusive vertical contracts would intensify downstream competition and transfer the benefits of premium programming to consumers*".[41]

In the *Newscorp/Telepiù* case and *BSkyB* case, it is explicitly referred to the fact that without a must-offer obligation, the availability of content to the public is restricted, and, thus, reduces their choice.[42] In contrast to these decisions, the Belgian Competition Council did not make any explicit reference to the benefits of this obligation for the viewers in the *Telenet/Canal+* decision. Neither did it in its 2008 decision when it decided to revise the scope of the must-offer obligation. However, the Court of Appeal, when annulling the 2008 decision of the Competition Council, and the Competition Council in its 2010 decision, referred to the interests of the public, particularly the existence of sufficient high-quality pay-television channels where the public can tune into to watch live games.[43] However, it should be regretted that the interests of the general public were not better taken into account. The Competition Council should have realised that Telenet, in order to avoid alternative platform operators to appeal to the must-offer obligation, would not buy all live packages. Given that the broadcasting rights are now split up between two service operators (Telenet and Belgacom), football fans that want to watch all matches of a particular match day are now obliged to subscribe to tow different platforms and instal two incompatible decoders. Hence, although this revised must-offer obligation has relative positive effects from a competition perspective, it may have rather negative effects for the wider public.

In the *BSkyB* case, Ofcom argued that the must-offer obligation "*would allow for the strengthening of competition between retailers and between platforms*".

38 Nicita and Ramello 2005, 384.

39 *Ibid.*, 385.

40 Hagiu and Lee 2008, 5.

41 Harbord and Ottaviani 2001, 3.

42 *Newscorp/Telepiù* case, para 151.

43 Court of Appeal 2008, para 89; Belgian Competition Council 2010, para 119.

Furthermore, it would "*maximise choice for consumers, both in terms of the range of price points and packages available, and in terms of the range of platforms open to them*".[44] Due to the must-offer obligation, Ofcom emphasised that "*consumers […] will benefit from increased choice, both through the ability to access highly attractive content on alternative platforms to those available today, and from the opportunity to purchase different types of packages potentially at different price […]*".[45] In addition, Ofcom stated that "*consumers that already subscribe to Sky's Core Premium Sports channels will be able […] to switch to alternative platforms that may better suit their needs. This may include subscribers trading down to cheaper, smaller bundles. […] There are clear consumer benefits as consumers are able to make choices that better fit their preferences—choices that are no longer restricted by the lack of availability of Sky's Core Premium Sports channels*".[46] Moreover, Ofcom estimated that, as a result of its decision, there could be around 1.5 to 2 million additional consumers of premium television channels by 2015.[47] In the long term, Ofcom expected that consumer's choice would also be increased due to technological innovation by retailers and platform providers.[48] Hence, in the future, the public would enjoy a greater range of innovative services following fresh investment by competing pay-television providers.[49] Although Ofcom's press release announcing the publication of the final conclusions of its investigation into the pay-television market was titled "*delivering consumer benefits in Pay TV*", Sky fundamentally disagreed. Sky argued that its rivals should not benefit from its big-money rights deals[50] and announced that it would fight this "*unwarranted intervention*". In short, Sky stated that 1) Ofcom has no jurisdiction to impose such an obligation, 2) the obligation imposed by Ofcom is disproportionate, 3) Ofcom made an error in considering the beneficial effects of the obligation and 4) Ofcom underestimated the adverse effect of the obligation.[51] Moreover, sports bodies have joined Sky in outlining their opposition to Ofcom's plans. The Premier League, for example, supported Sky's vision that it is unacceptable that platform operators who have been unwilling to invest in content themselves would get a free ride on the back of investments in content and innovation made by Sky.[52] Furthermore, the Premier League argued that the must-offer obligation would be highly detrimental to the public by significantly devaluing content rights, because it would reduce or remove the

44 Ofcom 2008, para 8.3. For a summary of expected effects on consumers, see: Ofcom 2010a, para 11.56.

45 Ofcom 2010a, para 11.63.

46 *Ibid.*, para 11.68.

47 Ofcom 2010b.

48 Ofcom 2009a, para 10.41; Ofcom 2010a, para 11.69.

49 Ofcom 2010b.

50 Sportcal.com 2009.

51 See e.g.: Demetriou 2010.

52 Sportcal.com 2009.

incentives on others to bid for exclusive broadcasting rights. Hence, given that the value of sports broadcasting rights would be significantly diminished, this will harm the Premier League member clubs, football and the consumers.[53] Although this obligation has provoked a lot of negative reactions, it also has been welcomed by new media operators who are in need of high-quality premium content.[54] For example, BT, the UK telecom operator, announced that it is ready to enter into a price war with Sky over the price charged for fans to watch premium sports events. It was prepared to undercut BSkyB by offering the latter's main sports channel for £15 a month, about £10 cheaper than charged by Sky.[55] However, for BT, Ofcom's decision did not go far enough and, thus, decided to appeal this decision. According to BT, Ofcom is wrong in not including Sky Sports 3 and 4 in the must-offer obligation and Ofcom erred in setting the maximum prices for supply.[56] During the interim relief, all parties have reached agreement at the Competition Appeal Tribunal (CAT). They agreed that the wholesale must-offer obligation will apply, but that they must pay into escrow the difference between the prices to be paid set by Ofcom and the prices charged by Sky.[57]

As already indicated above, the Newscorp-Telepiù merger would result in a quasi-monopolistic situation foreclosing "*access to content for third parties [...] and is likely to restrict availability of content to consumers, thus reducing their possibility of choice*".[58] Normally, a merger resulting in a near-monopoly in the pay-television market would not have been permissible under normal market conditions.[59] However, without this merger, there was a risk that Stream would exit the market. Therefore, the European Commission considered that "*the authorisation of the merger subject to appropriate conditions will be more beneficial to consumers than a disruption caused by a potential closure of Stream*".[60]

Hence, as can be concluded from the previous section, the viewer is especially seen in its role as an economic actor residing in a commercial market when must-offer obligations are/were imposed. In the different decisions, the competition authorities referred to the public and its economic interests, such as price and increased choice. Ofcom, for example, explicitly stated that the must-offer obligation would "*maximise choice for consumers, both in terms of the range of price points and packages available, and in terms of the range of platforms open to*

[53] See e.g.: BBC News 2010; Sportbusiness International 2010.

[54] See e.g.: Telegraph 2009; Geey and Ross 2008, 7.

[55] See e.g.: BBC News 2010; The Guardian 2010.

[56] See e.g.: Broadband TV News 2010b.

[57] Competition Appeal Tribunal 2010; Broadband TV News 2010a.

[58] *Newscorp/Telepiù* case, para 151.

[59] Scheuer and Schweda 2008, 7.

[60] *Newscorp/Telepiù* case, para 221; Rapid Press Releases 2003, IP/03/478.

them".[61] The fact that the public still has to pay an extra subscription fee in order to have access to premium packages, and thus, that these packages are not freely available, was not touched upon in these decisions.

11.3 Must-Offer Obligation: Wholesale Versus Retail Obligations

The main difference between, on the one hand, the *Newscorp/Telepiù* case and the *BSkyB* case and, on the other hand, the *Telenet/Canal+* case is that in the first two cases a 'wholesale' must-offer obligation was imposed and in the latter a 'retail' must-offer obligation. In general, the main difference between those two kinds of obligation is that when a wholesale must-offer obligation is imposed, the merged entity accepts to offer its premium broadcasting rights or content to other actors, while when a retail must-offer obligation is imposed, the vertically integrated operator makes its channels available to the subscribers of competitors on a 'self-distribution' basis.

11.3.1 Wholesale Must-Offer Obligation

In the *Newscorp/Telepiù* case, the merged entity had to offer "*third parties, on an unbundled and non-exclusive basis, the right to distribute on platforms other than DTH [satellite pay-television platform] any premium contents [...]*".[62] As a result, the competitors had the possibility to choose and unbundle specific contents from the vertically integrated entity's offer and to promote its own packages to their final subscribers.[63] The same goes for the *BSkyB* case. Ofcom required that Sky would "*provide wholesale access to particular content on regulated terms*".[64] Hence, in practice, the introduction of a wholesale must-offer obligation implies that the merged entity accepts to 'sublicense' its premium television channels at wholesale level on regulated terms to other actors.[65] This implies that sublicensed content becomes part of the packages offered by the other platform operators and that the latter may fix the price of that package. As a result, the same package can

[61] Ofcom 2008, para 8.3. For a summary of expected effects on consumers, see: Ofcom 2010a, para 11.56.

[62] *Newscorp/Telepiù* case, Annex Commitments to the European Commission—Part II—Substantive obligations, para 10.1.

[63] Nicita and Rossi 2008, 91.

[64] Ofcom 2009a, paras 1.49 and 8.22; Ofcom 2010a, para 9.27.

[65] Valcke 2004, 651; Ofcom 2009b.

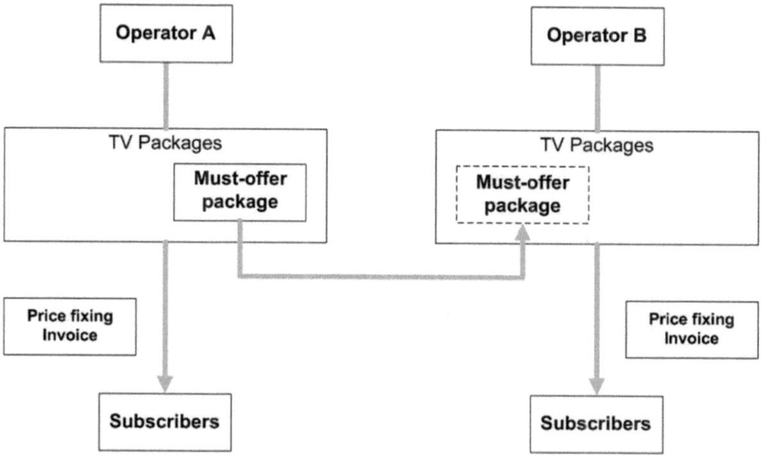

Fig. 11.1 Wholesale must-offer obligation

be offered at different prices by different platform operators. The wholesale must-offer obligation can be illustrated as in Fig. 11.1.

11.3.2 Retail Must-Offer Obligation

In contrast to the wholesale must-offer obligation, competition authorities may also require that premium television channels are made available to competing pay-television operators on a 'self-distribution' basis, i.e. retail must-offer obligation. In this setting, the competitor acts as an agent of the operator on which the must-offer obligation is imposed and the latter retains a direct relation with the subscribers of its competitor.[66] The must-offer obligation imposed in the *Telenet/Canal+* case, for example, was designed on a retail basis. This means that, although Telenet must enable alternative platform operators to include Telenet's premium content in their portfolio, Telenet retains control over the relation with subscribers to those alternative platform operators with regard to their channels.[67] Given that Telenet sets the retail price, there will not be any price difference between the different platforms. Thus, alternative distributors would *de facto* act as agents for Telenet: they would sell subscriptions to premium content on behalf of Telenet, at prices fixed by Telenet.[68] Although the vertically integrated company on which the must-offer obligation is imposed may not include its own name or promotion for its own services on the invoice of its 'must-offered' service to the

---

[66] Valcke 2004, 651; Colomo 2009, 5.

[67] Belgian Competition Council 2003, 2010, para 116.

[68] Valcke 2004, 650–651.

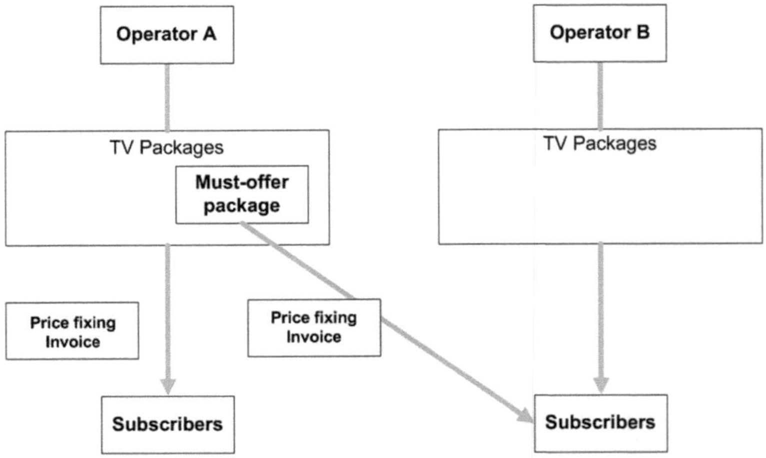

Fig. 11.2 Retail must-offer obligation

subscribers of the alternative platform operators,[69] it does not alter the fact that the alternative platform operators are selling subscriptions for the benefit of their competitor.[70] As a result, Valcke wondered whether alternative distributors would be inclined to sell subscriptions for the benefit of another operator.[71] The retail must-offer obligation can be illustrated as in Fig. 11.2.

In the different pay-TV consultation documents of Ofcom, it is indicated why the dominant operator, *in casu* Sky, had a preference for retail supply of its premium content, while competing retailers, wanting access to that premium content, indeed preferred a wholesale supply deal. Sky itself argued that its preference for retailing its own premium channels is not due to strategic considerations, but due to commercial *rationale*.[72] Sky stressed that it had a strong incentive to retail its own channels, due to *inter alia* its expertise in marketing its premium channels and television services generally and other retailers' desire to encourage subscribers to drop Sky channels if this was necessary to retain the customer for other services.[73] Other retailers, however, have strong reservations about allowing Sky to retail on their platforms. BT, for example, stated that "*a retail deal does not work for us*", because (1) it wanted to compete on price, (2) it wanted to offer customers flexibility on access to content, (3) given platform investment, BT wanted to control its own bundles and margins, (4) there were potential legal issues with agreeing retail pricing and discounts with a competitor on bundles, (5) this would lead to duplication of customer support—there would not be a one stop shop for customer

69 Belgian Competition Council 2003, 83.

70 Valcke 2004, 651.

71 *Ibid.*, 651.

72 Ofcom 2010a, paras 7.89 and 7.92.

73 *Ibid.*, para 7.91.

queries, 6) BT did not trust Sky to price competitively against itself, 7) BT had acquired all its other content wholesale.[74] Sky, when offering its premium channels on a retail basis, would maintain the customer relationship and owns the customer data. While there may be restrictions on the use of those data during the course of Sky's relationship with the alternative platform operators, those restrictions would cease to apply if Sky stopped retailing its channels over the alternative platforms. As a result, Ofcom stressed that Sky would have "*an opportunity to try to migrate customers to its satellite platform*".[75] In addition, if Sky would retail premium content on alternative platforms, this would prevent the other platform operator from being able to set bundle prices as it chooses, in combination with other products or stand-alone.[76] Therefore, Ofcom considered that Sky's preference for retail is due to "*a desire to retain control over packaging and pricing on other platforms, and therefore to avoid losing customers from its satellite platform*".[77] Ofcom further specified that if Sky would retail, "*it can benefit not only from its own satellite subscribers, but also from subscribers on other platforms [...]. Sky can influence the movement of subscribers between platforms through its retail packaging and pricing, thereby ensuring that it as far as possible locks consumers into its core satellite platform. If Sky wholesales to others, it [...] loses the control over cross-platform retail packaging and pricing, which means that it faces a greater risk of losing customers from its satellite platform*".[78] Consequently, Ofcom's view is that Sky derives two strategic benefits from keeping its retail competitors weak. On the one hand, Sky has the "*ability to manage competition between retailers on different platforms, in order to protect the position of Sky's own satellite platform*". On the other hand, Sky has the ability to "*prevent rival retailers from establishing a strong retail presence, which [...] could strengthen their position in bidding for content rights*".[79] Ofcom stressed that retailing via others' platforms potentially "*allows Sky the best of both worlds, in that it can drive some consumers to its own satellite platform, while charging a high price to those that would be unable to switch to satellite*".[80] To conclude, Ofcom indicated that even when Sky would retail widely on all platforms, it "*would not ensure fair and effective competition between retailers on different platforms, delivering choice, innovation and competitive prices to consumers, as there would only be one retailer of these important channels across platforms*".[81]

However, it should be noted that in Italy, years after the *Newscorp/Telepiù* decision, the wholesale must-offer obligation has spontaneously evolved to

[74] *Ibid.*, para 7.94.

[75] Ofcom 2008, para 6.128.

[76] *Ibid.*, paras 6.129–6.130.

[77] Ofcom 2010a, para 7.90.

[78] Ofcom 2009a, para 6.65.

[79] *Ibid.*, para 6.66; Ofcom 2010a, para 7.201.

[80] Ofcom 2008, para 6.121.

[81] Ofcom 2010a, para 7.226.

voluntary retail agreements. An impact assessment including an international comparison of wholesale must-offer remedies, done by Ofcom,[82] showed that the overall impact of the remedy had been mixed.[83] On the one hand, the main positive impact as a result of the wholesale must-offer obligation is increased choice for the public as a result of cross-platform availability of the packages of the merged entity. Hence, access to premium content has created the possibility for IPTV operators to offer the public other pay-television packages. On the other hand, several shortcomings concerning the wholesale must-offer obligation have become apparent. The primary problem raised by the IPTV platform operators was that the obligation only applies to premium content. They claimed that "*the absence of basic content from the conditions, coupled with Sky Italia's exclusive contracts with basic channel owners, placed a heavy restriction on IPTV operators' ability to deliver an attractive pay TV offer*". As a result, although the IPTV platform operators could offer the same premium content as Sky Italia, they could not attract many subscribers due to their weaker basic package. According to Value Partners, the clearest indication of the limitation of the wholesale must-offer remedy has been "*the shift away from taking up the wholesale must-offer to unregulated commercial agreements between Sky Italia and the IPTV players*". The latter have ceased their wholesale agreement and have entered into contractual agreements with Sky Italia, acting as distributors for both Sky's premium and basic packages. In this model, Sky Italia bills the subscribers directly and owns the customer relationship (cfr. *Telenet/Canal+* case). This could be seen as a positive evolution for the public, because they can access the same content on different platforms.

References

Legislation and Policy Documents

European Union

Commission Staff Working Document

Commission of the European Communities (2007) Commission Staff working document—The EU and Sport: background and context—accompanying document to the White Paper on Sport. 11 July 2007, SEC(2007) 935

---

[82] Ofcom 2009b, 13–15.

[83] Ofcom 2009a, 13.

Decisions

Commission decision of 2 April 2003 declaring a concentration to be compatible with the common market and the EEA Agreement (Case No COMP/M. 2876—Newscorp/Telepiù)

Press Releases

Rapid Press Releases (2003) Commission clears merger between Stream and Telepiù subject to conditions, 2 April 2003, IP/03/478

Speeches

Toft T (2006) Developments in European Law, Congress Sports & Law. 28 April 2006. http://ec.europa.eu/comm/competition/speeches/text/sp2006_003_en.pdf. Accessed 19 Aug 2010

UK

Consultations

Ofcom (2007) Pay TV market investigation—consultation document. http://stakeholders.ofcom.org.uk/binaries/consultations/market_invest_paytv/summary/pay_tv.pdf. Accessed 21 Aug 2010

Ofcom (2008) Pay TV second consultation—access to premium content. http://stakeholders.ofcom.org.uk/binaries/consultations/second_paytv/summary/condoc.pdf. Accessed 18 Aug 2010

Ofcom (2009a) Pay TV phase three document: proposed remedies. http://stakeholders.ofcom.org.uk/binaries/consultations/third_paytv/summary/paytv_condoc.pdf. Accessed 18 Aug 2010

Ofcom (2009b) Wholesale must-offer remedies: international examples—Annex 11 to pay TV phase three document. http://stakeholders.ofcom.org.uk/binaries/consultations/third_paytv/annexes/annex11.pdf. Accessed 18 Aug 2010

Ofcom (2010a) Pay TV statement. http://stakeholders.ofcom.org.uk/binaries/consultations/third_paytv/statement/paytv_statement.pdf. Accessed 19 Aug 2010

Press Releases

Ofcom (2010b) Delivering consumer benefits in Pay TV, 31 March 2010. http://www.ofcom.org.uk/consumer/2010/03/delivering-consumer-benefits-in-pay-tv/. Accessed 20 Aug 2010

Case Law

Belgium

Belgian Competition Council (2003) Decision no. 2003-C/C-89 of 12 November 2003. Tijdschrift van Rechtspraak van de Raad voor de Mededinging 4:72–83

Belgian Competition Council (2008) Decision no. 2008-C/C-11 of 25 March 2008. http://economie.fgov.be/fr/binaries/112008cc11_Verzoek_Telenet_herziening_pub_tcm326-35704.pdf. Accessed 19 Aug 2010
Court of Appeal, A.R. no. 2008/MR/7, Belgacom/Telenet and Liga Beroepsvoetbal
Belgian Competition Council (2010) Decision no. 2010-C/C-48 of 29 November 2010. http://economie.fgov.be/nl/binaries/48_2010CC48_Telenet_pub_tcm325-113664.pdf. Accessed 20 Dec 2010
Court of Appeal (2011) A.R. no. 2011/MR/1 and 2011/MR/2, 17 May 2011

UK

Competition Appeal Tribunal (2010). British Sky Broadcasting Limited supported by The Football Association premier League Limired v Office of Communication supported by Top-Up TV Europe Limited, Virgin Media Inc., British telecommunications Plc and Orange Personal Communications Services Limited, Case No: 1152/8/3/10 (IR), 29 April 2010. http://www.catribunal.org.uk/files/1152IR_BSKYB_Order_29.04.10.pdf. Accessed 20 Aug 2010

Doctrine

BBC News (2010) BT aims to undercut Sky on TV sport viewing packages, 17 January 2010. http://news.bbc.co.uk/2/hi/8464004.stm. Accessed 20 Aug 2010
Broadband TV News (2010a) CAT agreement partially imposes Sky wholesale plan, 29 April 2010. http://www.broadbandtvnews.com/2010/04/29/cat-agreement-partially-implements-sky-wholesale-plan/. Accessed 20 Aug 2010
Broadband TV News (2010b) BSkyB, BT and FAPL join Ofcom appeal, 11 June 2010. http://www.broadbandtvnews.com/2010/06/11/bskyb-bt-and-fapl-join-ofcom-appeal/. Accessed 20 Aug 2010
Colomo P (2009) Working paper—Ofcom's proposal to regulate access to premium television content: some thoughts. http://cadmus.eui.eu/dspace/bitstream/1814/10930/1/LAW_2009_03.pdf. Accessed 20 Aug 2010
Dejonghe T et al (2010) The Netherlands and Belgium. In: Hamil S, Chadwick S (eds) Managing football: an international perspective. Elsevier, Amsterdam, pp 409–436
Eufootball.biz (2010) Eredivisie Live to broadcast Jupiler League matches, 11 August 2010. http://www.eufootball.biz/Television/8520-eredivisie_live_broadcast_jupiler_league_matches.html. Accessed 24 Aug 2010
Evens T (2010) Challenging content exclusivity in network industries: the case of digital broadcasting. In: ITS Conference, Copenhagen, 13–15 September 2010
Geey D (2004) Collectivity v Exclusivity: Conflict in the Broadcasting Arena. Entertainment Law Review, vol 15, no. 1, http://www.danielgeey.com/pdf/a-ent-law1.pdf. Accessed 30 Dec 2011
Geey D, Ross V (2008) Ofcom consultation into premium pay-TV content. World Sports L Rep 10:6–8
Hagiu A, Lee R (2008) Exclusivity and control. http://www.hbs.edu/research/pdf/08-009.pdf. Accessed 20 Aug 2010
Harbord D, Ottaviani M (2001) Contracts and competition in the pay-TV market. http://129.3.20.41/eps/io/papers/0203/0203005.pdf. Accessed 20 Aug 2010
Lefever K, Evens T (2009) All sports for free! A difficult match? Right to information in the digital broadcasting era. Int Sports L J 3–4:29–33
Nicita A, Ramello G (2005) Exclusivity and antitrust in media markets: the case of Pay-TV in Europe. Int J Econ Bus 12(3):371–387
Nicita A, Rossi MA (2008) Access to audio-visual contents, exclusivity and anticommons in new media markets. Commun Strateg 71(3):79–101

Rowe D (2009) Submission to the sport on television review. http://www.dbcde.gov.au/__data/assets/word_doc/0012/121224/Professor_David_Rowe_main_submission.doc. Accessed 21 Aug 2010

Scheuer A, Schweda S (2008) Progress in the must-offer debate? Exclusivity in media and communication, Iris Plus. http://www.obs.coe.int/oea_publ/iris/iris_plus/iplus10_2008.pdf.en. Accessed 18 Aug 2010

Sportbusiness International (2010) Sports bodies slam Ofcom ruling on Sky, 1 April 2010. http://www.sportbusiness.com/news/174426/sports-bodies-slam-ofcom-ruling-on-sky?utm_source=sbinsl&utm_medium=email&utm_campaign=apr1. Accessed 20 Aug 2010

Sportcal.com (2008a) Eredivisie: new channel will not be another Sport7 Fiasco, 17 March 2008. http://sportcal.com/news/news_article.aspx?previouspage=news_list.aspx&pageno=114&articleID=48375. Accessed 20 Jan 2010

Sportcal.com (2008b) Eredivisie hands control of TV channel pricing to distribution partners, 22 July 2008. http://sportcal.com/news/news_article.aspx?articleid=61327. Accessed 20 Jan 2010

Sportcal.com (2009) Sports bodies get behind BSkyB in channel pricing row with Ofcom, 29 Oct 2009. http://sportcal.com/news/news_article.aspx?previouspage=news_list.aspx&pageno=16&articleID=70114. Accessed 20 Jan 2010

Telegraph (2009) Sky set for legal fight over pay-TV recommendation, 26 June 2009. http://www.telegraph.co.uk/finance/newsbysector/mediatechnologyandtelecoms/5653774/Sky-set-for-legal-fight-over-pay-TV-recommendation.html. Accessed 20 Aug 2010

The Guardian (2010) Ofcom orders Sky Sports price cut, 31 March 2010. http://www.guardian.co.uk/media/2010/mar/31/ofcom-sky-sports-price-cut. Accessed 20 Aug 2010

Valcke P (2004) Digitale Diversiteit. Convergentie van Media-, Telecommunicatie- en Mededingingsrecht. Larcier, Brussels

Chapter 12
Conclusion Part II

As a corollary to the ever-increasing prices paid for the coverage of popular sports events, especially football, the activities of selling, buying and exploiting of sports broadcasting rights and activities connected with it have attracted the attention of the European Commission and national competition authorities. Access to sports content is important for new media operators to enter and stay in the media market. As a result, not being able to acquire exclusive broadcasting rights to valuable sports content would deny them market access. In order to deal with these competition concerns, competition authorities have played an important role in shaping the conditions for selling, acquiring and exploiting these exclusive rights. The 'joint selling remedies' package, the sublicensing obligation and the must-offer obligation were imposed in order to establish open and effective competition.

In the past, sports associations sold all sports broadcasting rights in one large exclusive contract to a single broadcaster. This mechanism is better known as the joint selling practice. Over the last few years, the European Commission has accepted several agreements concerning the joint selling of sports broadcasting rights under the European antitrust rules, albeit with strings attached. While recognising that the practice of joint selling leads to efficiency gains, the European Commission indicated that this practice constitutes a restriction of competition under Article 101 (1) of the TFEU. Given that joint selling agreements could foreclose the market and, thus, limit viewers' choice, the European Commission intervened and the joint selling bodies amended their joint selling agreements. When addressing competition concerns related to joint selling arrangements, the European Commission applied a number of, as the European Commission calls them, standard remedies and if required by the concrete market situation, other remedies would be added.[1] The standard remedies are the following: unbundling of the rights, fall-back option, transparent tender procedure and limited duration of exclusive contracts. The additional ones are the following: 'no conditional

[1] Toft 2006a, 5–7; Toft 2006b, 7–9.

K. Lefever, *New Media and Sport*, ASSER International Sports Law Series,
DOI: 10.1007/978-90-6704-873-6_12,

bidding' commitment, 'no single buyer' commitment and monitoring by a trustee. In the *UEFA Champions League* case, *German Bundesliga* case and *FA Premier League* case, the European Commission decided that the amended joint selling agreement could be exempted under Article 101 (3) of the TFEU, because new media operators as well as viewers benefit from such agreements. Above all, the objective of the imposed remedies and commitments in the different joint selling agreement decision is to give new media operators the chance to buy exclusive broadcasting rights and, thus, the opportunity to enter the broadcasting market. However, the unequal treatment of innovative exploitation forms, such as the imposition of embargoes or limiting the coverage to clips, could make these new media services less attractive, might undermine market development and user take-up. Additionally, no attention is paid to the emergence of prosumers. Although digitalisation and access to Internet have created the opportunity for every citizen to create and distribute sports content, sports organisations will prevent them from doing so by concluding exclusive rights deals with professional media operators. Furthermore, in the press releases coinciding the three decisions, it was stressed that the amended joint selling agreements offer sports fans greater choice. For example, the European Commission emphasised that "*applying the competition rules to sport ensures that the interests of both fans and leagues are fairly balanced*".[2] However, when we take a closer look at the decisions, it can be concluded that the imposition of the joint selling remedies package is not strongly driven by a citizen-rationale. Although the European Commission takes into account the viewers' benefits, particularly their choice in the changed media environment, when exempting those agreements, it does not explicitly refer to the public's right to information and the public's access to sports events on free-to-air television. In fact, the European Commission only alluded to the general assumption that guaranteeing competition in the upstream market will ultimately result in benefits for the public.[3] Hence, as indicated in the Study on the Lisbon Treaty and EU Sports Policy, it seems that the exemption decisions were made with reference to the economic exemption criteria established in 101 (3) of the TFEU and not to wider social-cultural concerns, whether Treaty based or not.[4] However, national competition authorities have used antitrust rules as an instrument to foster competition while taking into account the public's right to information with regard to sports events. The German Competition Authority decision, for example, guaranteeing the broadcasting of highlights before 8 p.m. can be considered as an interesting example for the application of a more explicit citizen-orientated approach.[5] The same goes for the Belgian Competition Council. It has attached value to the principle that the public could see at least one live match on free-to-air television.

---

[2] Rapid Press Releases 2003, IP/03/1748.

[3] Lefever and Van Rompuy 2009, 256.

[4] Richard Parrish et al. 2010, 29.

[5] Lefever and Van Rompuy 2009, 267.

Another important competition issue could rise when broadcasters decide not to use the sports broadcasting rights they have acquired. When broadcasters choose not to broadcast the sports events, this could be in detriment to their competitors and the public. Their competitors do not get the chance to broadcast the sports events, because they do not have the rights and the public is denied coverage of those sports events. In order to deal with the warehousing problem of unused sports broadcasting rights, the European Commission imposed sublicensing obligations. The aim of the obligation to grant sublicenses is to benefit third parties that are interested to broadcast those sports events by reducing the harmful effects on competition due to the unused rights. In the *EBU/Eurovision system* case, the European Commission decided that the viewers were granted a fair share of the benefits of this Eurovision system, because they would have access to more high-quality sports programmes of both popular and minority sports. Hence, in this decision the public in its non-economic function was a significant component of the statement of reasons. Due to these benefits, the European Commission adopted a decision that granted an exemption to the arrangement. However, in order to be granted an exemption under Article 101 (3) of the TFEU, the European Commission required a revision of the existing sublicensing scheme. In doing so, it should be ensured that third parties (traditional as well as new media), via a set of sublicensing rules, would have sufficient access to jointly acquired broadcasting rights. It should be noted that with regard to the joint buying system, only in the first *EBU/Eurovision System* decision did concerns about the public's broad access to sport events prove to be a significant component of the statement of reasons and, thus, has accorded some importance to a non-economic concern.[6] However, this decision was overruled by the General Court. Furthermore, the General Court overruled a second exemption decision of the European Commission, because the sublicensing scheme did not guarantee competitors of EBU members, both traditional as new media, sufficient access to live broadcasting rights not used by the EBU members. In contrast to the *EBU/Eurovision system* case, in the *German public broadcaster state aid* case, no explicit reference was made to the viewers or the public. The European Commission's decision mainly focused on the fact that the financing of sports rights acquired by public service broadcasters should be limited to what is necessary for the fulfilment of their remit. Given that the European Commission did not consider unused rights as being necessary for the fulfilment of the public service task, it is necessary that the public service broadcasters' behaviour will sublicense unused rights to competitors and that this sublicense procedure will be made transparent and predictable for those third parties. Furthermore, the European Commission stressed that when public broadcasters bought rights which they are not allowed to use, such as pay-television rights, there is a risk that they would remain unused which is in detriment to their (existing and new) competitors.

---

6 Lefever and Van Rompuy 2009, 256.

Technological convergence has triggered a wave of horizontal and vertical concentration within and between the media and telecommunication sector. A problem could rise where a merged entity owns a portfolio of premium sports content being necessary to attract subscribers and, thus, forecloses third parties' access to this content, Furthermore, viewers wishing to have access to specific sports content are forced to subscribe to one specific platform at the (high) price established by that platform operator. In order to further the interests of the public and to give new media operators chance to enter the market, competition authorities have imposed must-offer obligations on the vertically integrated companies holding exclusive broadcasting rights of premium content. It is important to note that the imposition of a must-offer obligation does not imply that the broadcasting rights should be sold in a non-exclusive way. This obligation puts only a stop to the exclusive usage of broadcasting rights. As stated by Scheuer and Schweda "*there is no doubt that must-offer obligations serve to promote the development of new transmission methods*".[7] Moreover, greater consumer choice is also often referred to as a positive result of the must-offer obligations. However, Ofcom nuanced this: "*given that the must-offer obligations are frequently one part of a larger package of measures, [...] it is difficult to assess their specific impact in terms of consumer choice, prices and innovation*". Nevertheless, Ofcom agreed that, to some degree, "*must-offer remedies have been successful in increasing, or at least maintaining, retail competition and increasing consumer choice*".[8] In addition, overcoming exclusivity clauses would create new competitive opportunities in which different variables come into play, such as price, quality and programming, all to the advantage of the viewers as consumers.[9] Although it should be realised that the imposition is a very intrusive measure, Harbord and Ottaviani stressed that the competitive advantage of the industry leader is reduced, but that the additional surplus is captured by the public.[10] The latter is even truer when the dominant actor has the obligation to offer its rivals access to the broadcasting rights instead of channels. However, just as in the three European joint selling agreement decisions, in the must-offer decisions, the viewer is especially seen in its role as consumer, focussing on its economic interests (price, choice, etc.).

As indicated in Part I, public authorities are allowed under certain circumstances, under Article 10 of the ECHR, to intervene in order to protect the public's right to information with regard to live and full sports coverage (*supra*). Although some authors have stressed that competition authorities should take into account public interest objectives, such as the public's right to information, it has been indicated that those authorities are rather reluctant to do so. The preceding overview of the decision-making practice of different competition authorities has

---

7 Scheuer and Schweda 2008, 5.

8 Ofcom 2009, 3.

9 Nicita and Ramello 2005, 384.

10 Harbord and Ottaviani 2001, 2.

shown how those authorities attempted to foster competition in the markets for the sale, acquisition and exploitation of sports broadcasting rights and how this had an impact on the public's access to sports content. The first concern of competition authorities was to increase competition in the broadcasting market by guaranteeing new media operators access to sports broadcasting rights. According to the competition authorities, increased competition in the broadcasting market would also have a positive effect on the viewers, mainly in their role as consumer: increased choice, better quality, innovative services and lower prices. Apparently, the public, in those different decisions, is mainly referred to in its economic rather than in its social or political role. Donders, referring to Van Rompuy, says that the application of competition law seems to benefit organisations instead of consumers and that it, due to its inherent limitations, can only be indirectly beneficial for the citizens.[11] Although national competition authorities attached more weight to a non-economic consideration as the public's right to information (to sports events), this should be seen as a rather exceptional approach. In other words, in a vast majority of competition decisions, cultural objectives are subordinate to economic ones. Or, as indicated by Helberger, the consideration whether the public has access to important sports content generally lies outside the scope of competition assessments.[12] Furthermore, the European Commission has stated that "*[c]ompetition rules are neutral with respect to different types of broadcasters and do not provide a legal basis for favouring one category over another*".[13] As a result, competition law will not oblige rights holders to grant their broadcasting rights either to free-to-air broadcasters or pay-television operators.[14] Hence, with Article 10 of the ECHR in mind, competition law does not seem to be the proper regulatory instrument to take into account non-economic considerations specifically attached to the broadcasting sector, such as the protection of the public's right to information. Or as stated by Pons and Monti: "*[t]he solution is not always found in the application of competition law. Community or national legislation may seek to protect the public interest and to ensure the right for the largest number of viewers to have access to certain programmes*".[15] Consequently, in Part III, we will further explore the way media law is dealing with the public's right to information with regard to sports content in the changing media landscape.

[11] Donders 2010.

[12] Helberger 2005, 187.

[13] Wachtmeister 1998, 20.

[14] Bell et al. 2003, 417.

[15] Pons 1999, 15–16; Monti 2000, SPEECH/00/152.

References

Legislation and Policy Documents

European Union

Press Releases

Rapid Press Releases (2003) Commission reaches provisional agreement with FA Premier League and BSkyB over football rights, 16 December 2003, IP/03/1748

Speeches

Monti M (2000) Sport and competition. 17 April 2000, SPEECH/00/152
Toft T (2006a) EC competition law aspects: sports rights in a converging media technology environment. 30 March 2006. http://ec.europa.eu/competition/speeches/text/sp2006_002_en.pdf. Accessed 19 Aug 2010
Toft T (2006b) Developments in European law, congress sports & law. 28 April 2006. http://ec.europa.eu/comm/competition/speeches/text/sp2006_003_en.pdf. Accessed 19 Aug 2010

UK

Consultations

Ofcom (2009) Wholesale must-offer remedies: international examples - Annex 11 to pay TV phase three document. http://stakeholders.ofcom.org.uk/binaries/consultations/third_paytv/annexes/annex11.pdf. Accessed 18 Aug 2010

Doctrine

Bell A et al (2003) EC and UK competition rules and sport. In: Lewis A, Taylor J (eds) Sport: law and practice. Butterworths, London, pp 333–429
Donders K (2010) Under pressure? An analysis of the impact of European State aid policy on public service broadcasting. Marginalisation or revival as public service media?. PhD Thesis, Promotor: Prof. Dr. Pauwels Caroline, Brussel, in press
Harbord D, Ottaviani M (2001) Contracts and competition in the pay-TV market. http://129.3.20.41/eps/io/papers/0203/0203005.pdf. Accessed 20 Aug 2010
Helberger N (2005) Controlling access to content—regulating conditional access in digital broadcasting. Kluwer Law International, The Hague
Lefever K, Van Rompuy B (2009) Ensuring access to sports content: 10 years of EU intervention. time to celebrate? J Media Law vol. 2:243–268
Nicita A, Ramello G (2005) Exclusivity and antitrust in media markets: the case of pay-TV in Europe. Int J Econ Bus 12(3):371–387

Parrish R et al (2010) The lisbon treaty and EU sports policy—study. http://www.europarl.europa.eu/activities/committees/studies/download.do?language=en&file=32471. Accessed 14 Oct 2010

Pons JF (1999) Sport and European competition policy. http://ec.europa.eu/comm/competition/speeches/text/sp1999_019_en.pdf. Accessed 24 Aug 2010

Scheuer A, Schweda S (2008) Progress in the must-offer debate? exclusivity in media and communication, Iris plus. http://www.obs.coe.int/oea_publ/iris/iris_plus/iplus10_2008.pdf.en. Accessed 18 Aug 2010

Wachtmeister AM (1998) Broadcasting of sports events and competition law. Compet Policy Newslett 2:18–28

Part III
Media Law

There is no pressure. The team has to win and that's it.
(Nowinho, 2009)

In the previous Part, it was analysed how competition authorities have dealt with the development of new media operators and how their decisions have had an impact on the public's access to sports content, and particularly on the public's right to information. In doing so, different remedies imposed to deal with competition issues concerning the sale, acquisition and exploitation of sports broadcasting rights were discussed in depth. It was indicated that the development of new media has played an important role in the competition decisions. When imposing different remedies to boost the development of new media, the public's access to sports content has been taken into account. However, it should be emphasised that the different competition decisions could not be considered as being very citizen-oriented. In the different decisions, the public is mainly referred to in its economic rather than in its social or political role. Given that competition authorities are often reluctant to take into account non-economic considerations and that many-to-many communication does not automatically lead to increased access to information, another regulatory instrument, in particular media law, is still needed to protect the public's right to information. Or in other words, media law is still needed to protect the viewer in its role as citizen.

In this Part, one sector-specific measure focussing on the safeguard of the public's right to information, namely the 'list of major events' mechanism, will be critically analysed and discussed. As an introduction, the origin, the philosophy and the underlying theoretical rationale of this provision will be briefly touched upon. The aim of this chapter is to link the characteristics of the new media environment with the application of the traditional media legislation to evaluate in detail the 'list of major events' mechanism and to examine whether this mechanism is still adapted to guarantee the public's right to information in the digital media landscape. In this Part, the impact of the 'list of major events'

Quote of Jose Mourinho in December 2009 (Football Italia 2009).

mechanism on the development of new media will also be briefly touched upon. Before doing this, a closer look will be taken at the sector-specific regulation in general, namely the Audiovisual Media Services Directive. Finally, in an attempt to solve the limitations discussed, the introduction of a must-broadcast obligation will be proposed, which admittedly could itself raise some delicate issues.

It is not the aim of this book to discuss the general regulatory framework for audiovisual media services. Neither is it the objective to describe in-depth the right to short news reporting provision. Although the right to short news reporting also guarantees the public's right to information to short news reports of 90 seconds, this book will focus on the EU's action to ensure the public's access to live and full sports coverage. Live and full coverage of sports events will be the main focus of this book, because it seems that sport can mainly fulfil its social role, i.e. bringing people together, when sports events are experienced by a large number of people simultaneously and live. Or as described by Schoental *[t]he slow build-up of suspense which makes sports events so attractive and unique is [...] only present in the original broadcast.*[1] The European Commission paraphrased it as follows: *sports media rights are most attractive when broadcast live because once the outcome of an event is known the value of the right declines together with viewer interest.*[2] Therefore, this book starts from the hypothesis that guaranteeing the public's access to live and full coverage, and not just short news fragments, is an important value and objective in our democratic society. Furthermore, for all stakeholders involved, live and full coverage of sports events is crucial. For broadcasters, for example, live sports broadcasting rights are an important tool to attract viewers and, thus, to enter and stay in the broadcasting market. Given that people enjoy watching sports events on television, the coverage of sports events results in high viewing figures. The FIFA World Cup final in South Africa, for example, attracted more than 700 million viewers.[3] The battle for market share, viewers and subscribers has caused a substantial increase in prices paid for exclusive live sports broadcasting rights, ultimately benefiting the sports organisations and clubs selling their rights. For the viewers, sports events are the type of content that they still prefer to consume live. As this book is primarily concerned with the public's interest in experiencing live and full access to sports events, the right to short news reporting provision, which guarantees the public's right to information to short news reports, will not be described in detail, but will be touched upon when relevant.

[1] Schoental 2006.

[2] Commission of the European Communities 2007.

[3] Sportbusiness International 2010.

References

Schoental M (2006) Major events and reporting rights. IRIS Plus, 4:1–8

Commission of the European Communities (2007) Commission Staff working document—the EU and Sport: background and context—Accompanying document to the White Paper on Sport. 11 July 2007, SEC(2007) 935

Sportbusiness International (2010) FIFA: over 700m viewers for World Cup final, 12 July 2010. http://www.sportbusiness.com/news/178947/fifa-over-700m-viewers-for-world-cup-final?utm_source=sbinsl&utm_medium=email&utm_campaign=july12. Accessed 18 August 2010

Chapter 13
Content Regulation: General Introduction

13.1 Introduction

The single European market is one of the biggest achievements of European integration, and applies to television broadcasts as much as anything else.[1] The different national broadcasting regulations, however, contained disparities impeding the free movement of broadcasts within the European Union. To abolish these obstacles, in the hope to create a common market in the broadcasting sector, it was necessary to harmonise those national broadcasting laws. To do so, the European legislator embedded the regulation of the audiovisual sector in the Television without Frontiers Directive (hereafter: TWF Directive) in 1989.[2] The TWF Directive was substantially revised in 1997[3] and in 2007.[4] In 2010, the European legislator decided, in the interests of clarity and rationality of the Directive, to codify the different amending Directives. This codified version will be referred to as the Audiovisual Media Services Directive (hereafter: AVMS Directive).[5]

In 1997, the first revision of the TWF Directive was urged to take into account the new developments in the audiovisual market (*inter alia* teleshopping and sponsoring) and, more important, the access of the public to major (sports) events. Soon after this revision, economic developments and new technological evolutions, such as the convergence of technologies and markets, changed the media ecosystem profoundly. As a result of these changes, traditional broadcasters were increasingly challenged by both linear services on competing multimedia platforms and non-linear services offering the same audiovisual media content.[6] Whereas linear

[1] European Commission 2007, 8.
[2] Directive 89/552/EEC.
[3] Directive 89/552/EEC, amended by Directive 97/36/EC.
[4] Directive 2007/65/EC.
[5] Directive 2010/13/EU (hereafter: AVMS Directive).
[6] Commission of the European Communities 2005, COM(2005) 646 final, 2.

K. Lefever, *New Media and Sport*, ASSER International Sports Law Series,
DOI: 10.1007/978-90-6704-873-6_13,

services fell within the scope of the TWF Directive, on-demand services were only subject to the less strict E-Commerce Directive.[7] Because of this different legal treatment, the European Commission was of the opinion that competition in the common market could be distorted and considered a second review of the TWF Directive necessary.

In 2003, with the work programme annexed to the Fourth Report on the application of the TWF Directive,[8] the European Commission launched a first consultation round for the review of the TWF Directive. More consultation rounds and public hearings would follow. After 2 years, on 13 December 2005, the European Commission published its proposed changes to the TWF Directive.[9] In order to establish a modernised framework, the European Commission proposed *inter alia* to extend the scope of the Directive to all forms of audiovisual media services, including linear as well as non-linear services, to relax the advertising rules and to include the right to short reporting. After a long legislative process the amending Directive was finally adopted in December 2007, and entered into force on 19 December 2007.

13.2 Scope of the Audiovisual Media Services Directive

The scope of the TWF Directive was originally limited to television broadcasting services meaning "*the initial transmission by wire or over the air, including that by satellite, in unencoded or encoded form, of television programmes intended for reception by the public. It includes the communication of programmes between undertakings with a view to their being relayed to the public. It does not include communication services providing items of information or other messages on individual demand such as telecopying, electronic data banks and other similar services*".[10] In the *Mediakabel* case,[11] the Court of Justice was asked to interpret the notion of 'television broadcasting' in the light of the notion of 'information society services'[12] and with a view to qualifying (semi-)interactive media services like (near-)video on-demand. The Court of Justice clarified that '*a service comes within the concept of 'television broadcasting' [...] if it consists of the initial transmission of television programmes intended for reception by the public, that is, an indeterminate number of potential television viewers, to whom the same images*

[7] Directive 2000/31/EC.

[8] Commission of the European Communities 2003, COM(2002) 778 final, 3.

[9] Commission of the European Communities 2005, COM(2005) 646 final.

[10] Article 1 (a) of the TWF Directive.

[11] CJ, Mediakabel v Commissariaat voor de Media.

[12] Information society service is ''*any service normally provided for remuneration, at a distance, by electronic means and at the individual request of a recipient of services*'' (Directive 98/48/EC, amending Directive 98/34/EC).

are transmitted simultaneously. The manner in which the images are transmitted is not a determining element in that assessment'. 'The exclusion of 'communication services … on individual demand' from the concept of 'television broadcasting' means that, conversely, the latter concept covers services which are not supplied on individual demand'. Hence, one of the key characteristics of television broadcasting is that the programmes are transmitted in a linear fashion, so that the content items are transmitted consecutively and can consequently only be received at the same time.

The past decade, traditional broadcasters were facing increasing competition from other new actors in the media sector who were often subject to a different and lighter regulatory regime. These differences in regulatory treatment between the various forms of distributing (identical or similar media) content created an unlevel playing field in the market of audiovisual content delivery. To give all media the same opportunities in a competitive internal market, the European legislator extended the scope from television broadcasting services to all forms of audiovisual media services (AVMS), including linear and non-linear services. Hence, the new Directive abandons the idea of regulating different platforms separately and instead creates a platform-neutral framework. This implies that not the transmission method, but the nature of the service should determine the type of regulation that is applicable. It is thus irrelevant whether an AVMS is delivered via cable, air, satellite or ADSL, the same rules apply.[13]

Article 1 (1) (a) of the AVMS Directive defines an AVMS as "*a service as defined by Articles 49 and 50 of the Treaty which is under the editorial responsibility of a media service provider and the principal purpose of which is the provision of programmes in order to inform, entertain or educate, to the general public by electronic communications networks within the meaning of Article 2(a) of Directive 2002/21/EC. Such an audiovisual media service is either a television broadcast or an on-demand audiovisual media service*". As already indicated above, an AVMS includes linear as well as non-linear services. Television broadcast, i.e. linear audiovisual service, is defined as "*an audiovisual media service provided by a media service provider for simultaneous viewing of programmes on the basis of a programme schedule*".[14] In short, the media service provider decides upon the moment in time when linear services, such as classic television, near-video-on-demand and streaming, are transmitted and establishes the programme schedule. In other words, it is a push service, i.e. the programmes are pushed to the viewers who do not have any influence at all on the content of the broadcasting and the time they are displayed.[15] This kind of broadcaster is opposed to on-demand services, i.e. non-linear services, being "*an audiovisual media service provided by a media service provider for the viewing of programmes at the moment chosen by the user and at his individual request on the basis of a*

[13] Valcke et al. 2008, 77.

[14] Article 1 (1) (e) of the AVMS Directive.

[15] Chavannes 2005, 273.

catalogue of programmes selected by the media service provider (i.e. a nonlinear audiovisual media service)".[16] In contrast to the linear television broadcasting, the non-linear services are pull services, i.e. the user decides upon the moment in time when a specific programme is transmitted. In short, the difference between linear and non-linear services ultimately depends upon who decides when a specific programme is transmitted and whether fixed schedules exist.[17] It is also important to note that this Directive only covers economic activities and, thus, that non-economic activities, such as private websites or blogs which are not in competition with television broadcasting, are excluded from the scope of the AVMS Directive.[18]

13.3 Two-Tiered Regulation

Although non-linear services are also covered by the new AVMS Directive, the European legislator considered that a horizontal approach to content regulation would only be effective if linear and non-linear services follow a two-tier regulation system.[19] This graduated regulation implies that a basic tier of rules applies to all AVMS[20] and that linear services have to meet additional obligations.[21]

This different treatment has been introduced because of the difference in the degree of choice and control the user can exercise and by the different impact the services have on society.[22] Compared to non-linear services, the user has no real impact on the content of linear television schedules. The decision about what to see and when to see is vested with the broadcaster and content is received in real time as it is being disseminated. Thus, the viewer is a passive consumer of information.[23] Furthermore, it is argued that non-linear services have less impact on society, because the content is not viewed simultaneously by the public as viewers themselves determine the time of transmission.[24] This difference justifies the light-touch regulation for non-linear services.[25]

The 'list of major events' mechanism that will be analysed in the next chapter is included in the second tier of obligations (*infra*).

---

[16] Article 1 (1) (g) of the AVMS Directive.

[17] Rapid Press Releases 2006, MEMO/06/419, 5.

[18] Recital 21 of the AVMS Directive.

[19] Commission of the European Communities 2005a, b, COM(2005) 646 final, 5.

[20] Article 5–11 of the AVMS Directive.

[21] Article 14–17, 27–28 of the AVMS Directive.

[22] Recital 58 of the AVMS Directive.

[23] Valcke and Stevens 2007, 288.

[24] Council of the European Union 2006, 4.

[25] Recital 58 of the AVMS Directive.

13.4 Right to Information and the Audiovisual Media Services Directive

13.4.1 Introduction

Given that the European Union is committed to promote the right to information and freedom of expression, as enshrined in Article 10 of the ECHR and Article 11 of the Charter of Fundamental Rights (*supra*), these fundamental rights have to be kept in mind by the European legislator when drafting rules for the media sector, being the TWF Directive and AVMS Directive.[26]

As indicated by the European Commission, the TWF Directive provided a minimum harmonisation of national legislations applying to television broadcasting services across the European Union in order to serve two primary and interconnected objectives: 1) facilitating the free movement of television broadcasting services, and 2) ensuring the protection of fundamental public interest objectives. In addition to these two primary aims, the Directive also contributed to the fulfilment of wider complementary cultural and social aims, such as protecting European cultural heritage and diversity, and economic aims, such as encouraging the growth of a strong, competitive and integrated European audiovisual industry. Furthermore, the TWF Directive also needed to contribute to ensure the protection of fundamental human rights such as *inter alia* the basic right of freedom of expression and right to information. In doing so, the TWF Directive tried to balance the right to information with economic interests when the 'list of major events' mechanism was introduced in 1997 (*infra*). Given that the social and cultural goals of European regulation in the audiovisual policy field remain essentially valid for the future, the same principles and objectives were taken into account when drafting the different amending Directive. As a result, the new AVMS Directive reaffirms the importance of the 'list of major events' mechanism and introduced the right to short news reporting to guarantee the public's right to information.[27] As already indicated, only the 'list of major events' mechanism will be analysed. However, in the following subsection, in order to provide a sufficiently comprehensive overview, the short news reporting regulation will be highlighted. Given that this book focuses on live and full access to sports content, the 'list of major events mechanism' will be dealt with in detail in Chap. 2.

13.4.2 Short News Reporting

Exclusive rights deals can hinder non-rights holders to cover (sports) events. By excluding other media than those the organisers are able to control, the coverage of

[26] European Commission 2005a, b, 1.

[27] Commission of the European Communities 2005, SEC(2005) 1625/2, 21–23.

the event could lead to pure censorship: controversial images being 'deleted', negative publicity being covered up, access being limited to a very small delegation of the press paying the highest fee.[28] Additionally, the exclusion of non-rights holding media from events of public interest could have a negative effect on the public's choice and the diversity of content. It could limit the collection and dissemination of information to the largest broadcasters to the detriment of both their smaller competitors and the viewers.[29] According to the European Commission, for example, small broadcasters "*do not have sufficient technical means or financial resources to bear the cost of the systematic marketing of exclusive broadcasting rights to certain major events [...]*".[30] To moderate these negative impacts and to promote and guarantee access to information and pluralism, the 'right to short reporting' was introduced in the regulatory framework.

Already in 1991, the Council of Europe issued the Recommendation No. R. (91) 5 on the right to short reporting stimulating Member States to take measures in order to safeguard the right to information with regard to important events exclusively broadcast on one channel.[31] However, this Recommendation is not a legally binding instrument. Later, after the first revision of the European Convention on Transfrontier Television (hereafter: ECTT),[32] a new Article 9 was introduced in the Convention stating that "*each Party shall examine and, where necessary, take legal measures such as introducing the right to short reporting [...] to avoid the right of the public to information being undermined [...]*".[33] Hence, the right to short reporting became a binding provision for the parties of this Convention. At the second revision, this Article 9 was maintained.[34] In spite of this ECTT provision, a patchwork of different regulatory regimes has appeared. The European legislator was of the opinion that these differences could lead to internal market distortions, and introduced in Article 3k of the 2007 amending Directive a European wide obligation.[35] After the 2010 codification, this Article was renumbered to Article 15. It is important to note that the right to short news reporting is only applicable to linear services.

Article 15 of the AVMS Directive states that:

1. Member States shall ensure that for the purpose of short news reports any broadcaster established in the Community has access on a fair, reasonable and non-discriminatory basis to events of high interest to the public which are transmitted on an exclusive basis by a broadcaster under their jurisdiction.

---

28 Werkers et al. 2008, 51.

29 European Commission 2003, 2.

30 European Commission European commission 2005a, b, 2.

31 Council of Europe 1991.

32 Council of Europe 1989.

33 Council of Europe 1998.

34 Council of Europe 2008, para 60; Council of Europe 2009.

35 Commission of the European Communities 2005, SEC(2005) 1625/2, 19–20.

2. If another broadcaster established in the same Member State as the broadcaster seeking access has acquired exclusive rights to the event of high interest to the public, access shall be sought from that broadcaster.
3. Member States shall ensure that such access is guaranteed by allowing broadcasters to freely choose short extracts from the transmitting broadcaster's signal with, unless impossible for reasons of practicality, at least the identification of their source.
4. As an alternative to paragraph 3, Member States may establish an equivalent system which achieves access on a fair, reasonable and non-discriminatory basis through other means.
5. Short extracts shall be used solely for general news programmes and may be used in on-demand audiovisual media services only if the same programme is offered on a deferred basis by the same media service provider.
6. Without prejudice to paragraphs 1 to 5, Member States shall ensure, in accordance with their legal systems and practices, that the modalities and conditions regarding the provision of such short extracts are defined, in particular, any compensation arrangements, the maximum length of short extracts and time limits regarding their transmission. Where compensation is provided for, it shall not exceed the additional costs directly incurred in providing access.

In short, this provision obliges all Member States to ensure the possibility for non-rights holding broadcasters to report about events of high interest to the public which are transmitted on an exclusive basis. The notion 'events of high interest to the public' may not be confused with 'events of major importance of society' included in the 'list of major events' mechanism (*infra*). It is obvious that 'high interest' is a lower threshold than 'major importance for society' as required under Article 14 of the AVMS Directive.[36] These short extracts should not exceed 90 s.[37] A broadcaster should also be able to exercise this right through an intermediary acting specifically on its behalf on a case-by-case basis.[38] As a result, news agencies as such will not be entitled by Article 15.[39]

As the 'list of major events' mechanism (*infra*), the concept of the right to short reporting is also based on the notion of events. However, unlike the 'list of major events' mechanism, the right to short news reporting does not only apply to events of major importance, but also to events of high interest to the public, such as royal weddings, political events, cultural events, sports events, etc. Hence, Scheuer and Schoental formulated it as follows: "*in order to be covered by [Article 15] of the AVMS Directive, events only need to be of 'high interest' which is a lower threshold than 'major importance to society' as required under [Article 14]*".[40]

Any channel, including dedicated sports channels, can solely use those short reports for general news programmes. The concept of general news programmes does not cover the compilation of short extracts into programmes serving

[36] Scheuer and Schoenthal 2008, 930; Helberger 2005, 108.

[37] Article 15 of the AVMS Directive; recital 55 of the AVMS Directive.

[38] Recital 55 of the AVMS Directive.

[39] Scheuer and Schoenthal 2008, 931.

[40] *Ibid.*, 930.

entertainment purposes.[41] Furthermore, such extracts may be used in on-demand audiovisual media services only if the same programme is offered on a deferred basis by the same media service provider. In this way, media service providers are able to provide their live television broadcast news programmes in the on-demand mode (after live transmission), without having to tailor the individual programme by omitting the short extracts. This possibility should, however, be restricted to the on-demand supply of the identical television broadcast programme by the same media service provider. In other words, so it may not be used to create new on-demand business models based on short extracts.[42]

Member States should ensure that broadcasters can freely choose short extracts from the transmitting broadcaster's signal or by other equivalent means, such as access to the venue of these events.[43] As stated by Scheuer and Schoental, granting access to a recording of a programme and not to the signal of the event cannot be considered to be an equivalent, because it "*would not allow for an expedient use by the broadcaster exercising its right to short reporting and ensure a reasonable level of choice for, and quality of, the produced report*".[44] Member States need to define the modalities and conditions regarding the provision of such short extracts: compensation arrangements, the maximum length of short extracts and time limits regarding their transmission.[45] Such terms should be communicated in a timely manner before the event of high interest takes place to give other broadcasters sufficient time to exercise such a right.[46] With regard to the compensation arrangements, the Austrian Bundeskommunikationssenat asked the European Court of Justice to interpret Article 15 (6) of the AVMS Directive. The question is whether Article 15 (6) of the AVMS Directive is compatible with the property rights of the broadcaster who bought the exclusive broadcasting rights and its freedom to conduct business, included in Articles 17 and 16 of the Charter of the Fundamental Rights of the European Union[47] and Article 1 of the first protocol.[48, 49]

The country of origin principle applies to both the access to, and the transmission of, the short extracts. The country of origin principle is the cornerstone of the AVMS Directive. According to this principle, media service providers are only subject to the national rules of one single Member State. All other Member States (receiving states) are prohibited from exercising a secondary control. In a transfrontier case, this means that different laws should be applied

41 Article 15 of the AVMS Directive; Recital 55 of the AVMS Directive.

42 Article 15 (5) of the AVMD Directive; recital 57 of the AVMS Directive.

43 Article 15 (3)-(4) of the AVMS Directive; recital 55 of the AVMS Directive.

44 Scheuer and Schoenthal 2008, 932.

45 Article 15 (6) of the AVMS Directive.

46 Recital 55 of the AVMS Directive.

47 European Union 2000.

48 Council of Europe 1952.

49 Bundeskommunikationssenat 2011.

sequentially. First, for access to the short extracts, the law of the Member State where the broadcaster supplying the initial signal (i.e. giving access) is established should apply (to determine the conditions for access to the short extracts). And then, for transmission of the short extracts, the law of the Member State where the broadcaster transmitting the short extracts is established applies (to determine the conditions for transmission of the short extracts).[50]

When we take a closer look at the AVMS Directive and the Recommendation No. R. (91) 5 on the right to short reporting, we can derive from these two 'regulatory' instruments that the aim of the right to short reporting is purely informative. First, the AVMS Directive stresses that broadcasters, to safeguard the freedom to receive information, have the right to use short extracts.[51] Second, Recommendation No. R. (91) 5 often refers to the informative characteristics of short news reports. Short reports are, for example, defined as "*brief sound and picture sequences about a major event such as to enable the public [...] to have a sufficient overview of the essential aspects of such an event*". Secondary broadcasters are defined as "*any broadcasting organisation [...] wishing to provide information, by means of short reports, [...]*".[52] Principle 2 of this Recommendation states that "*any secondary broadcaster should be entitled to provide information on a major event by means of a short report*". Moreover, the fact that short extracts could only be used in general news programmes seems to further underline the purely informative aim of the short reports. The AVMS Directive stresses that the notion of general news programmes does not cover the compilation of short extracts into programmes serving entertainment purposes.[53] Furthermore, in the Explanatory Report of the ECTT, the definition of the term 'event of high interest' indicates that "*at least some aspects of the event justify short footage in a television programme providing information to the public*".[54] Hence, as emphasised by Helberger, it can be summarised that the right to short reporting supports the media in its mission to keep the public properly informed despite exclusive control over newsworthy content.[55]

---

[50] Recital 55 of the AVMS Directive.

[51] *Ibid.*

[52] Council of Europe 1991.

[53] Recital 55 of the AVMS Directive.

[54] Council of Europe 2008, para 229.

[55] Helberger 2005, 111.

References

Legislation and Policy Documents:

European Union

Charters

European Union (2000) Charter of fundamental rights of the European Union. *OJ* (2000) C 364/1

Directives

Council Directive of 3 October 1989 on the coordination of certain provisions laid down by law, regulation or administrative action in Member States concerning the pursuit of television broadcasting activities, 89/552/EEC. *OJ* (1989) L 298/23

Council Directive of 3 October 1989 on the coordination of certain provisions laid down by law, regulation or administrative action in member states concerning the pursuit of television broadcasting activities, 89/552/EEC, *OJ* (1989) L 298/23, amended by Directive 97/36/EC of the European Parliament and of the Council of 30 June 1997. *OJ* (1997) L 202/60

European Parliament and Council directive 98/48/EC of 20 July 1998 amending Directive 98/34/EC laying down a procedure for the provision of information in the field of technical standards and regulations. *OJ* (1998) L 217/18

European Parliament and Council directive 2000/31/EC of 8 June 2000 on certain legal aspects of information society services, in particular electronic commerce, in the Internal Market (Directive on electronic commerce). *OJ* (2000) L 178/1

European Parliament and Council directive 2007/65/EC of the of 11 December 2007 amending Council Directive 89/552/EEC on the coordination of certain provisions laid down by law, regulation or administrative action in Member States concerning the pursuit of television broadcasting activities. *OJ* (2007) L 332/27

European Parliament and Council directive 2010/13/EU of 10 March 2010 on the coordination of certain provisions laid down by law, regulation or administrative action in Member States concerning the provision of audiovisual media services (Audiovisual Media Services Directive). *OJ* (2010) L 95/1

European Parliament and Council directive of 10 March 2010 on the coordination of certain provisions laid down by law, regulation or administrative action in Member States concerning the provision of audiovisual media services (Audiovisual Media Services Directive). *OJ* (2010) L 95/1

Commission Staff Working Document

Commission of the european communities (2005) Commission Staff working document—Annex to the proposal for a directive of the European parliament and of the council amending council directive 89/552/EC on the coordination of certain provisions laid down by law, regulation or administrative action in Member States concerning the pursuit of television broadcasting activities impact assessment—draft audiovisual media services directive. 13 December 2005, SEC(2005) 1625/2

Proposals

Commission of the European communities (2005) Proposal for a directive of the European parliament and of the council amending council directive 89/552/EEC on the coordination of certain provisions laid down by law, regulation or administrative action in Member States concerning the pursuit of television broadcasting activities. 13 December 2005, COM(2005) 646 final

Reports

Commission of the European communities (2003) Fourth report from the commission to the council, the European parliament, the European economic and social committee and the committee of the regions on the application of directive 89/552/EEC "Television without Frontiers". 6 January 2003, COM(2002) 778 final

Press Releases

Rapid press releases (2006) The commission proposal for a modernisation of the television without frontiers directive: frequently asked questions, 9 Nov 2006, MEMO/06/419

Miscallanious

Council of the European union (2006) Proceedings audiovisual working party. (COD) 6994/06, 7 March 2006

European commission (2003) Discussion paper—review of the television without frontiers directive theme 6: access to short extracts of events subject to exclusive rights. http://ec.europa.eu/avpolicy/docs/reg/modernisation/2003_review/twf2003_theme6_en.pdf. Accessed 21 Aug 2010

European commission (2005) Why and how Europe seeks pluralism in audiovisual media. http://www.fub.it/files/Pluralism.pdf. Accessed 9 Feb 2012

European commission (2005) Issues paper for the audiovisual conference in liverpool—right to information and right to short reporting. http://ec.europa.eu/avpolicy/docs/reg/modernisation/issue_papers/ispa_shortrep_en.pdf. Accessed 20 Aug 2010

European commission (2007) Information society and media and communications: linking European policies. http://ec.europa.eu/information_society/activities/policy_link/brochures/documents/media.pdf. Accessed 20 Aug 2010

Council of Europe

Conventions

Council of Europe (1989) European convention on transfrontier television, CETS No. 132, 5 May 1989

Council of Europe (2008) European convention on transfrontier television—drafting group on the revision of the European convention on transfrontier television, T-TT-GDR(2008)002Rev5.

http://www.coe.int/t/dghl/standardsetting/media/T-TT/T-TT-GDR_2008_002Rev5_en%20 Preliminary%20Draft%20Expl%20Rep%20ECTT.pdf. Accessed 21 Aug 2010

Protocols

Council of Europe (1952) Protocol to the convention for the protection of human rights and fundamental freedoms as amended by protocol No. 11

Council of Europe (1998) Protocol amending the European convention on transfrontier television, 1 October 1998. http://conventions.coe.int/Treaty/EN/Treaties/Html/171.htm. Accessed 20 Aug 2010

Council of Europe (2009) Draft second protocol amending the European convention on transfrontier television and its explanatory report, T-TT(2009)007FIN_en, 24 September 2009. http://www.coe.int/t/dghl/standardsetting/media/T-TT/T-TT_2009_007FIN_en%20 second%20protocol%20amendment.pdf. Accessed 20 Aug 2010

Recommendations

Council of Europe ((1991) Recommendation No. R (91) 5 of the committee of ministers to member states on the right to short reporting on major events where exclusive rights for their television broadcast have been acquired in a transfrontier context

Case Law

Court of Justice

CJ, Mediakabel v Commissariaat voor de Media, 2 June 2005, Case C-89/04, ECR (2005) I-4891

Austria

Bundeskommunikationssenat (2011) GZ 611.003/0004-BKS/2011, http://www.bundeskanzleramt.at/DocView.axd?CobId=43863. Accessed 24 June 2011

Doctrine

Chavannes R (2005) Note under ECJ 02.06.2005, nr. C-89/04. Mediaforum, vol. 7(8):273–275

Football Italia (2009) Tetchy Mou rails against the Press, 8 December 2009

Helberger N (2005) Controlling access to content—regulating conditional access in digital broadcasting. Kluwer Law International, The Hague

Scheuer A, Schoenthal M (2008) Article 3k AVMSD. In: Castendyk O et al (eds) European media law. Alphen a/d Rijn, Kluwer Law International, pp 929–933

Schoental M (2006) Major events and reporting rights. IRIS Plus 4:1–8

Valcke P, Stevens D (2007) Graduated regulation of 'regulatable' content and the European audiovisual media services directive one small step for the industry and one giant leap for the legislator? Telematics Inform 24:285–302

Valcke P et al. (2008) Hoofdstuk 1. communicatierecht. In: Valcke P and Dumortier J (eds), Trends in Digitale televisie: Juridische Uitdagingen. die Keure, Antwerpen, pp 1–120

Werkers E et al (2008) One world one dream? Sports blogging at the Beijing Olympic games. ISLJ 3–4:42–51

Chapter 14
'List of Major Events' Mechanism

14.1 Introduction to the 'List of Major Events' Mechanism

This section begins with an explanation of the origin and philosophy of the 'list of major events' mechanism. After the delineation of the broader background of this system, two basic theoretical concepts will be introduced: events of major importance and live and deferred coverage. This section will describe which sports events are/could be considered as events of major importance and, thus, could be included in the list of major events. Additionally, this section will explain when such an event of major importance should be broadcast live or when deferred coverage would be sufficient. In doing so, it will be analysed in more detail whether Article 10 of the ECHR could be the legal basis to justify a claim to watch major sports events live and full.

14.1.1 Origin and Philosophy

Ever since the growth of pay-television in the late 1980s–early 1990s, there is considerable concern about the consequences of certain commercial practices in the exploitation of exclusive sports broadcasting rights. In the struggle for exclusive broadcasting rights, free-to-air broadcasters have lost, over the years, the bidding war to pay-television operators. This trend, however, could lead to important sports events, which were previously broadcast freely to the public, migrating to pay-television platforms. This shift is likely to cause the so-called siphoning effect that occurs "*when an event or programme currently shown on free-to-air television is purchased by an operator for the purpose of showing it on a subscription channel instead. If such a transfer occurs, the programme or event will become unavailable for showing on free television system or its showing on*

K. Lefever, *New Media and Sport*, ASSER International Sports Law Series,
DOI: 10.1007/978-90-6704-873-6_14,

free television will be delayed so a segment of the people [...] could be denied access altogether."[1] Although a proportion of households will be likely to switch to pay-television platforms, households unable or unwilling to pay an extra subscription fee could be deprived of access to those important events, which may endanger their right to information.

As indicated before, access to coverage of sports events is valued very high, because it can play an important role in bringing people together and creating social cohesion (*supra*). However, sport can only create a shared experience on one condition: a large number of people can follow the event on television. One can only sensibly discuss and debate a game with other people when they have also seen it and shared the experience.[2] Hence, guaranteeing that everybody has access to coverage of the event represents a prerequisite for such effects to occur.[3] Given that some sports events are seen as so vital and of heritage importance, public authorities considered that it was justified to intervene preventing those events from 'disappearing behind a decoder.' In order to safeguard the social role of sport, to limit the migration of sports events to pay-television and to foster the public's right to information, many countries have adopted laws whereby the national government mandates that certain events of national and cultural significance could only be shown in an exclusive way on free-to-air television.[4] Given that, in the EU, several Member States had different regulations, these differences could restrict the cross-border transmission of major sports (or other) events and the development of one integrated European market.[5]

Therefore, to promote the cross-border broadcasting transmission and to guarantee the public's right to information, the European Parliament proposed on second reading, at the first revision of the TWF Directive in 1997, to insert a new Article 3a relating to free access of the public to the broadcasting of major sports events.[6] Before taking position, the European Commission wanted to take a closer look at this problem,[7] resulting in two communications: a communication of Mr. Oreja[8] and a communication of the European Commission itself.[9] Those communications concluded that the different regulatory regimes resulted in a patchwork of different measures throughout the Union restricting the free circulation of television services and the construction of an internal market. Therefore, the European Commission concluded that, in order to avoid legal uncertainty and

1 Home Box Office, Inc v. FCC 567 F.2d 9 (D.C. Cir 1977).

2 Boardman and Hargreaves-Heap 1999, 173.

3 Gratton and Solberg 2007, 208.

4 Fraser and McMahon 2002, 2.

5 Fleming 1997, 282.

6 European Parliament 1996.

7 Castille 1997, 11.

8 Oreja 1997.

9 European Commission 1997, SEC(1997)0174/9.

market distortions,[10] it was necessary to harmonise these different regulations.[11] As a result, the European legislator decided to include this Article 3a, better known as the 'list of major events' mechanism, in the TWF Directive, allowing Member States to draw up a list of events of major importance for society that could only be broadcast in an exclusive way on free-to-air television (*infra*).

Inspiration for this new Article 3a of the TWF Directive was found in the old Article 9 of the European Convention on Transfrontier Television stating that "*each Party shall examine the legal measures to avoid the right of the public to information being undermined due to the exercise by a broadcaster of exclusive rights for the transmission or retransmission, [...], of an event of high public interest and which has the effect of depriving a large part of the public in one or more other Parties of the opportunity to follow that event on television.*" In 1998, when the ECTT was revised for the first time, the public's right to information was substantially enlarged and strengthened, introducing a new Article 9 *bis* establishing a framework which guarantees the public's free access to the broadcasts of major events similar to the TWF Directive.[12] In 2009, it was proposed, by a second amending protocol, to rename the ECTT in the European Convention on Transfrontier Audiovisual Media Services reflecting the widened scope of the Convention (hereafter: ECTAMS).[13] When amending this Convention, the provision related to the 'list of major events' mechanism was renumbered and became Article 10.[14] However, the revision of the Convention is officially discontinued following the termination of the negotiations of the Convention. Kroes, in a letter addressed to the Secretary General of the Council of Europe, underlined that the European Union has exclusive competence for the issues covered by the draft of the revised Convention and that EU member States are not allowed to become party to the Convention on their own. Furthermore, the letter indicated that the EU does not intend to become a party to the Convention as this would constrain the speed and scope of any future policy response in the areas covered.[15]

During the consultation rounds of the second revision of the TWF Directive, the European legislator and the different stakeholders had the opportunity to revise Article 3a. In the Fourth Report on the application of the TWF Directive, the European Commission stated that "*Article 3a of the TWF Directive was working satisfactorily.*"[16] Moreover, the majority of contributions received during the

[10] Recital 19 of the TWF Directive.

[11] European Commission 1997, SEC(1997)0174/9., para 3.

[12] Council of Europe 2001.

[13] Council of Europe 2009a, b, c.

[14] Council of Europe 2009c, 10.

[15] Council of Europe 2011.

[16] Commission of the European Communities 2003c, COM(2002) 778 final, 10.

consultation rounds also considered Article 3a of the TWF Directive to be "*useful, necessary, effective and proportionate.*" Hence, according to the European Commission, there was no urgent, pressing need for a revision of this provision.[17] At the Liverpool Audiovisual Conference "Between Culture and Commerce" in 2005, the majority of the participants also confirmed their support to the terms of Article 3a.[18] Therefore, although the TWF Directive was revised fundamentally, the provision about the 'list of major events' mechanism was not subject to modifications. The Article was only renumbered and became Article 14 of the AVMS Directive stating:

> *1. Each Member State may take measures in accordance with Community law to ensure that broadcasters under its jurisdiction do not broadcast on an exclusive basis events which are regarded by that Member State as being of major importance for society in such a way as to deprive a substantial proportion of the public in that Member State of the possibility of following such events by live coverage or deferred coverage on free television. If it does so, the Member State concerned shall draw up a list of designated events, national or non-national, which it considers to be of major importance for society. It shall do so in a clear and transparent manner in due time. In doing so, the Member State concerned shall also determine whether these events should be available by whole or partial live coverage, or where necessary or appropriate for objective reasons in the public interest, whole or partial deferred coverage.*
>
> *2. Member States shall immediately notify to the Commission any measures taken or to be taken pursuant to paragraph 1. Within a period of 3 months from the notification, the Commission shall verify that such measures are compatible with Community law and communicate them to the other Member States. It shall seek the opinion of the contact committee established pursuant to Article 23a. It shall forthwith publish the measures taken in the Official Journal of the European Union and at least once in a year the consolidated list of the measures taken by Member States.*
>
> *3. Member States shall ensure, by appropriate means within the framework of their legislation, that broadcasters under their jurisdiction do not exercise the exclusive rights purchased by those broadcasters following the date of publication of this Directive in such a way that a substantial proportion of the public in another Member State is deprived of the possibility of following events which are designated by that other Member State in accordance with paragraphs 1 and 2 by whole or partial live coverage or, where necessary or appropriate for objective reasons in the public interest, whole or partial deferred coverage on free television as determined by that other Member State in accordance with paragraph 1.*

In short, the 'list of major events' mechanism allows Member States to draw up a list with events, being of major importance for society, that can only be broadcast exclusively on a free-to-air television in order to ensure that a substantial proportion of the public would not be deprived of the possibility of following such events.

[17] Commission of the European Communities 2003b, COM(2003) 784 final, 16; European Commission 2005.

[18] DCMS 2005, 15.

14.1.2 Events of Major Importance for Society

14.1.2.1 No Objective Definition

Although only 'events being of major importance for society' (which may not be confused with 'events of high importance to the public' (*supra*)) should be broadcast exclusively on free-to-air television, it is not clear what is meant by this notion. The AVMS Directive does not contain an objective definition of the concept 'events of major importance for society.' This Directive provides little guidance in recital 49 and 52 to decide whether an event can be considered as an event of major importance. According to recital 52, "*events of major importance for society have to meet certain criteria, that is to say be outstanding events which are of interest to the general public in the European Union or in a given Member State or in an important component part of a given Member State and are organised in advance by an event organiser who is legally entitled to sell the rights pertaining to that event.*" Furthermore, recital 49 clarifies that "*the events of major importance for society that should be covered in the area of sports are events such as the Olympic Games, the football World Cup and European football Championship.*"

Given that this guidance is included in the recitals of the Directive, it is up to each of the Member States to specify the criteria to determine which event can be included in the list. Despite this freedom of interpretation, the criteria used by each Member State to include an event in the list vary to some degree, but display a considerable consistency. When we take a closer look at the criteria employed, in most instances it is enough for the event to satisfy two of the following criteria[19]: (1) the event is a pre-eminent national or international event,[20] (2) the event is of interest to those who do not normally follow that branch of sport on television,[21] (3) the event is generally followed by many viewers and is traditionally broadcast on free-to-air television,[22] (4) the event involves a national team or national representatives,[23] and (5) the sport of which it is a part has particular cultural

[19] Craufurd Smith and Bottcher 2002, 120.

[20] Example: Article 153, § 1, 2° of the Flemish Community Media Decree; Article I, § 4 (1), 3° of the Federal Act on the exercise of exclusive television broadcasting rights 2001.

[21] Example: Article 4, § 2 (1) of the French Community Media Decree; Article 1 (2) (a) of the Decision No 8/1999.

[22] Example: Article 153, § 1, 2° of the Flemish Community Media Decree; Article I, § 4 (1), 4° of the Federal Act on the exercise of exclusive television broadcasting rights; Article 2 (1) (d) of the Decision No 8/1999.

[23] Example: Article 2 (1) (c) of the Decision No 8/1999; Article 153, § 1, 2° of the Flemish Community Media Decree states.

significance for the country in question.[24] To stipulate those criteria, the Guidelines attached to the ECTT were used as inspiration.[25]

As to the third criterion, FIFA stressed that fulfilment of that criterion is merely an indicator of the importance of the event allowing consideration of the possibility of including it in the list.[26] The UEFA added the following: "*[this criterion] does not constitute an appropriate basis for measuring the importance of an event for society. In fact, before the development of pay television, this criterion would have applied to every sporting event that was televised.*"[27] However, the General Court stressed that "*[e]ven before the advent of pay television, many events were not broadcast on the free channels of the time, with the result that that criterion cannot be regarded as being automatically met today in respect of such an event.*"[28]

It is important to realise that sports events could only be included in the list if the different criteria are met. Therefore, the 'list of major events' mechanism and the possibility of a sports event to be included in the list may not be used as a means to pressure sports organisations to take specific initiatives. In Flanders, for example, Member of Parliament Decaluwé suggested (or even threatened) to add the play-offs of the Belgian Jupiler Pro League to the list of major events in order to convince the Pro League to abolish the controversial play-offs. According to Decaluwé, given that the play-offs, when they are listed, should be broadcast on free-to-air television, the value of the contract with pay-television operators would decrease. Decaluwé is hoping that the Pro League would prefer better financial conditions and, thus, would decide to return to a competition without play-offs.[29] Such an illegitimate use of the 'list of major events' mechanism should not be permitted.

Since there is no objective definition, state practice varies and differs mainly on two different levels: (1) national traditions and (2) amount of games per event.

A. National Lists

The events included in the national lists differ from Member State to Member State depending on their national traditions. Although all the notified lists contain the Olympic Games (though in Ireland only the Summer Games[30]) and a variety of

[24] Example: Article 2 (1) (b) of the Decision No 8/1999; Article I, § 4 (1), 2° of the Federal Act on the exercise of exclusive television broadcasting rights states; Article 153, § 1, 3° of the Flemish Community Media Decree 2009.

[25] Council of Europe 2002, para 10.

[26] GC, FIFA v European Commission, Case T-385/07, para 88.

[27] GC, UEFA v European Commission, para 113.

[28] *Ibid.*, para 140.

[29] De Morgen 2011b.

[30] Broadcasting (Major Events Television Coverage) Act 1999 (Designation of Major Events) Order 2003.

football events (e.g. Champions League, FIFA World Cup and European Football Championship), the Member States' lists reflect their own national interests and own social characteristics.[31] It comes as no surprise that only the Belgian list contains the World Cyclo-Cross championship[32] and that the Irish list reckons the Nation Cup at the Dublin horse show[33] as a major event.

Although a compulsory European list had been discussed, this idea was rejected for the 'national tradition' reason. First, a European list would not add any value, because some sports are less known in some Member States. Second, a European list would become too long if taking into account all the national characteristics.[34] And finally, the concept of a European list is seen as being in contradiction with the principle of subsidiarity.[35]

B. Amount of Games Per Event

As indicated by Weatherill, there is even a wide variation in connection with events which one would suppose would be of a more-or-less equally powerful interest. The finals of Football's World Cup and European Football Championship are listed in their entirety in the UK[36] and Belgium,[37] while Germany[38] and Austria[39] have only listed the final, semifinals, opening match and matches of the respective national team, and Italy[40] only the final and the matches of the national team.[41]

For *inter alia* this reason, the FIFA and UEFA have challenged the European Commission's decision declaring that the UK and Belgian lists are compatible with Community law (*infra*). According to the UEFA and FIFA, the European Commission's decisions are based on a manifest error of appreciation, as the European Commission concluded that matches not involving any home nation team in the European Football Championship or FIFA World Cup could be considered as events of major importance for the UK or Belgium.[42] Therefore,

---

[31] Reding 2004, 3.

[32] Article 1, § 1, 6° of the Order of the Flemish Government establishing the list of events of major importance to society.

[33] Broadcasting (Major Events Television Coverage) Act 1999 (Designation of Major Events) Order 2003.

[34] European Commission 1997, SEC(1997)0174/9.

[35] Commission of the European Communities 2003b, COM(2003) 784 final, 16.

[36] Ofcom 2008a, Annex 1.

[37] Article 1, § 1 (2) of the Order of the Flemish Government establishing the list of events of major importance to society.

[38] § 5a of the Interstate Treaty on Broadcasting.

[39] § 1 (2) of the Ordinance on events of substantial social interest.

[40] Article 2 of the Decision No 8/1999.

[41] Weatherill 2007, 236.

[42] GC, FIFA v European Commission, Case T-68/08; GC, FIFA v European Commission, Case T-385/07; GC, UEFA v European Commission,.

they argued that the listing of the entire European Football Championship and FIFA World Cup as a protected event is disproportionate. Although FIFA and UEFA accepted that 'prime'/'gala' matches, i.e. games involving the national teams should remain on free-to-air television, along with the final, the knockout rounds and the opening game, 'non-prime'/'non-gala' matches should be made available for pay-television broadcasters.[43] Although recital 49 of the AVMS Directive makes specific reference to the Football World Cup and European Football Championship, both FIFA and UEFA argued that there is no evidence that it was the Community legislature's intention to ensure that every match in those football tournaments should be regarded as being of major importance for society.[44] Although the European Commission agreed with the latter, it stressed that designating events as being of major importance for society is a matter of the Member States' judgment.[45] Furthermore, the European Commission argued that each Member State has some discretion for determining which events are of major importance for society, and that the application of that criterion has not been harmonised at Community level, implying that it is not for the European Commission to impose its views concerning the importance of a specific event for the Member States in question.[46]

Hence, the question is whether a match between, for example, France and Spain would be of cultural or social importance for citizens other than Spanish or French people, and therefore also should be broadcast on free-to-air television in the UK. Some argue that if the match France versus Spain is the determining match to decide whether England would go to the quarter finals, there would be an argument for that game being of cultural significance.[47] However, they express their doubt that this decisive match as such will create the same sense of belonging as a match played by the English team itself. Nevertheless, the guidance given by the UK on listed events indicates that it is sufficient for the event to be a 'pre-eminent international event in the sport.'[48] Hence, it is not required that the national team is involved. Since the FIFA World Cup offers access to world-class football, of interest whether one's national team is playing, Craufurd Smith and Bottcher argued that "*there is a plausible case for listing all the world cup finals matches.*" Moreover, football has become a much more cosmopolitan game. Domestic clubs now have players from around the world and fans are interested in watching them play, even if it is for an opposing national side. Therefore, given the status of the FIFA World Cup and the widespread interest in the development of the tournament, those authors argued

---

[43] GC, FIFA v European Commission, Case T-68/08, para 59; GC, FIFA v European Commission, Case T-385/07, para 64; GC, UEFA v European Commission, para 116.

[44] GC 2010a, paras 53, 54; GC 2010b, para 76.

[45] European Commission 2010.

[46] GC 2010b, para 82.

[47] Sportbusiness International 2008b.

[48] Ministry for Culture, Media and Sports 1997.

that it would be difficult to establish that the UK had incorrectly assessed the public interest in listing all the matches of the FIFA World Cup.[49]

According to the General Court, although the Football World Cup and European Football Championship are mentioned in recital 49 of the AVMS Directive, this does not mean that the inclusion of the Football World Cup and European Football Championship as a whole is automatically compatible with Community law.[50] However, the General Court indicated that this recital implies that "*when a Member State includes World Cup matches [or/and EURO matches] in the list it has decided to draw up, it does not need to include in its notification to the Commission specific grounds concerning their nature as an event of major importance for society.*"[51] Given that the World Cup and EURO should be seen as a single event rather than as a series of individual events divided into 'prime' matches and 'non-prime' matches,[52] the General Court explicitly emphasised that "*there is no valid consideration leading to the conclusion that, in principle, only 'prime' ['gala'] matches may be thus categorised and therefore included in such a list.*"[53] The General Court even indicated that not all 'non-prime' matches must be necessarily of major importance for society in order for the World Cup and EURO to be legitimately included, in its entirety, on the lists.[54] As long as those matches could have an influence on the fate of the national team in the tournament may depend on the results of 'non-prime' matches and that those matches could determine the opponents of the national teams,[55] their inclusion in a list is justified.[56] The fact that non-prime matches attract less viewers or that broadcasters decide not to broadcast those matches, neither does imply that those matches could not be included in the list of major events.[57] Additionally, the General Court stated that the importance of those 'non-prime' matches arises "*from the simple fact that they are part of the World Cup tournament [EURO tournament], just like other sports for which interest, usually low, is*

[49] Craufurd Smith and Bottcher 2002, 130.

[50] GC, FIFA v European Commission, Case T-68/08, para 56; GC, FIFA v European Commission, Case T-385/07, para 60; GC, UEFA v European Commission, para 52.

[51] GC, FIFA v European Commission, Case T-68/08, para 57; GC, FIFA v European Commission, Case T-385/07, para 61; GC, UEFA v European Commission, para 53.

[52] GC, FIFA v European Commission, Case T-68/08, para 70; GC, FIFA v European Commission, Case T-385/07, para 72; GC, UEFA v European Commission, para 103.

[53] GC, FIFA v European Commission, Case T-68/08, para 69; GC, FIFA v European Commission, Case T-385/07, para 71; GC, UEFA v European Commission, para 103.

[54] GC, FIFA v European Commission, Case T-385/07, para 102.

[55] GC, FIFA v European Commission, Case T-68/08, para 70; GC, FIFA v European Commission, Case T-385/07, para 72; GC, UEFA v European Commission, para 103.

[56] GC, FIFA v European Commission, Case T-68/08, para 120; GC, FIFA v European Commission, Case T-385/07, para 102; GC, UEFA v European Commission, para 136.

[57] GC, FIFA v European Commission, Case T-68/08, para 123; GC, FIFA v European Commission, Case T-385/07, paras 103 and 105; GC, UEFA v European Commission, para 127.

heightened when they take place in the Olympic Games."[58] As a result, the European Commission, in not questioning the view that it is not appropriate to distinguish between 'prime' and 'non-prime' matches for the purpose of determining the importance of the World Cup and EURO for the Belgian and UK society, did not make any error.[59] Moreover, the fact that the UK distinguished between 'prime' and 'non-prime' matches for other events, such as the Cricket World Cup, or that the other Member States only included 'prime' matches in their list, does not affect this finding.[60] It should be regretted that the General Court did not refer to the new Article 165 of the TFEU in order to attribute more weight to the important role that sports events could play for the society (*supra*). FIFA and UEFA decided to appeal this ruling.[61]

14.1.2.2 Lists Still up-to-date?

The question that often arises is whether those lists are still up-to-date. In the UK, for example, the Government decided to review the list of events (for the first time in 10 years) in 2009.[62] As formulated by Culture, Media and Sport Secretary Andy Burnham, it is important that "*the list moves with the times and people's tastes.*"[63] In the review of the listed events, two major questions were discussed: (1) do the current criteria remain appropriate or is there a need to revise those criteria, and (2) should there be any changes to the events currently listed?[64] Although recommendations to change the criteria and the events on the list were published in November 2009, the new UK Government decided to push back the final decision with regard to this topic until the whole country switches to digital television by the end of 2012. Boyle referred to this decision as: "*change of government, change of mood music.*"[65] Sports Minister Robertson said that "*with digital switchover concluding in 2012, this will result in the widespread availability of a significantly increased number of television channels, many of which will be free to air. Add to this [...] the Ofcom pay-TV review, and the broadcasting context for this decision is increasingly unclear.*"[66]

---

[58] GC, FIFA v European Commission, Case T-68/08, para 117; GC, FIFA v European Commission, Case T-385/07, para 99; GC, UEFA v European Commission, para 124.

[59] GC, FIFA v European Commission, Case T-68/08, para 118; GC, FIFA v European Commission, Case T-385/07, para 100; GC, UEFA v European Commission, para 125.

[60] GC, FIFA v European Commission, Case T-68/08, para 133; GC, UEFA v European Commission, paras 76 and 138.

[61] C-204/11 P pending case 2011; C-205/11 P pending case 2011; C-201/11 P pending case 2011.

[62] Department for Culture, Media and Sport 2009.

[63] Telegraph 2008a; Broadcastnow 2008.

[64] Department for Culture, Media and Sport 2009, 8; The Guardian 2008c; Telegraph 2008a.

[65] Raymond Boyle 2010.

[66] Sportbusiness International 2010; Sports-city 2010.

In a rapidly changing society, it is necessary that all Member States would review or at least take a look at their list. In Belgium, for example, the Queen Elisabeth Music Competition is included in the list of major events.[67] The European Commission has accepted that this music competition is included in the list, because "*the Queen Elisabeth Music Competition has a distinct cultural importance as a catalyst of Belgian cultural identity, due to the important contribution of Queen Elisabeth and her husband King Albert to Belgian history and to the extremely high quality and the worldwide significance of that cultural event.*"[68] Although it can be argued that the Queen Elisabeth Music Competition is a prestigious and important event for the music world, it is questionable that this competition still meets at least two of the four required criteria.[69] According to the first criterion, the event should have "*a special general resonance within the Member State, and not simply a significance to those who ordinarily follow the sport or activity concerned.*" Although it cannot be denied that the Queen Elisabeth Music Competition is a unique and important event, the attention given by non-culture-lovers for this competition has decreased over the years. Second, the event should have "*a generally recognised, distinct cultural importance for the population in the Member State, in particular as a catalyst of cultural identity.*" Given the fact that the interest for this event has faded over the years, this event could probably not be considered as having a significant impact on the building of the Belgian cultural identity. The third criterion requires that "*involvement of the national team in the event concerned in the context of a competition or tournament of international importance.*" In the Queen Elisabeth Music Competition of 2007 (piano) and 2009 (violin), two Belgian musicians reached the final. In the Queen Elisabeth Music Competition of 2008 (singing), two Belgians reached the semi-finals. Given that it is not guaranteed that a Belgian musician will be qualified to play or sing in the competition, this criterion is not always applicable. However, it should be said that this music contest is an international known competition. The fourth and last criterion requires that "*the event has traditionally been broadcast on free television and has commanded large television audiences." With regard this last criterion, it is important to note that it is difficult to assess 'a consistently large audience' or 'high ratings.'* Given that no threshold or percentage of the population is specified, the European Commission stresses that it is up to the Member States to assess, on a case-by-case basis, whether or not a large audience was reached.[70] Although the Queen Elisabeth Music Competition has been broadcast on free-to-air television, *in casu* the public broadcaster, it has not always

---

[67] Article 1, § 1, 10° of the Order of the Flemish Government establishing the list of events of major importance to society.

[68] Commission decision of 25 June 2007 on the compatibility with Community law of measures taken by Belgium pursuant to Article 3a(1) of Council Directive 89/552/EEC on the coordination of certain provisions laid down by law, regulation or administrative action in Member States concerning the pursuit of television broadcasting activities. *OJ* (2007) L 180/24, para 15.

[69] Article 153, § 1 of the Flemish Community Media Decree 2009.

[70] European Commission 2010.

been able to attract large audiences. Between 2001 and 2009, an average of 150.000 persons has been watching the Queen Elisabeth Music Contest for at least 10 min every year.[71] Hence, it seems that it should be studied in depth whether this contest does still meet at least two of the required conditions or whether it is no longer justified to be included in the list.

14.1.3 (Whole or Partial) Live or (Whole or Partial) Deferred

14.1.3.1 No Objective Definition

Each Member State needs to determine whether an event should to be covered (wholy or partialy) live or whether deferred coverage would be sufficient and justified. Just as for the notion 'event of major importance for society,' the AVMS Directive does not contain an objective definition of these concepts. Live coverage means that the viewers can follow the event in real time, as it takes place. Deferred coverage means that the event concerned is recorded and broadcast at a later point in time.[72]

The coverage and scheduling of programmes or events is often a commercial decision directed to attract the largest possible viewing audience in order to increase the potential to earn advertising revenue. This motivation results in the scheduling of events live or delayed, based on what the broadcasters consider will rate highest on that specific moment.[73] The basic principle of the 'list of major events' mechanism, however, should be that a listed event should be broadcast live and in full. The corollary to this is that if a (free-to-air) broadcaster decides not to broadcast an event live and in full, because other programmes would rate more highly, it could be argued that the event is not truly of national importance and therefore should not be listed.[74] But there are always exceptions to any rule...

According to Article 14 (1) of the AVMS Directive, a deferred coverage is acceptable "*where necessary or appropriate for objective reasons in the public interest.*" As Scheuer and Schoenthal make clear, once a Member State has opted for a list, "*it can no longer restrict the measures guaranteeing the public's access to merely deferred coverage without special justification.*"[75] The AVMS Directive, however, does not contain any guidance on how 'objective reasons in the public interest' ought to be interpreted. Scheuer and Schoental stressed that "*since the primary objective of prescribing non-exclusive coverage is to ensure the*

71 VRT 2009.

72 Scheuer and Schoenthal 2008, 423.

73 Department of Broadband, Communications and the Digital Economy 2009, 17; FACTS 2001.

74 Cricket Australia 2009.

75 Scheuer and Schoenthal 2008, 423.

participation of the vast majority of the population, any reasons given for allowing deferred coverage should be tested against this interest." Therefore, if audience figures demonstrate that a substantial part of the public is not following or cannot follow live coverage, deferred coverage may be the preferable option.[76] For example, in the cases of the 2002 FIFA World Cup co-hosted by South Korea and Japan or the 2008 Beijing Olympic Games, it simply could not be expected of sports fans to get up in the middle of the night to watch the competition. Additionally, according to Scheuer and Schoental, if two events of major importance take place at the same time, broadcasters may have recourse to deferred coverage.[77] Furthermore, para 16 of the ECTT's Guidelines clarifies that "*live coverage is naturally preferred by audiences, but may sometimes not be possible due to: the long duration of the event; the time at which an event takes place; the time difference between the State in which the event takes place and the State in which the event is designated. The above circumstances would seem to be an objective reason for deciding on deferred or partial live coverage of the event.*" However, FIFA states that "*the fact that two matches are played simultaneously does not justify the failure to broadcast one of them, since they can be broadcast by different channels, and sub-licences are also possible for this specific case.*"[78]

In Austria, for example, only specified events, such as the Summer or Winter Olympic Games, the FIS World Alpine skiing championships, the World Nordic skiing championships and the Vienna Opera Ball, can be broadcast deferred.[79] Moreover, deferred coverage of those events is only possible when the broadcast starts within 24 h after the beginning of the event.[80] In France, events of major importance may be broadcast in prerecorded form where they take place between midnight and 6 a.m., French time, on the condition that the broadcast in France starts before 10 a.m.[81] In the French Community of Belgium, television broadcasters may postpone the broadcasting of a listed event if it takes place between midnight and 8 a.m., Belgian time, if the event coincides with a news or current affairs programme normally broadcast by the service at that time or if the event comprises several elements taking place simultaneously.[82]

In the UK, though, Ofcom took the view that the interests of viewers lie in allowing them to participate in the event as it happens, as far as possible. This suggests that live television coverage of most sports events, including those taking place in different time zones, should be covered simultaneous with the event. However, Ofcom has also recognised that a certain degree of flexibility is

---

[76] *Ibid.*, 423.

[77] *Ibid.*, 423.

[78] GC, FIFA v European Commission, Case T-385/07, para 89.

[79] § 2 of the Ordinance on events of substantial social interest.

[80] Article I, §3 (1) of the Federal Act on the exercise of exclusive television broadcasting rights.

[81] Article 4, § 3 of the Decree No 2004-1392.

[82] Article 3 of the Order designating events of major importance and determining the procedures for making them accessible).

needed.[83] In the past, free-to-air broadcasters regularly faced difficulties in scheduling sporting events. To remedy this, in 1998, a list with A events and B events was introduced. Group A events (e.g. the Olympic Games, the FIFA World Cup Finals Tournament, the FA Cup Final, etc.) are those events which may not be covered live on an exclusive basis unless certain criteria are met.[84] In fact, this means that an A listed event, in almost all circumstances, must be broadcast live by a free-to-air broadcaster reaching 95 % of the population and that exclusivity of an A listed event is virtually impossible to (free-to-air) broadcasters not reaching the required 95 % (*infra*).[85] Circumstances where A listed events can be broadcast live on pay-television are: (1) where the event is non-exclusively broadcast on both terrestrial and pay-television, and (2) where no free-to-air broadcasters reaching 95 % of the UK population bid for the live rights and a pay-television operator obtains consent from Ofcom in the UK to broadcast the events.[86] Group B events (e.g. the Commonwealth Games, the World Athletics Championship, etc.) are those events that may not be broadcast live on an exclusive basis unless adequate provision has been made for secondary coverage (e.g. a second service provides edited highlights or delayed coverage amounting to at least 10 % of the scheduled duration of the event, subject to a minimum of 30 min for an event lasting an hour or more, whichever is the greater).[87] However, in the 2009 report on the review of free-to-air listed events, the Independent Advisory Panel argued that the division between Group A events and Group B events was no longer up-to-date. In the past, the 1998 Panel saw Group B as a safety net. The broadcasting of certain listed events could present serious scheduling problems for the broadcasters either because of their duration or because of the number of events involved. A decade after the 1998 report, the 2009 Panel assessed that broadcasters in 2009 put noticeably less emphasis on their problems of scheduling events of a longer duration. Today, broadcasters have the ability to use their digital portfolio to maximise the breadth and depth of their coverage of sports events. Therefore, the 2009 Panel concluded that, in the changed and still evolving broadcasting environment, guaranteeing highlights or delayed coverage was no longer a sufficient response.[88] The Panel formulated it as follows: "*[s]cheduling issues, for broadcasters who are now operating a range of new channels and outlets with scope for events to be broadcast behind the 'red button,' have significantly diminished in their relevance. Therefore, highlights or delayed coverage cannot be seen as a sufficient substitute for the live event in this generation.*"[89] As a result,

---

[83] Ofcom 2008a, para 1.12.

[84] *Ibid.*, para 1.3.

[85] Geey and Ward 2008, 4.

[86] Ofcom 2008a, paras 1.13–1.17; Geey and Ward 2008, 4.

[87] Ofcom 2008a, paras 1.3, 1.18, 1.19.

[88] Independent Advisory Panel to the Secretary of State for Culture, Media and Sport 2009, paras 140–149.

[89] *Ibid.*, para 145.

the Panel decided to recommend a single list of live events protected for free-to-air television.[90] However, it is important to note that, in November 2010, the Australian Government decided to divide the Australian list of events of major importance for society in Tier A and Tier B events (*infra*).[91]

To summarise, it has become clear that the concern is primarily focused on guaranteeing the public's access to (preferably) live sports events that are considered to be of major importance for society.[92]

14.1.3.2 Live Broadcasting on Free-To-Air Television

In Part I, it was stated that live sports coverage on television could be protected under Article 10 of the ECHR. However, it was indicated that attempting to make plausible that the public would have a right of access to full and live coverage on free-to-air television of any sports event that is transmitted, would probably be too challenging. However, some sports events could be more 'valuable' than others so their live coverage should be guaranteed on free-to-air television. And it is precisely the ultimate aim of the 'list of major events' mechanism to protect the public's access to events of major importance for society to live sports coverage on free-to-air television. Given that the sports events of major importance for society contribute to the development of our society (*supra*), Harrisson and Woods emphasised that ensuring free-to-air access to short reports to major sports events is important for the public to learn about the outcome of the event, but ignores the importance attached to watch sports events live.[93] This is all the more true if these sports events are considered by Member States, with approval of the European Commission, to be of major importance for society. Scheuer and Schoenthal formulated it as follows: "*[i]n principle, the Signatories of the Convention have to arrange their systems of information in a way that the individual citizen can be kept informed of the essential issues of society and, therefore, also of certain major events. The obligation to ensure access to the coverage of major events, thus, serves the accomplishment of a public interest [...].*"[94] Or as indicated by Hitchens, "*[s]port may not be regarded by all as being within this category but nevertheless there are certain types of sporting events that are commonly regarded as important to the general community for which access should be preserved.*"[95]

---

[90] *Ibid.*, paras 140–149.

[91] Department of Broadband, Communications and the Digital Economy 2010; Minister for Broadband, Communications and the Digital Economy 2010b; Minister for Broadband, Communications and the Digital Economy 2010c.

[92] Lefever et al. 2010, 400.

[93] Harrison and Woods 2007, p286–287.

[94] Scheuer and Schoenthal 2008, p417–418.

[95] Hitchens 2006, 224.

In this regard, the 'list of major events' mechanism has even been explicitly linked with Article 10 of the ECHR. Recital 49 of the AVMS Directive states that "*it is essential that Member States should be able to take measures to protect the right to information and to ensure wide access by the public to television coverage of national or non-national events of major importance for society.*" Likewise, the European Parliament's Resolution on the broadcasting of sports events considered it "*essential for all spectators to have a right of access to major sports events, just as they have a right to information.*"[96] The same goes for the Committee of the Regions with its Resolution on the broadcasting rights of major sport events.[97] In 2007, the European Commission declared that "*it will continue to support the right to information and wide access for citizens to broadcasts of sport events, which are seen as being of high interest or major importance for society.*"[98] In their comment on this regime, Scheuer and Schoenthal emphasised that "*it is the interest that the general public has access to the coverage of important events as a means of participating in the process of obtaining and imparting information, as well as the pursuit of public debate over such events.*"[99] Hence, full and direct access to major sports events can be approached as a means of promoting civil participation in our democratic society, by enabling citizens to participate fully in public discourse about these events (*supra*). This is recently affirmed by the General Court stating that the 'list of major events' mechanism is intended to protect the right to information and to ensure wide public access to television broadcasts of national or non-national events of major importance for society. And given that this mechanism relates to events which are of major importance for society, it is justified by overriding reasons in the public interest (*infra*).[100]

14.2 The 'List of Major Events' Mechanism and its Problematic Notions in a Digital Media Landscape

The 'list of major events' mechanism is included in the second-tier obligations of the AVMS Directive. This implies that the scope of this provision is limited to linear audiovisual media services. However, when we take a closer look at Article 14, it is clear that not all linear services fall under the scope of this provision. According to Article 14 (1) of the AVMS Directive, it should be ensured that events of major importance for society will not be broadcast on an exclusive basis

[96] European Parliament 1996.

[97] Committee of the Regions 1997, para 2.

[98] Commission of the European Communities 2007b, COM (2007) 391 final, 17.

[99] Scheuer and Schoenthal 2008, 410.

[100] GC, FIFA v European Commission, Case T-68/08, paras 51–53; GC, FIFA v European Commission, Case T-385/07, paras 55–57; GC, UEFA v European Commission, paras 47–49.

with the result that "a substantial proportion of the public" cannot follow those events on "free television."

Sections 14.2.1 and 14.2.2 will provide an orientation on the definition of the concepts 'free television' and 'substantial proportion of the public' and will explore how these two terms should be interpreted in a changing media environment. Section 14.3 will highlight the implications of the interpretation of those two notions on the economic freedom of the market players.

14.2.1 Free Television

14.2.1.1 Introduction

According to recital 53 of the AVMS Directive, free television refers to "*broadcasting on a channel, either public or commercial, of programmes which are accessible to the public without payment in addition to the modes of funding of broadcasting that are widely prevailing in each Member State (such as licence fee and/or the basic tier subscription fee to a cable network).*" The ECTT's Guidelines further clarifies that free television should be understood "*as the broadcasting of programme services which have near-universal coverage (as defined by the law of each Party) and are accessible to the public in their own language(s) without payment in addition to the modes of funding of broadcasting that are widely prevailing in each Party.*"[101] Although it is often stated that pay-television does not fall under the scope of this definition (*infra*), it is not exactly clear what should be understood by 'free (-to-air) television.' Moreover, since the definition is included in the recitals of the Directive, it is not guaranteed that free-to-air broadcasters will be of the same type in each Member State.[102]

To justify the *rationale* that those listed events should only be broadcast exclusively on free-to-air television, Helberger argued that states can have policy interests to preserve the public's access to important content and ensure that matters of interest can be received by the whole population rather than by a small circle of privileged subscribers (*supra*).[103] Harrison and Woods stressed that programmes and information, having social and civic assets (such as news, documentaries, sport, etc.), should be available to all and not be subject to payment barriers.[104]

[101] Council of Europe 2002, para 9.

[102] Harrison and Woods 2007, 282.

[103] Helberger 2005, 90.

[104] Harrison and Woods 2007, p7–10.

14.2.1.2 Pay-Television

A. Pay-Television Versus Free-to-Air Television

Due to technological developments, access to television programmes can be made dependent on an additional subscription fee. This evolution resulted in the emergence of a new kind of broadcaster: pay-television. Pay-television broadcasters could be defined as broadcasters offering every receiver the possibility to, with extra payment on top of the fee for the cable subscription or licence fee, to receive a selection of programmes. This implies that, while free-to-air television is usually financed by advertising or State contributions (*supra*), pay-television operators are usually funded through subscription fees.[105] However, it should be noted that the Belgian pay-television operator Belgacom TV decided to include advertising spots before, during and after football matches.[106]

Given that the public has to make an additional payment, i.e. extra subscription fee, to watch the programming offered by the pay-television operator, it is obvious that pay-television will not be labelled as free-to-air television. However, Scheuer and Schoenthal argued that a relatively low subscription fee, i.e. about the same level or even lower than the fee paid for cable transmission, does not automatically turn the channels into pay-television channels.[107] In Denmark (when the Danish list was still in force[108]), for example, pay-television broadcasters charging fees lower than DKK 25 per month (±3.4 EUR) were indeed considered free-to-air broadcasters.[109]

In the analogue past, there was a clear distinction between free-to-air television, on the one hand, and pay-television, on the other hand (*supra*). However, these distinctions are becoming increasingly blurred as pay-television and free-to-air television grow closer together.[110] In fact, channels are now commonly sold in bundles rather than individually.[111] Distributors bundle individual channels into different packages, then they sell those packages to the customers, and finally they distribute those packages via a network to the public (*infra*). Those distributors offer, on the one hand, basic packages including the traditional free-to-air channels, and, on the other hand premium packages containing sports and movies. The latter are commonly sold as part of a bundle with basic channels, via a mechanism known as 'buy-through.' This 'buy-through' requires consumers to purchase a

105 Commission of the European Communities 2000, Notification of 14 July 2000, para 20.

106 De Standaard 2008.

107 Scheuer and Schoenthal 2008, 415.

108 In 2002, the Danish Government decided to revoke the Danish Order including the listed the events (Revocation of the Danish Order on the use of TV rights to events of major importance to society. OJ (2002) C 45/7).

109 Section 4 (2) of the Order on the use of TV rights to events of major importance for society.

110 Commission decision, 2 April 2003, para 39.

111 Ofcom 2009, para 3.49.

basic package before they can even buy a premium package for an additional subscription fee.[112] In the past, it was clear that the basic package was the first and general package offered by the distributor while the premium package was always discretionary. Due to changing business models, this clear dividing line becomes blurred. The basic package, for example, can evolve to a very limited package only including the 'must-carry' channels (*infra*) at no extra cost beyond the minimum monthly subscription.[113] In addition to this package, distributors can offer, for a few extra Euros, another package including more commercial channels which were in the past included in the basic package. Additionally, distributors can also offer the public the opportunity to extend the basic package with a selection of an extra package reflecting their personal preferences (e.g. music channels, children programmes, etc.) for a fixed amount per month.[114] And, finally, distributors still offer the premium packages including sports and movies at a higher subscription price.[115] Hence, it is not clear anymore which package could be designated as 'basic' and freely available or as 'premium.' Furthermore, this would become even more problematic when, as proposed by Donders and Evens, operators would offer flex packages in which viewers can make their own package of preferred channels and can change this package in a more flexible way than is currently the case. That way, viewers would pay only for the content they really prefer.[116] Given that, in the future, the distinction between pay-television and free-to-air television could become more difficult to make, another approach is needed. In order to create more legal certainty in the changed media environment, the Flemish legislator has tried to come up with a solution: replacing the notion 'free-to-air television' by 'basic package of different aggregators' (*infra*).

B. Pay-Television Operators Acquiring Exclusive Broadcasting Rights

a. Europe

Although pay-television will (usually) not be referred to as free-to-air television, this does not imply that pay-television operators are not allowed to acquire the exclusive broadcasting rights on those listed events. The aim of the rule is to prohibit exclusive coverage on pay-television, and not the acquisition of the broadcasting rights by those pay-television operators.[117] This means that pay-television operators may broadcast those events on a non-exclusive basis as long as at the same time the free-to-air coverage is guaranteed. In Germany, for

---

112 *Ibid.*, para 3.49.

113 Frontier Economics 2009, 32.

114 European Commission 2002a, para 2.4.47.

115 Frontier Economics 2009, 32.

116 Donders and Evens 2010.

117 Scheuer and Schoenthal 2008, 414.

example, pay-television operators may broadcast major events if a broadcaster makes it possible, under appropriate conditions, for the event to be broadcast on a free and generally accessible television channel at the same time or, where individual events running in parallel make this impossible, slightly deferred.[118] In the UK, Group B events could even be shown on pay-television without live coverage of the whole events. Highlights on free-to-air television of those events were considered a sufficient secondary coverage (*supra*).[119]

In different Member States, pay-television operators may exercise the exclusive broadcasting rights after they have offered or sublicensed those rights to free-to-air broadcasters at reasonable market rates and no free-to-air broadcasters wished to acquire those sublicences.[120] When no free-to-air broadcaster declares itself willing to take sublicences, pay-television operators in the Flemish Community, for example, may make use themselves of the broadcasting rights acquired.[121] The same goes for Austria. When pay-television operators did all that could be reasonably expected under normal market conditions in an attempt to enable the event to be viewed on free-access television channels, they can broadcast those events themselves.[122]

The problem, however, is that no mechanism exists to determine what constitutes a fair price for those exclusive rights offered by pay-television operators or under which conditions pay-television operators have to grant such sublicences.[123] In 2008, in the UK, for example, football fans could not watch the FIFA World Cup qualifying match of England against Croatia after the pay-television broadcaster could not close a deal to sell rights to the free-to-air broadcasters. According to the pay-television broadcaster, the free-to-air broadcasters were unwilling to pay a fair price.[124] When we take a closer look at 'the list of major events' mechanism in the different Member States, only the Austrian and German rules do contain mechanisms to determine the 'fair price.' In Austria, for example, when no agreement is reached, the Federal Communication Senate shall decide whether the pay-television operator has fulfilled its obligations. In the event that the broadcaster has not adequately fulfilled these obligations, the Federal Communication Senate will determine the appropriate market price for the granting of broadcasting

---

118 Article 5a § 1 of the Interstate Treaty on Broadcasting.

119 Ofcom 2008a, para 1.18.

120 For example: Article 4 (1) of the Broadcasting (major events television coverage) Act 1999, *Statute Book* S.I. 28/1999; Article 3 of the Order of the Flemish Government establishing the list of events of major importance to society.

121 Article 3, § 3 of the Order of the Flemish Government establishing the list of events of major importance to society.

122 Article I, § 3 (3) of the Federal Act on the exercise of exclusive television broadcasting rights.

123 Parrish and Miettinen 2009, 28; Helberger 2005, 97.

124 See e.g.: The Guardian 2008a; BBC News 2008b.

rights.[125] In Germany, when parties fail to reach agreement on appropriate conditions, they shall agree to accept arbitration in due time before the event takes place.[126]

Furthermore, when pay-television operators would refuse to sell the acquired rights, the Directive does not contain a predefined sanction. Again, it is up to the Member States to decide what should happen when a broadcaster does not adequately fulfil its obligations. In Austria, for example, such broadcasters may be sued for damages in a civil action.[127] In Ireland, broadcasters can go to Court for an order restraining the other broadcaster from carrying on or attempting to carry on the prohibited activity, a declaration that the contract under which the other broadcaster received exclusive rights to the designated event is void, damages from the other broadcaster or a direction that the right to provide television coverage of the event shall be offered to the aggrieved broadcaster at reasonable market rates.[128]

b. Australia: Delisting Procedure

While in Europe, pay-television operators are not excluded from the bidding process, in Australia, pay-television operators are not allowed to participate in the first bidding procedure for the exclusive broadcasting rights of listed sports events. In fact, the Australian anti-siphoning regulation provides free-to-air broadcasters with the right of first refusal regarding the purchase of the rights to listed events.[129]

The Australian anti-siphoning legislation[130] gives free-to-air broadcasters priority over pay-television operators for the acquisition of all exclusive broadcasting rights (both free-to-air and pay-television rights) to listed events.[131] When free-to-air broadcasters choose not to make an offer to acquire those rights, "*listed events can be removed from the notice 2016 h before the start of the event, unless the Minister publishes in the Gazette before that time a declaration that the event continues to be specified in the notice after that time.*"[132] After the delisting of an event, pay-television operators are allowed to buy the exclusive broadcasting rights of that event. This automatic delisting won't take place when the Minister publishes a declaration that the event continues to be specified in the notice. The Minister may only publish such a declaration if he is satisfied that at least one

---

[125] Article I, § 3 (4) of the Federal Act on the exercise of exclusive television broadcasting rights.

[126] Article 5a, § 1 of the Interstate Treaty on Broadcasting.

[127] Article I, § 3 (4) of the Federal Act on the exercise of exclusive television broadcasting rights.

[128] Article 166 (1) (b) of the Broadcasting Act 2009.

[129] ACMA 2006, 2.

[130] Section 115 of the Broadcasting Services Act 1992.

[131] Australian Broadcasting Authority 2000, 5.

[132] Subsection 115 (1AA) of the Broadcasting Services Act.

commercial television broadcasting licensee or national broadcaster has not had a reasonable opportunity to acquire the right to broadcast the event.[133]

Before 2005, the delisting period was limited to 6 weeks (=1008 h). This six-week period, however, had proven to be insufficient time for pay-television operators to acquire the rights, as well as finalise schedules, negotiate advertising contracts and promote the event.[134] Although the revised 12 weeks period should provide adequate time for pay-television broadcasters to acquire and promote an event,[135] pay-television operators were complaining that this mechanism still creates delays and difficulties in the programming and promoting of delisted events.[136] Therefore, they proposed a delisting period of 26 weeks. According to pay-television broadcasters, this extended period would, on the one hand, better balance the interests of pay-television broadcasters and free-to-air broadcasters and, on the other hand, improve the efficiency of the delisting provision to the benefit of the viewers.[137] After the 2010 reform of this regulation, the delisting period will be extended to the requested 26 weeks.[138]

According to the free-to-air broadcasters, however, there is a loophole in the current regulation exploited by pay-television operators with the result that some listed events will not be shown on free-to-air television.[139] The Australian 'list of major events' mechanism is designated to prevent pay-television from acquiring rights to a listed event prior to a free-to-air broadcaster. However, due to the manner in which the rules are drafted, this intention is being circumvented. The problem, which is referred to by the free-to-air broadcasters, is that the pay-television licence conditions only apply to pay-television broadcasters.[140] The licence conditions state that pay-television broadcasting licensees will not acquire the right to televise, on a subscription broadcasting service, an event that is specified in a notice under section 115(1) unless: (1) a national broadcaster has the right to televise the event; or (2) a commercial television network covering greater than 50 % of the Australian population has acquired the rights to televise the event.[141] As a result, the Broadcasting Service Act does not prevent a company other than a pay-television broadcaster from acquiring the rights to broadcast a listed event before a commercial or national free-to-air television broadcaster. Hence, third parties associated with pay-television broadcasters, such as

[133] Subsection 115 (1AB) of the Broadcasting Services Act.

[134] Parliament of Australia 2004, Bills Digest No. 73 2004-05; Subsection 115 (1AA) of the Broadcasting Services Act.

[135] ACMA 2006, 2.

[136] Productivity Commission 2000, 435.

[137] ASTRA 2009; Basketball Australia 2009.

[138] Minister for Broadband, Communications and the Digital Economy 2010c.

[139] See e.g.: Parliament of Australia 1998a, Bills Digest No. 6 1998-99; Free TV Australia 2009, 22; Department of Broadband, Communications and the Digital Economy 2009, 6.

[140] Parliament of Australia 1998a, Bills Digest No. 6 1998-99.

[141] Paragraph 10 (1) (e) of Schedule 2 of the Broadcasting Services Act.

programme suppliers,[142] can buy those rights. Once they have acquired those exclusive broadcasting rights, these third parties can control the terms on which they want to offer those rights to interested broadcasters. In fact, they can impose terms which limit the amount, timing or scope of the coverage by free-to-air broadcasters with the result that the latter reject the offer. Then, they can trade those exclusive rights, when the event is delisted, to a pay-television broadcaster (i.e. 'on-selling'). The result is that a listed sports event will only be available on pay-television. In this case, the pay-television broadcaster, when deciding to broadcast the listed event, is not in breach because the prohibition is on acquiring the rights, not on broadcasting the content when the rights are held by someone else.

C. Digital Television

The last decade has been characterised by the transition from analogue television to digital television (*supra*). Currently, digital television signals are almost always displayed on analogue television sets connected to a digital receiver or set-top-box, which decodes those signals through the analogue SCART socket or connector.[143] Most television sets are equipped with a digital decoder in order to decrypt the encrypted television signals. However, these built-in decoders can often not be used, because platform operators have chosen to encrypt their signals in a specific way. As a result, viewers are forced to buy a specific decoder. Given that the essential condition to watch digital television is the acquisition of special technical equipment, the question rises whether digital television could be labelled as free-to-air television. In practice, viewers who do not have the necessary reception equipment would be excluded from accessing the events of major importance to society. Obviously, upgrading to digital television results in an extra expenditure for the public. Should this cost be interpreted as an additional payment on top of the basic subscription fee as a result of which digital television will not be considered as freely available?

In Member States there is no unanimous vision of how digital television should be interpreted. In the UK, for example, the 'list of major events' mechanism gives access to the broadcasting of events of major importance to society for no payment other than the television licence fee and the cost of receiving equipment.[144] The same goes for the French Community, where a broadcaster is considered to be free-to-air when the viewers do not have to pay, apart from the technical cost,

---

[142] There are three situations in which a person is a programme supplier of a commercial broadcaster: (1) the person supplies or may be reasonably expected to supply a commercial television broadcasting licensee with two-thirds of its sporting programmes, (2) the person is a related body corporate of the licensee, or (3) where the ACMA declares the person to be a programme supplier for the purposes of the 'must offer' rules (Section 146D (2)–(5) of the Broadcasting Services Act).

[143] Commission of the European Communities 2003a, COM(2003) 541 final, 17.

[144] Independent Advisory Panel to the Secretary of State for Culture, Media and Sport 2009, para 80.

another subscription fee other than the price of the basic cable package.[145] In Italy, the regulation about the listed events unequivocally states that the Italian public should have the possibility to follow the listed events on free television without incurring additional costs for the acquisition of technical equipment.[146] Hence, in Italy, digital television will not be interpreted as freely available. The same goes for Austria. The Austrian Federal Act on the exercise of exclusive television broadcasting rights defines free-access television channels as "*channels which viewers are able to receive without any additional [on top of the licence fee] or regular payments for the use of technical equipment for decoding.*"[147] As other Member States' legislators, the Flemish legislator has never clarified whether payment for technical equipment would be interpreted as an extra payment and, thus, how digital television should be qualified in the Flemish Community.[148] In 2010, Mrs. Lieten, the Flemish Minister of Media, stressed that she intended to take this issue into account when the Order of the Flemish Government establishing the list of events of major importance for society would be revised.[149]

One could argue that the designation of digital television as being not free-to-air is a stricter regulation than required by the AVMS Directive. Given that Article 4 (1) of the AVMS Directive allows Member States to "*require media service providers under their jurisdiction to comply with more detailed or stricter rules in the fields coordinated by this Directive provided that such rules are in compliance with Community law*," Member States are free to broaden the concept 'without payment in addition' to extra payment for the acquisition of technical equipment.

One should realise that, by the beginning of 2012 when the switch off of analogue terrestrial broadcasting throughout the Member States should be completed,[150] this question will probably become a non-issue. Given that digital television is only a further development of analogue television, the payment for a decoder is just a logical result of technological evolution and should, after the analogue switch off, no longer be considered as additional.[151] However, no deadline has been fixed yet for the analogue switch off of other platforms such as cable or satellite. This implies that the issue as described above will, in highly cabled countries such as Belgium or the Netherlands, remain much longer.

---

145 Article 4, § 3 of the French Community Media Decree.

146 Article 2 of the Decision No 8/1999.

147 Article I, § 3 (2) of the Austrian Federal Act on the exercise of exclusive television broadcasting rights.

148 Lefever and Evens 2009a, 32.

149 Commissie voor Cultuur, Jeugd, Sport en Media 2010, 6.

150 Commission of the European Communities 2005, COM(2005) 204 final, 9.

151 Lefever and Evens 2009b; Lefever and Van Rompuy 2009, 263.

D. Flemish Regulation: Basic Package of Different Distributors[152]

a. Introduction

Although the European Commission claimed that the 'list of major events' mechanism works satisfactorily (*supra*), the Flemish legislator decided to revise this provision, while transposing the AVMS Directive in national law, in order to create more legal certainty in the digitised world. The reviewed Article 153, §1 of the Flemish Community Media Decree states that "*the Flemish Government shall draw up a list of events considered to be of major importance for the public and which, for this reason, may not be broadcast on an exclusive basis so that a large part of the public of the Flemish Community cannot watch them live or deferred on television via the basic package of the different distributors.*" Although the Flemish legislator assumed that the replacement of the term "*free-to-air television*" by "*basic package of the different distributors*" would create more legal certainty, the question rises whether this assumption is correct.

b. Distributor

The old Flemish Community Media Decree had a two-layered foundation and only contained obligations for broadcasters (content layer) and network operators (network layer). Recently, though, a new key player has entered the broadcasting market, namely the 'distributor.' Distributors bundle individual channels into different packages, that are sold directly to the customers, and are distributed via a network. They do not necessarily have their own content or network, but do maintain a relationship with the public.[153]

Although distributors fulfil an important position in the media value chain, they were not regulated under the old Flemish Community Media Decree, and, thus, operating in a legal vacuum. Being convinced that the importance of these intermediaries between the broadcasters and network providers would grow in the future, the Flemish legislator decided, in order to create more legal certainty, to replace the 'two layer model' with a 'three layer model.' In this three layered model, in addition to the content layer and the network layer, a new and third layer was added: the distribution layer (distributors).

It is important to realise that companies can integrate two or three different functions, being a broadcaster as well as a distributor and/or network operator, meeting the respective obligations. In Belgium, for example, Belgacom and Telenet combine those three functions. Belgacom is the incumbent telecommunications operator (i.e. network provider), it has its own pay channel 'kanaal 11' (i.e. broadcaster) and it offers bundles to the public (i.e. distributor). Telenet is the

---

[152] This subsection is a revised, updated and more elaborated version of the following articles: Lefever and Evens 2009a, 29–33; Lefever et al. 2009, 513–520.

[153] Vlaams Parlement 2008, 16.

largest cable operator in Flanders (i.e. network provider), it has its own pay-television channel 'Sporting Telenet' (i.e. broadcaster) and it offers bundles to the public (i.e. distributor).

c. Basic Package

According to the new provision, a large part of the public should be able to watch major events on television via the basic package of the distributors. But what exactly does the Flemish legislator mean by 'basic package' and how should this term be interpreted?

The Flemish Community Media Decree itself does not contain a clear definition of the term 'basic package.' Although the Explanatory Memorandum defines basic package as "*the general or first package offered by the distributor*,"[154] this definition does not, however, offer real clarity and raises a lot of questions. The main question that arises is whether 'basic package' should be understood as a free basic package, which can be equalled to free-to-air television in the former regulation, and whether a digital supply could be labelled as basic package. Given that the *rationale* behind the events list regulation has not changed over time, it can be assumed that the 'free-to-air theory' could be applied *mutatis mutandis* to the revised Article 153 of the Flemish Community Media Decree. This would imply that the term basic package refers to the supply that every client gets when subscribing to the service of a distributor without any additional payment. Hence, it seems that premium packages offering additional content such as movie and sports channels could not be referred to as a basic package because the payment of an additional subscription fee is required. It should also be noted that the Order of the Flemish Government establishing the list of events of major importance to society does not offer any guidance on the interpretation of this new notion. When this Flemish Media Decree was revised, the Order was not amended. As a result, this Order still contains the notion of free-to-air television instead of the new notion 'basic package.'[155]

As regards the digital package, the reasoning applied for digital television can be repeated (*supra*). It is up to the Flemish legislator to decide whether the digital package should be labelled as a basic package. In other words, the Flemish legislator should specify whether only channels included in the analogue basic package of the distributors are allowed to show the major events in an exclusive way.

The last remark relates to the must-carry provision (*infra*). Article 186 of the Flemish Media Decree states that distributors making use of networks, which are the principal means to receive broadcasts for a significant number of end-users, are obliged to include some predefined channels in their 'basic offer.' Just as the Flemish Media Decree fails to define 'basic package,' the Decree does not contain

---

[154] *Ibid.*, 53.

[155] Article 2 of the Order of the Flemish Government establishing the list of events of major importance to society.

a definition of the term 'basic offer.' Moreover, the Explanatory Memorandum does not clarify this term either. Could or should this term be interpreted as a synonym of the 'basic package' mentioned in Article 153? In the explanatory memorandum of a draft proposal to amend the Flemish Media Decree,[156] it is explicitly stated that the notions 'basic offer' and 'basis package' could not be seen as synonyms. However, this explanatory memorandum does not contain any explanation about the difference between the two concepts. When we take a closer look at a recent decision of the Flemish Media Regulator,[157] the two notions seem to be closely linked. In its decision, the Flemish Media Regulator defines the basic offer of a distributor as its cheapest offer not only taking into account the subscription fee but also the costs for purchasing or renting technical equipment, such as a set-top box. *In this case*, this cheapest offer was the analogue offer. However, the Flemish Media Regulator did not rule out that a digital offer, depending on the facts, could also be classified as basic offer. Given that these two concepts are quite similar, it is up to the legislator to clearly define these concepts and to point out the differences in order to create more legal certainty.

E. Internet

In 2008, the International Olympic Committee launched an online channel, available on YouTube, to broadcast Beijing 2008 highlights. This new channel would be accessible in countries where digital video-on-demand rights were not been sold or were acquired on a non-exclusive basis.[158] In January 2010, YouTube confirmed its first live major sporting deal and announced that it would host live Indian Premier League (IPL) cricket matches in the UK. This deal gives YouTube the exclusive rights to stream IPL cricket matches online. In the past, the IPL declared that exclusive streaming deals would not be concluded in countries were television broadcast deals were taking place. However, a spokesman for the IPL said that negotiations for a television rights deal for the UK would go ahead.[159] Furthermore, YouTube is also in talks with European football leagues about securing live broadcasting rights.[160] However, it is not known whether sports organisations would only sell broadcasting rights to YouTube for territories where the matches do not take place.[161] Recently, Google stressed again that it is working on a major overhaul of YouTube. YouTube should be able to compete with traditional broadcasters and cable television. The website is planning a series of

156 Vlaamse Regering 2011a.

157 Flemish Media Regulator 2011.

158 Sportbusiness International 2008c.

159 The Guardian 2010a, b.

160 The Guardian 2011.

161 De Morgen 2011a.

changes to its home page to highlight sets of 'channels' around topics such as sports.[162] The question rises whether it is problematic if YouTube, or YouTube-like services, since YouTube itself is located in the United States and falls outside the scope of European media regulation, would acquire broadcasting rights of listed events?

As such, YouTube-like services are excluded from the scope of the AVMS Directive. A service will only be classified as an AVMS when the service falls under the editorial responsibility of a media service provider. Editorial responsibility is defined in Article 1 (1) (c) of the AVMS Directive as "*the exercise of effective control both over the selection of the programmes and over their organisation either in a chronological schedule, in the case of television broadcasts, or in a catalogue, in the case of on-demand audiovisual media services. Editorial responsibility does not necessarily imply any legal liability under national law for the content or the services provided.*" It is up to the Member States to further specify the definition of 'editorial responsibility' and 'effective control.'[163] As a result, service providers that do not have effective control over the content and only give the possibility for the distribution and uploading of audiovisual content generated by private users (user-generated content) for the purposes of sharing and exchange within communities of interest are excluded from the scope of the AVMS Directive. Providers of YouTube-like services do not actively select the content and do not control its organisation in a chronological schedule or a catalogue and, therefore, do not exercise editorial responsibility within the meaning of the AVMS Directive. Given that they only offer a portal and platform to users to make audiovisual content of their own available to a wide audience, those operators will not fall under the scope of the AVMS Directive.[164] The fact that YouTube and YouTube-like services exercise at least some secondary control over the content of their sites (the YouTube Community Guidelines, for example, state that "*YouTube staff review flagged videos 24 h a day, 7 days a week to determine whether they violate our Community Guidelines. When they do, we remove them*"[165]) does not result in the classification of those providers as audiovisual media service providers.[166] As long as the content is deleted *ex post*, acting on complaints of users or on the grounds of the rules of protection of minors or copyright, and does not involve an active selection *ex ante*, such control is not considered as editorial responsibility in the sense of the AVMS Directive.[167]

However, when YouTube and YouTube-like services decide to buy broadcasting rights and to compete with traditional broadcasters, they could no longer be classified as a platform provider, but have become media service providers.

[162] The Wall Street Journal 2011.

[163] Recital 25 of the AVMS Directive.

[164] Valcke et al. 2010, 276.

[165] YouTube 2011.

[166] Lefever and Werkers 2010, 217.

[167] Valcke et al. 2010, 276.

Furthermore, as already indicated above, live streaming could be classified as a linear audiovisual media service. As a result, YouTube-like services should also respect Article 14 of the AVMS Directive. Hence, the question that rises is whether a service offering live streaming would fall under the definition of free-to-air television. Just as it is the case with traditional television, it is up to the media service provider to decide whether he would offer access to live streamed sports events for free or whether he would require an extra payment. If the latter is the case, this service could not be labelled as free-to-air. Otherwise, when no additional payment is required, this service could be considered as broadcasting which is accessible to the public without payment in addition to the basic tier subscription fee.

14.2.2 Substantial Proportion

14.2.2.1 No Objective Definition

The 'list of major events' mechanism requires that it should be guaranteed that "*a substantial proportion of the public*" would have the possibility of following the listed events. Just as with the definition of 'event of major importance,' the AVMS Directive does not contain a definition of the term 'substantial proportion.' During the Liverpool Conference in 2005, experts were asked whether the concept of 'a substantial proportion of the public' should be harmonised. In the Issue Paper, the European Commission noted that there was a preference not to harmonise the concept of substantial proportion of the public, as this differed in accordance with the audiovisual landscape in each Member State.[168] Given that a compulsory interpretation of this notion is not considered appropriate, it is still up to every Member State to freely interpret the concept of 'substantial proportion of the public.' It is important to note, as indicated by ACMA, that this proportion does not refer to viewers actually watching the broadcast event, but instead to the number of viewers who would be able to watch the programme, should they choose to do so.[169]

In Austria, for example, the listed events should be seen on a television channel accessible by at least 70 % of the viewers.[170] In the UK, a free-to-air broadcaster wanting to broadcast listed events exclusively should be received by at least 95 % of the households of the UK.[171] Also in Ireland, 95 % of the households should be

[168] European Commission 2005.

[169] ACMA 2007.

[170] Article I, § 3 (1) of the Austrian Federal Act on the exercise of exclusive television broadcasting rights.

[171] § 98 (2) of the Broadcasting Act 1996; Ofcom 2008a, para 1.6.

reached.[172] Given that 95 % is a very high penetration rate, the Irish definition of the broadcaster that should reach 95 % of coverage is not confined to a single entity. Two or more broadcasters who enter into a contract or arrangement to jointly provide near universal coverage of a designated event shall be deemed to be a single broadcaster with respect to that event.[173] Therefore, a number of broadcasters, even of quite a small scale, who combined free-to-air coverage meets the required percentage, can qualify to provide coverage of a designated event.[174]

In the Flemish Community "*a large part of the population of the Flemish Community is considered to be able to follow an event of major importance to society on free-access television when the event [...] and can be received by at least 90 % of the population.*"[175] To guarantee that the rule has full force and effect and the attainment of the rule's objective would not be jeopardised, it is necessary that the verb 'can' is not interpreted as '90 % of the households have the possibility to watch those major events,' but as '90 % of the households should have actual access to those major events.' Otherwise, every new platform, at least after a certain rollout period, could be classified as in the possibility to reach a substantial part of the public (*infra*). Moreover, Mrs. Lieten, the Flemish Minister of Media, has recognised that this penetration rate of 90 % belonged to the analogue past, when 95 % of the population had access to analogue cable television. However, she acknowledged that, with the development of digital terrestrial, digital satellite and digital cable television and the coexistence of analogue and digital cable television, this 90 % requirement is no longer current.[176] Despite Lietens' statement, the Draft proposal amending the Flemish Media Decree still contains the 90 % requirement.[177]

14.2.2.2 Digital Television: Multi-Channels and Digital-only Channels

A. Introduction

The introduction of digital television is often hailed as a new revolution in today's media landscape as it provides a lot of new opportunities for content producers, advertisers and viewers. Digitalisation has created the possibility of transmitting more than one stream of programming over a single television channel at the same

[172] Article 1 (1) of the Broadcasting (major events television coverage) Act.

[173] Article 1 (3) of the Broadcasting (major events television coverage) Act.

[174] Irish Parliament 1999.

[175] Article 2 of the Order of the Flemish Government establishing the list of events of major importance to society.

[176] Commissie voor Cultuur, Jeugd, Sport en Media 2010, 6.

[177] Vlaamse Regering 2011b.

time, i.e. 'multi-channelling.'[178] This offers the broadcasters the opportunity to broadcast different digital-only channels alongside the traditional, 'primary' channel at the same time.[179] Furthermore, as emphasised by Ofcom, this allows those free-to-air broadcasters to compete more directly with premium sports channels being able to devote extended, in-depth coverage of a wide variety of sporting events on their digital channels.[180] Additionally, a free-to-air broadcaster could potentially show an event on a digital multi-channel at a time it may not otherwise show it on its main channel, due to the event's relatively low ratings and advertising earnings potential.[181] In addition, some events will be shown live on the digital channel and will be, later on, broadcast on the main channel.[182]

In Flanders, in 2008, the Queen Elisabeth Music Competition was broadcast on Canvas +, a digital-only channel of the public broadcaster, and the qualifying rounds of Club Brugge in the UEFA Europe League were broadcast on the digital-only channel EXQI Sport. However, the Queen Elisabeth Music Competition and the UEFA Europe League matches involving Belgian clubs are listed events.[183] The question that needs to be answered is whether this practice of broadcasting listed events on digital-only channels infringes the 'list of major events' mechanism.

B. Europe

Free-to-air broadcasters believe that the ability to carry listed sporting events on their digital-only channels exclusively would enhance the public's access to sports events by increasing the chances that audiences will be able to 'freely' view major sport. According to Free TV Australia, for example, "*there is no justification for any restriction on the ability of free to air broadcasters to show more free sport on multi-channels. Removal of these restrictions is in the public interest as it would deliver diversity and choice while helping the government to drive take-up of digital television in Australia, at no extra cost to the Government or consumers.*"[184] However, the *rationale* of the 'list of major events' mechanism would be undermined if they could do so.[185] In the analogue past, the free-to-air broadcasters provided their services to (almost) 100 % of the households. According to

---

[178] Department of Broadband, Communications and the Digital Economy 2009, 20.

[179] Productivity Commission 2000, 224.

[180] Ofcom 2009, para 4.74.

[181] Department of Broadband, Communications and the Digital Economy 2009, 20.

[182] Standing Committee on Environment, Communications, Information Technology and the Arts 2006, para 3.96.

[183] Article 1, § 1, 3° & 10° of the Order of the Flemish Government establishing the list of events of major importance to society.

[184] Free TV Australia 2009.

[185] Tennis Australia 2009.

different observers, as free-to-air broadcasters become digitised and are able to offer digital-only channels, there is a danger that those broadcasters—at least temporarily—will lose their universal character.[186] The point of listing events is that all citizens should be able to view those major events. Given the fact that the phrases 'free-to-air television' and 'substantial proportion of the public' are two cumulative conditions, free-to-air television broadcasters should continue to be restricted from showing listed events exclusively on their digital-only channels, since they do not (yet) reach the required part of the public.[187] In Flanders, for example, according to recent estimations and based on figures provided by digital television providers, the different distributors reached the milestone of 1 million connections by the end of 2008.[188] In June 2009, the total number of digital television households has been estimated at 1.2 million households.[189] In August 2010, a study indicated that digital television has a penetration rate of 55.7 %.[190] This implies that only about half of all Flemish households have access to digital television content and that the required coverage of 90 % is not met.[191] Although Flemish broadcasters infringed the' list of major events' regulation by broadcasting the Queen Elisabeth Music Competition and the qualifying match of Club Brugge on their digital-only channel, the Flemish Media Regulator, having the power to impose sanctions,[192] did not intervene.

C. Australia

The Australian Government has tried to anticipate this trend and introduced a special regulation with regard to the broadcasting of listed events on multi-channels and digital-only channels. In the past, before the 2010 revision, during the simulcast period, the licensee could not broadcast on a digital multi-channel a part of a listed event unless: (1) the licensee has previously televised the part of the event on its core service, or (2) the event is televised simultaneously on the core commercial television broadcasting service and the digital multi-channel, or (3) the broadcaster televises a part of the event in a news or current affairs programme on the digital multi-channel.[193] More recently, the Australian Government suggested that it was considering removing anti-siphoning restrictions on free-to-air multi-channels in order to drive the uptake of digital television[194]

---

186 See e.g. Rowe 2009.
187 Lefever and Evens 2009a, 33.
188 Studiedienst van de Vlaamse Regering 2009, 233.
189 De Tijd 2009, 7.
190 De Marez and Schuurman 2010, 16.
191 Lefever and Evens 2009a, 33; Lefever et al. 2009, 520.
192 Article 228 of the Flemish Community Media Decree 2009.
193 Subsection 41A of Schedule 4 of the Broadcasting Services Act.
194 X 2009, 16.

with the result that sporting events, present on the list, could be shown on new free-to-air digital channels (*infra*).[195] Although the free-to-air broadcasters supported this possible amendment,[196] other broadcasters opposed referring to the same arguments as mentioned earlier.[197]

Following the FIFA World Cup in South Africa, the Australian Minister for Broadband, Communications and the Digital Economy announced in May 2010 a change to the Australian anti-siphoning regulation. A notice would amend the Broadcasting Services Act and would remove eight group stage matches from the list. After this delisting procedure, SBS ONE could broadcast the non-delisted group matches, while the eight delisted matches could be broadcast live on the digital-only channel SBS TWO. Immediately after their live coverage on SBS TWO, SBS ONE has to replay each of the eight matches. Before the delisting procedure, SBS TWO would have been prevented from broadcasting listed events, because the anti-siphoning scheme precluded free-to-air broadcasters from premiering listed events on their digital-only channels. According to the Australian Minister for Broadband, Communications and the Digital Economy, this change will give viewers "*the opportunity to watch every match of the World Cup, irrespective of whether they receive the digital-only SBS TWO.*" Moreover, he hoped that this initiative will stimulate football fans to convert to digital television before the World Cup, so they have the ability to flick between key games.[198]

In November 2010, a series of reforms to the anti-siphoning regulation were announced.[199] The major change was the division of the list into two Tiers in order to allow greater use of digital-only channels. Tier A lists "*nationally iconic events*," such as the Melbourne Cup, Rugby Union World Cup Final, etc., while Tier B lists "*regionally iconic and nationally significant events*," such as Summer Olympics, Winter Olympics event, etc.[200] The Tier A events should be broadcast on the main channel of the free-to-air broadcasters, whereas the Tier B events could be broadcast on a free-to-air digital-only channel. According to the Government, because more than 70 % of Australian households watch digital television, the restriction on the use of digital-only channels to broadcast listed events could be relaxed.[201]

---

[195] Sportbusiness International 2008a; The Australian 2008.

[196] See e.g.: Free TV Australia 2009, 19–21.

[197] See e.g.: ASTRA 2009, 17–18; Basketball Australia 2009, 2.

[198] Minister for Broadband, Communications and the Digital Economy 2010a.

[199] These reforms will take effect from 1 January 2011 (Department of Broadband, Communications and the Digital Economy 2010).

[200] Department of Broadband, Communications and the Digital Economy 2010.

[201] Minister for Broadband, Communications and the Digital Economy 2010b, c.

D. Transitional Phase

This discussion will probably recur in every transitional phase that creates the possibility for the public to choose between different ways of watching television. At present, the public can choose between analogue television and digital television. Given that digital television is in its early stage of development, it is quite logical that digital-only channels will not yet reach the required percentages to broadcast listed events exclusively. It is apparent that the completion of digital (terrestrial) switch over in different Member States would increase significantly the numbers of channels reaching the required substantial proportion.[202] Hence, after the analogue (terrestrial) switch off, there is no doubt that digital television operators may exclusively broadcast listed events. However, one should realise that this would not be the case in highly cabled countries. In the meantime, the media sector is not static. The next step up in quality for digital television transmission is high definition television, offering enhanced picture quality, enhanced sound quality, a wide-screen display, etc. A prerequisite to watch high definition television is the acquisition of special high definition equipment, being a high definition decoder.[203] Without this decoder, it is impossible to watch those high definition channels. Hence, in the transitional phase from digital television to high definition television the same problems and questions will occur due to the 'substantial proportion of the public' criterion: as long as high definition television will not reach the required percentage, high-definition-only channels would infringe the 'list of major events' mechanism when exclusively broadcasting listed events. And although high definition television is the future of television today,[204] new ways of watching television (e.g. 3D television) will arise over the years and the question will rise again.

14.2.2.3 Internet

Even if live streaming could be considered as free-to-air television, YouTube-like services based in Europe would not (yet) be able to broadcast listed events exclusively. In Flanders, for example, 86.1 % of the citizens own a computer and 81 % have Internet connection.[205] As a result, just as digital television, streaming services over the Internet do not yet reach the required penetration rate. In other words, when YouTube-like services buy exclusive broadcasting rights of listed sports events, they should sublicense these rights.

---

[202] Independent Advisory Panel to the Secretary of State for Culture, Media and Sport 2009, para 39.

[203] EICTA 2008a.

[204] EICTA 2008b.

[205] De Marez and Schuurman 2010, 6, 7, 10.

14.2.2.4 Market Distortion?

Although the 'list of major events' mechanism's aim is to balance the industry's interest, on the one hand, and the individual's special interest in receiving information, on the other hand, it is, nevertheless, often argued that this mechanism has a significant impact on the economic freedom of the market players.[206]

A. Traditional Media Versus New Media

Due to the fact that access to listed events remains a privilege for linear broadcasters reaching a substantial proportion of the public, the FIFA raised in its 2007 complaint (*supra*) that the current 'list of major events' mechanism does not provide a fair opportunity to all audiovisual media providers, reserving live sports broadcasting rights to traditional media to the exclusion of new media services.[207] FIFA argued that the 'list of major events' mechanism restricts freedom of establishment as it prevents new media operators that wish to acquire exclusive rights for premium sports events, from establishing themselves on the Belgian broadcasting market. New media operators have only a limited penetration and, thus, do not fulfil the 'substantial proportion' criterion that is demanded by the Member States to broadcast those events exclusively. The UEFA claimed that the 'list of major events' mechanism represents a significant intervention in the market for the acquisition of sports rights, leading to a disproportionate and unjustified distortion of competition of the market.[208] In other words, according to the two governing bodies, the 'list of major events' mechanism privileges the traditional free-to-air broadcasters, to the detriment of new media providers and pay-television operators,[209] affecting FIFA's and UEFA's earning as organiser of these events.[210]

Although the idea that this system affects the bidding process and prevents new media operators and pay-television operators from acquiring broadcasting rights and from establishing themselves on the broadcasting market is supported by some authors, this way of thinking is not entirely correct (at least not for the Member States of the European Union). Although exclusive coverage of popular sports events is often regarded as being a prime incentive for people to subscribe to pay-television or other new media services, it seems questionable that the development of new audiovisual services would be hindered by the impossibility to broadcast those listed events exclusively. According to Ofcom, the listed events, due to the infrequency with which they are organised (e.g. the Summer Olympic

206 Council of Europe 2003, P. 21; Weatherill 2007, 237.

207 FIFA v. Commission, 4 October 2007, Case T-385/07. OJ (2007) C 315/41.

208 UEFA v. Commission, 5 February 2008, Case T-55/08. OJ (2008) C 107/28.

209 BBC News 2008a.

210 GC, FIFA v European Commission, Case T-68/08, para 165.

Games are organised every 4 years, the FIFA World Cup is organised every 4 years, etc.), are poor substitutes for sports content offered on pay-television services.[211] Hence, while irregular organised events are undoubtedly important for the public, they are not available on a regular basis, such as national premier league football, and could therefore be unlikely to drive up subscriptions to a pay-television business.[212] Hence, the success of pay-television or new media services is not only dependent on the exclusive broadcasting of listed events.

Furthermore, in Europe, the exclusive rights of listed events may be attributed to the highest bidder, being a free-to-air television, a pay-television operator or even a new media provider not reaching the required penetration rate. The General Court formulates it as follows: "*the 'list of major events' mechanism does not prohibit any broadcasters from acquiring the broadcasting rights for the World Cup or EURO, but only provides that some broadcasters are not allowed to broadcast those events on an exclusive basis.*"[213] The only requisite is that the broadcasters, not fulfilling the two criteria 'free-to-air television' and 'reaching a substantial proportion of the public,' cannot broadcast those events exclusively and, thus, have to offer or sublicense these rights to free-to-air broadcasters (*supra*). The fact that they cannot broadcast those events exclusively could indeed reduce their willingness to pay, could depress the price they are willing to offer, or could even deter them from bidding at all, leaving the free-to-air broadcasters to negotiate a lower price.[214] Furthermore, it is not proven that pay-television operators would pay a lot of money to acquire those rights and that free-to-air broadcasters can acquire those rights for a price that is significantly below the free market value. In the UK, for example, the Jockey Club argued that the BBC was placed in an overwhelmingly beneficial position, because the Grand National and Derby[215] is a Group A listed event. Over the last 5 years, the rights to both the Grand National and the Derby have declined in value by 70 %. However, the assumption that this was wholly because of the listed events status of both races, and that its removal would thereby lead to fiercer competition and a higher price for their rights, was undermined by BSkyB itself. BSkyB contended that one-off sporting events of whatever magnitude were of much lower priority for them than series of race meetings over a year that enabled them to build up a subscriber base.[216] For other listed events, whilst the 'list of major events' mechanism has been in operations, sports rights agreements have even risen in value

---

[211] Ofcom 2009, paras 4.78 and 4.163.

[212] Ofcom 2007a, para 5.28; Ofcom 2009, para 4.73.

[213] GC, FIFA v European Commission, Case T-68/08, para 178.

[214] Gratton and Solberg 2007, 213; Craufurd Smith and Bottcher 2002, 126; Weatherill 2007, 238.

[215] Ofcom 2008a, Annex 1.

[216] Independent Advisory Panel to the Secretary of State for Culture, Media and Sport 2009, para 76.

(*supra*).[217, 218] This way of thinking is confirmed by the General Court stating that, although this provision could be liable to affect to price paid for the broadcasting rights, it would not destroy the commercial value of those rights. According to the General Court, the sports federations are not obliged to sell the broadcasting rights on whatever conditions it can obtain and those federations are protected against collusive and abusive practices by Community and national competition law.[219] Furthermore, it should be noted that the General Court has recognised that the 'list of major events' mechanism affects FIFA's and UEFA's property rights, but that the latter may be restricted in relation to its social function. According to the General Court, the listing of events of major importance for society (even including all matches of the World Cup or the EURO) could be a justified restriction of FIFA's and UEFA's property rights.[220] Finally, it is important to note that Kesenne indicated that sports organisations should be aware of the fact that selling the broadcasting rights to pay-television operators would not always be more profitable than selling those rights to free-to-air television. Depending on the demand level and the price advertisers are willing to pay per viewer; free-to-air coverage of sports events could generate more revenues for the sports organisations. Not only are advertisers willing to pay more for advertising sports during the commercial breaks, they are also willing to pay more for shirt and board advertising.[221, 222]

Moreover, it can be argued that Member States, when drawing up their list, have already properly taken into account the pay-television operator's rights. When we take a look at the UK's list, the FA Cup Final is listed and not the Premier League matches.[223] The same goes for the Belgian list, were the Belgian Football Cup Final is listed and not the Jupiler Pro League matches. Although the European Commission argued that "*the Belgian Football Cup Final (men) is intended to bring together the two best Belgian clubs [...]*"[224] and that "*the FA Cup Final has a special general resonance in the U.K. as the pre-eminent single match in English domestic football,*"[225] it is very doubtful that this is really the case. In fact, the Football Cup is a knockout cup competition where also football teams from lower leagues take part. This could imply that, in the most extreme situation, two teams of a low league will play the final. Hence, it is apparent that

---

217 For example, since 1988, the value of the European television rights for the Olympics has increased at a rate of 65 % per summer event and 77 % per winter event (Ofcom 2007b, 53).

218 Free TV Australia 2009; GC 2010b, para 48.

219 GC, FIFA v European Commission, Case T-68/08, para 146; GC, FIFA v European Commission, Case T-385/07, para 142; GC, UEFA v European Commission, para 183.

220 GC, FIFA v European Commission, Case T-68/08, paras 141–145; GC, FIFA v European Commission, Case T-385/07, paras 137–141; GC, UEFA v European Commission, paras 178–182.

221 See business model of Formula One: *infra*.

222 Kesenne 2011.

223 Ofcom 2008a.

224 Commission decision, 25 June 2007, para 7.

225 Commission decision, 16 October 2007, para 7.

some matches of the national premier leagues (e.g. the matches between the top five teams), although they are not listed, have more resonance for the public than the Cup Final.[226] The only reason that could be given for the non-inclusion of the national premier leagues (or at least some matches of the league) is a financial one. It would be rather impossible for pay-television operators to attract subscribers if they cannot include the national premier league in their programming. Hence, when making the decision not to include the national premier leagues in the list; it seems that the Member States have already taken into account the industry's interest. In Spain, however, each week one match of the Spanish Premier League should be broadcast on free-to-air television. Although the clubs had feared that the power to choose the free-to-air match would be awarded to the Spanish Broadcasting Council, Consejo Estatal de Medios Audiovisuales, the right to choose was attributed to League itself.[227]

B. Let the Market Play…[228]

The 'list of major events' mechanism was born out of fear that events of major importance would be lost to free-to-air television. Some authors, however, argued that such fear is overstated.[229] According to them, governing bodies themselves are best placed to take the decision whether they want to sell the broadcasting rights to free-to-air broadcasters or pay-television operators,[230] by balancing, on the one hand, the importance of exposure to uphold the popularity and reputation of their sport, and, on the other hand, the importance of increased revenues to fund the fixed costs of their organisation. To ground their position that governing bodies would not only choose to sell their rights to the highest bidder,[231] they often refer to the same examples. In 1996, the IOC rejected a $1.8 billion bid from News Corp. and granted the European television rights for the 2000–2008 Olympic Games to the EBU for $1.442 billion. The decision to select EBU over Murdoch's company apparently reflects the IOC's concern that Murdoch might have placed key Olympic events on pay-television.[232] Another example is the Champions League Football rights' split between a live rights package for free-to-air broadcasters and a live rights package for pay-television operators (*supra*).[233] Moreover, the UEFA, when evaluating the bids for the broadcasting rights, will *inter alia* take into account "*the balance between free*

---

226 Conn 2009.

227 Sportcal.com 2010.

228 A complete economic impact assessment of the 'list of major events' mechanism falls outside the scope of this book.

229 ASTRA 2009; Basketball Australia 2009; Productivity Commission 2000, 443.

230 Zeffman 2009; Baron 2009.

231 Jeanrenaud and Kesenne 2006, 5.

232 Wise and Meyer 1997, 1805; The New York Times 1996.

233 Commission decision, 23 July 2003, para 33.

and pay-television."[234] Finally, Formula One, being a sponsored-led sport, needs to be broadcast on free-to-air television to meet their commercial partner's objectives. Therefore, for a pay-television broadcaster to win the rights to Formula One, it would need to offer a significantly higher price than a free-to-air channel, in order to make up for any shortfall in sponsorship revenues associated with its smaller audiences. So far, no pay-television operator has been willing to offer such an amount.[235] Recently, Ecclestone claimed that a shift from free-to-air television to pay-television for Formula One would be 'suicidal.'[236] However, between 2012 and 2018, in the UK, Sky Sports and BBC will share Formula One rights. Sky Sports will show every race, qualifying session and practice session live, while the BBC will air half the races live as well as the qualifying and practice sessions from those events.[237]

However, having all confidence to leave it up to the market and the sports bodies' decisions, weighing up the advantages of pay-television and the advantages of free-to air television can be very dangerous. As stated by Barnett, "*there is a real issue about the extent to which sports bodies can be trusted to represent the wider public interest [...] rather than the private interests of players and professionals who want a share of pay television's cash bonanza.*"[238] This can be proven by different examples. Although, in 1996, the then IOC director general, Carrard, stated that "*the IOC wants to secure the broadest possible broadcast penetration*"[239] and that the Olympic Charter compels the IOC to "*ensure the fullest coverage by the different media and the widest possible audience in the world,*"[240] in 2009, the IOC rejected EBU's bid for the exclusive broadcasting rights to the Olympic Games 2014 & 2016 and sold the rights (across all platforms) to Sportfive.[241] However, it should be noted that in the tender for the broadcasting rights, it is specified that the rights holder is obliged to provide at least 200 h of traditional[242] free-to-air coverage[243] of the Summer Games and at

---

234 *Ibid.*, para 30 (h).

235 Ofcom 2007b, 8; Zeffman 2009; Ogston 2009.

236 Sportbusiness International 2011a.

237 Sportbusiness International 2011b.

238 Barnet 2009.

239 The New York Times 1996.

240 Article 49 (1) of the Olympic Charter 2007.

241 MediaNetwork 2008; The Guardian 2008b; Telegraph 2008b; Sports City 2008; IOC 2009.

242 Traditional coverage includes, at a minimum, for each country, coverage of the Opening and Closing Ceremonies of the Winter Games and the Summer Games, any medal rounds or other significant events featuring a competitor from such country, and any other major events which have traditionally been among the highest in terms of viewer interest within such country (IOC 2008, para 2.3).

243 Free-to-air means broadcasting of audiovisual programming in a manner that approximately 95 % of television households within such country have access to and can actually receive such broadcasts, without any specific fee, charge or premium for the Olympic Games programming (IOC 2008, para 2.3).

least 100 h of traditional free-to-air coverage of the Winter Games.[244] Hence, Sportfive need to comply with the IOC's free-to-air coverage requirement and has to make sure that pay-television operators will sublicense the free-to-air broadcasting rights. Another example is cricket in the UK. In 1998, following strong lobbying from the English Cricket Board (ECB), the decision was made to move some cricket matches (including the Ashes[245]) to Group B of the listed events categories.[246] Although the Government's view was that the series would not migrate to pay-television, BSkyB outbid the free-to-air networks for the 2005 Ashes series during the first rights negotiation following delisting.[247] ECB's decision to sell the rights exclusively to BSkyB has dramatically cut the television audience for its sport. Four years ago, 7.4 million people watched England win the Ashes on free-to-air television. In 2009, nearly three quarters of the audience had vanished with only 1.9 million people following this sports event on Sky Sports.[248] Hence, according to Barnet, those examples show that sports bodies, earning money with their sport, do not always think of the wider public interest when they are making their decision.[249] Nicholas rephrased this as follows: "*what rights holders really want is some sort of balance between exposure and revenues for their rights and we try and put things into plan so that they can achieve those goals but let's be honest, it's 95 % about the revenues and 5 % about the exposure for most rights holders most of the time.*"[250] Therefore, according to some authors, market regulation aimed at preserving the major events being broadcast on free-to-air television might still be justified.[251]

14.3 The 'List of Major Events' Mechanism and its Implementation Problems

14.3.1 Introduction

Although the 'list of major events' mechanism's aim is well-intended, it seems inherently defective in guaranteeing the public free access to sports events on television, even events that are deemed of major importance for society. Hence, the unwanted result of the current system could be that the level of exposure that listed sports receive would be restricted. The aim of this section is to provide an

244 IOC 2008, para 2.3.

245 The Ashes is a Test cricket series played between England and Australia.

246 For more information, see: House of Commons—Culture, Media and Sport Committee 2006.

247 Free TV Australia 2009; Ofcom 2007b, 63.

248 Barnet 2009; The Guardian 2009; Free TV Australia 2009; Rowe 2009.

249 Barnet 2009.

250 Nicholas 2009.

251 Jeanrenaud and Kesenne 2006, 5.

overview of the different implementation problems. This section will also consider the Australian 'use it or lose it' principle as a means to guarantee the public's right to information in a more effective way. In addition, this section suggests the introduction of a 'must-broadcast' obligation in the regulatory framework in order to render the 'list of major events' mechanism even more effective.

14.3.2 A Voluntary Mechanism for Member States

Article 14 (1) of the AVMS Directive states that each Member State *may* take measures with regard to events of major importance for society. Hence, Member States have the right to draw up a list, but they do not have a legal duty to do so. As indicated by the European Parliament, the European Commission has stated that the 'list of major events' mechanism cannot be said to be a general principle which requires the Member States to ensure wide access by the general public to events of major importance at Community level.[252] If a Member State decides to create such a list, it shall do so in a clear and transparent manner in due time. According to the FIFA, the fact that all matches of the World Cup were included in the Belgian and UK list is characterised by a great lack of clarity, because the reasons for the choice were never disclosed. As a result, FIFA argues that this arbitrary method of composition of the list does not satisfy the requirements of clarity and transparency.[253] However, the General Court indicated that Article 14 (1) of the AVMS Directive "*does not set out specific matters which must feature in the procedures put in place at national level for the purposes of drawing up the list of events of major importance for society. That provision leaves the Member States a margin of discretion for organising the procedures in question as regards their stages, possible consultation of parties concerned and allocation of administrative competence, whilst stating that they must be clear and transparent as a whole.*" According to the General Court, the procedures should be clear and transparent, in the sense that "*they must be based on objective criteria which are known in advance by the parties concerned, so as to prevent the Member States' discretion for deciding on the specific events to include in their lists from being exercised in an arbitrary manner.*" The formulation of specific criteria to assess the importance of a certain event is an important element in order for lists to be drawn up in a transparent manner. The General Court concluded by saying "*that the requirement of clarity and transparency does not [...] oblige the competent national authority to set out the reasons why it did not follow the opinions or observations put forward during the consultation procedure.*"[254]

---

[252] European Parliament 2002, para 9.

[253] GC, FIFA v European Commission, Case T-68/08, paras 79–81; GC, FIFA v European Commission, Case T-385/07, paras 144–148.

[254] GC, FIFA v European Commission, Case T-68/08, paras 84–96; GC, FIFA v European Commission, Case T-385/07, paras 150–158; GC, UEFA v European Commission, paras 87–107.

Article 14 (2) further specifies that if a Member State has taken such a measure, it shall immediately notify the list to the European Commission. To date, only 8 countries have formally notified their list to the European Commission: Austria, Belgium, Finland, France, Germany, Ireland, Italy and the UK. In 2002, the Danish Government even decided to revoke the Danish Order that listed the events.[255] It is important to note that, although only 8 countries have formally notified their list to the European Commission, other Member States do also have lists of major events. In the Netherlands, for example, a list is attached to the Dutch Media Decree.[256] However, the list was not sent to the European Commission, because initial orientations in Brussels had shown that the European Commission thought that the list was too long.[257] The Polish media regulation too contains a list with important events for the Polish society.[258] The major difference between the notified and non-notified lists is that broadcasters from other Member States do not have to respect the latter. As Schoental rephrased this: "*at the heart of this provision is the mechanism of mutual recognition.*"[259] In more detail, when a Member State notifies its list to the European Commission, the European Commission shall, within a period of 3 months, verify whether the list is compatible with Community law, seek the opinion of the contact committee,[260] communicate them to the other Member States and publish the list in the Official Journal of the European Union. As a result, this publication enables the other Member States to comply with their obligations to mutually recognise the published lists.[261] More practically, the Member States are obliged to prevent circumvention, i.e. Member States must ensure that broadcasters under their jurisdiction do not exercise their exclusive broadcasting rights to circumvent the lists of events drawn up by other Member States.[262] Hence, a Member State must guarantee the respect of a notified list of major events of another Member State regardless whether it has drawn up such a list itself. Scheuer and Schoental put this mutual recognition principle in terms of 'rewarding' and 'penalising.' According to them, "*Member States which do so are 'rewarded' by the other Member States' obligation to enforce the list. Member States who decide not to draw up a list are 'penalized' with the obligation to enforce other Member States' lists, i.e. all those Member States will face the*

[255] Revocation of the Danish Order on the use of TV rights to events of major importance to society. OJ (2002) C 45/7.

[256] Articles 5.1–5.3 of the Media Act of 29 December 2008; Articles 18–21 of the Media Decree of 29 December 2008.

[257] ICRI et al. 2009a.

[258] Article 20b of the Broadcasting Act of 29 December 1992; ICRI et al. 2009b.

[259] Schoental 2006, 4.

[260] The contact committee is established pursuant to Article 29 of AVMS Directive.

[261] This principle of mutual recognition has been recognised in the TV Danmark case. For more information about this case, see: R. v. Independent Television Commission, ex parte TV Danmark 1 [2001] 1 WLR 74; House of Lords. R v. ITC, Ex Parte TV Danmark 1 Ltd, judgment of 25 July 2001, [2001] UKHL 42; Schoental 2006, 1–8; 2002, 107–133, Valcke et al. 2010, 296.

[262] Article 14 (3) of the AVMS Directive. Valcke et al. 2010, 296.

'disadvantages' of the mechanism regardless of whether they opt for the 'advantages'." According to them, this is a means of encouraging Member States to follow the procedure laid down in Article 14 when they adopt measures regarding access to major events.[263]

In the past, the European Commission informed the relevant Member State with a letter whether it had objections to the notified list and whether it would publish the list. Given that the letter closed the verification procedure which the European Commission is required to carry out; and the publication of the measures approved by the European Commission informs the other Member States of their existence, and, therefore, enables them to comply with their obligations to mutually recognise those measures, the letter produced legal effects for the Member States and, thus, is open to challenge before the European Courts. Hence, the verification now has to lead to a European Commission act (decision) adopted in accordance with its internal rules. Consequently, the results of such verifications done in the past, which took the form of letters from the Director General, had to be re-adopted in accordance with the correct decision-making procedures.[264]

With regard to this procedure, the FIFA and UEFA claimed that the European Commission failed to state reason when declaring the UK's and Belgian lists compatible with Community law, because the European Commission did not give any reasons to justify the inclusion of the World Cup and EURO as a whole in the lists.[265] Although the FIFA recognises that the World Cup is mentioned as an example of an event of major importance that does not mean that all the matches in the World Cup may automatically be included in the list.[266] Furthermore, the FIFA indicated the European Commission disregarded its obligation to conduct a detailed review of the compatibility of the lists with Community law, because its review of the included events was purely marginal and virtually redundant.[267] However, the General Court stated that the European Commission did not have to provide more detailed reasons for its appraisal in respect of the inclusion of 'non-prime' matches in the lists, because the World Cup should be regarded as a single event (*supra*).[268] Additionally, UEFA complained that the European Commission did not again verify the compatibility of the UK list after the Infront decision (*supra*) taking into account factors arising after the year 2000.[269] The General Court, however, stressed that the

---

263 Scheuer and Schoenthal 2008, 427.

264 For more information about this decision being a challengeable act, see: GC, Infront WM AG v Commission of the European Communities; CJ, Commission of the European Communities v Infront WM AG; Scheuer and Schoenthal 2008, 426, 427; Valcke et al. 2010, 296, 297.

265 GC, FIFA v European Commission, para 59; GC, FIFA v European Commission, Case T-385/07, para 64; GC, UEFA v European Commission, Case T-55/08, para 74.

266 GC, FIFA v European Commission, Case T-68/08, para 59.

267 *Ibid.*, para 60.

268 *Ibid.*, para 71; GC, FIFA v European Commission, Case T-385/07, para 73; GC, UEFA v European Commission, para 75.

269 GC, UEFA v European Commission, para 74.

European Commission "*could legitimately base itself on information gleaned from a consultation held prior to 1998 for the purposes of adopting the contested decision in 2007.*"[270]

14.3.3 A Voluntary Mechanism for Broadcasters

As said before, the 'list of major events' mechanism does not reserve the listed events for free-to-air television. Moreover, neither it compels free-to-air broadcasters to acquire the rights to listed events nor guarantees them exclusive rights to such events, nor does it oblige them to broadcast listed events to which they hold rights.[271]

14.3.3.1 No Obligation to use the Acquired Rights ('Hoarding Effect')

A. Introduction

This 'list of major events' mechanism does not actively encourage or oblige free-to-air television operators to broadcast the rights they have acquired, resulting in 'unused rights.'[272] In practice, those 'unused rights' can arise, for instance, in a situation where free-to-air broadcasters buy up rights to listed events and then refuse to show them.[273] Or, where broadcasters acquire the broadcasting rights for a sports event, including the rights for live transmissions, but only show summaries. Or where the potentially available broadcast minutes of an event exceeds by far the time which the broadcasters may actually show.[274] Or when free-to-air broadcasters have bought a bundle of rights including pay-television rights, although they are not in the position to exploit those rights.[275] Hence, even when free-to-air broadcasters have bought the exclusive rights of listed sports events, this 'list of major events' mechanism does not guarantee the effective broadcasting of those events on free-to-air broadcasters, limiting the viewer's access to sports events.[276] Attention should be drawn to the distinction between unused rights when broadcasters decide not to show the events and unused rights

[270] *Ibid.*, para 98.

[271] ACMA 2006, 2; Australian Broadcasting Authority 2000, 5.

[272] Perrine 2001, 25.

[273] Healy 2009, 222.

[274] European Commission State aid E 3/2005 (European Commission decision of 24 April 2007) (hereafter: *German public broadcaster state aid* case), para 301. (hereafter: *German public broadcaster state aid* case); Productivity Commission 2000, 437, 438.

[275] *German public broadcaster state aid* case, para 301.

[276] Productivity Commission 2000, 437.

as a result of rights holders not being able to sell their rights. In order to clarify the difference, the latter will be referred to as unsold rights while the former will be referred to as unused rights (*supra*).

In Flanders, for example, VT4 (a commercial broadcaster of the SBS Group) had bought the rights for the qualifying match Armenia–Belgium, but decided not to broadcast this listed event. The spokesman argued that the broadcaster did not want to change its regular programme schedule, because the public was not interested anymore in the matches played by their national team.[277] After missing EURO 2004 in Portugal and their failure to qualify for the FIFA World Cup 2006 in Germany and EURO 2008 in Austria and Switzerland, the Belgian national football team could not make it to South Africa even if they would win the match in Armenia. As a result, although all matches involving the Belgian men's football team are listed events, the public had not the possibility to watch the match on free-to-air television.[278] Recently, FIFA indicated that this broadcasters' practice of not fully exploiting the rights which they have acquired, limits the production and exposure of the FIFA brand.[279] According to FIFA, the fact that broadcasters themselves decide not to broadcast all matches (live) even demonstrates the disproportionate nature of the inclusion of these matches (*infra*).[280]

B. Australia: 'Use it or Lose it': Principle

a. Background to the Anti-Hoarding Regime

The objective of the Australian anti-siphoning regime is to prevent pay-television operators acquiring exclusive rights to broadcast important events for society.[281] To achieve this, the Minister may list specific events, the broadcast of which should be available free to the general public.[282] As a consequence, the Australian anti-siphoning regulation provides free-to-air broadcasters with the right of first refusal regarding the purchase of rights to listed events (*supra*).[283] Occasionally, however, those free-to-air broadcasters acquire exclusive broadcasting rights of the listed events, but, for commercial reasons, decide not to (fully) use those rights. A much-publicised example of 'hoarding' in Australia occurred in 1997 when the first session of the Ashes test (a Test cricket series played between England and Australia), being played in England, was not broadcast by Nine network, because the network chooses not to adjust its scheduled prime time programming. On

---

277 De Standaard 2009.

278 However, this match was broadcast on www.nieuwsblad.ne/sportwereld (Voetbalbelgië 2009).

279 GC, FIFA v European Commission, Case T-68/08, para 168.

280 GC, FIFA v European Commission, Case T-385/07, para 82.

281 Parliament of Australia 1998b, Regulation impact statement, para 1.

282 Subsection 115(1) of the Broadcasting Services Act.

283 ACMA 2006, 2.

another occasion, when the cricket clashed with Wimbledon, Nine decided not to broadcast the cricket matches and continued coverage of tennis.[284] Given that the practice of unused rights was considered as being to the detriment of the sport, the fans and subscribers,[285] the Australian Parliament realised that there was a need for an effective mechanism to combat hoarding.[286]

According to the Australian Parliament, the delisting remedy (*supra*) had been effective in addressing situations where free-to-air broadcasters were not interested in buying the rights to an event, but was less likely to be effective in situations where free-to-air broadcasters decided not to broadcast the listed events. Hence, it was apparent that the anti-siphoning legislation needed to be amended in order to provide an incentive for free-to-air broadcasters to only acquire live rights they will actually use, and to discourage the acquisition of live rights they are not planning to use on one television channel.[287]

In order to encourage free-to-air broadcasters to fully exercise their acquired rights, there were essentially three options proposed: (1) a 'must show' regime, (2) industry self-regulation, and (3) a 'must offer' scheme.[288] Given that the issue at stake involves free-to-air coverage of major sports events, it was emphasised that the chosen regulation would not directly affect the pay-television operators or adversely affect them. Therefore, the proposals dealt with the free-to-air coverage of sports events after the acquisition of their rights has taken place, while the anti-siphoning regime as such dealt with the acquisition of the rights.[289] Moreover, it is specified that the anti-hoarding regime will stand alone and will operate independently from the ant-siphoning regime, though the intention is to compliment and reinforce its purpose.[290]

In the following paragraphs the 'must offer' scheme and industry self-regulation will be addressed in more detail. The 'must show' regime will be discussed later.

Industry Self-Regulation

One of the options to persuade free-to-air broadcasters to use their acquired rights could be via industry self-regulation. Free-to-air broadcasters would be encouraged to develop a voluntary code of practice to address the hoarding issue. When choosing this option, broadcasters would still have the ability to determine how

---

284 Parliament of Australia 1998b, Regulation impact statement, para 5; Australian Broadcasting Authority 2000, 8; Australian Broadcasting Authority 2001, 23.

285 Broadcasting Services (Events) Notice (No. 1) 2004—Explanatory Statement, *Government Notices Gazette* 19 May 2004.

286 Parliament of Australia 1998b, Regulation impact statement, para 6; Australian Broadcasting Authority 2000, 8.

287 Parliament of Australia 1998b, Regulation impact statement, paras 5 and 27; Australian Broadcasting Authority 2000, 8.

288 Parliament of Australia 1998b, Regulation impact statement, para 11.

289 *Ibid.*, para 7; Australian Broadcasting Authority 2000, 8.

290 Parliament of Australia 1998a, Bills Digest No. 6 1998-99.

much of a listed event should be broadcast in order to satisfy the demands of their viewers.[291] The impact analysis, however, demonstrated that broadcasters are driven by commercial interests over their viewers' interests. In the impact analysis, it was formulated as follows: "*a broadcaster who has acquired exclusive broadcasting rights may see more of an advantage in withholding an event from a competing free-to-air broadcaster than in satisfying a marginalised public interest in their own broadcasting of the event.*"[292] Given these competitive pressures, it was argued that "*there is no evidence to suggest that broadcasters would be motivated to cooperate in a timely manner which would ensure that the objective of maximising the opportunities for the free-to-air televising of major events would be achieved.*"[293] Although the option of self-regulation has the least disruptive effect on competition, the Australian Parliament realised that this would also be the option that is least likely to solve the problem.[294]

Must-Offer Regime

Another option involved the introduction of a 'must-offer' regime.[295] The premise of this principle is specified as follows: "*that free-to-air broadcasters who have taken advantage of their privileged position under the anti-siphoning rules and acquired live rights to a designated event or events in a series should be made to bear the responsibility of that acquisition by providing free-to-air coverage themselves or enabling another national broadcaster to televise those events.*"[296] The impact assessment explicitly stressed that the must-offer obligation would not directly affect pay-television broadcasters, because "*[t]he 'must offer' regime concerns itself with how the free to air broadcasters use the live rights [...] after they have been acquired.*"[297]

In short, this must-offer regime requires commercial broadcasters to offer to the national public broadcasters the right to purchase, for a nominal charge, the free-to-air rights to an event they do not plan to transmit live. The national public service broadcasters must also offer unused portions of rights to each other (*infra*). The impact assessment identified the national public broadcasters as "*the appropriate facilitators of this regime as they are less constrained than commercial broadcasters by advertising arrangements and related scheduling decisions.*"[298]

---

291 Parliament of Australia 1998b, Regulation impact statement, paras 13 and 19.

292 *Ibid.*, para 20.

293 *Ibid.*, para 21.

294 *Ibid.*, paras 35, 36.

295 *Ibid.*, para 14.

296 *Ibid.*, para 22.

297 *Ibid.*, para 30.

298 *Ibid.*, para 23.

It was argued that one of the tasks of tax-payer funded national broadcasters is to guarantee free-to-air access to important events.[299]

According to the Australian Parliament, this mechanism would provide "*a direct incentive for free-to-air broadcasters to only acquire live rights they can actually use, and to fully utilise the rights they do acquire.*"[300] Given that the broadcasters have to offer their rights for a nominal charge, their investment won't be fully returned. As a result, "*the possible cost of this scheme is the disincentive to the initial acquisition of rights.*"[301]

Given that this system represents a balance between, on the one hand, the public's interest in the free-to-air coverage of the listed events and, on the other hand, the right of broadcasters to make programming decisions, the Australian Parliament preferred this option. Moreover, this option was found to be "*a practicable and workable model which best satisfies the objectives while only involving minimal reduction in competition.*"[302] This must-offer regime was introduced as a new Part 10A in the Broadcasting Services Act.[303]

b. Must-Offer Regime in Detail

Must-Offer Obligation

The anti-hoarding provision obliges commercial free-to-air broadcasters,[304] not intending to broadcast the whole or a part of the sports events live, to offer, before the offer time (*infra*), to the national public broadcasters (ABC and SBS) the right to purchase, for a nominal charge,[305] the free-to-air rights of those events. The offer must remain open for acceptance for a minimum period of 7 days.[306] The same goes for the national public broadcasters. They also have to offer unused (proportions) rights to each other for a nominal charge.[307, 308] This must-offer regime is also imposed on commercial free-to-air broadcasters' programme suppliers, usually acquiring broadcasting rights directly from the event owner.[309]

---

299 *Ibid.*, para 23.

300 *Ibid.*, para 27.

301 *Ibid.*, para 29.

302 *Ibid.*, para 37.

303 *Ibid.*, para 38; Parliament of Australia 1999a, Broadcasting Services Amendment Act (No. 1) 1999.

304 Commercial free-to-air broadcasters include Networks, 7, 9 and 10 (Parliament of Australia 1998a, Bills Digest No. 6 1998-99).

305 1 Australian Dollar (Section 146H (7) of the Broadcasting Services Act).

306 Section 146A of the Broadcasting Services Act.

307 1 Australian Dollar (Section 146N (6) of the Broadcasting Services Act).

308 Section 146A of the Broadcasting Services Act.

309 *Ibid.*; Section 146D of the Broadcasting Services Act; Parliament of Australia 1998a, Bills Digest No. 6 1998-99.

There are three situations in which a person is a programme supplier of a commercial broadcaster: (1) the person supplies or may be reasonably expected to supply a commercial television broadcasting licensee with two-thirds of its sporting programmes, (2) the person is a related body corporate of the licensee, or (3) where the ACMA[310] declares the person to be a programme supplier for the purposes of the 'must offer' rules.[311] Thus, in short, the anti-hoarding provisions seek to compel free-to-air broadcasters and their programme suppliers to actually use live broadcasting rights of certain events.[312]

The anti-hoarding rules are contravened if free-to-air (commercial or national) broadcasters, having the right to broadcast live a designated event (*infra*), either did not broadcast live any part of the (series of) event(s) or did broadcast live some, but not all of the (series of) event(s) and he did not offer the rights or the remainder of the rights before the offer time to the national public broadcasters.[313] The same goes for programme suppliers. A programme supplier contravenes the anti-hoarding rule either if he did not confer the right to broadcast live any part of the (series of) event(s) or he conferred the right to broadcast live in that area some, but not all, of the (series of) event(s), but after the offer time.[314]

Given that compliance with the anti-hoarding rules is a condition of a commercial television licence,[315] the ACMA has the power to issue a notice directing the commercial television licensee to stop the breach[316] or even to cancel or suspend the licence if commercial broadcasters breach their licence condition.[317] In addition, a maximum penalty of 2000 penalty units[318] could be imposed.[319] Programme suppliers, not subject to licence conditions, will be subject to a civil penalty of 2000 penalty units if found to have intentionally or recklessly contravened the anti-hoarding rule.[320] The national broadcasters do not hold licences, but are established under their own legislation: the Australian Broad-

---

310 ACMA is the Australian Communications and Media Authority. On 1 July 2005, the Australian Broadcasting Authority (ABA) was merged with the Australian Communications Authority to form the Australian Communications and Media Authority (ACMA).

311 Section 146D (2)–(5) of the Broadcasting Services Act.

312 Parliament of Australia 1998a, Bills Digest No. 6 1998–99.

313 Section 146E (1) & 146L (2) of the Broadcasting Services Act.

314 Section 146F (1) of the Broadcasting Services Act.

315 Paragraph 7(1)(h) of Schedule 2—Part 3 of the Broadcasting Services Act: "*the licensee will not use broadcasting services in the commission of an offence against another Act or a law of a State or Territory*".

316 Section 141 of the Broadcasting Services Act.

317 Section 143 of the Broadcasting Services Act.

318 2000 penalty units is currently 220,000 Australian Dollar (Australian Broadcasting Authority 2000, 11).

319 Section 139 (2) of the Broadcasting Services Act.

320 Section 139 (2) of the Broadcasting Services Act; Parliament of Australia 1998a, Bills Digest No. 6 1998-99; Parliament of Australia 1999b. Bills Digest No. 58 1999-2000.

casting Corporation Act 1983[321] and the Special Broadcasting Service Act 1991[322]. As a result, for the national broadcasters, breach of the anti-hoarding rule will be a breach of a statutory obligation. Although these anti-hoarding obligations arise under the Broadcasting Services Act, the ACMA has no direct sanctioning power over the national broadcasters. This is part of the preservation of independence of the national broadcasters.

It is important to note that a broadcaster has broadcast live the whole (series of) event(s), if the broadcaster broadcasts live all but an 'insubstantial proportion' of the (series of) event(s). The Broadcasting Services Act specifies an 'insubstantial proportion' as follows: "*interruptions for commercial breaks, news breaks, programme promotions, announcements or brief crosses to other live events.*"[323] In 2000, the former Broadcasting Authority emphasised that this does not include a regular news programme. ACMA regards those regular news programmes as a substantial proportion.[324] Furthermore, it is specified that when there are two or more events in a designated series, which wholly or partly overlap in time, and the free-to-air broadcaster or a programme supplier shows live one of them, they are supposed to have broadcast live the other overlapping events.[325] According to the former Broadcasting Authority, this would mean that if a broadcaster has the live rights to Wimbledon, and broadcasts the match on centre court, the broadcaster will be taken to have shown all the other matches taking place at the same time as the aired match.[326]

Designated Events and Designated Series of Events

Section 146C of the Broadcasting Services Act states that it is up to the Minister to make a disallowable instrument designating the events that are covered by the anti-hoarding provisions. It must be noted that designation has no retrospective effect, and, therefore, will only have an effect on events which rights are acquired after they have been declared as designated events by the Minister.[327] If a free-to-air broadcaster already holds rights to a designated event, the anti-hoarding provisions would not apply until the next time the rights will be auctioned.[328]

The criteria for designating an (series of) event to be subject to the 'must offer' regime are articulated in schedule 1 of the Explanatory Memorandum. The Minister may designate (series of) events where there is a widespread public expectation, based on past practice, that the (series of) event(s) will be broadcast

321 Australian Broadcasting Corporation Act 1983.

322 Special Broadcasting Service Act 1991.

323 Sections 146E (2) & 146L (3) of the Broadcasting Services Act.

324 Australian Broadcasting Authority 2000, 9.

325 Sections 146K (1) & 146Q (1) of the Broadcasting Services Act, 5.

326 Australian Broadcasting Authority 2000, 11 and 17.

327 *Ibid.*, 11; Australian Broadcasting Authority 2001, 24.

328 Australian Broadcasting Authority 2001, 24.

live and in full on free-to-air television, or the (series of) event(s) has grown in importance in the public's perception over time that it warrants full live free-to-air coverage.[329]

The 2002 and 2006 FIFA World Cup tournaments were the only events to have been designated under the anti-hoarding rules.[330] Accordingly, if a free-to-air broadcaster acquired the broadcasting rights of this competition and decided not to broadcast some matches, the rights of those games should be offered to one of the national broadcasters, and free-to-air audiences will continue to have access to the tournament as a whole.[331] As the 2002 and 2006 FIFA World Cup tournaments to which the 2000 Declaration applied have passed, this 2000 Declaration was formally revoked.[332] With regard to the 2010 Fifa World Cup in South Africa, eight group stage matches were removed from the list giving a digital-only channel the chance to broadcast these matches live (*supra*).

Offers to Transfer Rights

A commercial television broadcaster or a programme supplier is taken to have made an offer to transfer live broadcasting rights to national broadcasters only if they have offered to make an arrangement which in substance gives the national broadcaster the rights to broadcast live the whole or the part of the (series of) event(s).[333] In determining whether their arrangements would have such an effect, regard must be given to the practical effect of those arrangements.[334] Furthermore, the offer must be in writing[335] and must be given to the managing director of a national broadcaster[336] at or about the same time that a corresponding offer is given to the managing director of the other national broadcaster.[337] It is also necessary that contracts to acquire the broadcasting rights to broadcast live events must authorise the transfer of rights.[338]

It was the former Broadcasting Authority's view that "*an offer which is subject to a condition, such as participation or non-participation of Australians, would be excluded under the legislation.*" The Authority added that "*[s]uch an offer may*

---

329 Parliament of Australia 1998b, Regulation impact statement, Schedule 1—New section 146C; Australian Broadcasting Authority 2000, 14.

330 Broadcasting Services (Designated Series of Events) Declaration No. 1 of 2000; Australian Broadcasting Authority 2000, 9; Department of Broadband, Communications and the Digital Economy 2009.

331 Australian Broadcasting Authority 2000, 23.

332 Communications (Redundant Regulation) Instrument of Revocation (No. 1) 2009.

333 Section 146G (1) & 146M (1) of the Broadcasting Services Act; Australian Broadcasting Authority 2000, 10.

334 Section 146G (2) & 146M (2) of the Broadcasting Services Act.

335 Section 146H (2) & 146N (2) of the Broadcasting Services Act.

336 Section 146H (3) & 146N (3) of the Broadcasting Services Act.

337 Section 146H (4) & 146N (4) of the Broadcasting Services Act.

338 Section 146J & 146P of the Broadcasting Services Act.

not constitute an offer to make an arrangement which 'in substance' gives the rights to broadcast the event to the national broadcaster." Additionally, it was argued that conditional offers could present significant difficulties for the national broadcasters in terms of planning and promoting the changed schedule.[339]

Offer Time

The Minister does not only have to designate (series of) events, he also has the task to declare an offer time.[340] Section 146C (5) of the Broadcasting Services Act specifies that the offer time must occur 30 days or more before the start of the (series of) event(s), unless the Minister is satisfied that the offer time should occur closer to the start of the (series of) event. As the offer period must be open for at least 7 days, the minimum offer period must be 1 week before the start of the (series of) event(s).[341] According to the former Broadcasting Authority "*an offer period of at least 30 days recognises the time required by the national broadcasters to arrange for the broadcast of the event, to notify audiences about the change to the regular schedule and promote the new sports programme.*"[342]

Effectiveness

Again, the effectiveness of these provisions is questioned by different Australian broadcasters.

Although the anti-hoarding provisions force free-to-air broadcasters to offer broadcasting rights to the national public broadcasters under certain circumstances, the latter do not have to accept those offers. The minimum offer time of 30 days before the event, for example, makes it difficult to accommodate such events in the programming schedules of the other broadcasters. Hence, as indicated by the former Broadcasting Authority, "*the effective operation of the 'must offer' regime will depend on the ability of the ABC and SBS to accept transfers of rights to full and live coverage.*" The national broadcasters' decision to (not) accept the offer will be influenced by scheduling considerations, the potential viewer's reaction to changes to the programme schedule and the profile of the sport. Additionally, national broadcasters could be also confronted with practical difficulties when accepting an offer for certain sports events, such as transmission costs when the event is played overseas.[343]

---

339 Australian Broadcasting Authority 2000, 10.

340 *Ibid.*, 24.

341 *Ibid.*, 9.

342 *Ibid.*, 24.

343 *Ibid.*, 15, 16.

344 Perrine 2001, 26; Australian Broadcasting Authority 2000, 8; Productivity Commission 2000, 434.

Furthermore, the free-to-air broadcasters are not required to sell any pay-television rights they hold.[344]

Finally, the concept of 'use' is difficult to assess. Especially, in tournaments where there are multiple events or games such as the Olympic Games.[345] From 2007, ACMA will monitor and assess whether listed events have been 'used' satisfactorily.[346] To designate rights as being (un)used, the following criteria will be taken into account: (1) have broadcast rights been acquired by a free-to-air broadcaster, and what type of rights have been acquired; (2) did the broadcasters reach at least 50 % of the population; (3) was at least half of the total event broadcast; (4) was the event shown (near-)live; (5) would a delay in showing the event allow the event to be broadcast at a time of, or in a form, that would provide greater audience interest; (6) relevant contractual obligations with the rights holder; (7) were free-to-air rights sublicensed and were pay-television rights held by free-to-air broadcasters made available to a pay-television operator on a reasonable basis; and (8) other matters that may be relevant in individual circumstances.[347]

C. Must-Broadcast Obligation

a. Introduction

To remedy the negative effects of unused rights, the Australian 'use it or lose it'—principle is worth considering as a means to guarantee the public's right to information in a more effective way. However, as indicated above, the effectiveness of this system is questioned by different broadcasters. In order to deal with the lacunas of the Australian 'use it or lose it'—principle, a 'must-broadcast' obligation could be included in the current regulatory framework. As elaborated in a previous section, there exist some solid arguments in favour of recognition of a public right of access to (full and live) coverage of major (listed) sports events. In this regard, the proposed must-broadcast obligation could be approached as the realisation of a positive obligation for States based on Article 10 of the ECHR in order to more effectively safeguard this right of access (*supra*).[348]

This must-broadcast obligation would oblige broadcasters, who have bought the exclusive broadcasting rights of listed events, to broadcast (a substantial proportion of) those events live. It is not in the public's interest when broadcasters have a

---

345 Bruce Meagher, Director, Strategy and Communications Division, SBS cited in Standing Committee on Environment, Communications, Information Technology and the Arts 2006, para 3.103.

346 Australian Government 2006, 33, 34; Minister for Communications, Information Technology and the Arts 2006.

347 Standing Committee on Environment, Communications, Information Technology and the Arts 2006, para 3.99.

348 Lefever and Werkers 2010, 404.

warehouse of unused rights. Given that broadcasters are likely to broadcast those events or programmes they believe will attract the largest viewing audience in order to increase the potential financial return from advertisers,[349] this obligation could have a major impact on their economic freedom. Such obligation might seem very intrusive and, thus, its introduction requires a delicate balancing of the different interests at stake in order to determine its precise modalities.[350] Although it falls outside the scope of this book to carry out this balancing exercise in an accurate and extensive way, the contours of this discussion will already be drawn by taking a brief look at the tension between the proposed must-broadcast obligation and some interests that undoubtedly are conflicted by it: the freedom of services, on the one hand, and the freedom of programming, on the other hand.

b. Must-Broadcast Obligation Versus Freedom of Services

Introduction

The proposed must-broadcast obligation could restrict the broadcasters' freedom of services. The freedom of services, one of the four fundamental freedoms of the TFEU, is governed by Article 56 of the TFEU [ex 49 TEC]. This Article prohibits "*restrictions on freedom to provide services within the Union [...] of nationals of Member States who are established in a Member State other than that of the person for whom the services are intended.*" Although the TFEU and the provisions on freedom of services in particular do not contain any reference to broadcasting services, the European Court of Justice has declared that audiovisual services are subject to the provisions of the TFEU.[351] In the *De Coster* case, for example, it has been stated that "*the transmission, and broadcasting, of television signals comes within the rules of the Treaty relating to the provision of services.*"[352]

As a result, any national legislation (whether national, regional or local) of a Member State that discriminates against providers of broadcasting services established in another Member State will be prohibited under Article 56 of the TFEU [ex 49 TEC].[353] It is important to note that measures applying in a non-discriminatory way both to undertakings established in their national territory and to undertakings established in other Member States could also be considered a

---

349 Department of Broadband, Communications and the Digital Economy 2009, 17.

350 Lefever and Van Rompuy 2009, 267.

351 Böttcher and Castendyk 2008, 90; Valcke et al. 2010, 264, 265.

352 CJ, François De Coster v Collège des bourgmestre et échevins de Watermael-Boitsfort, para 28.

353 Valcke et al. 2010, 264, 265.

restriction on freedom to provide services within the meaning of Article 56 of the TFEU [ex 49 TEC] if those measures benefit certain undertakings established in that national territory.[354] However, in the *Debauve* case, the European Court of Justice stated that "*in view of the particular nature of certain services such as the broadcasting and transmission of television signals, specific requirements imposed upon providers of services [...] which are justified by the general interest and apply to all persons and undertakings [...] cannot be said to be incompatible with the Treaty.*"[355] To be justified as being in the general interest, (non-)discriminatory restrictions must be proportionate to the general interests protected and there must be no other alternative measures that are less restrictive of the inter-state provision of services that could be adopted.[356]

Hence, the question that needs to be answered is whether Article 56 of the TFEU [ex 49 TEC] would preclude a must-broadcast obligation or whether it could be a justified restriction of the freedom of services. Such obligation could be imposed if this is proportionate, transparent, and above all, necessary to meet clearly defined general interest objectives.

Public Interest Objectives

As mentioned before, restrictions of the freedom of services can only be justified by the protection of the general interest. The European Commission has explicitly stated that economic aims will not be considered general interest obligations.[357] One of the general interests that has been accepted and recognised by the European Court of Justice is the protection of the freedom of speech, the right to information and the plurality in the media.[358] Media pluralism is often considered to be an essential pillar for democracy and the development of citizens. In 2007, for example, Reding has once again stressed that "*maintaining media pluralism is crucial for the democratic process.*"[359] In the European Commission's understanding, ensuring media pluralism implies that citizens "*have access to variety of information sources and voices, allowing them to form opinions without the undue influence of one dominant opinion forming power.*"[360] Hence, to exercise informed choices, it is important to have a variety of sources and content, but it is more

[354] GC, FIFA v European Commission, Case T-68/08, para 49; GC, FIFA v European Commission, Case T-385/07, para 53; GC, UEFA v European Commission, para 45.

[355] CJ, Procureur du Roi v Marc J.V.C. Debauve, para 12.

[356] CJ, Commission v Kingdom of the Netherlands, para 19.

[357] European Commission 2002b, 7.

[358] See e.g. CJ, Stichting Collectieve Antennevoorziening Gouda et al. v Commissariaat voor de Media; CJ, United Pan-Europe Communications Belgium SA, Coditel Brabant SPRL, Société Intercommunale pour la Diffusion de la Télévision (Brutélé), Wolu TV ASBL v État belge (hereafter: *UPC Belgium* case).

[359] Rapid Press Releases 2007a.

[360] Commission of the European Communities 2007a, SEC(2007) 32, 5.

[361] Valcke 2004, 337.

important to ensure that citizens have access to those different sources.[361] In order to guarantee the latter, *inter alia* must-carry obligations were imposed in different Member States.[362] Must-carry obligations are a form of carriage obligation requiring network operators, used by a significant number of end-users as their principal means to receive radio and television broadcasts, to distribute certain radio and television channels. In the *United Pan-Europe Communications Belgium* case, the question was raised whether those must-carry obligations were a justified restriction on the freedom to provide services. The European Court of Justice agreed that must-carry obligations are liable to hinder the provision of services between Member States. Nevertheless, the European Court of Justice reaffirmed that a cultural policy aiming at safeguarding media pluralism "*may constitute an overriding requirement relating to the general interest which justifies a restriction on the freedom to provide services.*"[363] Hence, Article 56 of the TFEU [ex 49 TEC] does not as such preclude legal restrictions (such as the must-carry obligations), if these both pursue an aim of general interest, such as pluralism of television programmes, and are proportionate, transparent and non-discriminatory.[364] Furthermore, in the *Elliniki Radiophonia Tiléorassi* case, the European Court of Justice specifically stated that "*in order to justify rules which are likely to obstruct the exercise of the freedom to provide services, such justification, provided for by Community law, must be interpreted in the light of the general principles of law and in particular of fundamental rights.*"[365] Moreover, as regards rules relating to television, those limitations should be "*appraised in the light of the general principle of freedom of expression embodied in Article 10 of the European Convention on Human Rights.*"[366]

Recently, the General Court has explicitly stated that the 'list of major events' mechanism "*gave concrete expression to the possibility for the Member States to restrict the exercise, in the audiovisual field, of fundamental freedoms established by primary Community law, on the basis of overriding reasons in the public interest.*"[367] The General Court reiterated that the freedom of expression and

[362] At European level, the must-carry obligation is included in Article 31 of the 2002/22/EC (hereafter: Universal Service Directive).

[363] *UPC Belgium* case, para 41.

[364] *UPC Belgium* case, paras 47 and 51; Valcke et al. 2010, 266, 267.

[365] CJ, Elliniki Radiophonia Tiléorassi AE and Panellinia Omospondia Syllogon Prossopikou v Dimotiki Etairia Pliroforissis and Sotirios Kouvelas and Nicolaos Avdellas and others, para 43.

[366] *Ibid.*, para 45.

[367] GC, FIFA v European Commission, Case T-68/08, para 48; GC, FIFA v European Commission, Case T-385/07, para 52; GC, UEFA v European Commission, para 44.

[368] GC, FIFA v European Commission, Case T-68/08, paras 51 and 158; GC, FIFA v European Commission, Case T-385/07, paras 55 and 127; GC, UEFA v European Commission, para 47.

freedom to receive information is an overriding reason in the public interest which is capable of justifying restrictions.[368] Since the measures adopted under Article 14 of the AVMS Directive relate to events of major importance for society, the General Court argued that those measures are justified by overriding reasons in the public interest.[369]

As already indicated several times, the must-broadcast obligation would be introduced into the regulatory framework to make the 'list of major events' mechanism more effective and, thus, to guarantee the public's right of information in a better way. Therefore, the safeguard of the public's right to information, in particular access to certain events of major importance for society, could be a cultural policy objective that could justify a restriction on the broadcasters' freedom of services.

Proportionality

As indicated by Tichy, "*[t]here is no doubt that the enforcement of both fundamental rights and fundamental freedoms may cause conflict.*"[370] The question that rises is whether fundamental rights would automatically prevail over EU law. Tichy and Klabbers indicated that there could be a possibility that fundamental rights should be given priority over conflicting Community law.[371] However, they immediately nuance this. According to Tichy, for example, "*as a general rule, it should held as there not being a general primacy of fundamental rights over the fundamental freedoms.*"[372] Klabbers stated that the European Court of Justice does not proclaim that either human rights law or Community law prevails.[373] As a result, in cases where the exercise of an ECHR right clashes directly with an economic freedom (*in casu* the public's right to information must be weighed against the economic interests of the primary broadcasters) and where it is not a priori clear which right should take precedence, Dommering indicated that the proportionality test should apply.[374]

The principle of proportionality means that a public authority may not impose obligations except to the extent to which they are strictly necessary in the public interest to attain the purpose of the measure. In other words, this means that the imposed restrictions "*must in no case be disproportionate in relation to that aim*"[375] and that the manner in which it is applied "*must be subject to a*

[369] GC, FIFA v European Commission, Case T-68/08, para 53; GC, FIFA v European Commission, Case T-385/07, para 57; GC, UEFA v European Commission, para 49.

[370] Tichy 2004, 5.

[371] *Ibid.*, 5; Klabbers 2009, 151.

[372] Tichy 2004, 6.

[373] Klabbers 2009, 165.

[374] Dommering 2008, 76.

[375] *UPC Belgium* case, para 44.

[376] *Ibid.*, para 51.

transparent procedure based on objective non-discriminatory criteria known in advance."[376] para 51. More specifically, the new balance may not impose too burdensome obligations on economic actors in the broadcasting sector in order to guarantee the public's right to information or vice versa the public's right to information may not be brought in danger only to protect the economic interests of the actors.

Transparency

In the *UPC Belgium* case (supra), the European Court of Justice explicitly stated that "*such [must-carry] legislation [...] is not disproportionate in relation to that objective, which means that the manner in which it is applied must be subject to a transparent procedure based on objective non-discriminatory criteria known in advance.*"[377] Transparency should increase legal certainty. The European Commission emphasised that this condition "*will provide the market players concerned with the maximum legal certainty as regards the actual consequences of a given must-carry regime on their business [...].*"[378] As a result, as indicated by the European Commission, the fact that the must-carry obligation may only be imposed for the transmission of radio and television broadcast channels and services that are "specified,"[379] i.e. that they should be clearly identified in advance, should be viewed in this context.[380] The European Court of Justice stressed that "*each broadcaster must be able to determine in advance the nature and scope of the precise conditions to be satisfied [...].*"[381] According to the European Commission, a transparent designation procedure is necessary for broadcasters and network operators to know their rights and obligations.[382] In order to comply with this requirement, the rules with regard to the must-broadcast obligation should be explicitly included in the sector-specific media regulation.

---

376 *Ibid.*, para 51.

377 *Ibid.*, para 51.

378 European Commission 2002b, 8.

379 Article 31, § 1 of the Universal Service Directive.

380 European Commission 2002b, 8.

381 *UPC Belgium* case, para 46.

382 Rapid Press Releases 2009. Although Belgium amended the Electronic Communications Act of the bilingual region of Brussels-Capital in March 2007, the European Commission was of the opinion that it concerns on proportionality and transparency of the must-carry rules were not addressed (Rapid Press Releases 2008c, 2009).

Appropriateness

The principle of proportionality also requires that the means to attain an intended aim must be appropriate and should not go beyond that which is necessary in order to achieve that objective.[383] In other words, the means employed to achieve the aim must be both necessary and the least burdensome.[384] The European Court of Justice rephrased this as "*it must not be possible to obtain the same result by less restrictive rules.*"[385]

When the Australian Parliament was thinking about encouraging free-to-air broadcasters to fully exercise the rights they have acquired, it stated that a must-broadcast regime would lead to a maximisation of free-to-air coverage of sports events. However, it was added that "*this obligation would place a significant regulatory and commercial burden on the free to air television industry.*"[386] Given that the must-broadcast obligation has been appreciated as being the most interventionist of the three options (*supra*), and, therefore, would subvert competition to the greatest extent,[387] the Australian Parliament preferred the must-offer obligation (*supra*). Furthermore, although the FIFA argued that 'non-prime' matches could not be classified as of major importance for society because the legislation does not require broadcasters to broadcast those events,[388] the General Court indicated that the absence of a must-broadcast obligation for non-prime matches does not imply that those events are not of major importance for society. The General Court emphasised that the purpose of Article 14 of the AVMS Directive is "*not to force indirectly Member States wishing to provide for such protection to require a free channel provider to broadcast those events.*" The General Court even added that "*[i]f, in order to include legitimately an event in a list of events of major importance for society, the Member States had to require a free television service to broadcast it, the provision in question would produce effects going beyond the scope of its objective.*"[389]

At first, the introduction of such a must-broadcast obligation could be seen as very intrusive and disproportionate. However, it should be noted that the objective of the 'list of major events' mechanism could be better realised after the introduction of such an obligation. As indicated before, the Australian must-offer

[383] CJ, Stichting Collectieve Antennevoorziening Gouda et al.v Commissariaat voor de Media, para 15; CJ, Arbeitsgemeinschaft Deutscher Rundfunkanstalten (ARD) v PRO Sieben Media AG, para 51.

[384] European Commission 2002b, 7.

[385] CJ, Stichting Collectieve Antennevoorziening Gouda et al.v Commissariaat voor de Media, para 15.

[386] Parliament of Australia 1998b, Regulation impact statement, paras 16 and 34.

[387] *Ibid.*, para 36.

[388] GC, FIFA v European Commission, Case T-68/08, para 108; GC, FIFA v European Commission, Case T-385/07, para 86.

[389] GC, FIFA v European Commission, Case T-68/08, para 132; GC, FIFA v European Commission, Case T-385/07, para 111.

obligation has been criticised as being ineffective, as there is no requirement for the national broadcasters to accept the offers. Therefore, it is possible that a more intrusive obligation, such as the must-broadcast obligation, could be accepted as being proportionate, because it will be more effective in obtaining the objective.

The proportionality of this obligation will also depend on the discourse that is protected. As already indicated earlier, the type of debate in pursuance of major sports events is not as important for procedural democracy as political discourse. However, discourse in the public interest concerns not only speech the organisation of a democracy, but also concerning the culture of the society (*supra*). Given that live experience of important sports events can contribute significantly to the latter type of public discourse, by promoting civil participation in our democratic society, the imposition of a must-broadcast obligation with regard to listed sports events could be seen as a proportionate measure. Additionally, the inclusion of the must-broadcast obligation in the regulatory framework could make the 'list of major events' mechanism more proportionate, by limiting the negative effects (e.g. limited exposure) for the organisers of the event when broadcasters would decide not to fully exploit the rights they have acquired.

In addition, the sanction for non-compliance with this obligation should also be proportionate. An imprisonment sanction, for example, is deemed disproportional. A fine, deterrent enough to make broadcasters think twice about not using the acquired rights, could probably be proportionate.

Moreover, the obligation to broadcast the listed events only applies when a broadcaster decides to compete for exclusive broadcasting rights and when the rights will be assigned to that broadcaster. Given that the broadcaster has participated in the tender procedure, it would be difficult to argue that the must-offer obligation would force a broadcaster to show an event against its will.

In order to make the must-broadcast obligation more proportionate, it could be argued that, as in Australia, only a limited amount of listed events would be covered by this obligation. However, this would lead to the undesirable situation where some listed events would be designated as being more important than other listed events. Due to the fact that events could only be included in the list if they are of major importance for society, they should all be protected under the must-broadcast obligation.

c. Must-Broadcast Obligation Versus Freedom of Programming

Introduction

The freedom of broadcasters to frame their programmes independently is part of the wider right to freedom of expression as enshrined is Article 10, § 1 of the

[390] Castendyk 2008, 443, 444.

[391] ECHR, Groppera Radio AG and others v. Switzerland, para 55.

ECHR.[390] In the *Groppera* case, the European Court of Human Rights has explicitly stated that "*both broadcasting of programmes over the air and cable retransmission of such programmes are covered by the right enshrined in the first two sentences of Article 10 § 1.*"[391] Although the primary benefit of a must-broadcast obligation would be the absolute guarantee that listed events are shown on free-to-air broadcasters, this obligation would at the same time place a heavy burden on those broadcasters. This obligation would have a significant impact on the free-to-air broadcasters' ability to schedule their programmes freely. This system would force those broadcasters to broadcast events that they otherwise would decide not to show. Broadcasters have often argued that where they hold live rights and choose not to fully exercise them, they do so because their other programming is more popular.[392] As already indicated in Part I, the coverage and scheduling of programmes or events is often a commercial decision, primarily driven by the potential to earn advertising revenue. Hence, broadcasters are most likely to schedule programmes or events they believe will attract the largest viewing audience.[393] The question that rises is whether the inclusion of a must-broadcast obligation in sector-specific regulation is a justified restriction of the broadcasters' freedom of programming.

Given that the introduction of a must-broadcast obligation could be a restriction of the broadcaster's freedom of programming (as part of their freedom of expression), this obligation must be assessed in the light of Article 10 of the ECHR. Hence, it would only be justified if the threefold condition in the limitation clause (Article 10, § 2 of the ECHR) is met: the restriction must be 'prescribed by law,' pursue a 'legitimate aim,' and be 'necessary in a democratic society' (*supra*).

The Restriction has to be 'Prescribed by Law'

First, the restriction of the freedom of expression has to be 'prescribed by law.' This implies that the regulation must be adequately accessible and adequately foreseeable, i.e. it must be formulated with sufficient precision to reasonably foresee the consequences that a given action may entail.[394] An unpublished provision cannot satisfy the first condition; an unclear and contradictory rule cannot satisfy the second.[395] Since the requirement 'prescribed by law' is an equivalent of the above described transparency requirement, it can be repeated that if the must-broadcast obligation would be included in the sector-specific media regulation, this first requirement would normally be fulfilled.

---

392 Parliament of Australia 1998b, Regulation impact statement, paras 15, 16.

393 Department of Broadband, Communications and the Digital Economy 2009, 17; FACTS 2001, 13.

394 ECHR, Sunday Times v. the United Kingdom, para 49.

395 Dommering 2008, 43.

Legitimate Aims of Article 10, § 2 of the ECHR

Second, the restriction has to be in pursuance of one or more of the 'legitimate aims' listed in Article 10, § 2 of the ECHR: "*national security, territorial integrity or public safety, for the prevention of disorder or crime, for the protection of health or morals, for the protection of the reputation or rights of others, for preventing the disclosure of information received in confidence, or for maintaining the authority and impartiality of the judiciary.*"

As already indicated in Part I, broadcasting regulation contains different rules 'infringing' the broadcasters' freedom of programming. Quota regulation and advertising rules, for example, were considered justified in order to protect the rights of others, in particular the public (*supra*). Based on the analysis done in Part I, the 'list of major events' mechanism could be labelled as a justified State's intervention in order to protect the public's right to information. Given that the must-broadcast obligation would be introduced into the regulatory framework to make the 'list of major events' mechanism more effective, the public's right to information would be better guaranteed. Based on the observation that in the *Groppera* case and *Autronic* case, the European Court of Human Rights has incorporated the principle of media pluralism into the protection of the rights of others within Article 10, § 2 of the ECHR,[396] the must-broadcast obligation could probably be classified as a justified intervention under Article 10, § 2 of the ECHR.

Necessary in a Democratic Society

Third, the restriction has to be 'necessary in a democratic society.' The test of 'necessity in a democratic society' requires the European Court of Human Rights to determine whether the 'interference' corresponds to a 'pressing social need,' whether it was proportionate to the legitimate aim pursued and whether the reasons given by the national authorities to justify it are relevant and sufficient.[397] Voorhoof deduced from the case law of the European Court of Human Rights that the necessity test in a democratic society is the ultimate and decisive criterion.[398]

A Pressing Social Need

As already indicated in Part I, broadcasting regulation guaranteeing access to live and full coverage of sports events of major importance for society could be classified as necessary in a democratic society. Recital 5 of the AVMS Directive specifies that the growing importance of audiovisual media services for societies and democracy, in particular by ensuring freedom of information, diversity of

[396] ECHR, Groppera Radio AG and others v. Switzerland, paras 69, 70; ECHR, Autronic AG v. Switzerland, paras 58, 59; Marauhn 2007, 117.

[397] ECHR, Bladet Tromsø and Stensaas v. Norway, para 58; ECHR, Sunday Times v. the United Kingdom, para 62.

[398] Voorhoof 1995, 59.

opinion and media pluralism, justifies the application of specific rules to these services. More specifically, recital 49 of the AVMS Directive indicates that measures should be taken to "*protect the right to information and to ensure wide access by the public to television coverage of national or non-national events of major importance for society.*" In accordance with this incentive, different Member States have drawn up a list that should guarantee the broadcasting of those sports events on free-to-air television. As already described above, broadcasts of sports events are granted a major social role in bringing people together, providing people with a sense of belonging and uniting the nation. However, the free-to-air broadcasters did not always fully exercise the rights they have acquired. In order to provide an incentive for free-to-air broadcasters to not only buy rights, but also broadcast them, the must-broadcast obligation could be introduced. As a result, the right to information would be better guaranteed. Given that the right to information is often considered to be an essential pillar for democracy and the development of citizens (*supra*), this restriction of the freedom of expression could be considered as a 'pressing social need.'

Proportionality

In addition, the European Court of Human Rights should evaluate the proportionality of the restriction. In doing so, the European Court of Human Rights will examine whether a restriction is "*proportionate to the legitimate aim pursued.*"[399] As a result, any interference disproportionate to the legitimate aim pursued will not be deemed necessary in a democratic society.[400]

As regards the question whether this must-broadcast obligation achieves this legitimate aim, it must be noted that this obligation does not establish the right for broadcasters to freely decide which programmes they want to broadcast, but limits this right to the extent that when they would buy the broadcasting rights of major sports events that they would be obliged to broadcast them.

Since the requirement 'proportionality' is an equivalent of the above described proportionality requirement, the above reasoning can be referred to (*supra*).

14.3.3.2 No Obligation to Purchase Rights

A. Introduction

Helberger raised the question whether 'the list of major events' mechanism should be interpreted that, when a Member State has drawn up a list, the free-to-air broadcasters are forced to buy such rights, at all costs.[401] According to Scheuer

[399] See e.g. ECHR, Handyside v. the United Kingdom, para 49; ECHR, Perna v. Italy, para 39.

[400] Council of Europe 2007, 9.

[401] Helberger 2003, 81.

and Schoenthal, the answer is firm and clear, the measures to be taken cannot aim at the acquisition of the broadcasting rights, but are aimed at regulating the exercise of those rights.[402] Additionally, in the UK, the Department for Culture, Media and Sport explicitly stated that "*the inclusion of an event in the list does not mean that it has to be shown on television. What the law seeks to do is ensure that the rights to these events must be made available to free-to-air broadcasters on fair and reasonable terms. Hence, sports rights holders are not obliged to offer the events and free-to-air broadcasters are not obliged to bid for coverage of them.*"[403] Given that free-to-air broadcasters are not obliged to buy the exclusive broadcasting rights of the listed events, this might result, as indicated by Helberger, in a situation in which, even though the listed events are important for society, they might not be bought and, thus, not be transmitted.[404] In Flanders, for example, no broadcasters (free-to-air broadcasters nor pay-television operators) were interested in buying the rights for the home matches played by the Belgian national football team in the qualifying rounds for the FIFA World Cup 2010.[405] Consequently, the Flemish citizens were not able to follow these matches on the Belgian television, even though the matches involving the Belgian men's football team are included in the Flemish list.[406, 407]

B. Must-Buy Obligation

In order to deal with this problem, a must-buy obligation for the public broadcaster could be introduced in the regulatory framework. Just as the must-broadcast obligation, this must-buy obligation would be in conflict with both the freedom of services and the freedom of programming. But in contrast to the must-broadcast obligation, the must-buy obligation would probably not pass the proportionality test.

402 Scheuer and Schoenthal 2008, 419.

403 DCMS, http://www.culture.gov.uk/PDF/sport_on_television.pdf.

404 Helberger 2005, 106.

405 De Standaard 2009.

406 Football events involving national teams have a special general resonance in Belgium as they give Belgian teams the opportunity to promote Belgian football at international level (Commission decision of 25 June 2007).

407 Article 1, § 1 of the Order of the Flemish Government establishing the list of events of major importance to society.

a. Why Public Broadcasters?

According to a UNESCO definition, public broadcasters need to inform, educate and entertain citizens and need to serve as a cornerstone of democracy.[408] Hence, the mission of the public broadcaster is directly related to the democratic, social and cultural needs of each society.[409] Consequently, the programmes of the public broadcaster should contribute to the development of a democratic and tolerant society and the development of an active citizen.[410]

Furthermore, the coverage of sports events is recognised as being part of the public service broadcasters' remit. The Protocol on the system of public broadcasting in the Member States has recognised the Member States' competence to define the main parameters of their public broadcasting systems, namely their funding and remit.[411] Given that the European institutions have the obligation to respect its Member States' national identities,[412] Member States have a broad discretion with regard to defining the remit of their national public broadcasters.[413] In the UK, the mission of the BBC is *inter alia*: sustaining citizenship and civil society, representing the UK, its nations, regions and communities, bringing the UK to the world and the world to the UK.[414] In order to fulfil these missions, the Broadcasting Agreement further specifies that the BBC should have appropriate coverage of sport.[415] In addition, it is clarified that the BBC's coverage of sport in particular has a key role to bring together a wide range of people.[416] The same goes for the Netherlands where the Dutch authorities consider that broadcasts of popular and less popular sports fall within the definition of the main task of the public broadcasters.[417]

The European Commission, in different State aid decision, has agreed that the acquisition of sports broadcasting rights was part of the public broadcaster's

---

408 UNESCO, http://portal.unesco.org/ci/en/ev.php-URL_ID=1525&URL_DO=DO_TOPIC&URL_SECTION=201.html.

409 Protocol (No. 32) annexed to the EC Treaty on the system of public broadcasting in the Member States.

410 Ofcom 2008b, 23.

411 Protocol (No. 32) annexed to the EC Treaty on the system of public broadcasting in the Member States; Katsirea 2008, i.

412 Article 6 (3) of the EC Treaty.

413 Protocol (No. 32) annexed to the EC Treaty on the system of public broadcasting in the Member States; Ridinger 2009, 6.

414 Department for Culture, Media and Sport 2006a, Article 4.

415 Department for Culture, Media and Sport 2006b, Clauses 8 & 10.

416 BBC Trust 2007, 1 & 7.

417 Commission decision, 22 June 2006, para 79.

remit.[418] In the *German public broadcaster* case (*supra*), the European Commission stressed that sport can be part of a broadly defined public service remit to offer a varied and balanced programme.[419] Moreover, the European Commission agreed that a more detailed interpretation of the notion 'information' could refer to programme categories such as news, political information, regional information, but also sport.[420] In the *Irish public broadcaster* case[421] and the *Dutch public broadcaster* case,[422] the European Commission has reaffirmed that sport can be part of the public service mission in order to provide a balanced and varied offer. Also a couple of years earlier, in 2003, the European Commission has found the broad task and obligations of the French public broadcasters, including the transmission of sports events, legitimate.[423]

Finally, the EBU specifically singles out sport as a vital genre in the continued relevance of public service broadcasters.[424] In a speech in 2000, the then president, Wessberg, stated that "*public broadcasters cannot fulfil their cultural mission—a mission related directly to the democratic, social and cultural needs of each society—if they cannot broadcast sports events that are important to their audiences. […] It is therefore essential for public service broadcasters to be able to acquire rights to broadcast sports competitions and to produce high-quality programmes from these events.*"[425]

Given that the listed sports events are attributed an important social function, the broadcast of those events could probably be grasped under the public broadcaster's remit.

Proportionality Test

The broadcasting rights of international sports events, such as the Summer Olympics, FIFA World Cup or European Football Championship, are always extremely popular and wanted. Free-to-air broadcasters will also compete for the broadcasting rights of smaller sports events when those events are very popular with the general public, such as cyclo-cross in Belgium. The problem, however, rises when events are listed of which athletes are performing below par. Due to bad performances, neither the broadcasters nor the public is interested in those events. As a result, the broadcasting rights of those sports events remain unsold.

---

418 For more detailed information, see e.g.: Rapid Press Releases 2005a, b, 2006, 2008a, b; European Commission, 27 February 2008; Commission decision, 22 June 2006.

419 *German public broadcaster state aid* case, para 242; Rapid Press Releases 2007b, 2.

420 *German public broadcaster state aid* case, para 335.

421 European Commission, 27 February 2008, para 87.

422 Commission decision, 22 June 2006, para 23.

423 Commission decision, 10 December 2003, para 72.

424 Rowe 2004, 388.

425 Wessberg 2000.

Given that, a situation where broadcasting rights of listed events are not sold is rather seldom, it could be argued that a must-buy obligation for public broadcasters could be seen as a proportionate obligation. However, this should be nuanced. The introduction of a must-buy obligation would put organisations selling sports broadcasting rights of listed events in a strong position. They know that, in the end, those rights will be sold. Hence, they can push the price of those rights to a very high and unlimited level.

Instead of introducing this obligation, it seems better that the different governments would try to keep their lists up-to-date. As long as the included events are of special general resonance for the citizens, the broadcasters will probably be willing to buy those rights.

References

Legislation and Policy Documents

UNESCO

UNESCO, What is public service broadcasting?. http://portal.unesco.org/ci/en/ev.php-URL_ID=1525&URL_DO=DO_TOPIC&URL_SECTION=201.html. Accessed 23 August 2010

European Union

Protocols

Protocol (No. 32) annexed to the EC Treaty on the system of public broadcasting in the Member States. OJ (1997) C 340/109

Communications

European Commission (1997) Communication of the European Commission, on the initiative of Commissioner Marcellino Oreja, on exclusive rights for TV broadcasting of major (sports) events. 5 Febr 1997, SEC(1997)0174/9

Commission of the European Communities (2003a) Communication from the Commission to the European Parliament, the Council, the Economic and Social Committee and the Committee of the Regions on the transition from analogue to digital broadcasting (from digital 'switchover' to analogue 'switch-off'). 17 Sept 2003, COM(2003) 541 final

Commission of the European Communities (2003b) Communication from the Commission to the European Parliament, the Council, the Economic and Social Committee and the Committee of the Regions, The future of European regulatory audiovisual policy. 15 Dec 2003, COM(2003) 784 final

Commission of the European Communities (2005) Communication from the Commission to the Council, the European Parliament, the European Economic and Social Committee and the Committee of the Regions on accelerating the transition from analogue to digital broadcasting. 24 May 2005, COM(2005) 204 final

Decisions

European Parliament decision on the common position adopted by the Council with a view to the adoption of a European Parliament and Council Directive amending Council Directive 89/552/EEC on the coordination of certain provisions laid down by law, regulation or administrative action in Member States concerning the pursuit of television broadcasting activities (C4-0380/96—95/0074(COD)) (Codecision procedure: second reading). *OJ* (1996) C 362/0056

Commission decision of 2 April 2003 declaring a concentration to be compatible with the common market and the EEA Agreement (Case No COMP/M. 2876. Newscorp/Telepiù). *OJ* (2004) L 110/73

Commission decision of 23 July 2003 relating to a proceeding pursuant to Article 81 of the EC Treaty and Article 53 of the EEA Agreement, COMP/C.2-37.398—Joint selling of the commercial rights of the UEFA Champions League. *OJ* (2003) L 291/25

Commission decision of 10 December 2003 on State aid implemented by France for France 2 and France 3 (notified under document number C(2003) 4497). *OJ* (2004) L 361/21

Commission decision of 22 June 2006 on the ad hoc financing of Dutch public service broadcasters, C 2/2004 (EX NN 170/2003). *OJ* (2008) L 49/1

European Commission decision of 24 April 2007, State aid E 3/2005 (ex- CP 2/2003, CP 232/2002, CP 43/2003, CP 243/2004 and CP 195/2004)—Financing of public service broadcasters in Germany, C (2007) 1761 final

Commission decision of 25 June 2007 on the compatibility with Community law of measures taken by Belgium pursuant to Article 3a(1) of Council Directive 89/552/EEC on the coordination of certain provisions laid down by law, regulation or administrative action in Member States concerning the pursuit of television broadcasting activities. *OJ* (2007) L 180/24

Commission decision of 16 October 2007 on the compatibility with Community law of measures taken by the United Kingdom pursuant to Article 3a(1) of Council Directive 89/552/EEC on the coordination of certain provisions laid down by law, regulation or administrative action in Member States concerning the pursuit of television broadcasting activities. *OJ* (2007) L 295/12

European Commission State aid E 4/2005 (ex NN 99/1999)—Ireland. State financing of Radio Teilifís Éireann (RTÉ) and Teilifís na Gaeilge (TG4), 27 Febr 2008, C(2008)723 final

Directives

European Parliament and Council Directive 2002/22/EC of 7 March 2002 on universal service and users' rights relating to electronic communications networks and services (Universal Service Directive). *OJ* (2002) L 108/51

European Parliament and Council Directive 2010/13/EU of 10 March 2010 on the coordination of certain provisions laid down by law, regulation or administrative action in Member States concerning the provision of audiovisual media services (Audiovisual Media Services Directive). *OJ* (2010) L 95/1

European Parliament and Council Directive of 10 March 2010 on the coordination of certain provisions laid down by law, regulation or administrative action in Member States concerning the provision of audiovisual media services (Audiovisual Media Services Directive). *OJ* (2010) L 95/1

Notifications

Commission of the European Communities (2000) Notification of 14 July 2000 pursuant to Article 4 of Council Regulation (EEC), No 4064/89 (Case No COMP/M.2050—Vivendi/ Canal+/Seagram), 13 Oct 2000

Reports

Commission of the European Communities (2003) Fourth Report from the Commission to the Council, the European Parliament, the European Economic and Social Committee and the Committee of the Regions on the application of Directive 89/552/EEC "Television without Frontiers". 6 January 2003, COM(2002) 778 final

Resolutions

Committee of the Regions (1997) Resolution of the Committee of the Regions on the 'Broadcasting rights of major sport events. OJ (1997) C 379/67

European Parliament (1996) Resolution on the broadcasting of sports events. OJ (1996) C 166/109

Commission Staff Working Documents

Commission of the European Communities (2007) Commission Staff working document—Media pluralism in the Member States of the European Union. 16 January 2007, SEC(2007) 32

White Papers

Commission of the European Communities (2007) White Paper on Sport. 11 July 2007, COM (2007) 391 final

Press Releases

Rapid Press Releases (2005a) State aid: Commission requests Germany, Ireland and The Netherlands to clarify role and financing of public service broadcasters, 3 March 2005, IP/05/ 250

Rapid Press Releases (2005b) State aid: Commission closes inquiries into French, Italian and Spanish public broadcasters following commitments to amend funding systems, 20 April 2005, IP/05/458

Rapid Press Releases (2006) State aid: Commission requests Belgium to clarify financing of public service broadcaster VRT, 20 July 2006, IP/06/1043

Rapid Press Releases (2007a) Media pluralism: Commission stresses need for transparency, freedom and diversity in Europe's media landscape, 16 January 2007, IP/07/52

Rapid Press Releases (2007b) State aid: Commission closes investigation regarding the financing regime for German public service broadcasters—frequently asked questions, 24 April 2007, MEMO/07/150

Rapid Press Releases (2008a) State aid: Commission requests Austria to clarify financing of public service broadcaster ORF, 31 January 2008, IP/08/130

Rapid Press Releases (2008b) State aid: Commission closes investigation into financing of Flemish public service broadcaster VRT, 27 Febr 2008
Rapid Press Releases (2008c) Telecoms Rules: Belgium receives final warning on broadcasting "must-carry" rules, 6 May 2008, IP/08/699
Rapid Press Releases (2009) Telecoms: Legal action against Germany, the Netherlands and Sweden closed while Belgian must-carry rules case goes to Court, 8 Oct 2009, IP/09/1491

Speeches

Reding R (2004) Sport and television: ready to face new challenges? SPEECH/04/448

Miscellaneous

DCMS (2005) Final report on Working Group 2: rights to information and short extracts, Liverpool audiovisual conference—between culture and commerce, Liverpool, 20–22 Sept 2005. http://ec.europa.eu/avpolicy/docs/reg/modernisation/liverpool_2005/uk-conference-report-en.pdf. Accessed 20 August 2010
European Commission (2002a) Market definition in the media sector: economic issues. http://ec.europa.eu/competition/publications/studies/european_economics.pdf. Accessed 21 August 2010
European Commission (2002b) Working Document—Subject: 'Must-carry' obligations under the 2003 regulatory framework for electronic communications networks and services. http://ec.europa.eu/information_society/policy/ecomm/doc/current/broadcasting/working_doc_must_carry.pdf. Accessed 23 August 2010
European Commission (2005) Issues Paper for the audiovisual conference in Liverpool—right to information and right to short reporting, July 2005. http://ec.europa.eu/avpolicy/docs/reg/modernisation/issue_papers/ispa_shortrep_en.pdf. Accessed 20 August 2010
European Parliament (2002) Public hearing 'sports and audiovisual rights'—background note—subject: sports and TV rights. http://www.europarl.europa.eu/meetdocs/committees/cult/20020417/465312en.pdf. Accessed 2 Sept 2010
Oreja Marcellino (1997) Communication de M. Oreja à la Commission—Droits exclusifs pour la télédiffusion des événements majeurs, notamment sportifs, 3 February 1997

Council of Europe

Conventions

Council of Europe (2009b) Revision of the European convention on transfrontier television, Draft Council of Europe Convention on Transfrontier Audiovisual Media Services, T-TT(2009)013FIN_en, 24 Sept 2009. http://www.coe.int/t/dghl/standardsetting/media/T-TT/T-TT_2009_13FIN_en%20Provisional%20agreemt%20on%20draft%20amendts%20to%20ECTT+preamble.pdf. Accessed 20 August 2010

Protocols

Council of Europe (2009c) Draft second protocol amending the European Convention on Transfrontier Television and its explanatory report, T-TT(2009)007FIN_en, 24 Sept 2009.

http://www.coe.int/t/dghl/standardsetting/media/T-TT/T-TT_2009_007FIN_en%20second%20protocol%20amendment.pdf. Accessed 20 August 2010

Reports

Council of Europe (2003) Report by Dr Andreas Grünwald1 on possible options for the review of the European Convention on Transfrontier Television, 24 April 2003, T-TT (2003) 2. http://www.coe.int/t/dghl/standardsetting/media/T-TT/T-TT(2003)002_en.pd. Accessed 21 August 2010

Council of Europe (2009a) Draft Explanatory Report to the revised European Convention on Transfrontier Television updated following the consultation on 25–27 Febr 2009. http://www.coe.int/t/dghl/standardsetting/media/T-TT/T-TT_2009_009_en%20Preliminary%20Draft%20Expl%20Rep%20ECTT.pdf. Accessed 20 August 2010

Miscellaneous

Council of Europe (2001) Main lines of the convention—European Convention on Transfrontier Television. http://www.humanrights.coe.int/Media/topics/broadcasting/transfrontier/convention_on_transfrontier_tv.htm. Accessed 20 August 2010

Council of Europe (2002) Guidelines for the implementation of Article 9a European Convention on Transfrontier Television, 4 Dec 2002, T-TT (2002) 018. http://www.coe.int/t/dghl/standardsetting/media/t-tt/T-TT(2002)018rev1_en.asp. Accessed 20 August 2010

Council of Europe (2011) Transfrontier television: the revision of the convention discontinued, 4 Febr 2011. http://www.coe.int/t/dghl/standardsetting/media/t-tt/default_EN.asp. Accessed 15 March 2011

Australia

Legislation

Australian Broadcasting Corporation Act 1983. http://www.austlii.edu.au/au/legis/cth/consol_act/abca1983361/. Accessed 21 August 2010

Special Broadcasting Service Act 1991. http://www.austlii.edu.au/au/legis/cth/consol_act/sbsa1991254/. Accessed 21 August 2010

Broadcasting Services Act 1992. http://www.austlii.edu.au/au/legis/cth/consol_act/bsa1992214/. Accessed 21 August 2010

Parliament of Australia (1998) Broadcasting Services Amendment Bill 1998. Bills Digest No. 6 1998-99

Parliament of Australia (1998) Regulation impact statement, attached to the Explanatory Memorandum of the Broadcasting Services Amendment Bill 1998. http://www.austlii.edu.au/au/legis/cth/bill_em/bsab1998304/memo1.html. Accessed 21 August 2010

Parliament of Australia (1999) Broadcasting Services Amendment Act (No. 1) 1999, No. 197, 1999. http://www.comlaw.gov.au/ComLaw/Legislation/Act1.nsf/0/9FAA18A746474E87CA25743200099306/$file/19799.pdf. Accessed 21 August 2010

Parliament of Australia (1999) Broadcasting Services Amendment Bill (No. 1) 1999. Bills Digest No. 58 1999-2000

Broadcasting Services (Designated Series of Events) Declaration No. 1 of 2000. http://www.comlaw.gov.au/comlaw/Legislation/LegislativeInstrument1.nsf/0/5940AD4E8F02BADECA256F7B00110FE1?OpenDocument. Accessed 21 August 2010

Parliament of Australia (2004) Broadcasting Services Amendment (Anti-Siphoning) Bill 2004. Bills Digest No. 73 2004-05

Communications (Redundant Regulation) Instrument of Revocation (No. 1) 2009. http://www.comlaw.gov.au/ComLaw/Legislation/LegislativeInstrument1.nsf/0/0BD892DD094D216ACA25768C007E7760?OpenDocument. Accessed 21 August 2010

Standing Committee on Environment, Communications, Information Technology and the Arts (2006) Broadcasting Legislation Amendment (Digital Television) Bill 2006. http://www.aph.gov.au/Senate/committee/ecita_ctte/completed_inquiries/2004-07/cross_media/report/report.pdf. Accessed 21 August 2010

Reports

Productivity Commission (2000) Broadcasting Inquiry Report—Report No. 11. http://www.pc.gov.au/__data/assets/pdf_file/0003/26598/broadcst.pdf. Accessed 20 August 2010

Australian Broadcasting Authority (2001) Investigation into events on the anti-siphoning list—Report to the Minister for Communications, Information Technology and the Arts. http://fulltext.ausport.gov.au/fulltext/2001/aba/anti_siphRpt.pdf. Accessed 21 August 2010

ACMA (2006) Anti-siphoning Monitoring Investigation. Interim Report No. 1. http://www.acma.gov.au/webwr/_assets/main/lib101062/acma_anitsiphoning_interim_report_1_2006.pdf. Accessed 21 August 2010

ACMA (2007) Anti-siphoning Monitoring Investigation. Report No. 5. http://www.acma.gov.au/antisiphoningreport/5/start.htm. Accessed 21 August 2010

Investigations

Australian Broadcasting Authority (2000) Investigation into the implementation of the anti-hoarding rules—Issues paper. http://www.acma.gov.au/webwr/aba/newspubs/radio_tv/investigations/documents/general/ahi_ip.pdf. Accessed 21 August 2010

Miscellaneous

Australian Government (2006) Meeting the digital challenge—reforming Australia's media in the digital age—discussion paper on media reform options. http://www.archive.dcita.gov.au/__data/assets/pdf_file/0006/37572/Media_consultation_paper_Final_.pdf. Accessed 21 August 2010

Department of Broadband, Communications and the Digital Economy (2009) Sport on television: a review of the anti-siphoning scheme in the contemporary digital environment—discussion paper. http://www.dbcde.gov.au/__data/assets/pdf_file/0010/118864/Sport_on_Television_Review_discussion_paper.pdf. Accessed 19 August 2010

Department of Broadband, Communications and the Digital Economy (2010) Future anti-siphoning list, 25 Novemb 2010. http://afr.com/rw/2009-2014/AFR/2010/11/25/Photos/3808ab0a-f88f-11df-a2c9-b1a91965d87a_anti-siphoning.pdf. Accessed 29 November 2010

Independent Advisory Panel to the Secretary of State for Culture, Media and Sport (2009) Review of free-to-air listed events. http://www.culture.gov.uk/images/publications/independentpanelreport-to-SoS-Free-to-air-Nov2009.pdf. Accessed 19 November 2009 [no longer available]

Minister for Broadband, Communications and the Digital Economy (2010a) SBS to broadcast all 2010 FIFA World Cup Games live. 16 May 2010. http://www.minister.dbcde.gov.au/media/media_releases/2010/048. Accessed 21 August 2010

Minister for Broadband, Communications and the Digital Economy (2010b) Anti-siphoning scheme—frequently asked questions, 25 Novemb 2010. http://www.dbcde.gov.au/__data/

assets/pdf_file/0019/131464/101123_Anti-siphoning_Reforms_-_FAQs.pdf. Accessed 29 Novemb 2010
Minister for Broadband, Communications and the Digital Economy (2010c) Anti-siphoning scheme—fact sheet, 25 Novemb 2010. http://resources.news.com.au/files/2010/11/25/1225961/029472-anti-siphoning-factsheet.pdf. Accessed 29 Novemb 2010
Minister for Communications, Information Technology and the Arts (2006) 'Use it or lose it' guidelines released for anti-siphoning sport. http://www.minister.dbcde.gov.au/coonan/media/media_releases/use_it_or_lose_it_guidelines_released_for_anti-siphoning_sport. Accessed 21 August 2010

Austria

Legislation

Federal Act on the exercise of exclusive television broadcasting rights 2001 [Fernseh-Exclusivrechtegesetz], Austrian Federal Law Gazette I No 85/2001
Ordinance on events of substantial social interest [Verordnung der Bundesregierung über Ereignisse von erheblicher gesellschaftlicher Bedeutung], Austrian Federal Law Gazette II No 305/2001

Belgium

Legislation

Order of the Flemish Government of 28 May 2004 establishing the list of events of major importance to society [Besluit houdende vaststelling van de lijst van evenementen van aanzienlijk belang voor de samenleving], Belgian State Gazette, 19 August 2004
Order of 8 June 2004 designating events of major importance and determining the procedures for making them accessible, Belgian State Gazette 6 Sept 2004 [Arrêté désignant les événements d'intérêt majeur et fixant les modalités de leur accès]
Vlaams Parlement (2008) Explanatory Memorandum [Memorie van Toelichting—Ontwerp van Decreet betreffende de radio-omroep en televisie], 19 Dec 2008, 2014/1. http://docs.vlaamsparlement.be/docs/stukken/2008-2009/g2014-1.pdf. Accessed 21 August 2010
French Community Media Decree of 27 February 2003, Belgian State Gazette 17 April 2003 [Décret sur la radiodiffusion], last amended and renamed by the French Community Decree of 5 Febr 2009 into "French Community Audiovisual Media Services Act"; coordinated by the Decree of 26 March 2009, Belgian State Gazette 27 July 2009
Flemish Community Media Decree of 27 March 2009 [Decreet betreffende radio—omroep en televisie], Belgian State Gazette, 30 April 2009, modified by the Decree of 24 July 2009, Belgian State Gazette, 16 Sept 2009
Vlaamse Regering (2011a) Explanatory Memorandum of a draft proposal amending Flemish Media Decree of 27 March 2009 [Memorie van Toelichting—Voorontwerp van decreet houdende wijziging van diverse bepalingen van het decreet van 27 maart 2009 betreffende radio-omroep en televisie]
Vlaamse Regering (2011b). Draft proposal amending Flemish Media Decree of 27 March 2009 [Voorontwerp van decreet houdende wijziging van diverse bepalingen van het decreet van 27 maart 2009 betreffende radio-omroep en televisie]

Miscallanious

Commissie voor Cultuur, Jeugd, Sport en Media (2010) Parliamentary proceedings [Handelingen], 18 May 2010. http://docs.vlaamsparlement.be/docs/handelingen_commissies/2009-2010/c0m227cul31-18052010.pdf. Accessed 21 August 2010

Studiedienst van de Vlaamse Regering (2009) Vrind 2009. Vlaamse Regionale Indicatoren. Vlaamse Overheid: Brussel. http://www4.vlaanderen.be/dar/svr/afbeeldingennieuwtjes/algemeen/bijlagen/vrind2009/2009-07-01-vrind2009-volledig-blw.pdf. Accessed 21 August 2010

Denmark

Legislation

Order No 138 of 19 February 1998 [Bekendtgørelse om udnyttelse af tv-rettigheder til begivenheder af væsentlig samfundsmæssig interesse]. *OJ* (1999) C 14/6

Revocation of the Danish Order on the use of TV rights to events of major importance to society. *OJ* (2002) C 45/7

France

Legislation

Decree No 2004-1392 of 22 December 2004 applying Article 20-2 of Law No 86-1067 of 30 September 1986 on the freedom of communication [Décret no 2004-1392 du 22 décembre 2004 pris pour l'application de l'article 20-2 de la loi no 86-1067 du 30 septembre 1986 relative à la liberté de communication], French Official Gazette, 24 Dec 2004

Germany

Legislation

Interstate Treaty on Broadcasting of 31 August 1991, last amended by the Twelfth Interstate Treaty for Amending the Interstate Treaties of 18 December 2008 [Rundfunkstaatsvertrag], German Federal Law Gazette, 27 March 2008

Ireland

Legislation

Broadcasting (major events television coverage) Act. Statute Book S.I. 28/1999

Broadcasting (Major Events Television Coverage) Act 1999 (Designation of Major Events) Order 2003, Irish Statute Book S.I. 99/2003

Irish Parliament (1999) Parliamentary Debates—Major Events Television Coverage Bill, 1999: Second Stage (Resumed). http://historical-debates.oireachtas.ie/D/0505/D.0505.199906020005.html. Accessed 21 August 2010

Italy

Legislation

Decision No 8/1999 of 9 March 1999 [Delibera n. 8/99 modificata dalla delibera n. 172/1999], Official Gazette No 119 of 24 May 1999, as amended by Decision No 172/1999 of 28 July 1999, Italian Official Gazette No 192 of 17 August 1999

Poland

Legislation

Broadcasting Act of 29 December 1992 [Ustawa o Radiofonii i Telewizji]. Pol Off J 1993, No 7, item 34, 1993, as amended

The Netherlands

Legislation

Media Act of 29 December 2008 [Wet van 29 december 2008 tot vaststelling van een nieuwe Mediawet], State Gazette of the Kingdom of the Netherlands 2008/583
Media Decree of 29 December 2008 [Besluit van 29 december 2008 houdende vaststelling van een nieuw Mediabesluit], State Gazette of the Kingdom of the Netherlands 2008-585

UK

Legislation

Broadcasting Act 1996. http://www.opsi.gov.uk/RevisedStatutes/Acts/ukpga/1996/cukpga_19960055_en_11. Accessed 21 August 2010
Department for Culture, Media and Sport (2006a) Copy of Royal Charter for the continuance of the British Broadcasting Corporation. http://www.bbc.co.uk/bbctrust/assets/files/pdf/regulatory_framework/charter_agreement/bbc_royal_charter.pdf. Accessed 23 August 2010
Department for Culture, Media and Sport (2006b) An agreement between Her Majesty's Secretary of State for Culture, Media and Sport and the British Broadcasting Corporation. http://www.bbc.co.uk/bbctrust/assets/files/pdf/regulatory_framework/charter_agreement/bbcagreement_july06.pdf. Accessed 23 August 2010

Consultations

Ofcom (2007a) Pay TV market investigation—consultation document. http://stakeholders.ofcom.org.uk/binaries/consultations/market_invest_paytv/summary/pay_tv.pdf. Accessed 21 August 2010
Ofcom (2007b) Summary of UK sports rights—Annex 10 to pay TV market investigation consultation. http://www.ofcom.org.uk/consult/condocs/market_invest_paytv/annex_10.pdf. Accessed 18 August 2010
Ofcom (2008) Code on sports and other listed and designated events, 2 Sept 2008, http://www.ofcom.org.uk/tv/ifi/codes/code_sprt_lstd_evts/ofcom_code_on_sport.pdf. Accessed 20 August 2010
Ofcom (2008b) Ofcom review of Public Service Television Broadcasting (summary of phase 1 consultation responses). http://www.ofcom.org.uk/consult/condocs/psb/psb_resp_summary.pdf. Accessed 23 August 2010
Ofcom (2009) Pay TV phase three document: proposed remedies. http://stakeholders.ofcom.org.uk/binaries/consultations/third_paytv/summary/paytv_condoc.pdf. Accessed 18 August 2010
Department for Culture, Media and Sport (2009) Free to air—consultation introduction. http://www.culture.gov.uk/freetoair/consultation/introduction.html. Accessed 20 August 2010

Reports

House of Commons—Culture, Media and Sport Committee (2006) Broadcasting rights for cricket. Ashes to Ashes—the death knell for live Test match cricket on free-to-air TV? http://www.publications.parliament.uk/pa/cm200506/cmselect/cmcumeds/720/720.pdf. Accessed 21 August 2010
Independent Advisory Panel to the Secretary of State for Culture, Media and Sport (2009) Review of free-to-air listed events. http://www.culture.gov.uk/images/publications/independentpanel report-to-SoS-Free-to-air-Nov2009.pdf. Accessed 19 Novemb 2009 (no longer available)

Miscellaneous

DCMS, coverage of sport on television. http://www.culture.gov.uk/PDF/sport_on_television.pdf. Accessed 20 August 2010
Ministry for Culture, Media and Sports (1997) Communication—notes for guidance on the listing of major sports events, included in Commission Decision of 16 October 2007 on the compatibility with Community law of measures taken by the United Kingdom pursuant to Article 3a(1) of Council Directive 89/552/EEC on the coordination of certain provisions laid down by law, regulation or administrative action in Member States concerning the pursuit of television broadcasting activities. OJ (2007) L 295/12

Others

IOC (2007) Olympic charter. http://www.olympic.org/Documents/olympic_charter_en.pdf. Accessed 21 August 2010

Case law

Court of Justice

CJ, Procureur du Roi v Marc J.V.C. Debauve, 18 March 1980, Case 52/79, ECR (1980) I-833

CJ, Elliniki Radiophonia Tiléorassi AE and Panellinia Omospondia Syllogon Prossopikou v Dimotiki Etairia Pliroforissis and Sotirios Kouvelas and Nicolaos Avdellas and others, 18 June 1991, Case C-260/89, ECR (1991) I-2925

CJ, Commission v Kingdom of the Netherlands, 25 July 1991, Case C-353/89, ECR (1991) I-4069

CJ, Stichting Collectieve Antennevoorziening Gouda et al.v Commissariaat voor de Media, 25 July 1991, C-288/89, ECR (1991) I-4007

CJ, Arbeitsgemeinschaft Deutscher Rundfunkanstalten (ARD) v PRO Sieben Media AG, 28 October 1999, Case C-6/98, ECR (1999) I-7599

CJ, François De Coster v Collège des bourgmestre et échevins de Watermael-Boitsfort, 29 Novemb 2001, case C–17/00, ECR (2001) I-9445

CJ, United Pan-Europe Communications Belgium SA, Coditel Brabant SPRL, Société Intercommunale pour la Diffusion de la Télévision (Brutélé), Wolu TV ASBL v État belge, 13 Dec 2007, Case C-250/06, ECR (2007) I-11135

CJ, Commission of the European Communities v Infront WM AG, 13 March 2008, Case C-125/06, ECR I-1457

General Court

GC, Infront WM AG v Commission of the European Communities, 15 Dec 2005, Case T-33/01, ECR II-5897

GC, FIFA v European Commission, Case T-385/07, 17 Febr 2011 (not yet published in the ECR)

GC, FIFA v European Commission, Case T-68/08, 17 Febr 2011 (not yet published in the ECR)

GC, UEFA v European Commission, Case T-55/08, 17 Febr 2011 (not yet published in the ECR)

European Court of Human Rights

ECHR, Handyside v. the United Kingdom, 7 Dec 1976, Application no. 5493/72

ECHR, Sunday Times v. the United Kingdom, 26 April 1979, Application no. 6538/74

ECHR, Groppera Radio AG and others v. Switzerland, 28 March 1990, Application no. 10890/84

ECHR, Autronic AG v. Switzerland, 22 May 1990, Application no. 12726/87

ECHR, Bladet Tromsø and Stensaas v. Norway, 20 May 1999

ECHR, Perna v. Italy, 6 May 2003, Application no. 48898/99

Belgium

Flemish Media Regulator (2011) Willy Herpol vs. BVBA Coditel/Numericable, Decision 2011/007, 21 March 2011

UK

R. v. Independent Television Commission, ex parte TV Danmark 1 [2001] 1 WLR 74
House of Lords. R v. ITC, Ex Parte TV Danmark 1 Ltd, judgment of 25 July 2001, [2001] UKHL 42

US

Home Box Office, Inc v. FCC 567 F.2d 9, (D.C. Cir 1977)

Miscellaneous

FIFA v. Commission, 4 Oct 2007, Case T-385/07. OJ (2007) C 315/41
UEFA v. Commission, 5 Febr 2008, Case T-55/08. OJ (2008) C 107/28
European Commission (2010) Hearing before the General Court on 24 Febr 2010
GC (2010a) Reports for the hearing UEFA v. European Commission, Case T-55/08
GC (2010b). Reports for the hearing FIFA v. European Commission, Case T-385/07
C-201/11 P pending case, UEFA vs. European Commission, 27 April 2011
C-204/11 P pending case, FIFA vs. European Commission, 28 April 2011
C-205/11 P pending case, FIFA vs. European Commission, 28 April 2011

Doctrine

ASTRA (2009) Submission to the sport on television review. http://www.dbcde.gov.au/__data/assets/pdf_file/0010/121330/Australian_Subscription_Television_-and-_Radio_Association_main_submission.pdf. Accessed 21 August 2010
Barnet S (2009) Free-to-air events, Westminster Media Forum keynote seminar: the future for broadcast sports and free-to-air events, London, 27 Oct 2009
Baron F (2009) Free-to-air events, Westminster Media Forum keynote seminar: the future for broadcast sports and free-to-air events, London, 27 Oct 2009
Basketball Australia (2009) Submission to the sport on television review. http://www.dbcde.gov.au/__data/assets/pdf_file/0010/121231/Basketball_Australia_main_submission.pdf. Accessed 19 August 2010
BBC News (2008a) Uefa eyes change to free TV football. 6 June 2008. http://news.bbc.co.uk/2/hi/business/7438763.stm. Accessed 21 August 2010
BBC News (2008b) Free-to-air TV sport reconsidered, 26 Sept 2008. http://news.bbc.co.uk/2/hi/uk_news/7637518.stm. Accessed 21 August 2010
BBC Trust (2007) BBC public purpose remit: representing the UK, its nations, regions and communities. http://www.bbc.co.uk/bbctrust/assets/files/pdf/regulatory_framework/purpose_remits/nations.pdf. Accessed 23 August 2010
Boardman A, Hargreaves-Heap S (1999) Network externalities and government restrictions on satellite broadcasting of key sporting events. J Cult Econ 23:167–181
Böttcher K, Castendyk O (2008) Article 49 EC. In: Castendyk O et al (eds) European media law. Kluwer Law International, Alphen a/d Rijn, pp 85–122
Boyle R (2010) Citizen sport? Television, sport and national events in the U.K., IAMCR Conference, Braga, 19 July 2010

Broadcastnow (2008) Government to review sports 'crown jewels', 26 Sept 2008. http://www.broadcastnow.co.uk/news/multi-platform/news/government-to-review-sports-crown-jewels/1875021.article. Accessed 20 August 2010

Castendyk O (2008) Article 4 TWFD. In: Castendyk O et al (eds) European media law. Kluwer Law International, Alphen a/d Rijn, pp 429–455

Castille V (1997) De nieuwe Televisierichtlijn zonder Grenzen van 1997. A&M 1:5–15

Communications Law Centre (2009) Submission to the sport on television review. http://www.dbcde.gov.au/__data/assets/pdf_file/0011/121232/Communications_Law_Centre_main_submission.pdf. Accessed 21 August 2010

Conn D (2009) Competition in sports broadcasting, Westminster Media Forum keynote seminar: the future for broadcast sports and free-to-air events, London, 27 Oct 2009

Council of Europe (2007) Freedom of expression in Europe: case law concerning Article 10 of the European Convention on Human Rights. Council of Europe, Strasbourg

Craufurd Smith R, Bottcher B (2002) Football and fundamental rights: regulating access to major sporting events on television. Eur Public Law 8(1):107–133

Cricket Australia (2009) Submission to the sport on television review. http://www.dbcde.gov.au/__data/assets/pdf_file/0012/121233/Cricket_Australia_main_submission.pdf. Accessed 19 August 2010

De Marez L, Schuurman D (2010) Digimeter Rapport 2. http://drop.io/digimeter. Accessed 23 Sept 2010

De Morgen (2011) YouTube wil Europees voetbal live uitzenden, 25 Febr 2011. http://www.demorgen.be/dm/nl/5403/Internet/article/detail/1227842/2011/02/25/YouTube-wil-Europees-voetbal-live-uitzenden.dhtml. Accessed 4 April 2011

De Morgen (2011) Decaluwé wil play-offs voetbal kelderen via evenementenlijst, 15 March 2011. http://www.demorgen.be/dm/nl/5036/Wetstraat/article/detail/1236309/2011/03/15/Decaluwe-wil-play-offs-voetbal-kelderen-via-evenementenlijst.dhtml. Accessed 15 March 2011

De Standaard (2008) Belgacom TV introduceert reclame rond voetbal, 28 June 2008. http://www.standaard.be/Artikel/Detail.aspx?artikelId=QJ1TM38J&kanaalid=21. Accessed 28 June 2008 (no longer available)

De Standaard (2009) We willen ons normaal zendschema niet doorbreken, 9 Sept 2009. http://www.standaard.be/Artikel/Detail.aspx?artikelId=TR2EUPNM. Accessed 9 Sept 2009 (no longer available)

De Tijd (2009) Helft Vlaamse gezinnen kijkt digitale televisie, 4 August 2009, 7

Dommering E (2008) Article 10 ECHR. In: Castendyk O et al (eds) European media law. Kluwer Law International, Alphen a/d Rijn, pp 35–81

Donders K, Evens T (2010) Broadcasting and its distribution in Flanders, Denmark and the United States: an explorative and future-oriented analysis—a research report for SBS Belgium (not published)

EICTA (2008a) HD television? http://www.eicta.org/fileadmin/user_upload/document/EICTA_-_HD_factsheet_television.pdf. Accessed 21 August 2010

EICTA (2008b) The digital switchover & high definition TV. http://www.eicta.org/fileadmin/user_upload/document/EICTA_-_HD_factsheet_switchover.pdf. Accessed 18 August 2010

FACTS (2001) Australian broadcasting authority's inquiry into the anti-siphoning list submission from the Federation of Australian Commercial Television Stations. http://www.freetv.com.au/SiteMedia/w3svc087/Uploads/Documents/65db9424-80da-4a9b-b8e3-ba18b908ef12.pdf. Accessed 19 August 2010

Fleming H (1997) Television without frontiers: the broadcasting of sporting events in Europe. Entertain Law Rev 8(8):281–285

Fraser D, McMahon K (2002) When too much sport is barely enough: broadcasting regulation and national identity. Entertain Law 1(3):1–52

Free TV Australia (2009) Submission to the sport on television review. http://www.dbcde.gov.au/__data/assets/pdf_file/0015/121236/Free_TV_Australia_main_submission.pdf. Accessed 21 August 2010

Frontier Economics (2009) The impact of listed events on the viewing and funding of sports—a report prepared for the chair and review panel. http://www.culture.gov.uk/images/publications/FE-DCMS-Impactoflistedevents.pdf. Accessed 21 August 2010
Geey D, Ward J (2008) UEFA and FIFA challenge EU approved listed TV events. World Sports Law Rep 8:3–5
Gratton C, Solberg HA (2007) The economics of sports broadcasting. Routledge, London
Harrison J, Woods L (2007) European broadcasting law and policy. Cambridge University Press, Cambridge
Healy D (2009) Country reports: Australia. In: Blackshaw I et al (eds) TV rights and sport. legal aspects. T.M.C. Asser press, The Hague, pp 215–234
Helberger N (2003) Brood en spelen. De implementatie van de evenementenlijst van artikel 3a van de Televisierichtlijn. Mediaforum 3:78–84
Helberger N (2005) Controlling access to content—regulating conditional access in digital broadcasting. Kluwer Law International, The Hague
Hitchens L (2006) Broadcasting pluralism and diversity: a comparative study of policy and regulation. Hart Publishing, Oxford
ICRI et al (2009a) Independent study on indicators for media pluralism in the member states—towards a risk-based approach. final report—annex III: country reports—The Netherlands. http://ec.europa.eu/information_society/media_taskforce/doc/pluralism/study/netherlands.pdf. Accessed 21 August 2010
ICRI et al (2009b) Independent study on indicators for media pluralism in the member states—towards a risk-based approach. final report—annex III: country reports—Poland. http://ec.europa.eu/information_society/media_taskforce/doc/pluralism/study/poland.pdf. Accessed 21 August 2010
IOC (2008) Invitation to tender for European Broadcast Rights (not published)
IOC (2009) IOC Agrees European Broadcast Rights Contract for 2014 and 2016 Olympic Games, 18 Febr 2009. http://sochi2014.com/en/sochi-live/press-center/36723/. Accessed 21 August 2010
Jeanrenaud C, Kesenne S (2006) Sport and the media: an overview. In: Jeanrenaud C, Kesenne S (eds) The economics of sports and the media. Edward Elgar, Cheltenham, pp 1–25
Katsirea I (2008) Public Broadcasting and European Law: a comparative examination of Public Service Obligations in Six Member States. Kluwer Law International, Alphen a/d Rijn
Kesenne S (2011) Private television and sports broadcasting. Private television conference, Brussels, 28 April 2011
Klabbers J (2009) Treaty conflict and the European Union. Cambridge University Press, Cambridge
Lefever K, Evens T (2009a) All sports for free! A difficult match? Right to information in the digital broadcasting era. Int Sports Law J 3–4:29–33
Lefever K et al (2009) De Koningin Elisabethwedstrijd voor iedereen! Of toch niet? De evenementenlijst in het digitale televisielandschap. A&M 5:513–520
Lefever K, Evens T (2009) Sports content on the move. Regulating access to sports events on mobile platforms, EuroCPR 2009, Sevilla, 30 March 2009
Lefever K, Van Rompuy B (2009) Ensuring access to sports content: 10 years of EU intervention. Time to celebrate? J Media Law 2:243–268
Lefever K et al (2010) Watching live sport on television: a human right? The right to information and the list of major events regime. Eur Hum Rights Law Rev 4:396–407
Lefever K, Werkers E (2010) Digital sports content: the rise of new media players and the legal consequences in terms of obligations and liability risks. Entertain Law Rev 6:214–219
Marauhn T (2007) Freedom of expression, freedom of assembly and association. In: Ehlers D (ed) European fundamental rights and freedoms. De Gruyter Recht, Berlin, pp 97–129
MediaNetwork (2008) IOC rejects EBU's bid for rights to Olympic Games 2014 & 2016, 2 Dec 2008. http://blogs.rnw.nl/medianetwork/ioc-rejects-ebus-bid-for-rights-to-olympic-games-2014-2016. Accessed 21 August 2010

Nicholas B (2009) Digital sports rights, Westminster Media Forum keynote seminar: the future for broadcast sports and free-to-air events, London, 27 Oct 2009

Ogston A (2009) Competition in sports broadcasting, Westminster Media Forum keynote seminar: the future for broadcast sports and free-to-air events, London, 27 October 2009

Parrish R, Miettinen S (2009) Sports broadcasting in community law. In: Blackshaw I et al (eds) TV rights and sport. Legal aspects. T.M.C Asser Press, The Hague, pp 9–33

Perrine J (2001) Constitutional law challenges to anti-siphoning laws in the United States and Australia. Sports Adm 3:21–31

Ridinger M (2009) The public service remit and the new media. Iris Plus. http://www.obs.coe.int/oea_publ/iris/iris_plus/iplus6_2009.pdf.en. Accessed 23 August 2010

Rowe D (2004) Fulfilling the 'cultural mission': popular genre and public remit. Eur J Cult Stud 7:381–400

Rowe D (2009) Submission to the sport on television review. http://www.dbcde.gov.au/__data/assets/word_doc/0012/121224/Professor_David_Rowe_main_submission.doc. Accessed 21 August 2010

Scheuer A, Schoenthal M (2008) Article 3a TWFD. In: Castendyk O et al (eds) European media law. Kluwer Law International, Alphen a/d Rijn, pp 407–428

Schoental M (2006) Major events and reporting rights. IRIS Plus 4:1–8

Sportbusiness International (2008a) Australia considers changes to anti-siphoning law, 7 Febr 2008. http://www.sportbusiness.com/news/164149/australia-considers-changes-to-anti-siphoning-law. Accessed 21 August 2010

Sportbusiness International (2008b) UEFA challenge on sporting crown jewels, 19 June 2008. http://www.sportbusiness.com/britsport/167021/uefa-challenge-on-sporting-crown-jewels. Accessed 20 August 2010

Sportbusiness International (2008c) IOC launches new channel, 5 August 2008. http://www.sportbusiness.com/news/167608/ioc-launches-new-channel. Accessed 4 April 2011

Sportbusiness International (2010) UK free-to-air decision postponed to 2013, 22 July 2010. http://www.sportbusiness.com/news/179432/uk-free-to-air-decision-postponed-to-2013. Accessed 20 August 2010

Sportbusiness International (2011a) Pay-TV shift for F1 would be "suicidal", claims Ecclestone, 10 May 2011. http://www.sportbusiness.com/news/183591/pay-tv-shift-for-f1-would-be-suicidal-claims-ecclestone. Accessed 10 March 2011

Sportbusiness International (2011b) Sky Sports and BBC to share F1 rights, 29 July 2011. http://www.sportbusiness.com/news/184058/sky-sports-and-bbc-to-share-f1-rights. Accessed 1 August 2011

Sportcal.com (2010) Law will confirm Spanish league's right to choose free-TV match, 4 January 2010. http://sportcal.com/news/news_article.aspx?articleid=71202. Accessed 20 January 2010

Sports City (2008) IOC rejects collective European TV rights bid, 3 Dec 2008. http://www.sports-city.org/news_details.php?news_id=6464&idCategory=24. Accessed 21 August 2010

Sports-city (2010) Crown jewels' ruling deferred, 22 July 2010. http://www.sports-city.org/news_details.php?news_id=12456&idCategory=1. Accessed 20 August 2010

Telegraph (2008) Government to review sports 'crown jewels', 26 Sept 2008. http://www.telegraph.co.uk/sport/3085557/Government-to-review-crown-jewel-sporting-events.html. Accessed 20 August 2010

Telegraph (2008) BBC Olympic coverage under threat as IOC rejects bid by Europe's free-to-air stations, 3 Dec 2008. http://www.telegraph.co.uk/sport/othersports/olympics/3544110/BBC-Olympic-coverage-under-threat-as-IOC-rejects-bid-by-Europes-free-to-air-stations-Olympics.html. Accessed 21 August 2010

Tennis Australia (2009) Submission to the sport on television review. http://www.dbcde.gov.au/__data/assets/pdf_file/0014/121325/Tennis_Australia_main_submission.pdf. Accessed 21 August 2010

The Australian (2008) Anti-siphoning review may hand sport to free channels, 4 Sept 2008. http://www.theaustralian.news.com.au/story/0,25197,24290125-7582,00.html. Accessed 21 August 2010

The Guardian (2008a) Croatia v England talks end in stalemate, 9 Sept 2008. http://www.guardian.co.uk/football/2008/sep/09/englandfootballteam.worldcup2010qualifiers2. Accessed 21 August 2010

The Guardian (2008b) BBC facing battle to keep rights to Olympic Games after IOC snub, 2 Dec 2008. http://www.guardian.co.uk/media/2008/dec/02/bbc-sportsrights. Accessed 21 August 2010

The Guardian (2008c) David Davies to lead review of 'crown jewels' sports events on free TV, 10 Dec 2008. http://www.guardian.co.uk/media/2008/dec/10/crown-jewels-sports-tv. Accessed 20 August 2010

The Guardian (2009) Sky's limits leave cricket's fans in the dark and grass roots cut short, 15 July 2009. http://www.guardian.co.uk/sport/blog/2009/jul/15/test-cricket-broadcast-rights-sky/print. Accessed 21 August 2010

The Guardian (2010a) Live Indian Premier League cricket 'to be shown on YouTube', 19 January 2010. http://www.guardian.co.uk/technology/pda/2010/jan/19/ipl-youtube-live-cricket?intcmp=239. Accessed 4 April 2011

The Guardian (2010b) YouTube confirms worldwide deal for live Indian Premier League cricket, 20 January 2010. http://www.guardian.co.uk/media/2010/jan/20/youtube-live-indian-premier-league. Accessed 4 April 2011

The Guardian (2011) YouTube bids to become home of live sport online, 23 Febr 2011. http://www.guardian.co.uk/media/2011/feb/23/youtube-sports-nba-nhl. Accessed 4 April 2011

The New York Times (1996) Murdoch loses bid on Europe's TV rights, 31 January 1996. http://www.nytimes.com/1996/01/31/sports/olympics-murdoch-loses-bid-on-europe-s-tv-rights.html. Accessed 20 January 2012

The Wall Street Journal (2011) YouTube Recasts for New Viewers, 7 April 2011. http://online.wsj.com/article/SB10001424052748704013604576247060940913104.html?mod=WSJEUROPE_hpp_LEFTTopWhatNews. Accessed 8 April 2011

Tichy L (2004) Fundamental rights and fundamental freedoms: short remarks. In: Pernice I, Zemánek J (eds) A constitution for Europe: the IGC, the Ratification process and beyond. Baden-Baden, Nomos. http://www.ecln.net/elements/conferences/book_prag/TichyFinal.pdf. Accessed 24 August 2010

Valcke P (2004) Digitale Diversiteit. Convergentie van Media-, Telecommunicatie- en Mededingingsrecht. Larcier, Brussels

Valcke P et al (2010) The EU regulatory framework applicable to broadcasting. In: Garzaniti L, O'Regan M (eds) Telecommunications, broadcasting and the internet. EU Competition Law & Regulation, 3rd edn. Thomson Sweet & Maxwell, London, pp 263–330

Voetbalbelgië (2009) Toch live uitzending van Armenië-België, 9 Sept 2009. http://www.voetbalbelgie.be/nl/article.php?id=24700. Accessed 9 Febr 2012

Voorhoof D (1995) The media in a democratic society. Article 10 of the European Convention on Human Rights. In: Council of Europe (European Media Law Forum) (ed) Legal problems of the functioning of media in a democratic society. Llubljana, Slovenia, pp 39–74

VRT (2009) Koningin Elisabethwedstrijd—kijkcijfers (not published)

Weatherill S (2007) European Sports Law—collected papers. TMC Asser Press, The Hague

Wessberg A (2000) Sport, television and the Internet. http://www.ebu.ch/news/press_archive/2003_and_prev/press_news_1100a.html. Accessed 23 August 2010

Wise A, Meyer B (1997) International Sports Law and Business, vol 3. Kluwer Law International, The Hague

X (2009) Sports broadcasting in the digital era. Commun Law Bulletin 27(4):15–20

YouTube (2011) YouTube community guidelines. http://www.youtube.com/t/community_guidelines. Accessed 4 May 2011

Zeffman D (2009) Free-to-air events, Westminster Media Forum keynote seminar: the future for broadcast sports and free-to-air events, London, 27 Oct 2009

Chapter 15
Conclusion Part III

Over the years, free-to-air television has lost its status as primary vehicle for live sports coverage in favour of pay-television, which uses sports coverage as a crucial weapon in the struggle for market share. Although the public might benefit from this subscription supply if it would lead to an increase of channel quantity and choice, some households could be denied access to sports events of major importance for society, because these extra services require a supplementary subscription payment. In other words, households unwilling or unable to pay an extra subscription fee could be deprived access to these events. Hence, their right to information could be endangered. As the right to information constitutes one of the essential foundations of a democratic society, Article 14 of the AVMS Directive, containing the 'list of major events' mechanism, assures that events of major importance for society would only be exclusively broadcast on free-to-air television reaching a substantial proportion of the public.

Given that there is no clear definition of 'events of major importance for society', it is up to the Member States to designate events of major importance taking into account their own national and cultural characteristics. Due to the fact that the Member States have to justify why an event is included in the list, they should realise that they do not have a full freedom to include every event they want. To ensure that the listed events still have the possibility of bringing people together and creating social cohesion, it is up to the Member States to keep their list up-to-date and to decide, if events do not fulfil the criteria test, to delist events.

The sports events included in the 'list of major events' could only be broadcast in an exclusive way on free-to-air television. According to recital 53 of the AVMS Directive, free-to-air television refers to "*broadcasting on a channel, either public or commercial, of programmes which are accessible to the public without payment in addition to the modes of funding of broadcasting that are widely prevailing in each Member State (such as licence fee and/or the basic tier subscription fee to a cable network)*". Although the definition of free-to-air television differs in each Member State, in most Member States pay-television could not be classified as

K. Lefever, *New Media and Sport*, ASSER International Sports Law Series,
DOI: 10.1007/978-90-6704-873-6_15,

free-to-air. However, in the future, free-to-air television and pay-television could grow closer together blurring the distinction between these two services. A recent question that has arisen is whether digital television could be grasped by the definition of free-to-air television. In practice, viewers who do not have the necessary reception equipment, such as a decoder, would be excluded from accessing the events of major importance to society. Throughout the European Union, there is no unanimous vision on how digital television should be interpreted. In some Member States, digital television could fall under the definition of free-to-air television because free-to-air television gives access to sports events for no payment other than the television license fee and the cost of receiving equipment, while in other Member States digital television could not fall under the definition of free-to-air television because in these Member States sports events of major importance for society should be followed on television without an extra expenditure for technical equipment, such as a decoder. In Flanders, in order to create more legal certainty for broadcasters and platform operators in the digital media landscape, the government decided to replace the notion 'free-to-air' television by the notion 'basic package of the different distributors'. However, given that the Flemish Media Decree and the Explanatory Memorandum do not provide clear definitions of what is actually meant by 'basic package' and mainly due to the discrepancy between the Flemish Media Decree and the Order of the Flemish Government establishing the list of events of major importance to society, the revision could not put a stop to the uncertainty.

The 'list of major events' mechanism is inserted in the regulatory framework as a reaction to the development of new media: pay-television. In order to protect the public's right to information with regard to sports events of major importance for society, it should be guaranteed that those sports events could only be broadcast exclusively on free-to-air television reaching a substantial proportion of the public. In the different Member States, the substantial proportion goes from 70 to 95 % of the households. Given that new media providers have only a limited penetration and, thus, do not fulfil the 'substantial proportion' criterion, they are hindered from broadcasting listed sports events in an exclusive way. Recently, due to the digitalisation process, broadcasters have discovered the possibility to broadcast a digital-only channel alongside their traditional, analogue channel. As a result, there is a danger that these broadcasters, when broadcasting a listed event on their digital-only channels, would lose, at least temporarily, their universal character. As long as digital television does not reach the required penetration rate, digital-only channels are not allowed to broadcast listed events exclusively. However, the Australian Government has tried to find a new balance in the digital media landscape between, on the one hand, the public's right to information, and, on the other hand, the development of new media, such as digital television. Following the FIFA World Cup in South Africa, the Broadcasting Services Act was amended and some World Cup matches were removed from the list of major events allowing digital-only channels to broadcast previously listed events. Nevertheless, the free-to-air television has to replay the delisted matches immediately after the match was finished. The Australian Minister for Broadband, Communications and the

Digital Economy hoped that this initiative would stimulate football fans to convert to digital television. Given that 70 % of the Australian households watches digital television, this Minister announced, in November 2011, that the prohibition of using digital-only channels to broadcast listed events could be relaxed. In order to allow greater use of digital-only channels, the list of major events will be divided into two Tiers. Tier A events, being nationally iconic events, should be broadcast on the main channel of the free-to-air broadcasters, while Tier B events, being regionally iconic and nationally significant events, could be broadcast on a free-to-air digital-only channel. However, it should be realised that these changes to the 'list of major events' mechanism would have a significant impact on the public's right to information.

In order to guarantee the protecting of the public's right to information, it is important that Member States foresee, on the one hand, a proportionate sanctioning mechanism for broadcasters infringing the 'list of major events' mechanism or refusing to transfer or cede rights or that do so on unfair or unreasonable terms and, on the other hand, an effective controlling and enforcing power mechanism. Furthermore, it is also important to stress that policymakers can speed up the uptake of digital television in cabled countries without touching the core principle of the 'list of major events' mechanism and, thus, preventing free-to-air channels to show listed events exclusively on their digital-only channels. In order to stimulate the development of digital television, policymakers can decide to subsidise the sale of digital decoders. However, when doing so, they have to take into account possible competition concerns that could be created. In Italy, for example, the Italian Government decided to subsidise the sale of digital set-top boxes. However, the European Commission opened an enquiry into this subsidy for digital decoders in Italy. The European Commission decided that subsidies for digital decoders granted by Italy in 2006 did not violate the State aid rules as they are offered for all decoders, regardless of the transmission platforms, and proportionate to the objective of promoting the transition to digital television. However, the Italian subsidies provided in 2004 and 2005 to buyers of decoders for digital terrestrial television were found incompatible under the State aid rules as they were not technology-neutral and creating an undue distortion of competition by excluding satellite broadcasting.[1]

Although the 'list of major events' mechanism's aim is well-intended, the unwanted result of the current system could be that listed sports events would not be broadcast at all. In fact, this mechanism does not oblige free-to-air broadcasters to buy the rights to listed events nor does it oblige them to broadcast the listed events once they have bought the broadcasting rights. Hence, this might result in a situation in which listed events, even though they are labelled as important for society, might not be shown on television. Moreover, it is quite paradoxical that a broadcaster, broadcasting a listed event on its digital-only channel and reaching at least a small part of the public, infringes the rules about the 'list of major events'

---

[1] For more information about this case, see: Rapid Press Releases 2005, 2007a, b.

mechanism, while a broadcaster, having the exclusive rights on listed events, decides not to broadcast the events is not infringing the rules. As already stated by the EBU in 2003, it is important to reinforce this 'list of major events' mechanism to avoid the risk of being considered merely a 'paper tiger' and to operate satisfactorily.[2] Hence, it is up to policymakers to intervene and rethink this regime so that it would work satisfactorily. The Australian 'use it or lose it' principle, limiting the warehousing of broadcasting rights, could inspire the European and Member States' legislators in creating a better and more balanced 'list of major events' mechanism. According to the Australian Minister for Communications, Information Technology and the Arts, this principle is designed "*to ensure the anti-siphoning list works the way it was intended and does not produce the perverse effect of reducing rather than increasing the total availability of sport to consumers on both free to air and pay television*".[3] In short, this must-offer regime requires commercial broadcasters to offer to the national public broadcasters the right to purchase, for a nominal charge, the free-to-air rights to an event they do not plan to transmit live. However, the reason for existence and the effectiveness of this regime is questioned both by free-to-air broadcasters and pay-television broadcasters. The first group stated that the failure to broadcast an event live and in full is often wrongly equated with hoarding. As a result, they doubt the need for these rules. The second group has criticised the rules as ineffective, because there is no obligation for the national broadcasters neither to accept the offers nor to sell any pay-television rights they hold.

In order to deal with the lacunas of the Australian 'use it or lose it'—principle, the current EU regulatory framework could be complemented with a 'must-broadcast' obligation regarding the exclusive broadcasting rights of the listed events of major importance for society. Given that it is not in the public's interest when broadcasters have a warehouse of unused rights, this obligation would require broadcasters, once they have acquired rights of listed events, to effectively use those rights and broadcast the events. Because this obligation might seem very intrusive, its introduction requires a delicate balancing of the different interests at stake in order to determine its precise modalities.[4] As broadcasters are likely to broadcast those events or programmes of which they believe that they will attract the largest viewing audience in order to increase the potential financial return from advertisers, this obligation would have a major impact on their economic freedom and their freedom of programming. However, as other intrusive measures can be imposed in order to safeguard a public interest, it seems justified to restrict the broadcasters' freedoms, when necessary to meet clearly defined general interest objectives, proportionate and transparent. The introduction of a must-buy obligation for public broadcasters in order to make sure that the

[2] EBU 2003.

[3] Minister for Communications, Information Technology and the Arts 2006.

[4] Lefever and Van Rompuy 2009, 267.

broadcasting rights of listed events will be bought would probably not be proportionate.

References

Legislation and Policy Documents

European Union

Speechess

Rapid Press Releases (2005) State aid: Commission opens inquiry into subsidy for digital decoders for terrestrial TV in Italy, 21 December 2005, IP/05/1657

Rapid Press Releases (2007) State aid: Commission endorses subsidies for digital decoders in Italy, but only where technology-neutral, 24 January 2007, IP/07/73

Rapid Press Releases (2007) State aid: Commission endorses subsidies for digital equipment in Italy, 28 June 2007, IP/07/960

Australia

Miscallanious

Minister for Communications, Information Technology and the Arts (2006) Use it or lose it guidelines released for anti-siphoning sport. http://www.minister.dbcde.gov.au/coonan/media/media_releases/use_it_or_lose_it_guidelines_released_for_anti-siphoning_sport. Accessed 21 Aug 2010

Doctrine

EBU (2003) Public consultation by the European commission on the review of the television without Frontiers Directive—EBU contribution. http://ec.europa.eu/avpolicy/docs/reg/modernisation/2003_review/contributions/wc_ebu_en.pdf. Accessed 23 Aug 2010

Lefever K, Van Rompuy B (2009) Ensuring access to sports content: 10 years of EU intervention. Time to celebrate? J Media L 2:243–268

Chapter 16
Conclusion

Sport has the power to unite people in a way little else can. Sport can create hope where there was once despair. It breaks down racial barriers. It laughs in the face of discrimination. Sport speaks to people in a language they can understand

(Nelson Mandela quoted in Committee of the Regions 2007).

The last decade, due to technological changes, the media sector has changed fundamentally. In the digital media landscape, the content and information available continue to grow everyday. First, due to the increased transmission capacity, both the number of broadcasters and the hours spent to sports content has substantially increased. This digital evolution also allows the broadcasting of a wider variety of sports events to a niche public. Second, new platforms, such as Internet and mobile phones, have created the opportunity for content providers to expand their offerings. In the past, sports fans could only watch sports events at the venue or on a traditional television set in their living room or in a pub. Technological developments, however, have greatly affected the way how sports fans can follow sports events. During the day, fans can consult highlights on sports or news websites, receive news alerts or pictures on their mobile phone and listen to downloaded podcasts with the most recent news. In the evening, they can watch the game on their television set at home. As a result, the public can now be informed about sports events '24/7', accessible at any place and time that suits them. Third, the digitalisation process has drastically lowered the cost of content production. As a result, everybody has now the opportunity to become content producer, while in the past, the dissemination of information was the exclusive domain of the professional media. Hence, it comes as no surprise that these changes have fundamentally altered the relationships between the stakeholders of the sports/media complex. In the analogue past, the different stakeholders of the sports/media complex had clearly defined roles: sports organisations offered sports content and broadcasters bought exclusive sports broadcasting rights to deliver the games to the stay-at-home fans. However, in the digital media landscape, not only media organisations are interested in broadcasting sports events, commercial organisations, the public and the sports organisations are also offered the opportunity to produce their own sports content. Because sports content is wanted more than ever before, the digital evolution has resulted in new conflicting interests between the different stakeholders of the sports/media complex. One should realise

K. Lefever, *New Media and Sport*, ASSER International Sports Law Series, DOI: 10.1007/978-90-6704-873-6_16,

that the sports/media complex will continue to be affected by new evolutions in the media sector. Connected television, which allows viewers to access Internet via their television set, for example, will create new challenges for policy makers.

Besides its economic dimension, sport has been attributed an important societal significance. Sport can play different roles, going from an educational to a public health role or from a cultural and social to a recreational role. These specific characteristics are often referred to as the specificity of sport. Recently, the specificity of the sport has been officially recognised by Article 165 of the TFEU. As a result, when the European institutions would deal with the public's access to sports content, and in particular the public's right to information with regard to sports events, the societal role of sport can no longer be denied. It is important to indicate that sport plays an important role in bringing people together and contributing to social cohesion. Given that sport has the ability to create a sense of belonging, it has been argued that sports coverage could be protected under Article 10 of the ECHR. Article 10 of the ECHR guarantees the public's right to information and freedom of expression. According to the European Court of Human Rights, the notion information should be defined very widely. It encompasses everything that can play an important role in the development of a democratic society and the development of the citizens. Given that sport has the ability of representing and strengthening a nation, it can fulfil this role. In other words, sport contributes to the development of our society. As a result, there is no reason to assume that live sports coverage could not fall under the protection of Article 10 of the ECHR. Furthermore, Article 10 of the ECHR contains both a negative and a positive obligation for the States. The latter obliges Member States to actively protect fundamental rights of the citizens, while the former obligation prohibits States to intervene. When States would decide to actively protect the public's right to live and full sports coverage, the criteria of Article 10, § 2 of the ECHR should be respected. Based on the foregoing, public's access to live and full sports coverage could be protected by adequate sector-specific regulation or by competition authorities' interventions. Finally, it is important to indicate that the public's access to sports content is broader than guaranteeing access to sports coverage because it could play an important role for society. It also covers access to sports content in more economic terms, such as choice, price, innovation, etc. In other words, the public's access to sports coverage covers both the viewer's interests as a consumer (choice, price) and as a citizen (free access to live and full sports coverage).

Different legal instruments are regulating the broadcasting sector in Europe. When dealing with the public's access to sports coverage, both media and competition law play an important role. However, due to the recent changes in the media landscape, the relevance of media law has been questioned. For example, the digital media environment has provided the public with the opportunity to decide where, when and through which means they will watch (sports) content, while in the analogue past, the professional media decided which programmes and when they would be broadcast. As a result, some authors have been arguing that this shift from one-to-many to many-to-many communication undermined the *ratio legis* of media regulation. According to them, the basic principle of media regulation, i.e. spectrum scarcity and one-way selection of information at the level of traditional broadcasters could no longer be upheld. Hence, due to the increased participation of the public in creating and distributing content, government intervention in the broadcasting sector to guarantee the public's right to information would no longer be justified. Additionally, it was often argued that the regulation of the broadcasting market could be left to competition law.

The regulation of access to live and full sports coverage can only be left to competition law, if competition authorities, when dealing with the sale, acquisition and exploitation of sports broadcasting rights, (could) take into account the public's access to live sport on television. Unfortunately, different decisions of the European Commission and the national competition authorities have indicated that competition law is not the right tool in order to protect this normative objective. The main objective of competition law and the remedies imposed in the different decisions analysed in this book is to keep the market for the sale, acquisition and exploitation of sports broadcasting rights open and competitive. In their decisions, due to the inherent limitations of competition law, competition authorities mainly refer to the public as an economic actor (consumer) rather than a social actor (citizen). When imposing the "*joint selling remedies package*" in the *UEFA Champions League* case, *German Bundesliga* case and *FA Premier League* case, for example, the European Commission often stressed that the joint sale of broadcasting rights of sports events would provide advantages for the fans and the viewers. However, these decisions were not really an illustration of a citizen-oriented approach. Although the European Commission takes into account the viewers' benefits, particularly their choice in the changed media environment, when exempting the joint selling agreements, it does not explicitly refer to the public's right to information and the public's access to live and full sports coverage. Furthermore, although the objective of the remedies imposed in the different decisions was to guarantee small and new media operators' access to premium sports content, unequal treatment of innovative exploitation forms, such as the imposition of embargoes or limiting the coverage to clips, makes these new media services less attractive. In the *German public broadcaster state aid* case, when sublicensing obligations were imposed in order to deal with unused sports broadcasting rights, there was even no explicit reference made to the viewers or the public. Finally, in order to further the interests of the public and to give new media operators a chance to enter the market, competition authorities have imposed must-offer obligations on the platform operators holding exclusive broadcasting rights of premium sports content. However, just as in the three European joint selling agreement decisions, when must-offer obligations are imposed, the viewer is especially seen in its role as consumer, focussing on its economic interests (price, choice, etc.). Nevertheless, the German and Belgian competition authorities have shown that it is possible for competition authorities' decisions to reflect a more explicit citizen-oriented approach by explicitly taking into account the public's right to information. The German competition authority, for example, has attached value to highlights of matches being broadcast before

8 p.m. on a free-to-air channel, while the Belgian Competition Council has attached value to the principle that the public could see at least one live match on free-to-air television per match day. Furthermore, in the *EBU/Eurovision system* case, the European Commission explicitly stated that the viewers will benefit from a joint buying mechanism, because they will have access to more high-quality sports programmes of both popular and minority sports. Hence, in this decision the public's access to coverage of sports events played an important role when exempting the joint buying agreement. However, this decision was overruled by the General Court. Although these are examples of competition decisions attaching more weight to a non-economic consideration as the public's right to information (to sports events), this should be seen as a rather exceptional approach. In other words, in a vast majority of competition decisions, cultural objectives are subordinate to economic ones.

Not only have these decisions indicated that media law is still needed in order to guarantee the public's access to sports events. Even practice indicates that the concerns about access to sport content in the digital media environment remain valid. Although it is often argued that Internet would kill television, different studies indicate that traditional television consumption has even increased over the years and, thus, still remains the most important source of information. Furthermore, television is about shared emotions in familiar surroundings, whereas Internet is about individual media consumption. And practice shows that people prefer watching sports events on a big screen with their friends instead of alone. Furthermore, Internet has offered the public and the fans the opportunity to become both producer and receiver of information and content. This implies that sports fans could film during sports events and upload this content on their own website or user-generated content websites. At first sight, it seems that the evolution from one-to-many to many-to-many communication has offered the fans access to a plenitude of sports coverage and sports information. However, terms and conditions of different football teams and sports organisations contain the prohibition for ticket holders to bring recording material into the stadium. In June 2011, it was announced that Apple is developing software to stop iPhone users from filming live events, such as sports events or concerts, with their smartphone. Hence, these new evolutions limit the fans' and sports clubs' possibilities to upload audiovisual material of matches on the Internet. Given that traditional, linear television remains an important source of access to sports content, even in the Internet era, the basic principles and foundations of media law have not become redundant and media regulation is still needed to guarantee access to important and diverse content.

Therefore, we can conclude that it would be too dangerous to claim that the raison d'être of media regulation has disappeared. Or in other words, it could be argued that media law is still needed to guarantee the citizen's interests in the changing media landscape. However, one should realise that the current media regulatory framework, and in particular the 'list of major events' mechanism, needs to be modified or clarified in order to better protect the public's access to live sports coverage in a digital converging media environment. For example, it was observed that it is not clear whether digital television would fall under the notion "*free-to-air television*". Upgrading to digital television requires an extra expenditure for the subscriber: the acquisition of a set-top box in order to encrypt the television signals. Hence, the question that rises is whether this cost should be interpreted as an additional payment on top of the basic subscription fee as a result of which digital television would not be labelled as freely available. Moreover, only free-to-air broadcasters reaching "*a substantial proportion of the public*" are allowed to broadcast listed events in an exclusive way. In some countries, the digital television adoption does not (yet) reach the required substantial proportion. When a broadcaster would show a listed event live on its digital-only channel, this practice might infringe (currently) the 'list of major events' mechanism. Hence, it seems that free-to-air television broadcasters should continue to be restricted from showing a listed event exclusively on their digital-only channels until the switch from analogue to digital has been completed. However, in Australia, the restriction on the use of digital-only channels to broadcast listed events has been relaxed, because more than 70% of the Australian households watch digital television. Policymakers should realise that this discussion will probably recur in every "*transitional phase*" (from analogue to digital television, from digital to high-definition television, etc.) creating the possibility for the public to choose between different ways of watching television. During these transitional phases, it is important that the policymakers make a clear choice either for the public's right to information or for the development of digital television or other new media. However, it could be argued that the Australian Government found a new balance between the public's right to information, on the one hand, and the development of new media, on the other hand, when introducing the possibility to broadcast some listed events on digital-only channels. It should be noted that a major part of the Australian public (70 %) has already made the switch to digital television and, thus, that (only) 30 % of the households would be deprived access to live coverage of these events. However, in some highly cabled European Member States, such as Belgium and the Netherlands, only 50 % of the public have switched to digital television. As a result, such a measure could have a major impact on the public's right to information. Nevertheless, it seems that the exclusive broadcasting of sports events on new media could be an important tool in order to convince people to make the switch those new media. Without touching the core principle of the 'list of major events' mechanism, policymakers could also speed up the uptake of digital television in another way. In order to convince the public to take a digital television subscription, policymakers can decide to subsidise the sale of decoders, at least if this is done in a technological neutral way. Finally, in order to make the 'list of major events' mechanism more effective, the regulatory framework could be complemented with a 'must-broadcast' obligation, obliging broadcasters that have bought the exclusive broadcasting rights of listed events, to cover them live. Given that such an obligation might seem intrusive, its introduction requires a delicate balancing of the different interests at stake.

One final remark. In the past, exclusivity was the key word in the audiovisual media sector. Exclusive sports broadcasting deals were often seen as crucial to protect the value of the broadcasting rights for the rights holders and to maximise profitability for the broadcasters buying the exclusive broadcasting rights. Nevertheless, concerns have arisen about the negative effects those exclusive contracts could have on the public and new media operators. As a result, competition authorities and legislators have intervened in order to deal with these issues. Both must-offer obligations and the 'list of major events' mechanism, for example, deal with the way exclusive broadcasting rights should be exploited. Recently, however, the Dutch Eredivisie went even one step further and decided to, instead of selling its broadcasting rights exclusively, wholesale its own television channel to a number of distributors via various platforms. This non-exclusive strategy offers opportunities for both distributors and the public. Alternative distributors are able to include a sports channel in their package they otherwise would not have been able to afford. The viewers, in the past forced to choose a particular platform to access specific premium content, can subscribe to the platform of their choice. Sports organisations are often caught between, on the one hand, maximising exposure of their sport via free-to-air television to fuel interest and mass participation in their sport and, on the other hand, commercialising their product on pay-television limiting viewer numbers. A halfway house solution could be this multi-platform, non-exclusive approach that would reach more subscribers. Therefore, more research into the field of non-exclusive sports broadcasting rights deals would be of great value. Although non-exclusive rights deals could increase consumer's choice, it is important to examine the impact of such agreements on other players of the sports/media complex.

References

Legislation and Policy Documents

European Union

Opinions

Committee of the Regions (2007). Opinion of the Committee of the Regions on 'Equal opportunities and sport'. *OJ* (2007) C305/53

Index

K. Lefever, *New Media and Sport*, ASSER International Sports Law Series,
DOI: 10.1007/978-90-6704-873-6,

MIX
Papier aus verantwortungsvollen Quellen
Paper from responsible sources
FSC® C105338

If you have any concerns about our products,
you can contact us on
ProductSafety@springernature.com

In case Publisher is established outside the EU,
the EU authorized representative is:
Springer Nature Customer Service Center GmbH
Europaplatz 3, 69115 Heidelberg, Germany

Printed by Libri Plureos GmbH
in Hamburg, Germany